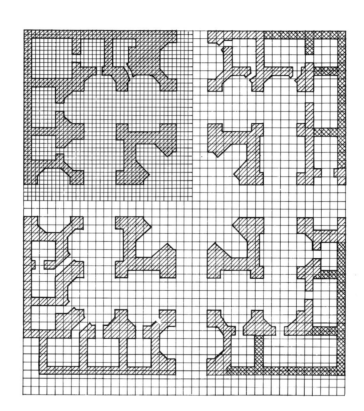

Architecture of the Islamic World

ITS HISTORY AND SOCIAL MEANING

*With a complete survey of key monuments
and 758 illustrations, 112 in colour*

Texts by ERNST J. GRUBE · JAMES DICKIE
OLEG GRABAR · ELEANOR SIMS
RONALD LEWCOCK · DALU JONES
GUY T. PETHERBRIDGE

EDITED BY GEORGE MICHELL

THAMES AND HUDSON

The half-title shows a redrawn version of one of the 16th-century plans from Uzbekistan mentioned in Chapter 4, unique survivals of Islamic architectural drawing. The originals are on paper made in Samarqand. The design is executed on a grid that represents the dirha, or cubit, while the grid of smaller squares establishes the size of the brick module for the builder.

The frontispiece is a detail of the north-west īwān of the Friday Mosque, Isfahan.

Designed and produced by Thames and Hudson, London
Managing Editor: Ian Sutton BA
Design: Ian Mackenzie-Kerr MCSD
Editorial: Marcy Bourne BA Susan Wagstaff BA
Picture Research: Deborah Pownall BA
Maps: Shalom Schotten MCSD
Plans: Garry Martin, Christopher Woodward DIPAA

Contents

Preface 7

GEORGE MICHELL

Co-ordinator of Studies in Oriental Architecture at the
Architectural Association, London, and editor of *Art and
Archaeology Research Papers*

Map 8, 9

___

Architecture and Society

Introduction 10

What is Islamic Architecture?

ERNST J. GRUBE

Professor of Islamic Art, Universities of Venice and Padua

Chapter one 15

Allah and Eternity: Mosques, Madrasas
and Tombs

JAMES DICKIE (YAQUB ZAKI)

Formerly Lecturer in Islamic Studies, University of Lancaster

Chapter two 48

The Architecture of Power: Palaces,
Citadels and Fortifications

OLEG GRABAR

Professor of Fine Arts, Harvard University

Chapter three 80

Trade and Travel: Markets and
Caravanserais

ELEANOR SIMS

Research Associate, Istituto Italiano per il Medio
e l'Estremo Oriente, Rome

Chapter four 112

Architects, Craftsmen and Builders:
Materials and Techniques

RONALD LEWCOCK

Fellow of Clare Hall, Cambridge

Chapter five 144

The Elements of Decoration: Surface,
Pattern and Light

DALU JONES

Editor of *Art and Archaeology Research Papers* and of catalogue for
'The Arts of Islam' Exhibition (Arts Council of Great Britain)

Chapter six 176

Vernacular Architecture: The House
and Society

GUY T. PETHERBRIDGE

Editor of *The Conservator*, journal of the United Kingdom Group
of the International Institute for Conservation of Historic and
Artistic Works

___

Key Monuments of Islamic Architecture

Arabia GEOFFREY KING RONALD LEWCOCK 209

Spain GEOFFREY KING 212

North Africa and Sicily GEORGE MICHELL 215

Egypt VIKTORIA MEINECKE-BERG 222

Syria, Jordan, Israel,
Lebanon JOHN WARREN 230

Turkey GODFREY GOODWIN 237

Iraq HELEN PHILON 245

Iran ANTONY HUTT 251

Central Asia and Afghanistan
YOLANDE CROWE 258

Indian subcontinent GARRY MARTIN 264

West Africa ALLAN LEARY 274

East Africa RONALD LEWCOCK 278

The Far East GEORGE MICHELL 279

___

GLOSSARY 281   BIBLIOGRAPHY 282   INDEX 284

Acknowledgments and Sources of Illustrations

The illustrations sections have been the responsibility of the publisher, though they have received unstinted help and advice from all the authors, both in the choice of pictures and in the wording of the captions. Professor Edmund Bosworth has kindly acted as adviser on the transcription and styling of Arabic words.

Page numbers are given first, the picture number follows in brackets.

Al Araby Magazine 17 (1). Peter Andrews 82 (4), 94 (35). Arthaud, Manuelle Roche 190 (35). Beirut, Institut Français d'Archéologie 54 (15). Berlin, Islamisches Museum 154 (25), 159 (45). BOAC photo archive 182 (17). E. Bohm 59 (27). Camera Press 83 (7), 155 (33). A. Costa 54 (16). Dr Yolande Crowe 53 (11), 58 (24), 60 (33), 93 (31), 95 (38), 156 (38), 158 (44), 159 (46), 189 (40), 193 (46). J. E. Dayton 57 (23), 59 (26), 93 (32), 116 (17). Dr James Dickie 19 (5), 20 (9), 21 (11), 22 (12–14, 16, 17), 24 (19), 35 (21), 26 (25), 27 (27, 28), 28 (29–31), 30 (36), 31 (37, 38), 60 (31), 157 (39). John Donat 89 (21), 126 (42), 184 (24). Olga Ford 25 (22), 50 (4), 53 (10), 117 (19), 120 (26, 28), 121 (29), 160 (48), 184 (25), 188 (35). Werner Foreman 21 (10), 63 (41), 124 (38), 125 (39, 40), 146 (3), 152 (23), 153 (24), 156 (36), 185 (27). Sonia Halliday 60 (29, 30, 32), 61 (34–36), 84 (9), 88 (19), 89 (21), 117 (20), 152 (22), 154 (31). Robert Harding Associates 20 (7), 29 (41), 49 (1), 53 (12, 13), 58 (24), 60 (33), 84 (8), 85 (11), 92 (27), 115 (14), 116 (16), 124 (37, 39), 145 (1), 148 (9), 149 (11), 152 (35), 156 (35), 159 (47). Angelo Hornak 51 (6), 56 (20), 64 (43), 149 (12), 154 (29). J. Housego 83 (6), 86 (14), 87 (17). Martin Hurlimann 31 (40). Tony Hutt 83 (5), 84 (12), 88 (20), 90 (24), 93 (30), 148 (6), 156 (27), 186 (36), 187 (33, 34). S. Jellicoe 146 (2), 156 (30). Dalu Jones 56 (21), 121 (31), 148 (7, 8), 150 (13, 14), 151 (17), 154 (25), 155 (34), 157 (40), 158 (41, 42). A. F. Kersting 22 (15), 26 (23, 24), 50 (4), 51 (8), 55 (17), 62 (38, 39), 118 (21, 22), 119 (25), 127 (45, 46, 50). R. Lannoy 63 (42). Allan Leary 191 (45). Leningrad, Oriental Institute 185 (28). Dr Ronald Lewcock 115 (9–13, 15), 116 (18), 118 (24), 120 (27, 30), 122 (32, 33), 123 (36), 180 (11). London, British Museum 82 (3), 114 (5). London, India Office Library 113 (1–4). London, Victoria and Albert Museum 114 (6, 8). Ayyub Malik 183 (20). Mas 54 (14), 127 (49), 155 (32). Dr V. Meinecke-Berg 91 (26). Middle East Archive 20 (6, 8), 158 (43). New York, Metropolitan Museum of Art, Fletcher Fund 30 (35). Oxford, Bodleian Library 63 (40). Paris, Bibliothèque Nationale 29 (33). Guy Petherbridge 182 (15, 18), 183 (21, 23), 187 (32), 189 (39), 190 (42). Helen Philon 24 (20). Josephine Powell 55 (18), 56 (22), 59 (28), 87 (18), 90 (25), 126 (44), 128 (51), 148 (10), 150 (15), 151 (18), 154 (28). Ronald Searight Collection 50 (2), 51 (7), 82 (2), 178 (2), 179 (5, 8). Ronald Sheridan 55 (19). E. Simpson 58 (25), 156 (37). Robert Skelton 84 (10), 95 (37). Ellen Smart 92 (28, 29). Jane Taylor, Sonia Halliday Photographs 52 (9). Tunisian Tourist Office 181 (13), 183 (22), 190 (41). Turkish Tourist Office 151 (19). John Warren 180 (10). E. Widmer 18 (2), 27 (26), 126 (43). E. Wilford 186 (29). Marion Wenzel 177 (1). Roger Wood 18 (3), 19 (4), 86 (15), 127 (47), 178 (4). Yan 81 (1), 127 (48).

The following have provided illustrations for the section headed 'Key Monuments of Islamic Architecture': Aerofilms Ltd; *Architectural Review*; Baghdad, Directorate General of Antiquities; Beirut, Institut Français d' Archéologie; Berlin, Staatliche Museum; E. Bohm; Boudot-Lamotte; Camera Press; Prof. J. Carswell; Dr Yolande Crowe; Paul Davies; J. E. Dayton; Dr James Dickie; Egyptian State Tourist Office; Olga Ford; Werner Foreman; Godfrey Goodwin; Sonia Halliday; Robert Harding Associates; D. Hill; Martin Hurlimann; Tony Hutt; Jerusalem, Israel Department of Antiquities; Dalu Jones; A. F. Kersting; Christel Kessler; Geoffrey King; Richard Lannoy; Allan Leary; Dr Ronald Lewcock; London, India Office Library; Garry Martin; Mas; George Michell; Middle East Archive; Paris, Documentation Français Phototèque; Paris, Musée de l'Homme; Josephine Powell; Turkish Tourist Office; John Warren; E. Widmer; E. Wilford; Cairo Dept. of Antiquities.

Preface

THE WEST has long admired the architecture of the Islamic world, but this fascination has mostly lacked any real understanding of the beliefs and way of life of those for whom these buildings were erected. Islamic architecture is more than just a spectacle of domes and minarets, perfumed pleasure palaces and exquisite turquoise tiles; it is a true expression of a rich culture that has unified countries as far apart as Spain and Java, Central Asia and sub-Saharan Africa, over some thousand years and more. Islamic buildings express the religious beliefs, social and economic structure, political motivation and visual sensibility of a pervasive and unified tradition. Underlying the variations from century to century and from region to region, a cohesive unity of architectural conception testifies to the power and breadth of Islam. From theology to commerce, from war to private pleasure, from mysticism to technology, the range of Islamic culture is expressed in a supremely assured series of buildings.

This is the first time that the architecture of the Islamic world has been placed in its cultural setting, thereby revealing both its relationship to Islamic society and the unity of its forms and decoration. This unity has long been recognized, but the complex interplay of theological, sociological, economic, political and technological factors in Islamic culture has never before been analyzed in terms of their influence upon architecture. Regional and chronological variations also form part of this architecture, and this book documents the diversifying elements encompassed by that tradition. A recognition of this unity and diversity, seemingly paradoxically combined, is the basis of any true appreciation of Islamic architecture.

The six chapters that make up the first part look at Islamic architecture from six different angles. In an introductory essay Ernst Grube surveys the whole field and isolates those features that make the architecture of the Islamic world distinctly Islamic. James Dickie (Yaqub Zaki) attempts a taxonomy of Islamic architecture, that is, a classification of religious buildings according to liturgical criteria. Oleg Grabar demonstrates the intimate connection between politics and architecture, describing the citadels and fortresses of a military élite as well as discussing the impact that powerful patrons had on architectural development. Eleanor Sims shows how commerce and trade influenced the evolution of a unique series of buildings that became an indispensable part of every Islamic city, the bazaar and caravanserai; Ronald Lewcock examines the building and craft traditions that flourished in these urban environments, thus promoting the development of sophisticated techniques. Dalu Jones analyzes the aesthetic of Islamic decoration in terms of light, surface and space – a combination of decorative elements which testifies to the diverse artistic influences that Islamic architecture incorporates. Guy Petherbridge shows that even non-monumental domestic buildings, especially those erected in timber or mud-brick, embody the same unifying principles.

The second part is a reference section and documentation of the first part: a gazetteer of key monuments, arranged according to region. This unique survey includes not only the central areas of Islam but peripheral areas such as Africa south of the Sahara and the Far East, where mosques and madrasas were often built in non-Islamic architectural styles. There is an introduction to the architecture of each region, followed by descriptions and specifications of the buildings, a chronological chart and map. Over 250 buildings are comprehensively treated and illustrated.

Architecture is more than a history of form and style: it is a product of cultural and environmental factors and an expression of the way of life of the people for whom it is built. The architecture of the Islamic world is the architecture of the Muslim people – from rulers and warriors, saints and teachers, merchants and travellers, to the modest family unit. Here is the story of these people and their buildings.

George Michell

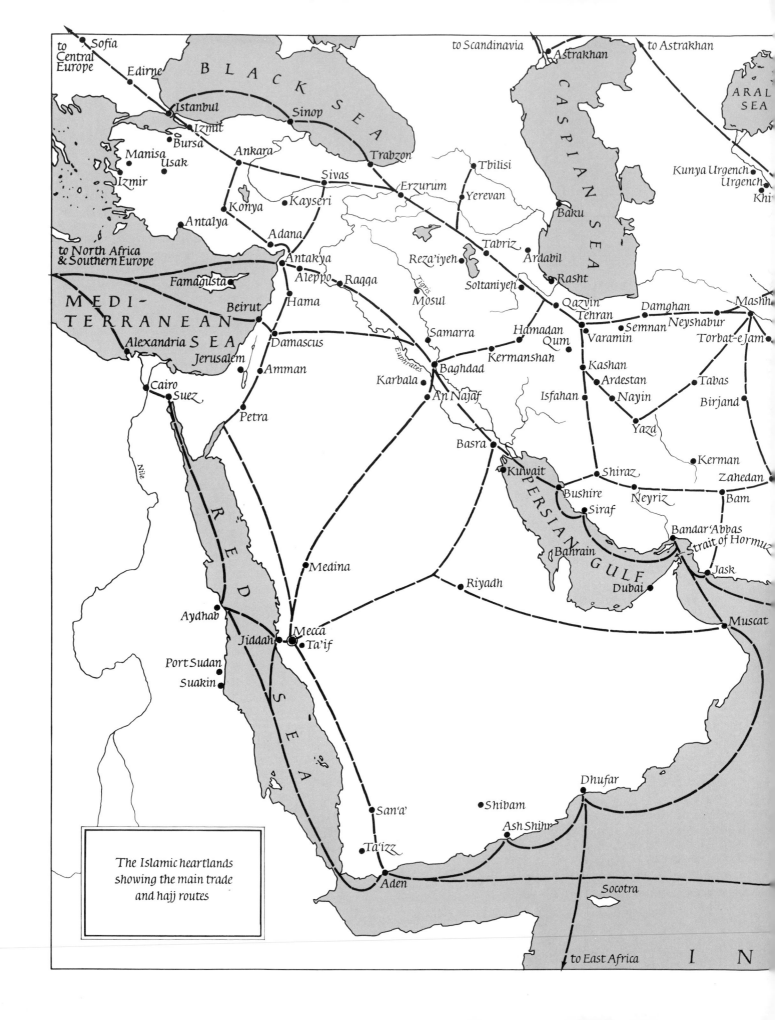

The Islamic heartlands
showing the main trade
and hajj routes

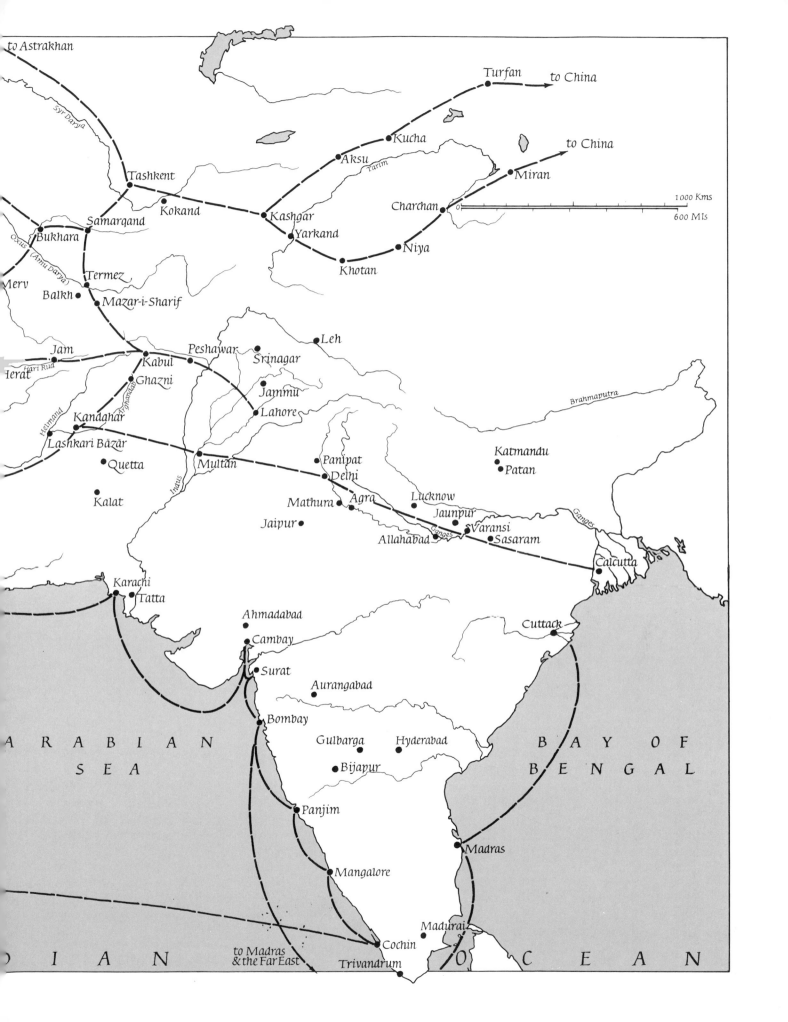

Introduction

As THIS BOOK is about Islamic architecture, the first question we must ask ourselves is whether there is such a thing as 'Islamic Architecture'. Do we mean the architecture produced for and by Muslims to serve Islam as a religion, referring, consequently, only to that architecture which *did* serve a religious function – the mosque, the tomb, the *madrasa*? Or do we mean all the architecture produced in Muslim lands? And if this should be so, what does 'Islamic' mean in this context? If 'Islamic' is not an adjective defining a religious quality, should it be understood as a word that identifies a special kind of architecture, that of a civilization reflecting, or determined by, special qualities inherent in Islam as a cultural phenomenon? Does such an architecture exist? Is there an architecture that can be recognized as different from other architectures created outside Islam? If the answer to this question is in the affirmative – and there seems little question that it must be – we are faced with the need to define those qualities that set Islamic architecture apart from non-Islamic architecture.

The following attempt at defining some of those qualities is, by force of circumstances, generalized, and many exceptions to the general 'rules' may be quoted. Yet such exceptions are perhaps not as numerous as we might think, and they can often be 'explained', at least to a degree, by showing that they are 'removed' in one way or another, even 'divorced', from the experiences that created those architectural forms here identified as specifically 'Islamic'. In sum, an attempt will be made to discuss those elements in Islamic architecture that appear to be typical, and that have to be explained as expressions of a culture created by Islam, differing in fundamental attitudes from other, non-Islamic architectural creations. And a suggestion will also be made that wherever these elements are weak or absent, something has happened in Islamic culture in the particular region where such monuments were produced to indicate a general weakening of the 'Islamicness' of the specific architecture in question.

Concentration on the Interior

One of the most striking features of all Islamic architectural monuments is their focus on the enclosed space, on the inside as opposed to the outside, the façade or the general exterior articulation of a building.

The most common and widely recognized expression of this attitude is, of course, the Muslim house; organized around an inner courtyard, it presents to the outside world high windowless walls interrupted only by a single low door. Often several houses are collected together into a larger walled complex accessible only through a single low doorway, which leads to an inner private passageway from which the individual dwellings can be reached. These houses, and in some cases even large building complexes, give the traditional Muslim city its peculiar unmistakable appearance, which still survives today in many examples of ancient town centres (the *qasbahs*, *medinas* and 'old cities' throughout the Islamic world).

This disregard for the outside appearance of a structure is often developed to the extreme whereby even a monumental structure, such as a congregational mosque, is completely hidden by being totally surrounded by secondary adjacent buildings (for instance a bazaar). This 'hiding' of major monuments goes hand in hand with a total lack of exterior indications of the shape, size, function or meaning of a building. Even if a structure has a visible façade or a portal, these features tell us little, if anything, about the building that lies behind it. In other words, rarely does a façade give any indication of the inner organization or purpose of the building in question, and it is rare that an Islamic building can be understood, or even its principal features identified, by its exterior.

To give but one example: a dome looms over the mass of a building, it is generally visible from afar but sinks into the maze of small cupolas and roofs of surrounding structures as we approach. The dome may indicate a mosque, a palace or a tomb; it may cover a prayer hall, a chamber at the end of a reception hall or a square, circular or octagonal tomb. It may be the principal feature of a structure designed around it; alternatively, it may be only a minor element in a vast structure that surrounds the domed area; it may also

What is Islamic Architecture?

ERNST J. GRUBE

be only one of several domes hidden, or half hidden, by other structures – parapets or inner portal frames. Instead of defining a specific kind of architecture, or a special building with a particular function, the dome appears to be a general symbol, signifying power, the royal city, the focal point of assembly; it can therefore serve both religious and secular purposes. Its outward visible appearance does not truly help us to understand, interpret or identify any building.

At all times and in all regions of the Muslim world we can find 'hidden architecture' – that is, architecture that truly exists, not when seen as monument or symbol visible to all and from all sides, but only when entered, penetrated and experienced from within. Despite the fact that exceptions do, of course, exist – and we will speak of them presently – 'hidden architecture' may be considered the main and dominant form of truly Islamic architecture. The Umayyad Great Mosque of Damascus is a typical example, the Dome of the Rock in Jerusalem a typical exception. The Great Mosque in Damascus follows an established type and helps to create a tradition; the Dome of the Rock, standing alone on its platform and visible from all sides, remains a unique building in Islamic culture, based entirely on pre-Islamic models, which were almost certainly taken over consciously. In the sense in which we would like the term to be understood, the Dome of the Rock is not a truly 'Islamic' building at all, in spite of the fact that it was built by Muslims (or at least at Muslim command) and served a function intimately connected with Islam's subjugation of its enemies: it is, in fact, a monument to this victory. Yet the formal architectural language of this monument is that of the vanquished, not that of the victors. What makes it an Islamic building is not its form but its intention, expressed, furthermore, not in an artistic language of its own, but by secondary, non-architectural means: Arabic inscriptions.

Of course, the architectural form of the Dome of the Rock, an isolated and clearly recognizable structure visible from all sides, is not without parallels in the later Islamic period. The tomb, especially the tomb tower and the free-standing Indian monumental tomb structure (culminating in the renowned Tāj Mahal),

may well be compared with the Dome of the Rock, at least from the purely formal point of view. The question might then be asked: are these buildings, though built for Muslims by Muslims and for Muslim purposes, truly Islamic buildings? Are they not atypical and, like the Dome of the Rock, really un-Islamic in their formal expression? If this is so, how can their existence be explained in a Muslim context?

Perhaps it is necessary at this point to interrupt our discussion to make a distinction between urban and non-urban Islamic architecture, because slightly different rules apply to these two different architectural expressions. Much Islamic architecture appears within the urban setting, though it must be added that a number of building-types were especially developed for the non-urban context, even if they frequently appear within the city as well. Most obvious is the caravanserai, which, in the majority of cases, appears in the open countryside along the principal travel routes. Next are the monumental tombs, which, almost without exception, appear as isolated monuments, whether in an urban situation or within a proper cemetery *extra muros* (most tomb towers, and types of funeral monuments such as the *īwān* of Pīr-i Bakrān). This is especially true when the monument commemorates an important personage; its very function as a commemorative structure makes 'visibility' and physical isolation imperative.

Other building-types that stand alone because of their specific function include fortified frontier structures (*ribāts* and *qasrs*), hunting lodges and utilitarian structures, such as bridges, watch-towers, gateways and fortifications, especially those of the major cities themselves. Even though most of the building-types just mentioned appear as isolated visible structures with clearly defined and undisguised exteriors, few 'break the rules'; that is, are developed into architectural forms that can be fully comprehended from the exterior. Few of these types, in fact, have truly developed exteriors and many, if not most, 'hide' behind high undecorated and unarticulated walls. Even where articulated exterior surfaces do appear, they have little, if any, relationship to the interior organization of the building. The

11

principle that a façade should be unrelated to the interior it fronts is quite common in Islamic architecture, and almost the general rule in buildings within the urban complex; the al-Aqmar Mosque in Cairo and the Mosque of ʿAlāʾ ad-Dīn in Konya, are only two of the most striking examples.

Two conclusions may be drawn: first, that very few building-types in the Muslim world articulate the interior space on their exteriors; and second, that these buildings are either totally functional – bridges, watch-towers – or true exceptions to the rule. In the case of the tomb tower or, for that matter, the mausoleum, we are in the presence of exceptional monuments that intrinsically demand to be clearly visible and free-standing. Of course, it is also true that many Muslim tombs, although built in tower form, are incorporated into a larger architectural complex which totally absorbs them (Natanz, the tomb of Shaykh ʿAbd al-Samad al-Isfahani).

Furthermore, although the origin of the tomb tower is still widely disputed, the suggestion that the royal tent provided at least a formal model and an initial stimulus to build in permanent materials is perhaps not to be discarded, especially as pre-Islamic burial rites in Asia often make use of the tent-cupola. In its pure form – a cylindrical body with a hemispherical or conical top – the tent always stands alone, especially the royal tent, monumental in size and thus symbolizing the power of the ruler. If the notion of the tomb tower should ultimately prove to have been derived from the tent, its unusual design (apart from its significance as a commemorative monument) would thus easily be explained. But whatever the derivation of the tomb tower, it would seem that its singular significance within the iconography of Islamic architecture necessitated its physical expression in an exceptional form.

To a large extent the same is true for the tomb mausoleum, usually a square or octagonal domed structure. To take the great Mughal monumental tomb as just one example, it might be said that its form, as that of its immediate predecessors (the Shīsh Gunbad in Delhi, the mausoleum of Shīr Shāh Sūr at Sasaram), derives directly from early Muslim and even pre-Muslim Indian buildings, which, though fused with imported ideas from Central Asia, were never entirely assimilated into a truly Islamic concept. Certainly these Indian mausolea have elements that are clearly Islamic, especially in their use of materials and decoration, but on the whole they are more closely tied to non-Muslim Indian traditions, just as the Dome of the Rock is tied to pre-Muslim Classical traditions. Neither tradition was ever entirely transformed; they continue to survive with only minor and superficial alterations provided by the Islamic approach to design. The architectural form as such remains, in cultural terms, a foreign element within Islamic architecture.

A detailed analysis of the other building-types listed above would, I believe, lead to similar conclusions. Always and everywhere in the Muslim world, forms of architecture were built that remained basically unaffected by the process of Islamicization of pre-Islamic or non-Islamic cultures; unabsorbed by Islamic art, these forms were consequently not an expression of Islamic culture but of the cultures from which they were originally derived. There may be exceptions to this general rule; that is, there may be cases in which the 'foreign' form may have been used consciously by the Muslim artist or patron to make a very specific point (the Dome of the Rock may well be such a building). But only an analysis of each individual case would make it possible to distinguish between the conscious use of a basically non-Islamic element in Islamic architecture, and the general use of unassimilated forms resulting from dominant cultural trends that have kept uninterrupted links with pre- or non-Islamic civilizations.

Form and Function

Closely related to the concept of a 'hidden architecture' is the striking and almost total absence of a specific architectural form for a specific function. There are very few forms in Islamic architecture that cannot be adapted for a variety of purposes; conversely, a Muslim building serving a specific function can assume a variety of forms.

The paramount example of this phenomenon is the four-*īwān* courtyard structure of Central Asia and Iran, which is also found in other parts of the Muslim world. These structures function equally well as palace, mosque, *madrasa*, caravanserai, bath or private dwelling; at different times and in different places, in fact, they were built to serve all of these functions. In other words, an Islamic building does not automatically reveal, by its form, the function it serves. It need not be designed to serve a particular purpose, but is, in most cases, an abstract and 'perfect' scheme that can be used for a great variety of functions without any difficulties. The strength of this preconceived 'absolute' scheme can best be demonstrated by the almost absurd insistence upon the monumental four-*īwān* plan for the mosque-madrasa of Sultan Hasan in Cairo, fitted into an irregular site that is singularly unsuited for it. Far from planning a building to fit the given space, the architects have here clung to a preconceived design, squeezing it awkwardly into the space available.

Generally, Islamic architecture is given to hiding its principal features behind an unrevealing exterior; it is an architecture that does not change its forms easily, if at all, according to functional demands, but rather tends to adapt functions to preconceived forms, which are basically the contained internal spaces. An analysis of the manner in which these internal spaces are defined and articulated should provide us with additional information concerning the specific quality of this architecture.

With the exception of the tomb, the mausoleum and other similar domed structures, Islamic buildings rarely display an inherent directional or axial quality. On the contrary, the actual physical direction of a building, if it has any at all, is often different from its functional direction. The visitor who enters a mosque, especially the courtyard of a mosque, is generally drawn alongside the prayer hall, down the width of the courtyard. This is often at right angles to the true metaphysical 'direction' as indicated by the *qibla* and, in turn, by the *mihrāb*, the absence of which would in many cases leave the visitor unsure of his orientation – something that would never happen in a basilica or a Classical temple.

If we try to account for this curious feature in Islamic design, we may recall the scheme of the Temple of Baal at Palmyra in Syria, a temple entirely built – apparently – in the language of Antiquity. Its cella is provided with the obligatory colonnade on all sides, heavy architraves and tympana on the narrow ends; the entrance, however, is not at one of the narrow ends but in the centre of one of the long sides, forcing the visitor, who thus finds himself confronted with a blank wall after crossing the threshold, to turn ninety degrees to either right or left in order to approach the two altars. Erected in the 4th century in a Hellenized Arab milieu, this temple serves well to indicate that the curious change of orientation (which represents a total contradiction of the logical sense of direction expressed in European architecture) is an ancient pre-Islamic concept, which appears to have survived, unaltered, into the architecture of the Islamic phase of Arab culture.

This lack of indication of a direction or focus in Islamic architectural design appears at all times and in all parts of the Muslim world; it is also clearly expressed in the lack of balance between the various parts of a building complex. European architecture is generally designed as a complete balanced plan; Islamic architecture usually shows no such basic structure, and additions to an original plan are, consequently, never hampered by an inherent principle governing the whole and conditioning all parts in an equal manner. It is true that balanced schemes do exist in Islamic architecture, the four-*iwān* plan being a case in point; but, firstly, that may be explained as being a pre-Islamic, Central Asian or Iranian concept adopted by Islam; and, secondly, it hardly ever survives in its pure state for long in the Muslim world. (The distortion of the plan in the mosque-madrasa of Sultan Hasan in Cairo has already been mentioned.) But much more important is the dissolution of this balanced plan within the totality of an Islamic architectural complex, its absorption into a maze of additional structure which, like accretions comparable to the natural growth of coral reefs or cell-structures of irregular form, accumulate around the nucleus of the original design, eventually engulfing it completely. The Friday Mosque of Isfahan, with its long and complex building history spanning almost a millennium, is a perfect example of this principle of organic growth.

It may then be said that Islamic architecture, with the exception of the four-*iwān* courtyard plan, is rarely, if ever, designed as a single balanced unit; where such a design was originally adapted, or even conceived, it soon disappears to become part of a greater complex. The very possibility of enlarging a given structure in almost any direction by adding units of almost every conceivable shape and size to the original scheme, totally disregarding the form of the original structure, is a characteristic that Islamic architecture shares with that of no other major culture. Its most impressive manifestation occurs in Muslim palaces, a context where financial, legal or other material considerations cannot ever have been the cause for the incredible 'irregularity' of planning (e.g. the Topkapi palace, Istanbul, or Fatehpur Sikri, India).

Interior Space

Enclosed space, defined by walls, arcades and vaults, is the most important element of Islamic architecture. This is emphasized not only by the phenomenon that little attention is paid to outside appearance or even visibility of any structure, but especially by the fact that most decoration (with the notable exception of the dome and the entrance portal) is reserved for the articulation and embellishment of the interior.

Decoration in Islamic architecture serves several functions, but its main effect – and very likely its main purpose – appears to be the creation of non-tectonic values, the dissolution of all those elements that in other architectural traditions emphasize the structure, the balance and counter-balance of loads and stresses – the actual mechanics of a building. Islamic architecture at its best, and at its most 'Islamic', is truly a negation of architecture as conceived in Europe, that is, of structure; it aims at a visual negation of the reality of weight and the necessity of support. The various means by which the effect of weightlessness is created, the effect of unlimited space, of non-substantiality of walls, pillars, and vaults are all well known. They range from the use of mosaic and painted decoration to tiles – especially lustre and painted polychrome – and from moulded and deeply cut stone or plaster to actual openwork and pierced walls, vaults and even supporting pillars. The multitude of decorative treatments of surfaces in Islamic architecture, the use of almost every conceivable technique and the development of a rich repertory of designs – from geometric abstract shapes to full-scale floral patterns, from minutely executed inscriptions in a full variety of calligraphic styles to the monumental single words that serve as both religious images and decoration – is without parallel in the architecture of the non-Muslim world. Its effect is extraordinary and its function quite unmistakable. It goes hand in hand with the non-directional plan, the tendency to an infinite repetition of individual units (bays, arches, columns, passages, courtyards, doorways, cupolas) and the continuous merging of spaces without any specific direction or any specific centre or focus. And if a definite spatial limit is reached, such as a terminal wall, the surface that should stop the progress of anyone moving through the building will be decorated with patterns that repeat themselves, leading on visually beyond the given limit of the wall surface, vault or dome.

The epitome of this concept of architecture is reached in the Alhambra, at Granada. Though a royal palace, it is not given a centre or focus to emphasize power. Instead, it is a maze of rooms and courtyards, of passages and corridors, of water basins and canals that link the open and covered spaces, of fountains and of decorations that are undoubtedly among the most extraordinarily complex and technically accomplished in all Islamic architectural design. Looking up into the suspended *muqarnas* canopy that forms the great dome of the Hall of the Two Sisters, we are truly aware of being in the presence of an architecture that is distinctly and unmistakably different from any other ever created by man. Its spirit is clearly 'readable'; in fact, in this example it is actually explained – at least in part – by inscriptions that run around the base of the dome. It is that of a metaphysical concept of the world, rooted in the religion that created it – Islam.

If Islamic architecture is distinctly different from non-Islamic architecture, and must be interpreted as one of the many emanations of the spirit of Islam, the adjective 'Islamic' is fully justified. The interpretation of it as a whole as well as the understanding of its specific parts can only be successful and meaningful if seen against the background of Islam as a cultural, religious and political phenomenon, and only in the precise relation to the specific circumstances that led to its creation. It is certainly impossible to present in this brief introductory note anything approaching an interpretation of those characteristics that we have tried to identify as being essential to Islamic architecture.

In fact, such an attempt would be premature, apart from the fact that it would be far beyond the capacities of a single scholar. It will still take many years of research, hardly in its infancy at the present time, satisfactorily to 'explain' the phenomenon of Islamic architecture, that is to say, to correlate the physical appearance of Islamic architecture in the various parts of the Muslim world with the 'spirit' of Islam as it prevailed in any given region and period. Such an interpretation must eventually be attempted if we ever want to go beyond the mere cataloguing and describing of the surviving monuments, although such precise cataloguing must, of course, form its basis. Much groundwork is still to be accomplished before we may safely venture forward, and only a true collaboration between the political, religious, economic and literary historians on the one hand and the art historians on the other may bring us nearer the desired goal of a more complete and accurate understanding of Islamic architecture.

This book is intended to serve as a first step in this new direction.

1 Allah and Eternity: Mosques, Madrasas and Tombs

JAMES DICKIE (YAQUB ZAKI)

The earliest indicator of the direction of Mecca was the spear. On this coin, struck during the reign of the Umayyad caliph, 'Abd al-Malik (685–705), a spear-like object is shown standing upright within the niche, which by this time had become normative as the liturgical indicator.

To THE MUSLIM the concept of *dīn*, or religion, embraces three elements: *īmān*, *'ibādāt* and *ihsān*, which may be loosely translated as 'belief', 'religious obligations' and 'right doing'. In Western terms these could be said to equate with dogma, ritual and ethics. In Islam, as in any coherent religious system, these components exist in an organic and mutually complementary relationship. Fundamental to *īmān*, or dogma, are belief in God, in His unity and His unicity, in His self-disclosure to a sequence of prophets culminating in the revelation of the Qur'ān to Muhammad, and in the finality of the latter's prophethood. After the Unity of God this last, known as the Seal of Prophethood, is the cardinal doctrine of Islam. As God's first and only prophet to all mankind Muhammad brings to a close all previous, scattered revelations, which are now rendered otiose in virtue of his universality. For thirteen centuries the finality of Muhammad's prophethood has stood for Islam as a secure foundation preventing the disintegration of the Faith, since any person who subsequently claims prophetical status within it must, *ipso facto*, be an imposter. This doctrine operates both forwards and backwards in time, not only annulling claims in advance but rescinding all previous revelations. Such, in sum, is the dogmatic content of the *Shahāda*, or Creed (literally, 'attestation of faith'), which comprises only two clauses, known from their fundamentality as *kalimas*, or 'words'. The first *kalima* reads, 'I believe that there is no god apart from the *the* god'; and the second, 'and that Muhammad is the messenger of God'.

Islam is pre-eminently the religion of unity on all levels: ontological, social, political. Socially and politically, the term used to describe that unity is *umma*, which is not susceptible of translation by a single word. Socially, it denotes the Muslim community, while politically the *umma Muhammadiyya* denotes 'Muhammad's nation', a revolutionary concept whereby, for the first time in history, the criterion of belief, or conscious act of election, replaced the genetic accident of birth as the criterion of nationality. The cosmogony of Islam posits a God-centred universe of which only the source, God Himself, can be said to be real; everything else is contingent being.

Knowledge of this unique, creative source can only be through the Names He ascribes to Himself in the Qur'ān and in such of His acts as manifest His Attributes. But in Himself God remains an unexpressed (and inexpressible) mystery; the essence, *dhāt*, of God is inapprehensible to a being such as man whom He so totally transcends. His nature can be apprehended only by His Names, because the Attributes they connote may be recognized from the same qualities present in the created world and familiar to us from experience. For instance, sovereignty we can appreciate from observation of a king: this enables us to understand the sovereignty of God and what it entails. Each subdivision, or *sūra*, of the Qur'ān begins with the formula 'In the name of God, the Compassionate, the Merciful', because the revelation of the Qur'ān is an act of mercy, of compassion for man who otherwise would lack a clear road to salvation.

The Attributes of God add up to the magical total of ninety-nine, derived from the Ninety-Nine Names of God, which are present in the Qur'ān either *in esse* or *in posse*. The Muslim rosary has ninety-nine beads in response to the Qur'ānic passage (Sūra vii, 180) where the believer is enjoined to use invocatory prayer: 'God's are the Most Beautiful Names so call on Him by means of them'. From meditation upon the qualities of God there may accrue not only an understanding of His actions but also a desire to endow oneself with these same qualities, a course which if embarked upon can even lead to gnosis, *ma'rifa*. Many of the Names are self-explanatory; others, like 'the Outwardly manifest' and 'the Inwardly Hidden', are abstruse and form the starting-point of Sūfism, which is an interiorization of Islam. Perhaps the most basic are the seven Rational Attributes, for it is they that explain the creation of man. God, when creating man, imparted to him seven of his own Attributes: life, knowledge, will, power hearing, seeing and speech, the totality of which make up a rational being. It is obviously this that is the meaning of the statement of the Prophet, 'God created man in His form'. Inasmuch as the Qur'ān is God's speech, it is a manifestation of His seventh Attribute.

This brings us to the second *kalima*, 'and that Muhammad is the messenger of God', because the purpose of prophethood is communication of truth, the record of which is scripture, written law. In Islam the sources of infallible religious truth are three: the Qur'ān; the *hadīth*, or prophetical tradition; and *ijmā'*, the principle of communal consensus, applied to contingencies not covered by either scripture or tradition (alternatively: *vox dei, vox prophetae* and *vox populi*). The two last merely supplement the authority of the first, the Qur'ān, for in contrast to other scriptures, which are only inspired, the Qur'ān bases its infallibility on its being the literal word of God, dictated to the world through the mouthpiece of a messenger, a chosen one, or *mustafā*. Qur'ān, which means simply 'a reading' (from *iqrā'*, 'read', the first word of the first revelation to Muhammad), is then the literal word of God, uncreate and co-eternal with Him. Although it may be said to have come into being in time, when the Archangel held out the tablet to Muhammad in the cave of Hira and invited him to read by saying '*iqrā'*', the text of the verses revealed then and subsequently was a transcription of an archetype known as the Preserved Tablet. This may be understood as a metaphor for the mind of God, but the point is that as the thought of God, the Qur'ān partakes of His nature; it is His utterance, *kalām Allāh*, made visible or audible and hence apprehensible. It is for this reason that in the hierarchy of the arts Islam accords the highest rank to calligraphy, because it is the art that embellishes God's speech.

Islam, frequently translated as 'submission' (though 'unconditional surrender' comes nearer the semantic content of the word in Arabic), is a contractual relationship between man and God, whereby man acknowledges the overlordship of God, a recognition that logically entails his own vassalage or slavehood. The terms of the contract are spelled out in the Qur'ān, which is not only a charter for the individual intent on his own salvation but a constitution for the state. Like the Torah, the Qur'ān is a book of law, and it is also the Criterion, *al-Furqān*, whereby man is enabled to distinguish right from wrong, lawful from unlawful, ritually pure from ritually impure. Entry into this contractual relationship with one's Creator is by pronouncing the *Shahāda*, 'attestation of faith', whereby one is become *mukallaf*, or subject to ritual obligations, and all the rest of the Law follows, beginning with the observance of the Five Pillars.

At the heart of Islamic Law stand the Five Pillars (the Arabic means, literally, 'corners'). This does not mean that the edifice of faith is pentagonal, for the Pillars are disposed in the pattern of a quincunx, with the First Pillar, the *Shahāda*, at the centre to which the remaining four are peripheral: *salāt* (prayer), *siyām* (fasting), *zakāt* (payment of the poor-tax) and *hajj* (pilgrimage). Textually present in the Qur'ān, the Five Pillars are accordingly obligation, with the partial exception of the *hajj*, performance of which is contingent on one's means. The Pillars that concern architecture are the Second and the Fifth.

Liturgical orientation and the mosque

One definition of a mosque could be a building erected over an invisible axis, an axis which is none the less the principal determinant of its design. The Muslim world is spread out like a gigantic wheel with Mecca as the hub, with lines drawn from all the mosques in the world forming the spokes. These lines converge on a city and within that city on a point. The city is Mecca, and the point is the Ka'ba at its centre. Mecca, the birthplace of Muhammad, is Islam's holy city and the goal of pilgrimage. The Ka'ba, a hollow cube of stone, many times rebuilt, the original of which goes back beyond the time of Muhammad, is the *axis mundi* of Islamic cosmology. It is diagonally oriented, with its corners facing the cardinal points of the compass. Like the conical Omphalos in Delphi it is the centre of the world, because it is the primordial symbol of the intersection between the vertical axis of the spirit and the horizontal plane of phenomenal existence. During the pilgrimage ceremony the pilgrim circumambulates the Ka'ba seven times, and this gyration of the great crowd round the Ka'ba, with its curious swirling, liquid movement, when seen from a minaret resembles nothing so much as an immense whirlpool. This rite finds its echo in the circumambulation of the tomb of a saint, likewise against the sun, so as to achieve the maximum exposure possible to the *baraka*, the invisible psychic fluid that emanates from any sacral object, be it a holy tomb or its occupant when alive, or his relics, such as his clothes and his rosary, when dead. It is precisely this which accounts for the design of the oldest extant Islamic building, the Dome of the Rock in Jerusalem, which is octagonal in plan and incorporates ambulatories to facilitate the movement of the hosts of pilgrims whom its builder, the caliph, 'Abd al-Malik, was hoping to attract.

At the centre of Islam, both geographically and spiritually, stands the Ka'ba. The *mihrāb* of every mosque is aligned with it, and to it every Muslim turns to pray; thus the whole of Islam can be seen as a wheel with the spokes radiating from the Ka'ba. But as well as this horizontal axis there is a vertical one, that of the spirit. At the Ka'ba the two intersect, so that it is the only non-directional religious building in the Muslim world. The circular motion of the rite of circumambulation (one of the requirements of the *hajj*) is visible here not only in the movements of the pilgrims round the Ka'ba but in the lines inscribed on the pavement. In the distance can be seen a mosque whose *mihrāb* must be the closest of all to its physical goal. (1)

The mosque

Prayer is established at four levels: the individual, the congregation, the total population of a town and the entire Muslim world. For three of these there are distinct liturgical structures. The first is the *masjid*, a mosque used for daily prayer by individuals or small groups but not for the Friday worship; it therefore has a *mihrāb* but no *minbar* (pulpit). The prayer-rug also corresponds to this level. The second is the *jāmi'*, the congregational or Friday mosque; used for the main weekly service, it is normally much larger than a *masjid* and provided with a *minbar*. The third is the *'īdgāh* ('place of prayer'), illustrated in pl. 5. Within these liturgical types a range of architectural variation is possible, and this page illustrates three of the most important.

The Ottomans developed the monumental centralized mosque, covered by a dome and buttressed by semi-domes. The mosque of Sultan Ahmet in Istanbul, known as the Blue Mosque (*above*), was begun in 1609 and finished in 1617. Four minarets flank the sanctuary, and two more the courtyard to the right, though liturgically only one is needed. In the foreground are the *madrasa* and the mausoleum of the pious young sultan, who, during the construction, laboured every Friday beside the builders. (2)

In North Africa and Spain an older type of mosque is found, consisting of a vast rectangular hall, the interior divided by rows of columns. At Qairouan, in Tunisia, the Great Mosque was built in the middle of the 9th century. Outwardly plain and lacking in architectural distinction, its only striking features are the minaret and domes over the entrance and the *mihrāb*, marking the terminal points of the *qibla īwān*, or axial aisle, which is elevated above the other aisles. (3)

The Iranian mosque is cruciform with a domed 'kiosk' at the *qibla*. The centre of each side has a huge open porch, or *īwān*. In Isfahan (*above*) the courtyard is entered through the *īwān* on the left. To its left and right, matching *īwāns* lead to *madrasas*; the right-hand one has a complicated sundial designed by the great 17th-century mathematician, Shaykh Bahā'i. (4)

The place of community prayer, the *'īdgāh*, is a mosque reduced to its bare essentials – a great open praying area with nothing but a *qibla* wall and a *mihrāb*. Here the whole population of a city can assemble for the two major festivals, the Breaking of the Fast and the Sacrifice of Abraham. This example (*right*) is at Nizamabad, Karachi; one has mentally to ignore the modern buildings behind the wall. (5)

Entrance, courtyard and fountain

Two ancillary structures are necessary for Islamic worship: the minaret, from which the muezzin gives the call to prayer (*right*), and a fountain for ablution. The worshipper has to be in a state of ritual purity before he starts to pray. This may mean taking a bath, but normally washing certain prescribed parts of the body is sufficient. *Below:* worshippers preparing themselves for prayer outside a mosque in Fez. (6, 7)

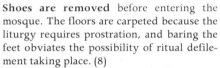

Shoes are removed before entering the mosque. The floors are carpeted because the liturgy requires prostration, and baring the feet obviates the possibility of ritual defilement taking place. (8)

The elderly or infirm may perform their ablutions inside the mosque, using a marble jar with a basin and taps. (9)

The courtyard afforded an opportunity for architectural display, which the Ottomans, the Safavids and especially the Mughals seized with enthusiasm. In Delhi (*above*), the courtyard of the Jāmi' Masjid is surrounded by finely sculptured arches. There is an ablution tank in the middle. (10)

Fountains could also be works of art. In this mosque at Istanbul, each tap is set in a finely worked niche. In front are stone stools so that the worshipper can isolate himself from the ritually impure floor. (11)

The axis of prayer

Inside the mosque the chief feature is the *mihrāb*, a niche in the centre of the *qibla* wall to define the direction of Mecca. This view of the Basīlī Mosque in Alexandria (*left*) shows all the basic liturgical requirements. From left to right: a clock for regulating services, a door into the sacristy, the *mihrāb* with a prayer-mat filling the concavity, surmounted by a round window to show its position externally and with a sanctuary lamp in front of it, and the *minbar*, or pulpit. The top step of the *minbar* (*right*) is reserved for the Prophet; the *īmām* stands on the second step and uses the top one as a seat. (12,13)

The masjid is distinguished from the *jāmi'*, or congregational mosque, by having no *minbar*, as in the Mosque of the Serpents, at Hama, in the Orontes Valley (*above*). (14)

The dikka is a platform usually in line with the *mihrāb* to hold muezzins chanting in unison the responses to the īmām's prayers, thus transmitting the particular stage of the liturgy to those out of earshot. At the Selīmiyye Mosque at Edirne (*above*), the *dikka* shelters an interior fountain. (15)

The working mosque: this lithograph by ▷ David Roberts, of the Mu'ayyad Mosque in Cairo in 1849, shows the mosque in use for teaching. The *mihrāb* is on the extreme left, with the *minbar* alongside. On the other side a teacher addresses a crowd from the high *dikka*, at the foot of which stands a *kursī*. (18)

Between ritually pure and ritually impure intervenes a low barrier, glimpsed here through the door admitting to the ablution zone in the Basīlī Mosque, Alexandria (*left*). (17)

A lectern (*kursī*) for the cantor stands next to the *dikka*. In Cairo, at the mosque of Rifā'i, it is large enough to hold a lectionary type Qur'ān. (16)

The madrasa

Education was always closely connected with worship, and from the beginning mosques could be used for both prayer and instruction (as in the lithograph by Roberts, pl. 18). The two functions eventually diverged, however, and the result was the collegiate mosque, or *madrasa*. Its plan, which seems to go back to the houses of Khurasan, resembles the Iranian mosque layout illustrated in pl. 4: a rectangular courtyard with an *īwān* in the centre of each side. Teaching takes place in the *īwāns*, and the students live in cells arranged along the intermediate walls. *Below:* the restored Mustansiriyya in Baghdad, an archetypal *madrasa* without pulpit or minaret (the minaret here belongs to another mosque), designed as a university and not as a place of worship. *Right:* the ancient *madras* in Isfahan where Avicenna once taught, a building that predates any actual *madrasa*. It is probably the oldest purpose-built structure for Islamic education extant. (19, 20)

24

The most sumptuous of Iranian *madrasas* is the Madrasa-i Shāh at Isfahan, a royal foundation dating from 1712–18. This view shows a corner of the large courtyard devoted to students' accommodation. A water channel running through the courtyard connects the *madrasa* with a caravanserai maintained in perpetuity by a religious endowment. *Right*: students studying in an alcove. They have removed their shoes and squat in a circle. Teaching takes place in a similarly intimate group, the teacher sitting against a pillar in the middle. (21,22)

The monastic mosque

To retreat from the world had been a feature of Islam from its inception. By the 11th century, communities of dervishes were established and monastic mosques were being built to serve their needs, though they follow no consistent pattern. For the Bektashīs, as for the Buddhists of Japan, landscape was part of the meditation technique. A view through the pergola on a terrace of Mount Muqattam (*above*), overlooking Cairo, shows how skilfully they sited their foundations. (23)

Unique in Islam, the so-called Barqūqiyya, outside Cairo, combines the forms of mosque, *madrasa* and monastery. It is cruciform in plan but substitutes hypostyle halls for *iwāns*, while the dervishes are housed in a three-storey block of cells (*above left*). The two domes cover separate funerary chapels for males and females. The collapse of the corridor floors (*above right*) allows one to see the entrances to the cells. (24,25)

Bektashiyya and Mawlawiyya are two of the major orders, both founded by great mystics. *Above left:* the dancing floor of the Bektashī convent of Hājjī Bektash, with the tombs of the Babas or heads of the order on galleries at either side. *Above right:* what was a spot in the middle of the carpet in the previous hall has grown into a pillar in the Bektashī foundation of Merdivenköy. The vertical axis has supplanted the horizontal, producing a completely centralized building. *Below:* the Mawlawiyya headquarters at Konya. The cells of the eighteen celibate dervishes form an L-shaped cloister in the foreground; in the middle distance is their *masjid*, with minaret and ablution fountain; at the back the ceremonial hall and the tomb of the founder, Rūmī. (26,27,28)

Memorial mosques dot the field of the historic Battle of the Ditch, when the supporters of the Prophet successfully defended Medina. Five mosques commemorate the sites of the command posts occupied by the leaders. That on the right was the Prophet's, and is predictably crowded with pilgrims, their heads covered as a sign of reverence. (29)

In a cemetery on the outskirts of Edirne, the architect Sinān built a tomb for his granddaughter. This view shows the oratory with an open trellis-work *mihrāb* enclosed in the typical keel-type arch favoured by the Ottomans, with the tombs lying beyond on the same axis. The floor is uncarpeted, as funeral prayers do not involve prostration, and the places where they are said are not subject to the same canons of purity as obtain in a mosque. *Far right:* two 'anthropomorphic' headstones in the same cemetery. The symbolic tops indicate the professions of those buried beneath. (30,31)

The celebration of death

Traditional Islam has developed rituals associated with death to a remarkable degree. Rules for burial are elaborate and strict, and the architecture of tombs and mausolea includes many masterpieces of Islamic art.

Funerals follow the pattern laid down by the Prophet. A 13th-century miniature from Baghdad (*above*) vividly depicts the committal ceremony in all its grisly detail, from the wailing women to the less involved gravediggers, who are introducing the shrouded corpse head first into the prepared vault. A prismatic coping stone marking the axis of the body's position in the grave is seen head on. More elaborate domed mausolea figure in the background. A modern photograph (*above left*) taken at the Şişli Mosque in Istanbul shows a state prior to this, when the bier, covered with a green, embroidered pall, awaits performance of the funeral prayer. (32, 33)

A modern interpretation of the traditional Mughal tomb is the mausoleum (*left*) designed by the Hyderabadi architect, Zain Yar Jung, for the poet-philosopher Iqbal and completed in 1951. The standard recumbent stone lies on a low plinth, or *suffa*, and there is a detached headstone bearing the epitaph. The marble is of such translucency that a person standing behind the headstone is visible through it. Both stones are inlaid with lapis-lazuli and bedecked with garlands. (34)

29

Cemeteries of Islam

Burial customs are conditioned by beliefs concerning salvation and resurrection. Bodies are placed in a recumbent position at right angles to the *qibla*, so that if turned on their right side they would face Mecca. Coffins are optional but a vault is essential, since the body must be able to sit up and reply to the Angels of the Grave.

Cats were probably the Prophet's favourite animal, and enjoy special privileges in Islam. One of them appears in the manuscript on the left, and they are still a common sight in cemeteries today. (36)

A funeral procession (*left*) approaches the gate of a tomb enclosure. Professional mourners accompany the coffin, while a standard-bearer stands to one side. Inside the enclosure surrounding the tomb of a saint – identifiable by the green pall and lamp – gravediggers are lining a freshly dug grave with stones to form a vault, while masons prepare the mortar. The cat is in the upper left-hand corner. This painting is by one of Islam's greatest artists, Bihzad. (35)

The qibla wall, being closest to Mecca, has more *baraka* than the others and tombs tend to crowd against it, leaving the centre empty. In the tomb for males in the Barqūqiyya, the exterior of which is shown in pl. 24, the graves are, as always, in the correct position at right angles to the *qibla* axis. (37)

The open sky was a fitting vault for a tomb, leaving it exposed to the blessing of rain and dew. The Köprülü tomb in the Divan Yolu in Istanbul is an example of the 'bird-cage' tomb, its beautiful bronze grille forming transparent walls. (38)

'Only the grass shall cover my grave, for grass suffices for the grave of such a pauper as I': the epitaph of the dervish princess, Jahānārā, in Delhi (*above*). One end of her earth-filled grave is seen on the right. (39)

Exquisitely carved, this squat pillar (*left*) stands on the roof of Akbar's mausoleum at Sikandra to hold incense. Next to it is the imperial tomb, but it is empty; Akbar's body lies in another chamber far beneath. (40)

31

The funerary garden remains one of the most profound and satisfying symbols in Islam. In essence it is the Paradisal Garden, which is itself none other than the Primordial Garden which man lost through sin. Grass, flowers and trees are inseparable from the Muslim cult of the dead. The tomb of Humāyūn outside Delhi (dating from 1555–65) is one of the finest funerary monuments in the world, a central mortuary chamber in which the second ruler of the Mughal dynasty rests, with subsidiary chambers round it occupied by less important members of the imperial family. The whole is set within a formal garden, and marks the focal point where the axes intersect. (41)

Liturgically, the mosque may be said to have as its starting point two verses in the Qur'ān; the second reads:

'We have seen the turning of your face towards the heavens [for guidance, O Muhammad]. And now We will turn you indeed towards a qibla which shall please you. So turn your face [in prayer] toward the Sanctified Mosque, and ye [O Muslims], wheresoever ye find yourselves, turn your faces [likewise] toward it' (Sūra ii, 145).

When these verses were revealed in a mosque that still exists on the outskirts of Medina, the congregation obediently turned around and prayed facing south towards Mecca instead of, as formerly, north towards Jerusalem. Picturesquely sited atop a rocky knoll on the outskirts of Medina, this mosque rejoices in the unique title of Masjid al-Qiblatayn (Mosque of the Two Qiblas). When, in the year 629, Mecca replaced Jerusalem as the focus of prayer, Islam gained a religious capital (though not a political one) in addition to a goal of pilgrimage. The notion of a directional axis operates on two levels: socially, as a focal point in relation to which the entire community, umma, is balanced; and liturgically, as the focus of prayer.

Prayer, the Second Pillar, can be construed as use of the horizontal axis by which one relates oneself to the vertical axis as represented by the Ka'ba. In its simplest terms, a mosque is a building erected around a single horizontal axis, the qibla, which passes invisibly down the middle of the floor and, issuing from the far wall, terminates eventually in Mecca. Reduced to essentials, therefore, a mosque is no more than a wall at right angles to the qibla axis and behind, or rather before, that wall there can be anything. This may be seen from the musallā, or 'īdgāh, which is nothing but that: an expanse of ground with a wall at the end, a wall with inserted niche and engaged pulpit. The Prophet's Mosque in Medina formed the prototype to which all subsequent Islamic religious building adhered, establishing the bipartite division of the mosque as well as this principle of axial planning. At the point where the qibla axis meets the far wall of the mosque an indentation is produced, a directional niche called the mihrāb, which is nothing less than the liturgical axis made visible. The mihrāb takes the shape of an arched niche, mostly framed by one or more pairs of colonnettes. Being the visual as well as the liturgical climax of the mosque, where the imām stations himself to lead the congregation in prayer, the mihrāb is usually the object of much lavish ornamentation. If a mosque have a lateral chapel, a flanking balcony, a royal or imperial loge, or īwāns on the transversal axis, then these auxilliary areas, too, are provided with mihrābs, though on a proportionately humbler scale, in much the same way as each chapel in a church has its own altar.

The earliest mosques had no mihrāb; and in the Prophet's Mosque at Medina a block of stone on the floor served the purpose of indicating the direction. This stone may have stood in for the Black Stone of the Ka'ba, which, as a sort of foundation stone, it symbolically represented.

When, however, Muslim armies fanned out from Medina in all directions and established the Islamic Empire, a means had to be devised to cope with the problem of prayer en route. The solution arrived at had the simplicity of genius; it was to trace in the sand with a spear the plan of an ad hoc mosque and then to thrust the spear, haft downwards, into the sand at the point occupied by the stone in the mosque in Medina. Once the worshipper had stepped over the boundary thus demarcated he was within a sanctified area in which all the Qur'ānic taboos governing ritual purity were in operation. The spear, then, was the first general liturgical indicator in Islam, although within a few decades the niche, introduced for the first time at Medina, became the standard means of indicating the direction of prayer. The spear survives, iconographically, in the coinage of the Umayyad dynasty. On a dirham struck during the reign of 'Abd al-Malik, a spear is shown standing upright within the niche, which by this time had become normative as liturgical indicator.

The mihrāb is an early innovation in Islamic architecture, and its origins have been the object of controversy. The concave mihrāb entered Islamic architecture in 707–9 when the caliph-to-be, 'Umar ibn 'Abd al-'Azīz, brought Coptic masons to Medina for the purpose of rebuilding the Prophet's Mosque. These masons fashioned a niche in the qibla wall similar to those in the Coptic churches they had worked on, with the difference that what had been a devotional niche now became directional. A mihrāb is an acoustic device, a resonator for the voice, shaped to bounce the sound back and magnify it at the same time. The concave mihrāb was, therefore, no fortuitous innovation but the consequence of an order that the Muslim overseers must have given the Copts. Flat mihrābs, where they exist, are for the purpose of private, recollected devotion not public address, because their shape would disperse the sound instead of trapping it. The *mihrāb* promptly became the central feature of any mosque and, indeed, of all sacred art and architecture in Islam. The same principle of directionality governs the design of mosques, mausolea and prayer-rugs, all of which feature the *mihrāb*. Divested of liturgical significance, the niche figures as a design motif throughout the Islamic fine arts, from textiles to tombstones, where it is anomalous.

The *mihrāb* has little in common with the altar of a Christian church; indeed, in all essential respects it is its antithesis. Whereas an altar is convex, or at least protuberant, the *mihrāb* is concave and this concavity, the symbolism of which requires that it be kept empty at all times, opposes itself aesthetically to the cluttered surface of an altar *mensa*. It is not the niche that is sacred but the direction it expresses; and precisely for this reason the *mihrāb* is accorded extraordinary respect. As a corollary, while mosques are oriented towards the *qibla*, bedrooms and privies are deliberately disoriented to obviate the possibility of inadvertent sacrilege. Very occasionally the connection between the *mihrāb* and its goal is made explicit: probably unique is the inclusion of stone fragments of the Ka'ba in the *mihrāb* of the mosque of Sokollu Mehmet Paşa at Kadırga in Istanbul; and certain prayer-rug designs include miniature representations of the Ka'ba, fitted under the apex of the *mihrāb* arch.

External features of the mosque

It is in relation to the *qibla* axis that the principal items of liturgical furniture are distributed, but considering the stages involved in the liturgical action it makes better sense to outline the external features of the mosque before moving inside. These features comprise minaret, dome and ablution fountain, the last of which occupies an intermediate position between external and internal features.

When Islam solidified into its present liturgical forms in Medina, some means of summoning people to prayer had to be devised, particularly for the congregational prayer at noon on Fridays, which involves the obligatory attendance of all adult males and the optional attendance of adult females. Muhammad disliked the Jewish use of the *shofar*, or ram's horn, and the Christian use of wooden clappers, both of which sounded cacophanous to his ears. After a dream in which one of the Prophet's companions saw a man chanting a summons to prayer, Muhammad turned to his Abyssinian freedman, Bilāl al-Habashī, and said, 'Mount up, Bilāl, and call the people to prayer'. Bilāl, who was noted for the sweetness of his voice, was therefore the first muezzin in Islam. The muezzin's office is to chant the *adhān*, or summons to prayer, which, in the prelapsarian days before the loud-speaker, used to flow over the rooftops and never failed to impress travellers with its plangent, fragile beauty. This was not, of course, the origin of the minaret but only the motivation for its invention; it was the need for height from which to broadcast the call that led to the development of the minaret. The muezzin's balcony is analogous to the belfry: the higher one gets the greater the area over which the sound can be distributed. As K. A. C. Creswell has shown, the minaret developed out of the corner towers of the temenos of the Church of St John the Baptist at Damascus, when the entire area was taken over to build the Umayyad mosque; here, however, the resemblance to Christian architecture ends, for church towers have to be sturdily built to take the immense weight of the bells, which is why minarets are more slender and graceful.

Though the column, the arch and the dome have been described as the trinity of Islamic architecture, the crowning glory of Islamic art is undoubtedly the dome, even if liturgically it is of minor significance. The earliest domes were small affairs erected over the *qibla* to define it externally and to light it internally. At a later stage the dome was used to cover the mortuary chamber in which the founder's body rested; then the dome moved from this lateral position to a central one, and grew in volume until it covered the entire sanctuary area around the *qibla*. And the mosque gained in utility what it lost in numinous impression, such as that conveyed by the Great Mosque at Cordoba; but, liturgically, either position had the effect of ensuring the visibility of the *imām* to his congregants. In early mosques he was highlighted against a dark interior; in later mosques he stood out less but everyone could read, not just those sitting near the windows. The dome is, of course, a cosmic symbol in almost every religious tradition; and, symbolically, in Islam the dome represents the vault of heaven in the same way as the garden prefigures Paradise.

Since the dome stands for heaven, the Paradisal Tree provides an appropriate motif for the decoration of its interior surface. An outstanding example of such decoration is found in the Dome of the Rock, where a highly stylized Cosmological Tree – which in Islam grows upside down – spreads downwards from the apex of the dome to embrace all the widening stages of heaven by the time it reaches the foot. The use of the *arbor inversus* may seem odd, but in Islam Paradise is the opposite, or mirror image, of this world. The principle of reversibility recurs throughout Islam; thus, the visible Qur'ān is but a reflection of the Preserved Tablet, the supernatural archetype which is laid up in heaven. Similarly, from the four quarters of the globe and in Mecca itself, one prays towards the Ka'ba. But once inside the Ka'ba one prays in the reverse direction, that is, outwards to any of the four walls. But perhaps the best example of such reversal is from the rich fund of anecdotage left by the Turkish folk hero, the inimitable Nasr ad-Dīn Khōja, who said: 'When I am dead, bury me upside down so in the next world I may appear the right way up.'

Intermediate between external and internal features is the ablution fountain, generally located in the centre of the courtyard to emphasize the initiatic function of water in Islam, exactly as the font in Christianity is located just inside the west door to emphasize that it is through the sacrament of baptism one enters Christ's Church. Similarly, in Islam water is the vehicle of purification and enjoys an almost sacramental status. In addition to a courtyard fountain, supplementary ablution facilities may be provided inside the mosque, often in the shape of a colossal marble jar with basin and taps so that the elderly may comply with the law without risk of exposure to the inclemency of the elements. Ablution may be either total or partial depending on the state of ritual impurity in which the worshipper finds himself. Normally, partial ablution suffices, but carnal intercourse ranks as a major defilement, and in this case a bath is mandatory. Whether total or partial, ablution must be performed with running water. Among its amenities, the fountain has taps for lukewarm water and low stools so the user can isolate himself physically from the ritually impure floor. This latter factor is the reason why, if the taps, together with showers and latrines, be in an area of their own, this wet zone should be separated from the rest of the mosque by a low balustrade. This defines the boundary between the areas of ritual purity and impurity, the former being invariably carpeted for the comfort of the congregants and kept scrupulously clean.

Likewise, at the entrance to the mosque stands another barrier with identical purpose: to demarcate pure and impure areas, in this case the street or public thoroughfare. It is at this barrier that congregants doff their footwear before entering the sanctuary or crossing it to reach the ablution zone. This is to obviate the possibility of ritually impure substances adhering to the soles and being deposited on the mosque floor. Shoes are accommodated in racks at the entrance or against the walls, or in wooden troughs on the floor. In addition to doffing his footwear the worshipper should properly cover his head, which is the Oriental way of showing respect. On being admitted to audience with a caliph or sultan one would cover one's head out of respect for the royalty of the Presence; so in a mosque one covers out of respect for the Divinity. Any brimless headgear that does not interfere with prostration is permissible, although a skullcap is preferable.

Prayer and the liturgical basis of mosque design

Formal prayer in Islam consists of repeated sequences of standing, bowing, prostration and genuflection; prayer is thus not only mental and verbal but also physical, thereby involving the whole being. Behind this practice lies the central Islamic concept of God's overlordship; and the physical postures represent progressive degrees of acknowledgment of this fact, culminating in the total abasement of prostration.

Prayer is established on four levels. Firstly, the daily prayers, which may be performed in congregation but are usually carried out individually. This office is held at the five liturgical hours of dawn, noon, afternoon, sunset and evening. Secondly, the congregational prayer on Friday at noon, which replaces the noon office for that day. Thirdly, community prayer on the two major festivals, ʿĪd al-Fitr (Feast of the Breaking of the Fast) and ʿĪd al-Adhā (Feast of the Sacrifice of Abraham). Fourthly, the annual ritual of the pilgrimage, which is a congregation of all the Muslims of the world. The four levels of prayer operate on an ascending scale: firstly, the individual; secondly, any congregation; thirdly, the total population of a town or city; and lastly, the entire Muslim world. Every level except the last has a corresponding sacred structure: for the first it is a *masjid*; for the second a *jāmiʿ*; and for the third a *musallā*, place of prayer, or *ʿīdgāh*, place of ʿĪd, an immense, open praying area with nothing but a *qibla* wall with a *mihrāb* and an open-air pulpit – in other words, a mosque reduced to its essentials. The Second and Fifth Pillars of Islam interact to produce a convergence on one day in the year, which is the climax of the liturgical calendar: the anniversary of the Sacrifice of Abraham, when the climax of the pilgrimage rites in the Plain of Arafat outside Mecca coincides with the ʿĪd prayers being said throughout the Islamic world. Thus the ʿĪd ritual is a local reflection of the pilgrimage.

Just as the third level necessitated a *musallā*, so it is the second, or congregational, level which is the motivation for the mosque. And it is the congregational factor – that is, how to regulate an immense crowd in accordance with the needs of the liturgy – that entails an aetiology of mosque design to explain why each piece of liturgical furniture occupies a specific station on the floor, as well as how these pieces of furniture and the offices corresponding to them interlock to form the liturgy. Also, the morphology of the liturgical action determines what categories are embraced within a typology of mosques according to two criteria: the functional (e.g. collegiate, memorial, etc.) and the geographic or cultural (e.g. not just Iranian but Seljuq, Mongol or Tīmūrid).

The directionality of prayer is fundamental to the

liturgical principles around which a mosque is constructed. A temple is a building designed to house a liturgical function. Churches developed as long, narrow buildings equipped with aisles as a result of the need to cope with a processional liturgy, whereas the mosque evolved as a square or rectangular building because it had to cope with a radial liturgy. For the architect of the mosque, two contradictory principles are involved. One of these stems from the insistence of Prophetical Tradition on the priority of the first row; that is, the first row of worshippers enjoys greater proximity to the source of blessing because it confronts the wall nearest to Mecca. There is then a *prima facie* case for extending the mosque laterally to accommodate as many as possible in the first row. But with a radial liturgy, the officiant in the middle would be invisible and inaudible at the extremities. As a result, two axes are in conflict; the primary liturgical axis of the *qibla* and the transversal axis, because of the superiority of the front row and the progressive inferiority of the rows behind. The success of a mosque architect may be measured by the degree to which he succeeds in reconciling these conflicting principles, taking into consideration the two axes and distributing mass and volume accordingly, to produce that impression of total equipoise which a successful mosque never fails to convey.

While for the daily prayers an oratory with no more than a *mihrāb* suffices or even merely a prayer-rug, which is really a portable mosque ensuring the ritual purity of the spot where the prayer is offered, there are small mosques known as *masjids*, literally, 'places of prostration', where such prayers are regularly performed behind an *imām*. A *masjid* should have no *minbar* because it is not used for Friday worship; this is the case in Turkey, where, practically alone in the Muslim world, the distinction between *masjid* and *jāmi'* is still recognized and the respective terms correctly used. The mosque par excellence, however, is the *jāmi' masjid*, that is, 'collective' or 'assembly' mosque, whose primary function is the Friday service, and hence is known in Iran as *the masjid-i Jum'a*, or Friday mosque, Friday being *Yawm al-Jum'a*, or 'Day of Assembly'. Having to cope with such numbers, and influenced by the precedent of the Prophet's Mosque (which had a covered portion supported on palm trunks), as well as the sheer expediency of utilizing the plethora of columns from redundant churches, the early *jāmi'* took the form of an immense hypostyle hall preceded by a courtyard.

Liturgical furniture of the mosque

What chiefly distinguishes the Friday service from the daily liturgy is the inclusion of a sermon. Thus, in addition to the omnipresent *mihrāb*, a *jāmi'* rejoices in the possession of a pulpit, *minbar*, to the right of the niche, so that the prayer-leader, or *imām* (properly, on this occasion an *imām khatīb*, or preaching *imām*), can address the congregation. In early Islamic times, the sermon was political rather than dogmatic in content, which helps to explain why the shape of the *minbar* has nothing in common with the Christian ambo. In origin it was the throne of the leader of the community, set up in the place of assembly, from the top of which he, Muhammad, pontificated as lawgiver. Having completed the sermon, he would descend the pulpit and enter the niche to lead the prayer, for as leader he represented the people to God and led the prayer in that capacity. This double role is expressed in the practice whereby to this day it is the same man who delivers the address as leads the prayers. The *minbar* is, therefore, a symbol of authority as much as an acoustic elevation, and in the case of the *imām*, of delegated authority. Conceivably, this may account for the fact that at a later stage of its evolution it acquired a canopy or dome, the canopy being an attribute of the ruler and even, in Indian iconography, of divinity. Moreover, the *imām* always delivers his address not from the top but from a lower step, and it may be that the empty, canopied space stands for the absent Prophet, exactly as in primitive Buddhism there was no image of the Buddha, a canopy sufficing to indicate his presence. Similarly, the practice of flanking the pulpit with standards not only emphasizes the intimate connection between politics and religion in Islam, but goes back to the Prophet, who walked to the *minbar* flanked by standard-bearers.

The first *minbar* was a rudimentary affair of three steps fashioned from tamarisk wood, from the topmost of which Muhammad addressed the Companions. Out of respect, Abū Bakr, the first caliph, occupied the intermediate step, and 'Umar modestly used the lowermost; but 'Uthmān said, 'Shall we descend into the bowels of the earth?', and thereafter everyone has used the first step from the top. During the reign of Abū Bakr, and even more with the sensational conquests of 'Umar, regional mosques proliferated, especially in the garrison towns of the Islamic armies. In these places the governor would lead the prayers, deputizing for the caliph in the same fashion as the latter deputized for the Prophet. The term *imām* survives with the meaning of prayer-leader, but as an exclusively religious office it dates only from the 'Abbāsids. Until that time, the conduct of public worship was one of the attributes of the ruler. When the governor of a province placed himself at the head of the community assembled for prayer it was clear to everyone that he was the caliph's representative. Islam does not distinguish between spiritual and temporal power. The juxtaposition of the *mihrāb* and *minbar* expresses their co-identity in the ambivalence of the *imām*, who uses both.

Pulpits are frequently of wood, richly carved and glowing with incrustation of nacre and ivory. Marble is no less common, and limestone and even iron have on occasion been used. Iran evinced a decided preference for the low pulpit, and the Indo-Pakistan subcontinent knows no other. In most countries the *minbar* became architecture in its own right, with folding doors admitting to a stairway crowned with a canopy or a bulbous cupola and topped with a crescent finial. But the most dramatic development took place in Turkey, where the stupendous Ottoman interiors required, both visually and acoustically, tall elegant structures, no less than ten metres high.

Of almost equal importance in the liturgy is the respondents' platform, or *dikka*. This usually straddles the *qibla* axis at a point about the middle of the mosque. But, since in a radial liturgy the first prerequisite is the visibility of the officiant in his niche, the *dikka* can also be positioned off the axis to the right. Although resorted to frequently in Turkey, this measure sensibly reduces the efficacy of the *dikka*. It is another prerequisite, not so much the visiblity of the *imām* as the audibility of his voice, that forms the *raison d'être* of the *dikka*. The *dikka* is a very early innovation and was already in widespread use by the 8th century, increase in congregation size having decreed its invention. Its closest approximation, outside Islam, is the choir stalls of a church. The respondents are known as *muballighūn*, human amplifiers (of the *imām's* voice), but it is not an office in its own right, for in a mosque every muezzin doubles as a respondent. Their function, from their vantage point atop the elevation of the *dikka*, is to copy the posture of the *imām* and chant in unison the appropriate exclamation or response, thereby transmitting that stage of the liturgy to the ranks behind, for whom the *imām* is neither visible nor audible. To regulate the movement of the congregation, liturgical signals are used, the most important being the *takbīr*, or Magnification, *Allāhu akbar*; and the importance of the *muballighūn* lies in the fact that by means of these signals they co-ordinate and synchronize the movements of all parts of the congregation.

With the advent of the loudspeaker, platform and respondents alike fell into desuetude, at which point Islam embarked on its present course of liturgical decadence. Their function was absorbed into that of the *qāri'*, or cantor, whose lectern flanked the *dikka*. Known as *kursī 's-sūra*, 'chair of the *sūra*' – because from it the cantor chants the Eighteenth Sūra of the Qur'ān in the half hour that elapses between the first and second *adhans* – this is the last item of liturgical

furniture to be considered. The art of *tajwīd*, or cantillation of the Qur'ān, is one of the most cultivated arts in Islam, being the phonic equivalent of calligraphy, the Islamic art par excellence. Most mosques have always had at least one lectern, or *kursī*. In Egypt the earliest-dated *dikka* bears the name of the 15th-century ruler, Qāyitbāy, but the earliest *kursī* goes back to Fātimid times (in the mosque within St Catherine's Monastery, Sinai). Like the earliest *minbars* (which ran on wheels), the *kursī* is a moveable item of furniture, albeit ponderous and awkward to shift. Made of wood with the habitual lavish incrustation, the standard *kursī* incorporates a little platform on which the cantor kneels facing the *qibla* as well as, optionally, a V-shaped slot to hold a copy of the Qur'ān. Mosque Qur'āns are gigantic and are comparable to lectionaries and antiphonaries, sometimes requiring two men to carry a single tome of a thirty-volume Qur'ān. Cantors are assigned in greater numbers to colleges and mausolea: in the former case so that students may learn the approved methods of reading the Qur'ān, and in the latter so that the deceased may benefit from the *baraka*, or spiritual power that inheres in the words.

In addition to niche, pulpit, respondents' tribune and cantor's lectern, a mosque abounds in quasi-liturgical items, such as folding stools to keep the Qur'ān off the floor, out of respect; safe receptacles, known as *kursīs*, used for holding the Qur'ān; reliquaries; sanctuary lamps; another, but differently shaped, *kursī* for instruction; and prayer-rugs, either single or serial; as well as candlesticks which flank the *mihrāb*, and which when lit during Ramadān envelop the *qibla* in an atmosphere of cultus. But all these count more as furnishing than furniture and command no place in the liturgy comparable to the intermeshing functions of *mihrāb*, *kursī* and *dikka*. The latter in pre-electronic mosques now stands forlorn, lamentable to behold, while in the modern mosque it does not even exist. Its abolition, with consequent dislocation of the *kursī* due to the development of electronics, has been a catastrophe, for it entails a loss of the stereophonic character of the liturgy. St Augustine wrote that architecture and music were the highest arts because they were 'the sisters of numbers', an admission which shows he was a Pythagorean at heart. The aesthetic significance of the mosque resides not in the architecture alone but in the fact that it was a place where that art was always to be found in the company of its sister.

The collegiate mosque, or madrasa

The functional criterion applied to a typology of mosques yields, in addition to separate structures for daily, congregational and community prayers, such other types as memorial, tomb, shrine and cemetery mosques as well as the monastic mosque, and one other type almost equal in importance to the *jāmi'*: the *madrasa*, or collegiate mosque. The problem in Islam is that nomenclature is never other than confused and different categories overlap. Not only did the *madrasa* plan ultimately furnish a model for the monastic mosque but the monastic mosque at an earlier stage of its development may have influenced the plan of the first *madrasa*. This was in Khurasan whence the new plan was to embark on a career of conquest, revolutionizing society and architecture alike.

In Islam, higher as well as elementary education is based on the religious sciences and related philological disciplines. The elementary school functions inside mosques, some of which, such as al-Azhar at Cairo, include facilities for higher education; in such places one can see a master on a *kursī* next to a pillar, his pupils forming a circle at his feet (hence the *halqa*, or 'circle', system of education). The credit for inventing a purpose-built structure incorporating lecture theatres and residential facilities for the students along with some basic liturgical features almost certainly belongs to Khurasan (of earlier *madrasas* at Ghazni, c. 1000, nothing is known); and its subsequent diffusion thence was in response to the prevailing political situation. By the time the Seljuqs appointed themselves guardians of the 'Abbāsid caliphate in 1055, practically the entire Muslim world had lapsed from Sunnī orthodoxy. Almost everywhere heresy was triumphant: the Fātimids (Sevener Shī'īs) had an anticaliph enthroned in Cairo whence they controlled a vast empire; no less vast was the empire of the Būyids (Twelver Shī'īs), based in Baghdad, the seat of the orthodox caliphate, which they stopped short of abolishing, and covering Iran as well as Mesopotamia. But they did not control the key province of Khurasan, which was virtually the only area where orthodoxy had not succumbed, with the result that the great Seljuq vizier, Nizām al-Mulk, decided to rally here the forces of orthodoxy: the key to his strategy was the *madrasa*.

The Prophet's house, or more accurately its courtyard, had supplied the model for the *jāmi'*; and now it was another domestic courtyard that was adapted for the needs of the *madrasa*. The typical Khurasanian house was cruciform in plan, with four arched openings, known as *īwāns*, off a central courtyard. Quite fortuitously, this layout coincided with the ideal framework within which to teach the four legal schools of orthodox Islam that enjoyed canonical status: the Hanafī, Shāfi'ī, Mālikī and Hanbalī rites. The space between each *īwān* and the corner of the courtyard could be extended to accommodate the students in cells arranged in one or two storeys. It is the residential factor that relates the collegiate to the monastic mosque, but whatever its

origins Khurasan thus witnessed the birth of a structure combining pragmatism and beauty to a degree seldom seen. The typical Khurasan *madrasa* consisted of two tiers of cells, or *hujras*, preceded by diminutive *īwāns* running around a courtyard, each side of which was punctuated in the middle by an *īwān* rising the full height of the façade or projecting in a frame above the line of the roof. The *qibla īwān* was given more prominence than the other three so it would serve as an oratory, *qibliyya*, without a pulpit however, as well as accommodating, between the liturgical hours, whichever was locally the most prominent of the rites. Such a building was at once symmetrical and yet articulated towards a focal point.

A *madrasa* courtyard can be viewed as a scenario with the façades broken at intervals by the huge axial *īwāns* in which the rhythm of the rows of small *īwāns* culminates, since they describe the same outline but on contrasted scales. The relationship in which they exist to each other is also modified by the very different spatial relationship that obtains between them and such accents as minarets and domes. It is not surprising that the new invention soon eclipsed the less spectacular *jāmi'*, even on its own ground, the liturgical.

Probably the first *madrasas* were simply the houses of the teachers, whereafter the idea was reproduced on a monumental scale appropriate to the Seljuq Empire whose needs the new installation was intended to serve. The great vizier, Nizām al-Mulk, who was the real ruler of the empire during the reign of Malik Shāh, realized the unique potential of the *madrasa* for training cadres of administrators without which the state could not hope to combat the heresies which menaced its existence. But it would be wrong to view the *madrasa* as no more than a tool of Sunnī (orthodox) reaction. From its inception, indeed from the very first word of the first revelation to Muhammad, Islam had the character of a literary and, therefore, learned civilization; in such a context the acquisition of knowledge and its transmission were paramount. Of these twin aims the *madrasa* was the instrument, and a network of *madrasas* was soon established, providing higher education in almost every urban area in the Islamic world.

The most famous Islamic university, the Nizāmiyya of Baghdad, was established in 1067. In jurisprudence it was Shāfi'ī and in theology Ash'arī: indeed, the role of the *madrasa* in speculative theology may have been decisive in canonizing Ash'arism as the official theology of Islam. Given its fame, we might have expected to know more about the Nizāmiyya of Baghdad, but the site of Islam's greatest university remains unexcavated, although there is no lack of evidence about its location. As a single-rite (Shāfi'ī) *madrasa*, with some six thousand students, it may have had no more than one *īwān*. The Nizāmiyya was eventually eclipsed by the rival establishment of the Mustansiriyya, the al-Mustansir Madrasa, founded in Baghdad in 1234. Excellently restored, the four-rite four-*īwān* Mustansiriyya represents the new genre in the perfection of its first flowering, before the collegiate function was overtaken by the liturgical. In teaching all four rites the Mustansiriyya was something of an exception; of some thirty *madrasas* in Baghdad all save two, the Bashariyya and the Mustansiriyya, taught but one rite. Nonetheless, one Nizāmiyya, that of Khargird, disclosed on excavation a perfect cruciform plan, as did another excavated at Rayy. In early *madrasas* there seems to be no correlation between size and the number of *īwāns*, and probably the number of *īwāns* responded to local conditions or even political considerations. Pending further evidence, one can only assume that single and multiple *madrasas* ran in parallel until, in the end, the latter prevailed.

Madrasas built by the Seljuqs of Rum are both simple and multiple. A three-*īwān* version resulted in the T-plan mosque, which was standard for the early Ottoman period and was superseded only by the centralized, dome-dominated mosque that emerged in Edirne (the Üç Şerefeli Mosque) and then triumphed in Istanbul. A gradual evolution is discernible even at the Bursa stage. Based on Seljuq precedent, the Bursa mosque had a domed courtyard, which, by contraction of the *īwāns*, suddenly discloses itself a Selīmiyye in miniature, anticipating Sinān's mosque of that name in Edirne by about two centuries. The apsidal structure containing the *mihrāb* in the latter mosque can even be interpreted as a residual *īwān-i qibla*. Seljuq *madrasas* on the full-scale plan, as at Sivas, Divriği and Erzurum, are colossal structures; however, the single-*īwān madrasas*, such as the Büyük Karatay and the Ince Minare, both in Konya, were small enough to allow the roofing of the courtyard, not, as in Egypt, with a lantern but with a dome, which resulted in a very harmonious design. The Seljuq art of Anatolia began with blunt, almost brutal forms expressive of power to an uncommon degree and ended in the grace of these two *madrasas*, which would be peerless were it not for the presence in the same city of the exquisite Sirçali ('glass') Madrasa. It began in grotesqueries on the façades of Sivas and Divriği, reminiscent of the Romanesque at its most bizarre, and ended in the refinement of the Ince Minare portal, whose sculptural quality sublimates the inherent beauty of Seljuq design without diminution of its powerfulness. This sense of power is the first impression to be conveyed by a Seljuq building, be it the mausoleum of the princess Khwānd Khātūn at Kayseri in Anatolia or the tomb tower of Qābūs at Gorgan, near the Caspian.

It was the Seljuq rebuilding of Isfahan's *jāmi'*, after the fire of 1121, in the shape of a four-*īwān madrasa* that set Iranian architecture on a course from which it has never subsequently deviated. Not even the Safavid accession in the 16th century and the consequent proclamation of Shī'ism as the state religion, with the coercive conversion of the country's Sunnī population, affected the supremacy of the *madrasa*. The standard Iranian mosque results from a fusion of the local 'kiosk' mosque, congregational in purpose, with the *madrasa*, collegiate in purpose; and to the product of this strange *mésalliance* are added minarets and dome. The dome surmounts the kiosk, to which the *qibla īwān* now forms a vestibule, and its importance is further emphasized by the addition of minarets at the side. The presence of a dome was accounted mandatory after the construction of the mosque at Zavare in 1135. That an invention so resolutely Sunnī should become normative in the most Shī'ī country in the Muslim world is a baffling paradox. Whatever its functional drawbacks when adapted to congregational purposes (visibility of the *imām* in an Iranian mosque being practically nil), aesthetically the emended *madrasa* is a vast improvement on the hypostyle *jāmi'*, which at best never had more articulation than that imparted to it by an axial aisle higher than the aisles to either side. The Tīmūrid development of this hybrid proved incomparable, producing in Transoxiana, Iran and India buildings that have no peer. The axially-planned Mughal mosque is derivative from the Iranian mosque but differs from it in details. Three, sometimes five, pyramidally arranged domes replace the single dome of Iran; the minarets return to the corners of the building to define the entire composition with an emphatic vertical accent; the two tiers of cells are reduced to single-storey porticoes whose low profiles throw into high relief the centre *īwāns*, which in their turn assume the function of entrance gates; and finally the whole is elevated on a tremendous plinth, known as a *kursī*, giving the mosque a monumental character unsurpassed elsewhere.

Syria takes us back to the heartlands of *dār al-Islām*, where Seljuq influence was no less paramount. In Syria, the earliest *madrasa* of which anything survives is a T-plan Hanafī *madrasa* of 1136, in Busra. The famous Nūriyya Madrasa in Damascus, whose quondam splendour can be guessed at from the only intact portion, the tomb of Nūr ad-Dīn Zangī, has a single (Hanafī) *īwān* facing an oblong, laterally extended oratory; but Nūr ad-Dīn's hospital has four *īwāns*. Infirmaries, or *māristāns*, follow the *madrasa* plan, which caught on to such an extent that it was indifferently used for madhouses, palaces, caravanserais, monasteries and even observatories, as well as colleges and hospitals. Indeed, from extant remains it is sometimes difficult to say which of these functions a cruciform building had.

One of the consequences of Saladin's defeat of the Fāṭimids in 1171 was the transposition of the *madrasa* from Syrian to Egyptian soil, where it flourished perhaps more than anywhere else. The new Ayyūbid *madrasas* were patterned on the one- and two-rite *madrasas* of Zangid Syria, which had in turn been the link with the art of the Great Seljuqs to the east. The majority of the Egyptians had remained unaffected by Ismā'īlī propaganda and were still Sunnīs of the Shāfi'ī persuasion. The first *madrasa* to be erected in Egypt, in 1216, was a two-*iwān* college, of which the mausoleum of Abū Manṣūr Ismā'īl still stands. The next building in Egypt to use the *iwān* principle was the Kāmiliyya Madrasa; but the first to have four *iwāns* was a curious twin *madrasa* (with two *iwāns* apiece) erected by al-Malik aṣ-Ṣāliḥ in 1241–2. The first to have all four normally disposed around a central courtyard was the Zāhiriyya of 1263, built by the same Baybars responsible for the other Zāhiriyya in Damascus. These royal patrons initiated a series of *madrasas* in unbroken succession down to the Ghūriyya, built by Qānṣūh al-Ghūrī, the penultimate Mamlūk sultan. After the last sultan was hanged at the Zuwayla Gate in 1517 the native style yielded to the imported Ottoman mosque. The modern Egyptian mosque results from a fusion of the Mamlūk style with the spatial insights of the Ottoman architects. Before its expiry, Mamlūk architecture had produced some of the finest Islamic buildings to be seen anywhere. The apotheosis of the *madrasa* in Cairo is that of Sultan Hasan. Afterwards, by reducing the courtyard in relation to the space occupied by the four *iwāns*, it was found possible to cover the courtyard and crown the building centrally with a lantern. This development, for which the Circassian Mamlūks take the credit, resulted in a unified design perfectly adaptable for congregational purposes, as is proved by its occasional contemporary revival (such as the Ramla Station Mosque in Alexandria) in which no function other than the liturgical is intended. In such cases, contraction of the lateral *iwāns* (or their adaptation to quasi-liturgical purposes such as ablution) ensures the visibility of the *imām* as he officiates in his niche. Indeed, except for rare revivals, in Egypt the *madrasa* may be said to have supplanted the *jāmi'*.

The monastic mosque, or khānaqāh

Nor is the collegiate mosque the sole Islamic institution that Egypt owes to that paladin of orthodoxy, Saladin: he it was who introduced the monastic mosque in Egypt, founding the country's first *khānaqāh* in a private house, the Dār Sa'īd as-Su'ada', in 1173–4.

Obviously, there is a close connection between the monastic mosque and the collegiate mosque, for they have in common the instructive and disciplinal factors as well as the residential, with all its concomitant facilities. But nomenclature at this point becomes a major problem, for in addition to *khānaqāh* numerous other terms are used: *takkiyya* (Turkish, *tekke*); *buq'a* (retreat); *dargāh* (lodge); *zāwiya* (converted house); and *ribāt* (monastic fortress).

The development of the monastic mosque cannot be considered independently of monasticism in Islam. As in Christianity, this was not contemporaneous with the foundation of the Faith but a later development. Yet, just as Christian monasticism has its roots in Christ's example if not his prescription, so Islamic monasticism goes back to the *sunna* of the Prophet whose habit it was to go into retreat, or *i'tikāf*, for ten-day periods.

Islamic monasticism is of two kinds, eremitical and coenobitic. The second was to give rise to specific architectural forms. From earliest times mosques had to provide facilities for retreatants in the shape of cells. These were temporarily occupied, but it was also customary for an ascetic to reside permanently in a minaret (*sawma'a*, one of the words for minaret, can also mean cell or hermitage), a practice which cannot but remind one of the stylites. Al-Ghazālī, Islam's most famous theologian, lived for a time in the west minaret of the Umayyad Mosque at Damascus, whither he had travelled after resigning his chair in the Nizāmiyya Madrasa at Baghdad. Such practices provide a basis for coenobitic monasticism, but all this time eremitical monasticism was offering an alternative kind of ascesis.

Still following the *sunna*, hermits would take up residence in caves, in imitation of the Prophet's regular withdrawal to the cave in Mount Hira outside Mecca, where in fact, after much fasting, Muhammad experienced the first revelation. In Egypt, Mount Muqattam was much favoured for this purpose and, in Spain, the mountains near Almería. This practice continued even after the institutionalization of asceticism in the shape of the first monastic establishments, or *khānaqāhs*, which emerged in response to the solidification of Sūfism into institutional forms of expression designed to ensure the transmission of a mystical method. These are the dervish orders, which first appeared in the late 12th century. Differing widely in their organization and rules, some are celibate, some are not, others only partly so. Celibate orders require kitchens and refectories in addition to cells. One order of itinerant dervishes, the Qalandariyya, needs no permanent residential provision but only begging bowls. In many respects, indeed, the closest equivalent to the Sūfī is not the Western monk but the *staretz* of the Eastern church. In fact, of all the myriad forms of Christianity, closest to Islam in spirit is the Russian Orthodox Church, with which it exhibits not a few parallels: apart from the obvious Sūfī/*staretz* correspondence, the 'holy fool' (known in Arabic as *majdhūb*) is common to both traditions; likewise the concept of the *batal*, or hero-saint; even the period of forty days' intensive mourning; while perhaps the most significant of all is the resemblance of *tasbīh* (use of the rosary) to the Jesus Prayer.

As the orders are extraordinarily fissiparous, *khānaqāhs* abound in Muslim cities; or, rather, abounded, because since the orders are foci of hostility to policies of Westernization they are a prime target for secular governments intent on erasing the influence of Islam. In consequence, their number has diminished dramatically, and it is not always easy to discern any consistent pattern among extant structures, even between houses of the same order. All of them consist, however, of the addition to a mosque of various dependencies such as ceremonial hall, cells, kitchen, refectory, punishment cell, library, special quarters for the shaykh and a guest house, but their arrangement is by no means as consistent as the organization of chapter-house, slype, dorter, lavatorium and refectory around a Christian cloister. In Egypt, *khānaqāhs* often employ the *madrasa* plan, with one of the *īwāns* serving as the ceremonial hall. This is vividly illustrated by the *khānaqāh* of Baybars al-Jashnakīr, in Cairo, completed in 1309, which could easily be mistaken for a *madrasa*. In fact, the two are often found side by side. It is often difficult to identify which orders occupied which *khānaqāhs* and one reason may be that the rulers changed them at will, thereby keeping the control of these sensitive establishments in their own hands.

The Ottoman combination of *madrasa*, *khānaqāh*, mausoleum and fountain, *sabīl*, within a single foundation really begins in Cairo and Baghdad. There is a steady stream of such foundations, usually royal, from the 14th century. The complex of Barsbay, in Cairo, is woefully ruined but the beautiful façade and rooms of the lower storeys are intact and would richly reward examination. This *khānaqāh* had the added distinction of a famous intendant: no less than the great historian, Ibn Khaldūn. Another famous historian, al-Maqrīzī, was an inmate of an even more imposing monastic establishment nearby, the *khānaqāh* of an-Nāsir Faraj ibn Barqūq. This, the flawed masterpiece of the architect, Sharka ash-Sharanbulī, is unique in the world of Islam: a *jāmi'* which imitates a *madrasa* yet is a *khānaqāh*. It uses the cruciform plan but substitutes hypostyle halls for *īwāns*, while the dervishes are housed in a three-storey block of sixty cells flanking the north hall. The monument contrives to combine beauty with austerity in a manner reminiscent of a Cistercian abbey, an impression to which the melancholy solitude of its (former) location materially contributed.

The question of location becomes much more important after the Ottoman conquest of Egypt in 1517, because thenceforward the Ottomans introduced their own orders, some of which enjoyed a special relationship with the state. The Mawlawiyya, or Mevlevīs, for instance, is an establishment order to which many of the Ottoman judiciary and even several of the sultans belonged; one of them, Selīm III, even composed a setting for the Mawlawī liturgy. Their *khānaqāh* is located in the Hilmiyya quarter of Cairo and forms an appendix to the 14th-century mosque known as Hasan Sadaqa, which eliminates the need for a special mosque. Its chief feature is an enormous ceremonial hall, *samā'-khāna*, for the performance of the characteristic whirling dance. This is a circle described in a square, with the circular dancing floor railed off to leave room for the spectators. More spectators were accommodated in the balconies on the first floor, including screened balconies for women; a special balcony for the orchestra projected over the dancing floor on the chord of a circle, so that the musicians could feed the music down to the dervishes whirling below. The balconies afforded a view of the spectacle from above, from which the astronomic symbolism of the dance patterns was apparent. Outside, there is a cloister with two tiers of cells and a fountain in the centre of the garth.

The urban setting of this *khānaqāh* has no particular significance, but in the next example location is paramount. The Bektashī *khānaqāh*, in the precincts of the cave of al-Maghāwirī, is so situated on Mount Muqattam as to command a breathtaking prospect of Cairo and the Nile. The Bektashī order requires its establishments to be located where there is a fine view. As with Taoist monasteries and certain Buddhist orders, landscape forms part of the meditational technique. The green garden amidst the lunar landscape of Muqattam resembles nothing so much as the Hollywood stereotype of an oasis. And the mountain is honeycombed with grottoes lined with the exquisitely sculptured tombs of those who desired to be buried in proximity to al-Maghāwirī's holiness.

Although the monks here were Albanian, for the Bektashiyya is the most popular order in Albania, the headquarters of the order is at Hājjī Bektash, in Cappadocia, one of the most interesting religious sites in Asia. The *khānaqāh* is arranged in the form of three courtyards that contract in size as they increase in sanctity, in accordance with a very ancient pattern, as they lead to the climax of the *kırklar meydân*, the Bektashī term for ceremonial hall, off which opens the tomb of Hājjī Bektash, the semi-legendary founder of the order. This is overlooked outside by another Seljuq mausoleum, that of Bālim Sultān, who refounded the order as an esoteric sect in the 16th century. The second court contains the cells and common rooms of the dervishes. On podia to either side of the hall, all the heads of the order, in sequence, are buried under green catafalques overlooked by the insignia of the order and specimens of the unique Bektashī calligraphy.

Also in Cappadocia, at Konya, lies the mother convent of the Mawlawiyya order. The order's founder, the mystical poet Jalāl ad-Dīn Rūmī, had been a protégé of the Seljuq sultan, Kayqubād I: so much so that he was buried in the sultan's rose garden. Around the beautiful Seljuq mausoleum where he lay grew up a highly complex monastic foundation in which an L-shaped cloister of eighteen cells (the number of celibate dervishes allowed to reside within a Mawlawī *tekke*) leads to a 'double' mosque of two domes. The first dome covers the mosque proper, indicated as such by the attached minaret, while the second covers the ceremonial hall for the performance of the dance. From the dancing floor, Rūmī's tomb is visible, and, beside his, the sepulchres of an entire spiritual dynasty, his successors in the headship of the order in unbroken succession, or *silsila*. The interior has that rare property of looking much larger than it is, and so tangible is the *baraka* that the visitor cannot fail to feel he has entered a power-house or accumulator charged with psychic energy.

Little seems known of Iranian *khānaqāhs*, and the numerous modern ones (18th century onward) follow the layout of the typical Iranian house. Three earlier sites exist: Pīr-i Bakrān, near Isfahan, Bistam and Natanz, the last of which, dating from the 14th century, would repay excavation. Belonging to the same century is the Tīmūrid *khānaqāh* of Khwāja Ahmad Yasawī, in Soviet Turkestan, which is quadripartite like a *madrasa*, with cells replacing the two lateral *īwāns*. At Mahan, the mother convent of the Ni'matullāhiyya order is housed in a series of late buildings disposed around two courtyards, with the 17th-century shrine of Shāh Ni'matullāh in the middle. It is a popular shrine and, as the order is vigorously alive, the *khānaqāh* could be studied in operation. The high degree of spirituality attained by the inmates does not seem to correspond to the highly developed forms of organization deducible from the great monastic complexes of Egypt and Turkey.

Even less studied still are the Indo-Pakistan *khānaqāhs*; and nothing could be more ironic, for India owes its Islamicization to the Sūfīs and not to the rulers, who mostly neglected to convert the subjects they ruled. The proselytization of the subcontinent was undertaken by four dervish orders, the Qādiriyya, the Suhrawardiyya, the Naqshbandiyya and Chishtiyya, all of which originated outside India. Proceeding from the heartlands of the Islamic world, places such as the Yemen and Iraq, Sūfīs belonging to these orders would cheerfully emigrate to distant India, where they settled in Hindu villages or towns, the holiness of their way of life instantly attracting attention: in a word, conversion by example. The risks they took did not deter them, for in Islam emigration, *hijra*, in imitation of the Prophet's emigration (from Mecca to Yathrib, thereafter known as Medina), has always ranked as a virtue second only to martyrdom. When such a man died, his tomb would attract pilgrims, a custodian or *mujawir* would be appointed and in no time at all a *khānaqāh* would grow up around the shrine. Again, it does not seem that these places matched the complexity of similar foundations in Egypt and Turkey.

The most distinctive feature of the dervish liturgy in nearly all its forms is, of course, the dance. This is a circular rotation, invariably anti-clockwise, which in several orders, chiefly Central Asian, Turkish and North African, becomes a highly sophisticated choreography. Such a ritual can be seen as implicit in the Islamic world-view. Alongside the horizontal axis, which has determined the whole course of Muslim architecture, there has always existed a vertical axis, implicit rather than explicit. The central building of all Islam, the Ka'ba, is, as we have seen, a vertical axis around which the pilgrims revolve; indeed it is the Islamic *axis mundi*. It was, however, in the halls designed to accommodate dervish ceremonies that the vertical axis assumed its most explicit form. In the Mawlawī order a dervish gyrates on his own axis and, simultaneously, in orbit around an invisible central axis representing the *qutb*, or 'pole', the title applied to the founder of the order, Jalāl ad-Dīn Rūmī, and also to his successors. In the fourth dance sequence, or *salām*, the living *qutb* leaves his *post* (the red sheepskin rug which is the emblem of his authority) and gyrates down the Equator, the name given to the *qibla* axis in the ceremonial hall, until he reaches the centre where he stops and turns on that spot. That is to say, for the duration of that phase in the ritual the identity of the *qutb* and that of his living representative coincide. In the Bektashiyya order the axis is expressed either in the design of the carpet (as at Hājjī Bektash itself) or as a pillar, which rises from the floor and merges with the groined vaulting of the roof (as at the Merdivenköy *khānaqāh* near Scutari on the Bosphorus).

In these rituals, esoteric Islam is only making explicit something present in the religion from earliest times, beginning with the Ka'ba and the Dome of the Rock. The latter, the earliest Muslim building to survive, is a shrine designed to enclose a sacred rock with ambulatories for pilgrims to go around it. Likewise, circumambulation is standard practice in any shrine or tomb, and the building is constructed on a square, hexagonal or circular plan to facilitate this ritual. It is obvious that in esoteric Islam a vertical axis tends to supplant the horizontal; and the closer one moves, dogmatically, to the periphery of Islam, increasingly it replaces it. All these movements are performed anti-clockwise, that is against the sun in the direction of the cosmic dance. It is hardly surprising, therefore, that whenever the sun wheel appears in Islamic iconography it is the female swastika (and not the male swastika, as in Buddhism). The point of intersection of the two planes represents the vertical axis, or *axis mundi*. In the same way, prayer, the expression of exoteric Islam, is a way of using the material world's horizontal axis to relate oneself to the vertical axis of the *Ka'ba* and ultimately to *Sūfism*, the esoteric dimension of Islam.

The 'tomb mosque', memorial mosque and mortuary chapel

Few rulers followed the example of Murād II, who renounced the Ottoman throne and retired to Manisa to don the woollen habit of a dervish. Many, however, wished to associate themselves with a religious order after their death.

The presence of dynastic tombs in a *madrasa* is evidence of the esteem accorded to learning in Islamic society, as well as an expression of the very human desire to have one's name perpetuated by being visibly associated with charitable works. The merit thereby acquired might materially affect one's spiritual destiny in the next life. Similarly, the garden should be considered as an expression of the eschatological hopes entertained by the person buried in it. Burial in a *khānaqāh* may likewise be construed as a manifestation of the high value that Islam places on sanctity, but it may be something more. In Christendom monarchs always preferred that their tombs should be in the keeping of holy men, and the general function of the Church as guardian of the dead was, in royal cases, restricted almost exclusively to abbeys. Apart from obvious cases, such as the dynastic burial-places of St Denis and Westminster, it is worth remembering that the rulers of Castille, Aragon, (united) Spain, Portugal, Scotland, Burgundy and the Hapsburg Empire all opted for burial in monastic foundations. Muslim monarchs still prefer to lie in the proximity of holiness. In modern Egypt members of the royal family were interred in the Rifā'ī Mosque in which the shrine of 'Alī Rifā'ī is situated; and in Samarqand after his horrendous conquests, Tīmūr reposes humbly at the feet of the saint, Nūr Sayyid Baraka, in a complex of buildings including a *madrasa* and a *khānaqāh*.

In neither of these two types of mosque, the collegiate or the monastic, however, does a mausoleum figure as an integral part of the structure. Probably the earliest 'tomb mosque', if the meaning be restricted to a place of worship that includes the founder's tomb, is the mosque of al-Juyūshī, perched on the cliff-edge of Mount Muqattam overlooking Cairo. Dating from 1085, it is too remote to be congregational and too inaccessible to be collegiate; it is a *masjid*, pure and simple, but with the added distinction of being the first mosque to have a tomb as an integral part of the design. Although commonly known as funerary mosques, such places are more precisely funerary foundations. Tombs are to be found in any of the mosque-types we have been discussing. Where, as is not infrequently the case, the tomb is an afterthought, in no sense can the establishment be designated a 'tomb mosque'. Even where it is intended to receive a body, with a purpose-built sepulchral chamber, or in the rarer instances where the mosque has grown around a tomb already in existence, the funerary function is always secondary. What is vulgarly known as the 'tomb mosque' is properly either a congregational, collegiate or monastic foundation with ancillary funerary function.

An influential body of opinion in Islam has all but convinced the 20th century that there is something inherently wicked in tombs, but such a belief finds no support in the Qur'ān. In Sūra xviii, 21, for instance, we read, *à propos* the Seven Sleepers: 'In like manner We [i.e. God] disclosed to them [the inhabitants of the city] that they might know that the promise of Allah is true, and that, as for the Hour, there is no doubt concerning it. When they [the inhabitants] disputed of their case [i.e. the Sleepers'] amongst themselves, they said: "Build over them a building; their Lord knows best concerning them." Those who won their point said: "Indeed we will build a mosque over them."'

It is interesting to note that at one of the three sites purporting to be the cave of the Seven Sleepers, that on Mount Qasyūn overlooking Damascus, the tombs of the protagonists, the shepherd and the dog, are in a garden at the entrance while the cave itself introduces a relatively minor category of building: the memorial mosque, which is altogether different from the so-called 'tomb mosque', with which it is frequently confused. Apart from the altruism involved in building a mosque, anyone who plans one to include his sepulchre expects (1) that this precaution shall ensure the maintenance of his tomb, as it is integral with the architecture; and (2) to benefit supernaturally from the prayers of the grateful users and also by the *baraka* issued by the Qur'ān every time it is recited. Endowments, *waqfs*, ensured that reciters were attached to important burial places. A memorial mosque, on the other hand, is intended to perpetuate a site or enclose an already existing object. For instance, the places occupied by the early Muslim commanders at the Battle of the Ditch in defence of Medina against the Meccans are commemorated by five mosques erected on eminences commanding the scene of the action. South of Damascus is the Masjid al-Qadam, or Mosque of the Footprint, which covers a stone with the impression of the Prophet's foot at the point at which he stopped before reaching the city with his trading caravan, saying, 'A man may only enter Paradise once'. A pitcher is provided beside the stone so one can pour water into the depression in the rock, then splash it on one's face to benefit from the *baraka*. All these mosques were erected to commemorate a site or to house something substantial; small sacral objects are contained in a reliquary, and sometimes, when the relic is of uncommon value, a special mosque may be built to house it in an atmosphere of prayer. Such a mosque is the Khirqa-yi Şerīf, erected in Istanbul in 1851 to accommodate a mantle of the Prophet. Usually memorial mosques are small and class liturgically as *masjids*, thus distinguishing them from 'tomb mosques', which can belong to any category.

Yet another variant is the mortuary chapel, not to be confused with the mortuary chamber of a 'tomb mosque'. Funeral prayers are normally performed at the mosque of the quarter where the deceased resided, after which the body is carried to the cemetery for the committal ceremony. If, however, the mosque be closed when the procession arrives, the service can be held at a special oratory attached to the cemetery, known as a *musallā* or *namāzgāh* (respectively, Arabic and Persian for 'place of prayer'). This is not a mosque but an open structure with an uncarpeted floor, since all three parts of the funeral prayer are performed in the standing position without prostration and with the bier in front at right angles to the *qibla*. The mourners need not even doff their footwear. Frequently, stone bearers or sleepers are provided beside a mosque, on which a bier may be deposited prior to the funerary service. Sometimes these bearers take the shape of a table, facing the *qibla* in the position the deceased will occupy when buried, and as a rule slanting towards the foot.

Burial and its dogmatic basis

Traditional Islam has developed to a remarkable degree the arts associated with death. Of special interest are the burial rites of saints and martyrs. The Islamic term for a martyr is *shahīd*, a witness, one who witnesses to the truth of Islam with his blood. For such a man the rules governing burial are relaxed; instead of the threefold linen shroud, a martyr must be buried, without washing, in the clothes in which he has died, because the blood and the dirt are evidences of his state of glory. Glory, because in Islam martyrdom entails automatic annulment of all sin: 'And do not call those who are slain in the way of God, "dead",' says the Qur'ān. 'Nay, rather they live, but ye do not see them' (Sūra ii, 154).

Not only are martyrs alive but also saints, *awliyā'*, who, on account of being in election, *wilāya*, may be presumed to share the same state of glory. The concept of the living saint is pivotal in Islam. People visit him to seek his intercession, *shafā'a*, and popular tombs are crowded with suppliants. Even when the visitor does not have a petition it is a mark of respect to visit a saint's tomb. On leaving, the visitor should be careful not to turn his back on the catafalque because a saint's tomb is his court, or darbār, and the proprieties of royal etiquette must be observed. A chain is suspended across the doorway at a height that obliges the visitor to bow on entering; this chain is also found in many mosques.

During his lifetime a saint exudes *baraka* and this continues to emanate from his grave. Even the pall covering the tomb is highly prized because it is saturated with *baraka*. The saint is present both physically, since his body remains incorrupt in the grave, and psychically. People consult him. The present writer vividly recalls seeing, at the shrine of Gazurgāh, outside Herat, a man kneeling against the plinth of the tomb with his forehead level with the sill, his lips visibly moving, then motionless while he listened to the saint before resuming the dialogue. But, saint or sinner, the grave is the point of psychic contact. When the mystical poet, Farīd ad-Dīn 'Attār, wished to settle the much-debated issue of 'Umar Khayyām's orthodoxy, it was from a clairvoyant, taken to the poet's tomb, that the answer came. The tomb, in fact, is conceived as the dwelling-place of the deceased and so, as in Ostia so in Cairo, it assumes the form of a house. Domesticity of context is easier if the civilization be one which practises inhumation. And at this point it is worth pausing to reflect on the dogmatic basis of burial in Islam. Again, this is Qur'ānic, for that God intends man to bury his dead is clear from Sūra v, 31, which deals with the first time man confronted the problem: when Cain had killed Abel he could not think what to do with the corpse; 'Then God sent a raven scratching up the ground, to show him how to hide his brother's naked corpse. He said: "Woe to me! Am I not able to imitate this raven and thus hide my brother's naked corpse?"' A coffin is optional, but a vault, no matter how simple, is indispensable, for the body must be able to sit up and reply to the Angels of the Grave, Munkir and Nakīr, who interrogate it on the first night after burial. Separate vaults are recommended for males and females. Axial burial is even more important in Islam than in Christianity. Graves, like mosques, operate liturgically and are, architecturally speaking, expressions of the horizontal axis. Bodies are buried in a recumbent posture at right angles to the *qibla* in such a way that they would face Mecca if turned on their side. Thus the believer enjoys the same physical relationship with the *qibla* both in life and in death. Bodies are rarely lowered vertically, but introduced into the vault end on and head first. In Egypt the entrance to the vault is always on the north side, whereas in Pakistan it is on the south. Bihzād gives a very clear picture of a funerary enclosure. The funeral is shown approaching the cemetery gate, while, inside, a freshly dug grave alongside an older burial is being lined with stones. The two tombs stand on a plinth, or *suffa*, a frequent feature in certain countries. The burials are in proximity to a holy tomb, the sanctity of which is indicated by a flag and the pall. The charming cat in the picture reminds us that this animal was often the companion of saints and that cats enjoyed a privileged status in Islam, even having a mosque of their own at Damascus where meals were provided for them out of special *waqf*, or endowment.

The position of the vault beneath is indicated on the surface by a recumbent stone whose shape reflects the grave. This stone may boast a headstone or footstone, or both, and this is known as a witness, *shāhid*, because the superscription testifies to the identity of the occupant. If there be a headstone it carries the epitaph leaving the recumbent stone free for Qur'ānic quotations. The most popular is the majestic Throne Verse (Sūra ii, 255), although in Muslim India the Ninety-Nine Names runs it a close second. Where, as in Turkey, both headstones and footstones are used, the recumbent portion of the tomb diminishes in importance until, by the start of the 18th century, it has contracted to a mere slab while the vertical portions have grown into gravity-defying shapes blending with the sweet curves of the Baroque. This period was responsible for the introduction of some decadently attractive forms, such as ovoid headstones and cylinders that taper downwards. Conventionally, headstones and footstones face the foot of the grave so as to be legible from that end; but should the deceased be buried alongside a pathway or road, one or both of his stones turn on their axes to address the passer-by. In Iran and the Indian subcontinent the headstone is equipped with a recess to hold a candle, a symbol of the soul.

A monograph could be written on the iconography of Turkish tombs, the headstones of which became well nigh anthropomorphic. The Ottoman Empire was perhaps the most elaborately ordered society in history. Until the sartorial reforms of Mahmūd II in the 19th century, it was possible to identify scores of professions and the rank of any member of the civil, religious and military establishments merely by their costume and headgear. This hierarchic vision was projected into death itself and survives petrified in the cemeteries: Grand Vizier, eunuch, concubine, all participate visibly in an Islamic *danse macabre*, and may still be readily identified because the headstone terminates in a carved representation of the kind of turban or other headgear proper to the rank of the deceased, if a man; while if the deceased were a woman, the headstone was carved in imitation of a flower, perhaps in recognition of her decorative function. Sometimes a person could lay claim to more than one symbol of rank. Thus 'Itrī, the great composer, wears on his tomb not the vase-shaped hat of felted camel hair of the Mawlawī order of dervishes, to which he belonged, but the turban of state, to which he was entitled as court musician. Sinān, the great architect, as a Janissary officer could have had the characteristic sleeve-shaped Janissary head-dress, but opted for the turban of state to show he was exalted as a Slave of the Gate.

Tombs are sometimes left uncovered, even when inside a mausoleum; and the Ottomans evolved a curious 'birdcage' structure in which the grave is exposed. Examples are the Yeni Valide tomb at Scutari and the Köprülü tomb in the Divan Yolu at Istanbul. The motive behind this architectural paradox was the conviction that a grave not exposed to the rain and the dew was unblessed; again, moisture is seen not only as a vehicle of purification but as a source of nourishment. This belief, which in the Mughal Empire seems to have found concrete expression in a ritual decree, probably was based on the beautiful Qur'ānic passage: 'He it is who sends the winds as tidings of His impending mercy, until, when they carry a heavy cloud to a dead land, We give the land to drink thereof' (Sūra vii, 57). When the tomb is inside a mausoleum, the recumbent stone is replaced by a wooden catafalque, known as a *tābūt*, which is a duplicate of the Islamic coffin, frequently on a magnified scale corresponding to the moral stature of the deceased. The protection afforded by the roof allows the otherwise perishable wood to be covered with rich stuff, such as Kashmir shawls or silk brocades specially woven for the purpose, or even, on occasion, the clothes of the deceased. These silk brocades were either green or the lovely Ottoman burgundy in colour, with Qur'ānic quotations in chevroned bands. Another pall, equally rich and sometimes woven with appropriate inscriptions, covered the coffin beneath. Both in this and the catafalque arrangement the same duplicative principle is at work, which in India produces the two-tier (crypt and ground floor) arrangement of Mughal tombs. Islamic coffins invariably have a gable-section top and taper towards the foot. The same conditions that permit the use of textile tomb-covers allow a real turban to be wound on a short pole at the head of the catafalque and, again, it is the turban proper to the profession of the deceased. The catafalque is Ottoman, but a saint's tomb rarely assumes any other form, sometimes with facilities for incensation in the shape of an incenser, or *mabkhara*. An unusually elaborate *mabkhara*, consisting of an exquisitely carved squat pillar with the top scooped out to receive the frankincense, stands at the head of Akbar's symbolic gravestone, or cenotaph, on the top floor of his mausoleum at Sikandra. Seldom does a holy tomb stand in the open air, but when it does a sacred flag flaps eerily in the breeze atop a long pole. Inside, however, an intensely devotional atmosphere prevails, with numerous votive lamps of silver suspended over the grave, which is always protected by a grille or screen. Such a screen, or *maqsura*, is of silver in the case of a saint and wood or marble in the case of anyone else. In the Tāj Mahal the screen is of pierced marble, and in addition the cenotaph has a canopy of mother-of-pearl. Such ciboria occasionally occur in Indo-Islamic architecture where the scale of the interior demands, as in the Gul Gunbad at Bijapur.

The purpose of a mausoleum is to protect the grave and ensure the perpetuation of the historical fact committed to its care. When not erected by the occupant or his family, a mausoleum is a tribute to the fame of the deceased. Although the grave it contains expresses the horizontal axis, a mausoleum is almost always a centrally designed building constructed around a vertical axis, with the tomb in the centre facing the *mihrāb* or just the plain *qibla* wall. Mausolea are commonly square or octagonal but can even be duodecagonal, like that of Shāh ʿAbbās II at Qum, or even polygonal. It seems strange that the *īwān*, which appears the ideal form for a tomb, should be so rarely used – the Gömech Khātūn mausoleum, at Konya, is practically unique; and the rectangular mausoleum, which is also appropriate since its shape follows the line of the tomb, is infrequent.

Graves may never be reused, and disturbance of the remains, even to remove them to another site, is objectionable. Provisional burial is known as *amāna*, or 'deposition in trust', and in such a case a coffin is mandatory. A simple dirt grave enclosed within curbs or filling the hollowed-out recumbent stone is greatly approved as expressive of humility. In the case of a mausoleum, a hole in the dome allowing the rain to fall on the earth, an arrangement found at the tomb of the Mughal empress Rabīʿa ad-Dawrānī, at Aurangabad, or at Bursa, where the pious sultan Murād II is buried, fulfils the same purpose. Tombs are the object of great respect: one must be careful never to tread upon a grave or let footwear come into contact with it, although this rule does not obtain among the Shīʿa. The dead should be frequently visited, especially on the two major festivals but also on two weekdays: Thursday evening and Friday morning. On these days any road leading to a cemetery presents a picturesque sight, with people carrying palm branches to deck the graves. In Spain myrtle was preferred, and this plant is conspicuous in funerary gardens because odoriferous plants are notoriously nostalgic and evocative. Other rituals include asperging the graves with rose-water and scattering rose-petals in addition, of course, to reciting the Qurʾān.

Cemeteries

Trees planted in cemeteries are evergreens, and Muslim graveyards have none of the lugubrious appearance that deciduous planting imparts to the cemeteries of northern Europe. The commonest tree is the cypress, although in funerary gardens other species are found. In Turkey it was believed that the height to which a tree grew was in proportion to the degree of glory in Paradise of the person buried nearest to it; and people used to be seen scaling cypresses to assess their respective degrees of growth over the past year. The funerary garden, or *rawda*, operates within a framework of eschatological reference in which the role of such symbols is crucial. This is evident from the Khwānd Khātūn complex in Kayseri, where the garden is reduced to mere symbolic space. Here, in an extraordinarily subtle arrangement, the tomb of the princess is visible from the mosque but (internally) inacessible; whereas, from the *madrasa* it is accessible but (externally) invisible. Thus the *rawda* is the key that locks the entire composition in a triumphant unity.

Cemeteries expand as a process of organic growth around a focus of grace, *baraka*, the focus in the great majority of cases being the tomb of a saint. It can also be the sepulchre of any distinguished person: one of the Companions (someone who, belonging to the first generation of Muslims, saw the Prophet with his own eyes), a martyr, a hero, a ruler, a poet or a mystic. In Istanbul, the biggest cemetery is that beside the tomb of Abū Ayyūb al-Ansārī, who is doubly attractive, a magnet to the prospective dead as martyr and Companion. But across the Bosphorus is another and even bigger cemetery, the Karaca Ahmet Mazarlık, where, for the price of only a ferry fare, one could be buried on the continent of Asia and thereby rest in the same earth as the Prophet. No more than one body may occupy a grave and cemeteries are invariably populous. Indeed, in Turkish graveyards the crowded headstones and footstones contrive to give the impression of a host of silent witnesses or sentinels, almost a visual metaphor for the words of the *imām* in the Friday service when, during the bidding prayer, he bids the congregation pray for 'the Muslim men and the Muslim women, the believing men and the believing women, the living amongst them and the dead', reminding the beholder that the concept of the *umma* embraces its dead as well as its living members.

The connection between burial and landscape is a topic that would repay closer study. In Turkey, a country with an outstanding naval tradition, admirals are buried beside the sea. Barbarossa's tomb stands prettily in a garden on the seashore at Beşiktaş, where formerly the galleys moored; at Tophane, the mosque and *türbe* of another admiral, Kiliç Ali Paşa, occupy a similar position. Other tombs stand proud of their surroundings on an eminence. Of such is the mosque of al-Juyūshī, already referred to, in Egypt.

By far the most eloquent mausoleum sited so as to command a prospect, is the appropriately poetic tomb of Süleyman Çelebi, author of the most famous *mawlid*, or nativity hymn, in Islam, who lies superlatively buried on a terrace overlooking the road from the quondam capital to the village of Çekirge. In fact, Islam, which is a religion of poets, knows better than most how to create a sympathetic ambience for a dead poet, as is evident from the Hāfiziye in Shiraz, where Hāfiz lies in eternal communion with the nature he loved.

If Islam is a religion for poets, it is no less a faith for warriors, with an almost Shinto-like emphasis on holy war and martyrdom. It comes, therefore, as no surprise that it can produce a tomb tower like the Gunbad-i Qābūs, than which no more perfect tomb for a warrior could be conceived, although the tomb of Ghiyāth ad-Dīn Tughluq, with its battered walls inside a miniature fort, runs it a close second. On a different scale but no less eloquent of power are the dynastic tombs of the great Mughals, of which four rank as perhaps the finest funerary monuments in history: the tombs of Humāyūn, Akbar, Jihāngīr and Shāh Jihān, the last commonly known as the Tāj Mahal. The plans of the first and last tombs group subsidiary chambers around a central mortuary chamber reserved for the founder, implying that the mausoleum was to serve a dynasty, in the same way as the mausolea of Augustus and Hadrian in Rome, and, like them, is intended to proclaim the power of the dynasty.

The funerary garden

Each of these four funerary monuments is conceived within a formal garden scheme as the focal point where the axes of the garden intersect. The art of landscape gardening in Islam is the product of both climatic factors (which account for the regional variations) and cosmological concepts (which account for the simi-larities). The basic similarity lies in their modular plan. A square or rectangular area divided into four quadrants by two axes forming a cross produces a unit known as the *chahār bāgh*, or fourfold plot. These units are subdivisible into four or nine. The repetition of the module results in a pattern immediately visible on account of the raised grid formed by the paths that separate the sunken flower beds.

Gardens were both functional and recreational, yielding their owner profit as well as pleasure, but when the time came for him to keep his appointment with the worm the encounter transpired in the same pavilion where formerly he caroused. Serais, or purpose-built enclosures, surviving outside imperial sepulchral gardens prove that these gardens were frequented by considerable numbers of people, entailing special accommodation facilities. This suggests that durbars were held at these courts of death. Courtiers must have dismounted in the serai and then processed inside to salute the silent Presence. A somewhat different imperial cult grew up around the tombs of the other Islamic emperors, the Ottomans. In the *türbe* at Bursa of the eponymous founder of the dynasty, Osman, captured standards and other trophies would be deposited; and the *türbe* of Fātih in Istanbul would receive a visit from the reigning sultan before he embarked on a campaign, in the hope of being endowed with some of the Conqueror's valour.

If the garden was conceived as a microcosm of the physical world axially organized in accordance with basic cosmological ideas, the tomb in the centre epitomized those ideas: the square plinth stood for the material universe, the dome for the circle of eternity, while the octagon could symbolize the transition from the one to the other being experienced by the deceased. Another kind of mausoleum was in vogue for a short space of time, and in India alone. This was the pyramidal mausoleum, best exemplified by Akbar's tomb at Sikandra, diminishing in stages, with a symbolic tombstone on the roof directly above the real tomb in a crypt beneath.

When a mausoleum stands in isolation within a funerary garden the effect is incomparable: aesthetically and conceptually, it transports the beholder to the frontier of emotional experience. Islamic art is in essence the vision of the Paradisal Garden, which is none other than the Primordial Garden which man lost through sin but whose image is recoverable from aboriginal memories submerged in the memory of the race. Far from being a coincidence, that the people who used these places were in no doubt as to their meaning or purpose is clear from the inscription over the gate of one, Akbar's garden at Sikandra: 'These are the Gardens of Eden: enter them to dwell therein eternally.'

2 The Architecture of Power: Palaces, Citadels and Fortifications

OLEG GRABAR

The expression of power has always been one of the functions of architecture. In Islam that function is less easy to isolate since the same features recur in buildings of every type. But it is nonetheless real; Akbar was as alive to it as Louis XIV. Through their palaces, their ceremonial gateways, their fortresses and their burial places, the powerful of the Islamic world proclaimed their glory in forms that outlasted their own lives and those of their dynasties. Akbar's new capital of Fatehpur Sikri, founded in 1569 to celebrate the birth of his son Jihāngīr, is perhaps the grandest of all such monuments. Laid out on a new site near Agra, it included a magnificent series of palaces, baths, kitchens, stables, treasuries, markets and mosques. The Gate of Victory (*opposite*) leads into the courtyard of the Great Mosque, containing the tomb of the city's patron saint, Shaykh Salīm Chishtī. It is the supreme example of the symbolic gateway in Islam, an assertion of the monarch's power and splendour far in excess of any functional need. Ironically, it was also among the shortest-lived. Akbar, fighting on the fringes of the Mughal Empire, neglected Fatehpur Sikri, which was abandoned after his death. (1)

Gates

A gate serves to admit and to exclude. It is also a symbol – of strength, of security, of wealth.

Granada: the Gate of Justice (*left*) in the Alhambra leads through the southern wall to the palace enclosure. Carved in the keystone of the arch is an upraised hand, probably a symbol of divine protection. (2)

Baghdad: The Talisman Gate (*above*), dating from 1221, was unusual in having dragons carved above the door. When this photograph was taken it had already been walled up; it was destroyed in 1917. (3)

Rabat: the Gate of the Wind (*above*), built in the 12th century, is among the most richly decorated of Moroccan gateways. A band of calligraphy encloses the whole. (5)

Jerusalem: St Stephen's Gate (*left*) may originally have incorporated animal sculpture representing either magical protection or the arms of the reigning prince. (4)

Aleppo: the double gates of the citadel (*above*), connected by a bridge over a moat, proclaim impregnable strength. (6)

Cairo is among the best preserved of Islamic cities and several of its ancient gates are intact. The Gate of God's Help (*left*) and the Gate of Conquests (*right*) were both built in the 11th century to traditional designs – basically straight passageways with heavy doors – and differ only in the shape of their towers. Above the first is carved the Muslim profession of faith in *kufı* letters and an inscription giving the date, 1087. (7,8)

Walls and towers

Military architecture is the most direct expression of power. At Diyarbakir (*opposite*), inscriptions and sculpture also reinforce the physical strength of its black basalt walls.(9)

Skoura in Morocco (*above*) and **Baku** in Soviet Azerbaydzhan (*below*) show how regional variations diversify what is basically the same architectural form. Brick patterning softens the severity of many North African buildings, while the citadel at Baku contained an open pavilion behind its lowering ramparts. (10,11)

From Yazd in Iran (*top*) to **Rumeli Hisar** on the Bosphorus (*bottom*), the type of defensive work with crenellated walls punctuated by towers remained standard. The walls of Yazd go back to the 14th century; they surround a desert city in an oasis, dependent for water on miles of underground conduits. Rumeli Hisar, by contrast, approaches more nearly a European *château-fort*; it was built as part of the Ottoman defence of Istanbul and already takes account of new developments in artillery. (12,13)

The citadel

Almost every ancient Islamic urban centre was dominated by its citadel, a city within a city. The nearest Western equivalent is the Russian Kremlin, which also contains palaces, churches, barracks and offices cut off from the rest of the city by strong walls. The **Alhambra** (*left*), built by the kings of Granada as the last expression of Muslim power in Spain, is the most perfectly preserved. *Opposite*: the citadels of Cairo, Herat and Jerusalem. **Cairo** (*top*) dates, in its present form, from the 12th century but is now overshadowed by the enormous 19th-century mosque of Muhammad ʿAlī. **Herat** (*centre*), in Afghanistan, was a pre-Islamic stronghold, which attained its greatest glory under the Tīmūrids. The citadel of **Jerusalem** (*bottom*), once the palace of Herod, has also been fortified since remote Antiquity. The last rebuilding of the walls was under the Ottomans in the 16th century. (14,17,18,19)

Bam, in Iran (*above*), commanded an important trade and invasion route. Its virtually impregnable citadel was rebuilt in the 16th and 17th centuries. (16)

Aleppo (*left*) has the most spectacular of all citadels. Built on a partly artificial mound in the centre of the city, it is surrounded by a massive wall and entered by the elaborate gate already illustrated (pl. 6). Inside the enclosure the planning was haphazard, but it contained an audience hall, a mosque, baths, living quarters and all the amenities of an independent town. (15)

The mausoleum

Outliving death, the power and glory of Muslim rulers was given public expression in a series of magnificent tombs. Despite a lack of orthodox religious sanction, these tombs are characteristic of virtually all Islamic dynasties. In **Cairo**, the Qarāfa cemetery (*above*) is a competitive display of family wealth. The **Gunbad-i Qābūs** ('Dome of Qābūs'), near Gorgan in Iran (*upper right*), was built by this local ruler in 1006 to house his remains and commemorate his name. In the second objective he succeeded, but his body, which is said to have been suspended in a coffin some 50 metres above the ground, has long since disappeared. (20,21)

At Sasaram, India, stands the mausoleum of Shīr Shāh Sūr, an Afghan who temporarily ousted the Mughals between 1540 and 1545. Less famous than the Tāj Mahal, it is nevertheless its rival in dignity and monumental effect. The dome, reflected like that of the Tāj in an artificial lake, rises more than 50 metres above the water. (22)

Soltaniyeh was founded by the Mongol rulers of Iran early in the 14th century and was for a brief period their capital. Like many greater cities, including Baghdad and Cairo, it is an example of an entire city conceived as an expression of the monarch's power, and was originally intended as a centre of pilgrimage. Most of its glories have disappeared, leaving only this vast mausoleum of Öljeytu, who died in 1316. Dominating the village sited on the remains of his once remarkable city, Öljeytu's tomb still suggests past splendours, when its eight minarets encircled the huge pointed dome covered in blue glazed tiles. (23)

Outside the cities

Closer to palaces as understood in the West are the complexes of buildings erected by Islamic rulers in remote areas away from the cities. Their purpose was primarily for administration or private pleasure. From outside they are often indistinguishable from fortresses, but inside they are furnished with every luxury.

Opposite: **Ukhaydir** (*top*) is perhaps the most impressive of the early Islamic palaces. Probably built by an 'Abbāsid prince in the 8th century, it is a huge rectangle, the walls being articulated by closely set buttresses. Inside, it must have been a miniature city, with an elaborate palace complex on the north side. **Mshattā**, in Jordan (*centre*), lies near the pilgrim route from Damascus to Mecca, and was also built in the 8th century. The palace was decorated with highly sophisticated carved panels, now in Berlin. **Lashkari Bāzār** (*bottom*), in Afghanistan, is a monument to Ghaznavid power of the 11th and 12th centuries. Behind its massive towers lay rich apartments, originally adorned with paintings and figure sculpture. (26,27,28)

Morocco (*top*) contains a series of such feudal castles situated away from urban centres. The architectural style is local and vernacular – the internal fittings have mostly disappeared. **Doğubayazit** (*above*), in eastern Anatolia, is an extraordinary mixture of Ottoman and European details; it was built by Işāq Paşa in the 18th century. (24,25)

Palaces: the Topkapi, Istanbul

For the centre of the mighty Ottoman Empire, the Topkapi seems at first surprisingly unassertive. Indeed, it is not a palace at all in the European sense, but a series of small buildings arranged informally and furnished with the utmost luxury. *Above*: Selīm III gives audience at the Gate of Felicity. *Right*: a bird's-eye view from the west, with the main gate in the foreground, the Gate of Felicity facing it, and the harem on the left. (29, 30)

The harem, or women's quarters, consists of a warren of small rooms, halls and passages tightly segregated from the rest of the Topkapi – a palace within a palace. The range on the left housed the black eunuchs. The domes on the right belong to the Divan. (31)

The younger brothers of a sultan, who were fortunate if they escaped execution, were immured in a separate building known as 'the Cage'. Here we are looking out into the Courtyard of the Cage: on the right is the 'Golden Road' between the men's quarters and the harem. (32)

The bedroom of Murād III (*right*), immediately next to the Cage, is one of the most luxurious chambers in the palace. It is lined with coloured tiles and roofed with a high dome. Round the upper part of the room runs an inscription in *kūfī*. (34)

The Baghdad kiosk was built by Murād IV to celebrate his capture of that city in 1638. It is preceded by a typical pool with a fountain, and beyond lies open to the Bosphorus and the Golden Horn. (33)

The kitchen occupied a whole wing of the first courtyard. There were ten large double kitchens, each with its chimney. In 1534 they employed fifty cooks, as well as hundreds of more menial servants. (36)

The Chīnili kiosk (*left*) lies outside the walls of the Topkapi proper but formed part of the palace complex. It is especially notable for the magnificent glazed Iznik tiles with which its entire surface is covered. (35)

61

The palace: Granada, Isfahan, Agra

The Islamic palace was built both for ceremony and for comfort, for public ostentation and for private pleasure. In the halls and courts of the Alhambra at Granada (*right, top and bottom*: the Court of Mexuar and the Court of the Lions) and in the garden pavilion of the Hasht Bihisht at Isfahan (*below*) we can still catch some echo of that exquisitely contrived world. (37,38,39)

Akbar, founder of Fatehpur Sikri (see pl. 1), was unique among Islamic rulers in his vision of a universal state drawing upon the best in all cultures and all religions. That vision was symbolized in his audience hall (*right*), in which the emperor's throne was placed upon a central pillar connected by bridges. Beneath him, visitors, philosophers and politicians met and argued. (41)

Shāh Jihān, Akbar's grandson, held court in the Red Fort at Agra, where he built the Dīwān-i-ʿAmm (*right*). A contemporary miniature (*above*) shows him receiving an embassy there. The emperor's throne was on a raised alcove of white marble, and the room was surrounded by pierced stone screens through which ladies could watch the proceedings. (40, 42)

The powerful at home: it was traditional for the rich families of most Islamic countries to make public display of their wealth in charitable foundations and tombs, but for their domestic life they preferred seclusion. As with the royal palaces, the exteriors give no hint of the riches within. The 'Azam family mansion at Hama, in Syria, (*opposite*) consists of a series of lavishly furnished rooms arranged informally, like a Topkapi in miniature. (43)

Palaces, Citadels and Fortifications

OLEG GRABAR

THE EXPRESSION OF POWER is in many ways an automatic attribute of monumental architecture. The quarrying of stones, the firing of bricks, the planning of buildings and the organization of work gangs, the acquisition of often expensive material for decoration, these and many other activities required by any large-scale construction demanded financial means and a legal authority that was generally available in the past to only a few rich ruling princes. Even public and collective monuments such as mosques and caravanserais reflected the glory, vanity, and power of the sultans, caliphs, or amirs, under whose reigns they were erected and whose names are permanently celebrated in their inscriptions. From Qairouan in the 9th century to Cordoba in the 10th, Isfahan in the 11th, or Delhi in the 13th, the great congregational mosques of Islam were provided with a totally or partially secluded area, the *maqsūra*, which was brilliantly decorated and at times innovative and inventive in both construction and composition. It was the place of the prince, the visible presence of earthly power in the building belonging to the whole community of believers. And it is probably not an accident that the earliest remaining monumental caravanserai in Islamic architecture, Qasr al-Hayr East in the Syrian steppe, was part of a complex of buildings built on direct orders of the caliph Hishām, and that its façade is hardly distinguishable from the façade of a palace. In later centuries Seljuq caravanserais in Anatolia or Safavid ones in Iran reflected and broadcast, by the sheer quality of their masonry and decoration, the strength and glory of their princely patrons, even if their real purpose was mercantile.

Whatever its social or personal functions, there hardly exists a major monument of Islamic architecture that does not reflect power in some fashion. Even the gilt domes of Shī'ī sanctuaries in Iran and Iraq are symbols both of holy places and of their wealthy royal patrons. Ostentation is rarely absent from architecture and ostentation is almost always an expression of power.

It is an obvious conclusion that power is inherent in architecture, and a consideration of the topic of power in Islamic architecture could consist merely in isolating those architectural motifs and practices that are most particularly associated with rulers or with the expression of wealth and of force. This is what I shall try to do in the first part of this chapter, narrowing the definition of power to its most obvious meanings of physical and symbolic control. But then in the second part I shall turn to the powerful rather than to power and identify the characteristics of the architecture sponsored or inspired by those who were in positions of power or possessed considerable wealth, whether or not these monuments were intended to express or serve power in its narrow meaning. This distinction can be understood as the difference between the architecture of a culture, and the architecture of individuals within a culture; and in another sense it is a distinction that makes possible the exploration of the range between private and public, or official, architecture.

There is a fundamental question raised by the consideration of power in architecture and for that matter by secular architecture in general. Since its functions are for the most part universal, to what extent and in what ways does it really illustrate cultural peculiarities? Palaces or fortifications are not restricted to Islam; how then do Islamic palaces or fortifications characterize this particular civilization? In the third and concluding part of this chapter, I shall turn to the forms of power in Islamic architecture. Islam was in many ways like Imperial Rome, a unified formal culture, with many regional and chronological variations, but with a coherent sense of its identities, of a *dār al-Islām* different and separated from other, barbarian or merely alien, realms. Were there forms that automatically expressed these differences, or is any architecture that is so closely tied to wealth and authority formally universal, and only cosmetically different?

Power

Monuments directly expressing power can be studied chronologically, emphasizing technical developments; regionally, explaining the forms imposed on architecture by local conditions; or, preferably, by isolating a typology of power architecture as it is likely to have

65

occurred throughout the Muslim world, and combining it with a study of both chronological and regional distinctions. The grouping of architectural types that I suggest begins with primarily military and defensive architecture, continues with certain kinds of urban developments and official palaces, and ends with the more elusive category of symbolic expressions of power. Rough though it is, this grouping corresponds to a scale of complexity that ranges from simplest to most elaborate. It should, however, be kept in mind that many monuments or types of monuments belonged to several categories at the same time and especially that they often changed in significance and use over the centuries. For instance, the walls and gates of Fātimid Cairo first separated a dynastic city from an older urban system, but then were transformed into real or imaginary barriers between social groups; and in the Alhambra, a citadel, which was a city, became the remote abode of princes.

Military architecture, the expression of physical power

When the frontiers of the Muslim world became stabilized around the middle of the 8th century, a more or less formalized system of defence was established almost by necessity. We know from the historian Balādhurī for instance that, as early as during the rule of the caliph 'Uthmān (644–66), there was someone in charge of the fortresses of Armenia. Whether or not such an early date is likely for the creation of an official inspectorate of frontier defences, sooner or later, from Spain or the Moroccan confines of the Sahara to the Steppes of Central Asia, a system of military protection was certainly developed. Insofar as its physical character can be imagined from written sources, it was initially centred almost exclusively on fortified cities. We have considerable information about the building and rebuilding of frontier towns, especially in Cilicia, where almost every early 'Abbāsid caliph seems to have been involved in fortifying and garrisoning towns such as Tarsus or Massissa. In North Africa small forts seem to have been constructed primarily, either to control Berber tribes or to protect the coastline against Byzantine incursions. In Spain, similar forts (Merida, Tarifa, Gormez) overlooked the major roads to the north. Information about other areas is scantier for early centuries, mostly because in Nubia, the Caucasus, or Central Asia the new Muslim frontier roughly coincided with older traditional cultural frontiers. All the Arabs had to do was to take over Sasanian, Soghdian, or Byzantine fortifications, and there is no apparent record in literary sources of unusual building activities or of novel functions.

Archaeological and visual information on all these defensive establishments is quite scanty for several centuries. Many of the tall tower-like buildings of packed earth and occasionally mud-brick, which were found in Central Asia by several Soviet expeditions, may for instance have been forts protecting main roads and settlements rather than feudal estates, as has been argued by several scholars, but the evidence is too unclear to allow definite conclusions. In any event, whether on the Central Asian frontier or in Spain, whether in new frontier areas or in traditional ones, it is reasonable to assume that the early Muslims simply followed the older, prevailing types of military architecture. This continuity in planning, technique, and construction is clearly apparent in two instances about which we are somewhat better informed: Diyarbakir, the ancient Amida on the upper Euphrates, and Merv in Khurasan. Furthermore, these two cities permit us to identify some of the standard components of Islamic military architecture, as it developed over the centuries.

In Diyarbakir the walls of the city are still remarkably well preserved and, thanks to an unusual wealth of Muslim as well as earlier Roman and Byzantine inscriptions, the history of the walls and of their massive towers can be roughly worked out. The key point is that the layout of the walls and their elevation were late Classical, as was the citadel, which was located in the north-eastern corner of the fortified city. Mighty gates, bearing the names of the cities towards which they are directed, were set at strategic points in the walls. A peculiarity of the walls and gates of Diyarbakir is the unusually rich decoration of sculptures that adorns them, which will be described in another context. Located in the middle of an immense oasis surrounded by deserts, Merv in Khurasan (today in the Soviet Republic of Turkmenistan) bears little visual resemblance to Diyarbakir. Like all Iranian cities, Merv occupied a huge area rather than the restricted space of a northern Mesopotamian town. But there also it was the pre-Islamic Merv, with its massive walls and characteristically Soghdian articulated buttressing, that became the first Muslim town; it contained a citadel at its northern side and in all likelihood pre-Islamic functions were initially continued by the Arab conquerors. The originality of Merv lies in the fact that, possibly as early as the late 8th century, a new Muslim city was being built alongside the older one and it reproduced most of the structural features of its predecessor. As in Diyarbakir, gates served as focal points in each wall and their names reflected local topographical features.

Diyarbakir and Merv make it possible to define, early in Islamic history, three consistent components of Islamic military and defensive architecture: walls and towers, gates, citadels. Initially, it seems, these features were almost exclusively characteristic of frontier areas and only appeared in the centre of the empire in rare instances such as Baghdad, where their importance was symbolic rather than practical. But from the late 9th or 10th century onwards, as central authority weakened and political power was taken over by large numbers of local dynasties frequently fighting with each other, military architecture spread to almost every urban centre, and in many ways established itself as a consistent component of Islamic cities until artillery made such defences superfluous, and the remains were transformed into nodal points within the growth of cities.

Walls and towers: As early as the 9th century the complex of cities known as Raqqa, on the Euphrates in Syria, was provided with a fortified enclosure. The walls of the present-day city of Raqqa, massive mud-brick constructions preceded by a moat, may indeed be remnants of early ʿAbbāsid walls, although their exact date still requires archaeological investigation. But the still unexplored circular city of Hiraqla, to the north of modern Raqqa, may in fact be a creation of Hārūn al-Rashīd and, as air photographs and cursory ground surveys show, it was provided with impressive walls. It is still uncertain whether the presence of defensive walls at Raqqa was the result of the direct impact of the capital Baghdad, of the fact that one of Raqqa's functions was to be an assembly point for military expeditions against Byzantium, of attempts to protect it against nomadic incursions, or of the proximity of Classical and Byzantine fortified cities in what used to be a frontier area before Islam. Arguments exist for any one of these interpretations but a positive answer requires additional literary and archaeological investigations.

No such problem of interpretation exists for cities after the 10th century. Hardly a town of any significance existed without fortified walls, mighty towers, and elaborate gates – often new ones, as in Herat, Yazd, or Damascus, but frequently totally or partially refurbished pre-Islamic ones, as in Jerusalem or Istanbul. From a purely architectural point of view not much can be said about these walls and towers. Mostly they are massive constructions built in materials characteristic of the region in which they are found: unbaked brick or packed earth in eastern Iran, stone in Syria and Palestine, various mixtures of brick and stone in Spain. Round, square, or elongated towers served as buttresses, lodgings, arsenals, or whatever other military purpose may have been required. Crenellations, walkways, machicolations, and, occasionally, small protective cupolas at key intersections of walls were probably stock elements in the construction of most of these walls and towers. But, although there are instances of major changes in wall

construction – as in the switch from brick to stone in 11th-century Egypt or in the bewildering masonry types found on the walls of Jerusalem – the purely defensive military walls of Islamic architecture are on the whole hardly novel or original, even if at times, as in the walls of Diyarbakir, the Alhambra, or the much later Iranian city of Bam, they are quite spectacular.

Gates: Matters are more complicated when we turn to gates. Two types of plan predominate: the straight gate, which was primarily a passageway even when provided with massive doors; and the bent entrance, which has obvious defensive uses, becoming in a few instances, such as the Gate of Justice in the Alhambra, a double bent gate. Both types of gates have a long pre-Islamic history and, although the bent gate became more common in obviously military architecture and in the western parts of the Muslim world, both tended to be used quite indiscriminately, especially in later centuries.

More interesting aspects of gates are their construction, their decoration, and the names given to them. Because they are so frequently dated, gates are one of our best examples for the history and development of vaults. For instance, in 11th-century Cairo or 14th century Granada the gates were built with an unusual number of different techniques of vaulting. Squinches coexist with pendentives, barrel vaults with cross vaults, simple semicircular arches with pointed or horseshoe arches. Gates can serve as a sort of gauge of the most common construction techniques and easily available materials of any one time. This is particularly so in areas where stone predominated, as baked brick was less frequently used in large-scale military monuments or has not been as well preserved. It is even possible that certain innovations in Islamic vaulting techniques, especially the elaboration of squinches and of cross vaults, were the direct result of the importance of military architecture, for which strength and the prevention of fires, so common in wooden roofs and ceilings, were major objectives.

The decoration of gates is tied to the broader question of the symbolism of gates. Certain official city gates did acquire symbolic associations and, as we shall see, were provided with appropriate visual expressions. Whether the more common and purely defensive gates were similarly decorated is a moot point. There is the evidence of the animal sculptures on the gates of Diyarbakir or on St Stephen's Gate in Jerusalem, for both of which it is possible to suggest either a magic meaning of protection or a symbolic meaning of the sovereignty of individual princes. A few literary references on early Islamic Isfahan tantalizingly suggest the possibility of astrological symbolism, and there is little doubt that further searches in written sources will yield additional examples of the same sort. But there does not seem to be a clear and consistent pattern to a visual symbolism of purely defensive gates in Islamic lands and each exception should be seen and explained independently.

A similar question concerns the names of gates, and is answered in a similar manner. Most names are topographical, involving either the local characteristics of a city or of its suburbs (Gate of Tanners or of whatever tribe settled nearby, as occurs in Marrakesh), or the nearest major centre (Jaffa Gate in Jerusalem). Sometimes there are references to real or mythical events associated with the gate, as occur in some examples in Jerusalem. Most of these are once again unique instances. But many more cities had a *bāb al-sirr*, a secret gate, possibly simply the means by which an army could easily leave or enter a city, rather than the gate of betrayal as some have interpreted it. A consistent name of gates is the Gate of the Lion, and it is true that on city gates in Derbend in the Caucasus or in Hamadan in Iran there seem to have been reused ancient sculptures of lions. It is, however, still difficult to determine whether these examples had a consistent and fully developed symbolic value at all levels, and not merely at a popular one.

Citadels: A more original development of Islamic military architecture is the citadel, *qal'a*, *kuhandiz*, or, more frequently in the western Islamic world, *qasaba*. A fortified defensive unit, occupied by a king or by a feudal lord and located in an urban centre, is of course not a new development, for it is found in ancient Assyrian cities like Khorsabad, and probably from that time onwards it became the typical landmark of most Near Eastern cities. In all likelihood the Arabs took over existing citadels in the areas they conquered, but it is only in north-eastern Iran that the literary evidence is clear on this point, perhaps because citadels were more common there in pre-Islamic times than elsewhere in the Middle East. We shall see later on that another type of government building appeared in western and central provinces of the empire. As the authority of the caliphate declined and the Turkish military became the main, if not the exclusive, ruling force in most of the Muslim world, old citadels were refurbished, for instance, in Jerusalem or Aleppo, and new ones were built, in Cairo and probably Damascus. Beginning in the 10th or 11th centuries, practically every town of any importance from Transoxiana, for which we have the geographer Ibn Hawqal's description of Bukhara's citadel, to Egypt, even including many secondary cities such as Homs in Syria or Hisn Kayfa in Turkey, acquired seats of power. These took the form of a forbidding, fortified area, usually built astride the city's walls, but sometimes tucked away in a commanding corner of the city or, much more rarely, situated outside the city. The most spectacular and best preserved of these citadels is the one in Aleppo, located on a partly natural and partly artificial mound overlooking the whole town. A superb stone glacis emphasizes the height of the monument, which can only be reached through a handsome bridge over a moat. Inside, ornate, formal audience halls adjoin mosques, baths, living quarters, even a religious sanctuary dedicated to Abraham, cisterns, granaries, and prisons. There is something very haphazard about the internal arrangements of Aleppo's citadel, possibly because of the rugged requirements of the terrain, but also because there was no set plan for citadels, nothing comparable to the formal order of Roman camps for instance, and Aleppo's citadel grew according to the whims of individual local rulers.

Few citadels are as impressive as Aleppo's, but most of them were located in such a fashion that both practically and symbolically they dominated the urban centres that they controlled. Interior organization varied enormously. The Alhambra, in addition to the celebrated palaces, was originally a whole city with houses, a mosque, baths, and other amenities normally required by an urban system. Ibn Hawqal describes Bukhara in the same manner, as a small city. The Cairo citadel included several palaces and mosques, and the citadel of the Shīrvān-Shāhs in Baku contained a unique open pavilion more typical of garden palaces than of defence monuments. Other citadels, the one in Damascus for instance, were more exclusively military, with barracks, arsenals, granaries, jails, a small oratory, and occasionally a slightly more formal apartment or reception area.

The variations in size and importance complicate any attempt to define the architecture of citadels as a whole. Another factor is that all of them have been so frequently modified over the centuries (many are still used today for purposes akin to their original ones) that elaborate archaeological investigations are needed before we can properly understand the character of their original constructions and the changes that were introduced. It can be hypothesized that, initially, citadels were strictly military, serving to accommodate alien soldiery away from the city's population. The reason why so many early citadels are found in Iran, especially in the eastern provinces, may be that in these areas of limited Arab presence it was particularly important to maintain the contrast between conquerors and conquered during the first centuries of Muslim rule. As the version of feudalism peculiar to Islam developed and as local dynasties were founded, some amenities of life were introduced into citadels, as well as official reception halls and other symbols of

0   10   20

Section through the citadel of Aleppo, showing the fortified gate, the bridge, the massive barbican defending the entrance and the reception hall built over it. (1)

power such as fancy inscriptions on walls and gates – for example the spectacular monumental inscriptions on the 15th-century citadel of Herat, and the sculptures of lions and snakes on Aleppo's citadel. Eventually the citadel became the palace of local rulers or of governors appointed from elsewhere. It is as dynastic centres of authority that one should understand the late Islamic citadels of Bukhara and Khiva. They convey the prestige and fear developed around another type of architecture of power to be discussed later. The tales of horror connected with them in the 19th century are the last vestiges of a far more elaborate way of life from a different age.

Formally, the constituent elements of citadel architecture were drawn from the wide repertoire of forms and functions created elsewhere: baths from the city, reception halls from palaces, walls and towers from defensive architecture. It is unlikely that there was a compositional order for citadels, except possibly in the eastern Iranian world where they were the predominant form of princely architecture. The originality of the Islamic citadel lies rather in the fact that so many very different kinds of monuments – the magnificent rooms of the Alhambra or the equally impressive cisterns of Aleppo – were found combined together in the same ensembles.

Walls with towers, and gates and citadels serve primarily military functions and are constructions that, different though individual examples may be from each other, are found all over the Muslim world and lend themselves to some sort of generalization.

Two other types of primarily military monuments should be mentioned, although the evidence for and about them is more spotty. One consists of single forts or other elaborate defence systems that were located outside major settlements and cities. With a few exceptions, in the Levant (Ajlun in Jordan for example) under the impact of the Crusaders, and in the forbidding mountains of northern Iran where the Assassins built their castles (Alamut is the most celebrated example), the Islamic world did not develop the isolated *château-fort* so typical of Western feudalism. From the frontiers of Central Asia to the shores of the Bosphorus or to the Atlas Mountains, however, various rulers erected forts at key places in the regions under their rule, simply as protection for small garrisons. These are frequently quite spectacular, as in the Ottoman fortifications on the Bosphorus, the Castle of Sighs at the entrance of the Bamiyan Valley in Afghanistan, or the eagle's nests of the southern Moroccan mountains, but architecturally they are hardly original.

The other type of military architecture consists of massive walls protecting certain key paths of invasion, in the manner of the Great Wall of China. Although little-known archaeologically, and not as common, they seem to have been built in pre-Islamic times both between the Caucasus and the Caspian Sea and in Central Asia. These walls penetrated into myth, especially in Iran, in the form of the striking wall of iron built by Alexander the Great against the barbarians of Gog and Magog. Whether anything similar was constructed or even attempted under Muslim dynasties is not clear, but on the whole it seems unlikely.

Naval fortifications, including arsenals with walls blocking sea passages, covered docks for ships, and storage spaces, form a special type of their own. These have been studied, in varying states of preservation, in Mahdia (Tunisia) and in Alanya on the south-eastern shore of Turkey. A reference in the geographical compendium of Ibn Hawqal indicates that similar but probably less elaborate protected harbours existed even on the Caspian Sea.

My last example of military architecture is a uniquely Islamic one: the still little-understood *ribāt*. Technically this was a fortified place reserved for temporary or permanent warriors for the Faith who committed themselves to the defence of frontiers and to proselytizing. Several early examples are known archaeologically in Tunisia; the one in Sousse bears many resemblances to early Islamic palaces, but its interior arrangement of large halls, with a sizable mosque and a minaret, identifies its special needs for meetings, keeping arms, and prayer. *Ribāts* existed also on the Byzantine frontier and in Central Asia, but no examples have been identified with enough certitude to allow for any kind of generalized formal definition.

The city as an expression of power

Islamic culture has always been primarily urban, and it is therefore not surprising that whole cities or parts of them were either conceived as expressions of power or, as I shall try to show, became the settings for various means of expressing power.

The very early Islamic cities of Iraq and elsewhere could be interpreted as expressions of power. Basra, Kufa and Fustat were called *mu'askar*, military camps, and served to separate the early community of the Faithful from the rest of the population. As far as one can discover, however, there is little evidence that any of the physical characteristics of these camps reflected their function, and for the most part they were planned as egalitarian communities rather than as visible expressions of physical or symbolic power.

The earliest clear example of a change is known only through texts: the city of Wasit, built in Iraq in 702 or 703 to become the capital of this frequently unruly province. Its location, equidistant from the three main earlier Muslim settlements in Iraq, was symbolic of its peace-enforcing role. The doors of its gates were taken from earlier pre-Islamic cities, thus indicating that it took its place in a long succession of capital cities. Its major monument was a Green Dome similar, at least in name, to the dome that existed in the imperial palace in Damascus. The ideas developed in Wasit by the great Umayyad governor, al-Hajjāj, culminated a few decades later in the foundation of Baghdad in 759. Astronomers presided over the tracing of this round city, roughly a mile in diameter. A mighty wall with four axial gates, bearing the names of the provinces or cities towards which they led, enclosed an outer ring of living and commercial quarters, and, in the centre, a mosque and the imperial palace. The latter was provided with two superimposed domes, the symbolic centres of the city and of the universe. The uppermost dome was green, topped with the statue of a rider, and it was echoed by four gilt domes, one over each gate. Nothing survives of this Baghdad and it did not last very long in its ideal state. Contemporary or nearly contemporary literary sources, however, are sufficiently precise to allow a reasonable reconstruction of a city whose geometric perfection, rationally conceived order, and even its name – the City of Peace – served as a physical demonstration of the new empire's power and universal claims.

The theme of a new city as an expression of power ran through much of Islamic history. When Cairo was founded in 969 as the dynastic capital of the missionary and exclusive Fātimids, some of the procedures used in Baghdad were repeated and the Egyptian capital became known as the Victorious One, al-Qahira – although there is an alternate explanation that its name refers to the planet Mars. As an example of urban design Cairo was less impressive than Baghdad, although there too the palaces occupied roughly the central part of the city, and living quarters for selected groups of followers were set in the rest of the enclosure. The remains consist of stone walls and three gates, two of which are known as Gates of Victory, belonging to an 11th-century reconstruction. To the idea of a city as an expression of power Cairo added the notion of power as expressed in the separation of a royal city from the urban centre proper. Gates or walls become curtains, dividing the community rather than, as in Baghdad, enclosing the whole community, from its leaders down to the poorest members. And perhaps it is no accident that, whereas the very name of City of Peace implies universal ecumenism, al-Qahira, like its immediate Tunisian predecessors, al-Mansuriyya or Mahdia, was one of the new cities whose names either glorified their founders or perpetuated a specific idea of power and victory. This particular development may be the result of the Fātimid peculiarity of belonging to a minority sect with a religious mission, or perhaps by the 11th century a sense of the universality of the Muslim world no longer was applicable.

Although Baghdad and Cairo are the most obvious and most celebrated cities of power, they are not the only ones that were founded during the early centuries of Islamic history. The ideas they exemplify are found in varying degrees of forcefulness in several other instances. Samarra, for example, was developed in the 9th century along the Tigris, a city of palaces, about which more will be said later, and of military settlements. On the whole, Samarra was less a city expressing power than one that housed power by removing the Turkish armies and the government from the cantankerous urban centre of Baghdad. More interesting are the monuments planned by Ahmad ibn Tūlūn in his military extension of his own town of Fustat in Egypt. His main creation, unfortunately known only through texts, was a large *maydān*, or open space, with formal gates leading to official or ceremonial buildings. Other examples of cities expressing, in parts or as a whole, the power of princes may have occurred in the eastern provinces of the Muslim world, as at Bust in Afghanistan, but very little is known about the layout and uses of these new capitals of Turkish dynasties.

A more original manner of expressing power occurred in cities through the location and design of monuments that in themselves are not directly connected with the functions of authority. The point can most easily be demonstrated in a street such as the shāri'a bayn al-qasrayn in Cairo. Originally the central artery of the restricted Fātimid city, it became one of the main axes of a bustling metropolis after the fall of the dynasty. Over the centuries, wealthy patrons who were endowing pious foundations of all sorts (*madrasas*, schools, hospitals, convents) or building warehouses and hostels for mercantile activities sought to justify their expenditure by conspicuously exhibiting its presence along a major street in the city. Thus an unparalleled succession of façades and minarets, whose main buildings are squeezed into whatever space was available, appear to broadcast the wealth and power of their patrons like a succession of neon signs in a modern Western town. The Cairene phenomenon is particularly spectacular but is not unique; in Damascus, Jerusalem or Aleppo, façades of pious monuments similarly adorn streets without necessarily revealing their full size or their purpose. In Isfahan, and probably in several other Iranian cities, façades and especially minarets proclaim the power and the wealth of their sponsors more than the pious purposes of the buildings. And in Ottoman times the great *külliyes*, buildings serving a wide range of practical social functions around a mosque, also expressed the power of individual sultans. The interesting point about these examples is that one or two characteristic forms of buildings, most frequently façades, gates or minarets, became the formal expressions of the presence and importance of their sponsors rather than of the purposes of the buildings.

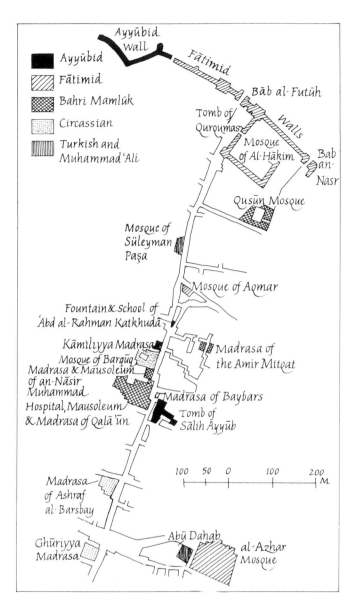

The shāri' a bayn al qasrayn, one of the main arteries of Fātimid Cairo, is lined with pious foundations endowed by rich patrons – to the glory of God, but also partly to their own. The buildings date from the 11th to the 19th centuries. The oldest is the mosque of al-Hākim (1013), the latest that of Süleyman Paşa (1839). (2)

71

This point had further implications for the forms of power in Islamic architecture.

Imperial power

The official palaces of the great age of Islamic civilization are poorly preserved and known mostly through literary sources. But even these sources are far from easy to interpret, and information is more adequate about the terminology used for parts of the palaces than for the buildings as a whole. We know of the existence of one or more *majlis*, or reception halls; of a *dār al-'āmma*, or formal area, where prince and people could meet; of an *īwān*, which could be either the whole palace or its most formal part; but it is almost impossible to imagine these elements as actual physical buildings. Although less formally worked out than in Rome or Byzantium, the major ceremonies around caliphs, sultans, or provincial governors usually imply a setting with some consistent requirements: a prominent place for the ruler, often with some symbolic feature like a baldachin or a cupola; a curtain separating him from the audience; passageways, which were generally only known to palace servants; treasure rooms and archives; wardrobes; gardens, often supplied with wild animals.

While historical or geographical accounts and imaginative literature such as the *Thousand and One Nights* do provide considerable, if unsystematic, information about the terminology of palaces and about the activities carried out in them, it is much more difficult to relate this information to the traces of buildings revealed by archaeology. The Umayyad palaces in Damascus and Rusafa were celebrated for their green domes. In Baghdad and early Merv there was an impressive cupola over the place of the throne, and in all likelihood this domed room was preceded by a long hall and by a court in which visitors and attendants gathered. Somewhat more precise information exists about the several large palaces of Samarra, Madīnat al-Zahrā' near Cordoba, and the Fātimid palaces of Cairo. All of them seem to have been sprawling conglomerates of many separate units, ranging from very functional and specific elements, such as baths and dwellings, to formal audience halls (cruciform in Samarra, basilical in Spain), gardens, and vast areas with no concretely identifiable purpose. In the 9th-century palaces of Samarra there were compositional axes in the main parts of the buildings, perhaps corresponding to a ceremonial order of progressive remoteness. Such axes do not appear in Cairo or Madīnat al-Zahrā', and each one of their known units should probably be considered as a self-contained, discrete monument. The implication in almost all of these palaces is that their recognition as monuments of official power lay less in their individual architectural characteristics than in their general presence as walled enclosures, separating the world of power from the world of the common man.

Matters changed after the Mongol conquest, especially in Iran and India, when new and wealthy dynasties, changes in the political and economic importance of various provinces, influences from Mongolia and China, and a conscious but somewhat romanticized awareness of a traditional Islamic past combined to revive an imperial desire for cities symbolizing and expressing power. Such was the Soltaniyeh developed by the Mongol ruler Öljeytu in the early 14th century. Only his spectacular mausoleum remains, and only ruins of the Ghāzāniyya and Rāshidiyya quarters in Tabriz. The Samarqand that Tīmūr and his immediate successors rebuilt next to the older Afrasiab fulfilled a similar purpose.

For most of these examples only fragmentary visual evidence exists, and even the descriptions and observations of curious travellers or of contemporary chroniclers are not sufficient to reconstruct the plans and characteristics of these cities. Two later and better preserved examples do illustrate the continuity of the tradition, even though they are stylistically and functionally very different from each other. One is the Isfahan of Shāh 'Abbās, where commercial centre, royal mosque, personal sanctuary, and palace entrance meet around a huge open space, *maydān*, used for ceremonies, games, parades, executions, and common urban activities. The other example is Fatehpur Sikri in India, created in the early 17th century by the Mughal king Akbar. Its triumphal arch, its sanctuaries, houses, offices, and especially its private and public audience halls, all served to make the power of the emperor permanently visible. Akbar's vision of the world is summed up in its extraordinary audience hall, which has in the middle a platform supported by a single column and connected with the four corners of the room.

Whole cities that visually express the power of the empire or of an individual emperor were but one aspect of an architecture of power within an urban context. In addition, there were kinds of buildings, as well as attitudes towards architectural monuments, that expressed various types of power within the city. In the early decades of Muslim rule an urban building appeared that seemed to be peculiar to Islam. It is known in texts as the *dār al-imāra* and its closest contemporary parallel would be a government centre containing financial, judicial, and all generally administrative offices, as well as the living quarters of a governor. The *dār al-imāra* was not usually found in capital cities but only in provincial headquarters. Two are known through archaeological investigations: at Kufa in Iraq and, perhaps less obviously identified, at

Isfahan was laid out in the time of Shāh 'Abbās I as a series of linked rectangular spaces based on the traditional Iranian garden.
A, *Chahār Bāgh, the main artery of the city;* B, *Allāhavardi Khān's Bridge;* C, *the Maydān-i Shāh, or Imperial Square;* D, *'Alī Qapu;* E, *Masjid-i Shāh;* F, *Masjid-i Shaykh Lutfullāh;* G, *Chihil Sutūn.* (3)

Qasr al-Hayr East in Syria. In both instances we are dealing with buildings that appear as houses or small palaces and in which minor modifications (somewhat more elaborate decoration, multiplicity of entrances suggesting easy access, a clear separation between purely living quarters and official ones) that have been made to otherwise typical arrangements can best be explained as ways to accommodate administrative and public requirements. By the end of the 8th century references to a *dār al-imāra* disappear from texts. Its functions were taken over by purely administrative buildings, usually known as *dīwāns*, about whose physical shape archaeology provides no information. In fact, evidence from 13th-century miniatures suggests that *dīwāns* were hardly distinguishable from regular houses. Thus began a tradition that is still part of the Middle Eastern scene: the perfectly neutral and undistinguished building serving as the most visible symbol of the state's bureaucracy.

Modified by evolutions in taste and by local architectural traditions, the themes of these 9th- and 10th-century palaces remained throughout the centuries. Lashkari Bāzār in Afghanistan exhibits a strongly symmetrical order with a carefully thought-out plan, and lends itself to reasonable guesses about the functions of official rooms. The Alhambra's two remaining complexes explode with brilliant interior decoration without exterior counterparts; the functions of the various halls and courts are less clear. Later Safavid palaces in Isfahan demonstrate, as in the 'Alī Qapu, a brilliant transformation of the palace gateway into a ceremonial and pleasure hideway; while the Chihil Sutūn and Hasht Bihisht are the only remaining examples of garden pavilions used both for official and for private purposes. All these motifs appear in the last and most modern of all palace complexes, the Topkapi in Istanbul, still in use at the end of the 19th century. Surrounded by high walls, entered through one major formal gate, and impressively located on a hill over the Bosphorus, it consists of a large number of pavilions, formal as well as private dwellings, reception halls, treasuries, and practical establishments such as kitchens. It was built over the centuries, without formal compositional order but according to a subtler order of ceremonial and practical use. Almost every one of the palace's parts must be considered as a separate monument and some, for example the Revan or Baghdad kiosks, are exquisite works of art. The quality and excitement of the Topkapi, just as in earlier palaces, can only be appreciated from within, from living there and participating in palace activities, not from its forceful impact on the surrounding world, like Versailles or the Winter Palace in St Petersburg.

73

The Topkapi palace in its final form, as it evolved over four centuries. (4)

1 The Ortakapi or Middle Gate
2 Palace water-works
3 Kitchens and cooks' quarters
4 Mosque of Beşir Ağa
5 Stables and harness rooms
6 Barrack of the Halberdiers
7 Hall of the Divan
8 Offices of the Divan
9 Inner Treasury
10 Gate of Felicity
11 Quarters of the White Eunuchs
12 Throne room
13 Ahmet III library
14 Privy kitchen
15 Cook's house
16 Mosque of the school, now the library
17 Harem mosque
18 Quarters of the senior students and officers of the household
19 Court of the Room of the Robe
20 Room of the Robe of the Prophet
21 Rooms of the Relics of the Prophet
22 Hall of the Treasury
23 Hall of the Pantry
24 Pavilion of Mehmet II, now the Treasury
25 Disrobing chamber of Selim II hammām
26 Site of Selim II hammām
27 Site of Selim II hammām boilers
28 Hall of the Expeditionary Force
29 Forehall of the Room of the Robe
30 Circumcision kiosk
31 Terrace and bower
32 Pool
33 Baghdad kiosk
34 Pool
35 Revan kiosk
36 Tulip garden
37 Mustafā Paşa kiosk
38 Physician's tower
39 Abdül Mecid kiosk
40 The Third Gate
41 Entry to residential area (a) Shawl Gate (b) Carriage Gate

42 Mosque of the Black Eunuchs
43 Court of the Black Eunuchs
44 Barrack of the Black Eunuchs
45 Princes' school
46 Quarters of the Chief Black Eunuch
47 Quarters of the Treasurer
48 Quarters of the Chamberlain
49 Aviary Gate
50 Main Harem Gate
51 Courtyard of the women of the Harem
52 Kitchen of the women
53 Hammām of the women
54 Stairs to bedrooms
55 Commissariat
56 Laundry
57 Women's dormitory
58 Apartments of senior women
59 Stairs to Harem garden
60 Court of women's hospital
61 Hospital hammām
62 Hospital kitchen quarters
63 Sultan Ahmet kiosk
64 Harem garden
65 Valide court
66 Valide's salon
67 Valide's antechamber
68 Valide's dining room
69 Valide's bedroom
70 Valide's oratory
71 Music room of Selim III
72 The Valide's hammām
73 Kadin's quarters
74 Hall of the Hearth
75 Harem Treasury
76 Hall of the Fountain
77 The Golden Road
78 The Jinn's consultation hall
79 The Cage
80 Anteroom of Murad III
81 Murad III bedchamber
82 Ahmet I library
83 Ahmet III dining room
84 The Throne Room Within
85 The Sultan's hammām
86 Boiler room
87 Bedchamber of Abdülhamit I
88 Salon of Selim III
89 Osman III Terrace
90 Osman III kiosk
91 Boating pool
92 Terrace of Selâmlik Garden

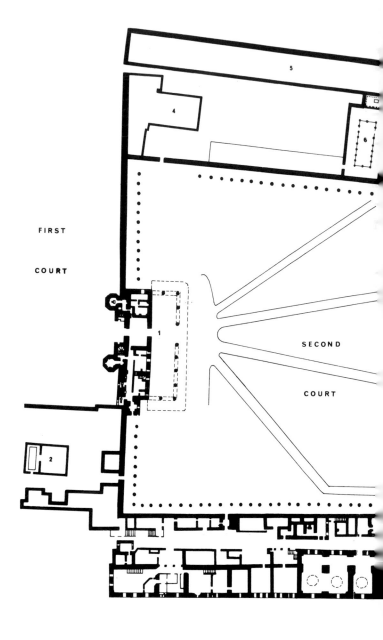

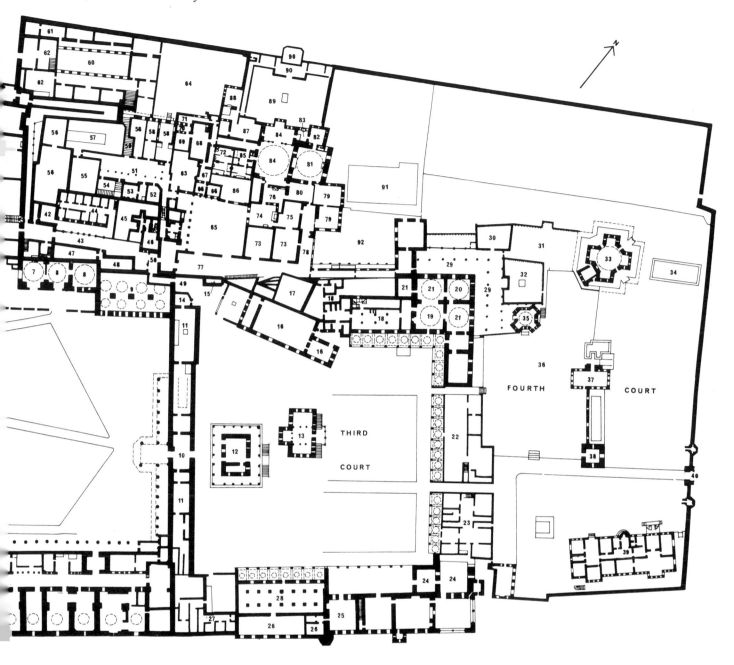

Symbolic power

Until the pre-modern empires of the Ottomans, Safavids, and Mughals, Islamic civilization is supposed to have avoided elaborate external symbols of its power and presence. In reality, of course, no continuous culture with a long history and a complicated past can avoid expressing its collective and individual successes, or its glory. Islamic civilization was no exception, even though it did not develop the coherent system of architectural forms of power found in Imperial Rome.

The earliest remaining major monument of Islamic art, the Dome of the Rock in Jerusalem, was meant initially to be a visual proclamation of the new Faith in the city of Judaism and Christianity. In Cairo the so-called Juyūshī Mosque, located on top of the cliffs overlooking the city, was built in the latter part of the 11th century to celebrate the end of a period of internal revolts and dissensions. The exact meaning of magnificent towers such as the 12th-century minaret in Jam (Afghanistan) or the 13th-century Qutb Minār is still the subject of some uncertainty. They were not really places for the call to prayer, but stunning proclamations of the power of the Faith and of its royal instruments in the wilderness of an Afghan valley or in

75

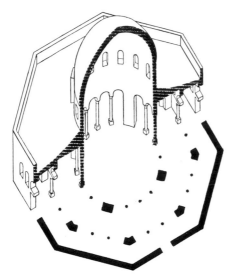

The Dome of the Rock in Jerusalem is Islam's first major monument, but not a typical example of Islamic architecture. Its model is a Christian martyrium and its function was primarily that of a symbol, a visual proclamation of the new Faith. (5)

a crowded Indian urban centre. Even the complex of the Court of the Lions in the Alhambra, and the so-called Puerto del Vino, outside the main palace complex, can be explained in part as architectural symbols of a rare Muslim victory over Christians in 1369.

In all these examples the forms of the architecture differ enormously: the Dome of the Rock and the Juyūshī Mosque are octagonal martyria with high cupolas; the minarets are tall towers; the Court of the Lions is a square hall around a porticoed court; the Puerto del Vino is a gateway. And in all of them it is inscriptions that provide the clue to the building's interpretation. Most frequently they are Qur'ānic passages, suggesting directly or metaphorically the meaning of the monument; at other times they are poems written for the occasion. It is therefore the applied decoration, rather than the architectural forms, that actually defines the building's initial purpose. With the passing of time, this purpose was either simply forgotten or its associations were modified. This is what happened to the Dome of the Rock, where pious meanings took over after the original motivation for the monument was gone. The Juyūshī Mosque in Cairo also became a mausoleum and a sanctuary.

Symbolic expression of authority is also found in royal or dynastic mausolea. A small dynastic mausoleum like the 9th-century Sāmānid one in Bukhara may have been more of a private monument than a public display of power. But enormous monuments like the mausoleum in Soltaniyeh (early 14th century), Tīmūr's tomb in Samarqand (early 15th century), or

the Tāj Mahal (early 17th century) were all deliberate and conspicuous displays of personal or dynastic wealth and glory. Many of them were focal points in the layout of cities and, curiously enough, all four of them incorporated striking technical innovations in their construction and decoration. It is even possible to interpret the succession of mausolea in a sanctuary such as the Shāh-i Zinda in Samarqand or the Qarāfa cemetery in Cairo as a competitive display of personal or family power and wealth around a holy place — much in the manner of late medieval private chapels in the West. Human vanities and ambitions often prevailed over the strictures of the Faith.

The powerful

I stressed earlier the difficulty of distinguishing between an architecture directly and exclusively dedicated to the expression and functions of power and that which ministered to the more private and temporary whims and requirements of wealthy and important individuals. Official and formally impressive monuments such as the Tāj Mahal, the Alhambra, Cairene religious complexes, or the palaces of Isfahan are, in varying degrees, permeated with details and meanings that reflect the taste of a patron, his unique personality and habits, or are a tribute to memories that are only remotely related to power. A number of monuments exist whose primary purpose was for personal satisfaction or expression, although some of them also have more official and formal associations with power. They differ from purely vernacular architecture in that each one of them tends to be unique and that the quality of almost every one required a financial and technical investment not available to everyone.

The earliest examples of an architecture of the powerful are provided by the Umayyad palaces of Syria, Jordan, and Palestine. Qasr al-Hayr West, Qusayr 'Amra, Mshattā, Khirbat al-Mafjar and Khirbat al-Minya are only the best known examples of what seem to have been dozens of country residences built in the large estates that were taken over by the new Arab aristocracy of the Levant. Typologically, and in many ways formally, they can be related to the country villas of Roman Antiquity. They included living quarters, common areas, a bath, and a small mosque. Almost all of them were also provided with official halls, usually varied in their shapes. Some scholars have argued that these were for formal receptions, that they were throne rooms of official palaces. Others have felt that, even though their forms are closely related to those of throne rooms, they were more probably entertainment rooms, reflecting no doubt the semi-official character of princely pastime. The most interesting feature of the main Umayyad palaces is their wealth of decoration. Paintings, mosaics, stucco or stone ornament covered most walls, but vary enormously in quality. In most instances that have been recovered so far, all sorts of representational themes (people, animals, narrative scenes) are found alongside pure ornament. Many of these themes have not yet been deciphered and explained; they include official scenes (enthroned princes, alien ancestors of Muslim rulers), private events (uniquely Arabian hunting scenes), routine symbols of pleasure and fun (hunting, women), copies of older monuments (Palmyrene sculptures at Qasr al-Hayr), and possibly even reflections of contemporary literature. This very variety of representational motifs is partly the result of the sudden and recent impact of the rich Classical heritage. The absence of such themes in the monuments found in cities suggests that these Umayyad palaces illustrated primarily the private world of a nouveau riche Arabian aristocracy.

Matters become somewhat more complicated as we try to follow the evolution of this particular tradition in later times and in other areas. In Central Asia, it is true, there is some evidence for the existence of a comparable phenomenon of country estates, although their dates are quite insecure and they did not seem to have been nearly as fancifully decorated as their Mediterranean counterparts. Another group of monuments that possibly may be related is found in North Africa. The *qal'a* of the Banī Hammād and Ashir are the two best examples of 11th-century feudal castles located away from a major centre. In part they can be placed in the same category as the forts discussed previously, but the *qal'a* of the Banī Hammād was provided with such unusual amenities of aristocratic life as a large artificial pool for boating, and its walls were decorated with some of our earliest known examples of what will become *muqarnas*-work. It is possible that during the 10th and 11th centuries the Būyid dynasty of western Iran and Iraq also built private country estates, but there is almost no archaeological evidence.

Remote hideouts were built in secluded areas until fairly recent times. One of the most spectacular is the palace of Işāq Paşa in Doğubayazit in eastern Anatolia. Completed in about 1784, it was the residence of several semi-independent governors and its style is a fascinating mixture of traditionally Ottoman and new Western Baroque details. Less well known but apparently equally spectacular is the Qal'a-yi Nādirī in the mountains north-east of Mashhad, also an 18th-century creation. The Iranian countryside still possesses several palaces in private estates, which have not been studied and therefore it is not really possible to know whether echoes of the Umayyad pleasure palaces still lingered on during the Qājār period.

As well as fortified and unfortified country and mountain mansions, the rich and powerful also built in cities. One aspect of their urban architecture has already been mentioned: the façades, minarets, and domes that adorn pious foundations, creating in many cities competing clusters of monumental complexes, each fulfilling the same social functions and looking alike, but identified with different individuals or social groups. These complexes are most readily observable in Cairo, but also exist elsewhere. In 14th-century Yazd, for instance, the sponsors of the major local monuments, mostly members of the local patriciate, also built for themselves gardens with pleasure, or living, pavilions, *bāgh*; and with apparently formal portals, *dargāh*, in which official business was transacted. Yazd demonstrates that surburban and urban developments were intimately tied to each other both economically and in terms of monumental constructions.

It is only in very recent years that scholars have begun to investigate the economic bases of urban architecture, although significant differences existed between large Iranian monuments and smaller Syrian ones based on different types of land ownership. Further studies will probably show that the power, wealth, and importance of individual patrons is reflected in the dimensions and location of their pious constructions as much as in the forms they chose for them. This peculiar situation has been made possible in the Muslim world by the legal provisions of *waqf* endowments, whereby the wealthy were encouraged to invest their income in socially useful pious constructions available to the whole community. How and when the system grew is still very unclear. As early as in the 9th century, the Darb Zubayda, the great caravan road from Iraq to Mecca, whose scientific archaeological investigation has just begun, was endowed with caravanserais, wells, bridges, and possibly even small palaces by Hārūn al-Rashīd's wife, presumably from her own personal funds. A 10th-century *waqf* from Samarqand gives a wonderful description of the complicated mosaic of owners in this particular city. Even though it says very little about individual monuments, it does suggest that they reflected the power structure of the town. By then it can be assumed that the legal system of traditional Islam was sufficiently well established for almost all major Muslim cities to have developed nodes of monumental ensembles, reflecting local or imported power and wealth. Foreign amirs established themselves locally by endowing schools and sanctuaries, while local patrician families competed with them and with each other by sponsoring the same functions.

In simplified terms there emerges the picture of a unique relationship between patronage and architecture, whereby the latter served as a guarantor of the former's prestige and power. But the whole subject still needs much investigation.

While this aspect of pious architecture as an expression of power was originally an Islamic phenomenon, a more universally consistent one lay in the palaces and houses built in cities by the powerful and the wealthy for their own personal use, rather than for official functions. Of these, hardly any erected before the 12th century have been preserved, and it is only through literary sources that we are aware of the mass of private palaces built all over Baghdad by the caliphs, their families, and major viziers. The inscriptions of the palaces bore wonderful names like 'Crown', 'Pleiades' and 'Bride', but practically nothing is known of their forms. For the bourgeoisie, the accounts of a writer such as Tanūkhī about the foibles of Baghdad's establishment are almost impossible to put in their appropriate setting. Even in the Cairo of the Fātimids we can only imagine the garden pavilions to which the caliph and his entourage would frequently repair; and the handsomely decorated house from Afrasiab, recently reconstructed by Soviet archaeologists, is difficult to set within its proper historical and aesthetic context. The many fragments of houses and their decoration found in Neyshabur also needed to be analyzed.

Not before the 15th century does enough information remain to construct the life and setting of the wealthy and powerful individuals of the Muslim world. And it is only from Ottoman times that the whole range of their physical setting begins to appear. In Damascus the ʿAzam palace is a superbly preserved mansion of a powerful local leader. Almost invisible from the rest of the city, tucked away in the midst of a winding bazaar, it is a sudden oasis of greenery within the dusty city. Its buildings, like those of the Topkapi palace, are a series of separate units, with different functions, strewn around a beautiful garden. A similar but less impressive palace built by the same family remains in Hama, and a whole group of such private dwellings is still standing in Cairo. In Isfahan or Nayin, Iranian versions of urban dwellings for the rich have been preserved; and the culmination of the tradition may be seen in the beautiful *yalis* of Istanbul, where normally inward-centred houses open up to beautiful views over the Bosphorus.

The forms and functions of power

This survey of the major monuments and functions that reflect power or serve as settings for power leads to a number of conclusions and observations, concerning both definitions of an architecture of power and whatever originality the Muslim world brought to it.

Because of its universal uses military architecture is rarely original in themes or techniques and Muslim examples are no exception. The appreciation of monuments like Aleppo's citadel, the outer walls of Cairo and Diyarbakir, the gates of Rabat or of Marrakesh lies more in a fascination for their impressive location, or for their unusual state of preservation, than in an awareness of their technical achievements. In most other ways these monuments simply continue a long tradition of military architecture already fully developed in ancient Middle Eastern empires and in Rome. In construction or decoration they reflect prevailing local tastes, with occasional tendencies toward grandiloquence. Certain characteristic Western military structures, such as the totally independent *château-fort* with its elaborate internal arrangements, are rare in Islamic architecture, although Crusader castles like the Crac des Chevaliers or Kerak were taken over by the Muslims and imitated in a few instances. A more original Muslim development may have been the growth of urban citadels. Although known elsewhere (the Kremlin for instance), the elaborate fortified palace-city, containing the whole gamut of living amenities and activities as well as administrative and coercive functions, might be called a uniquely Islamic phenomenon, if for no other reason than its ubiquity from Spain to Central Asia.

While it is probably true that the functional originality of Islamic military architecture lies only in a comparatively small number of technical modifications – for instance the development of bent gates or various improvements in arrow slits and machicolation – there is one area where military architecture may possibly have played an important role within the evolution of Islamic architecture in general. It is curious to note that major changes and inventions in techniques of vaulting and roofing roughly coincided with the increase in the number of fortresses, citadels, city walls, and other primarily military monuments in the 10th and 11th centuries. Possibly the practical concerns of defence architecture required experimentation and invention in stone and brick vaulting, and as a result of its immediate feudal needs a new tone was given to the conceptual and technical effort of the whole culture.

A wide question that may be asked about an architecture of power is: can its forms be defined according to any cultural ideological categories? At one level it may be argued that there was no uniquely Islamic formal system to reflect authority or wealth, except on the purely cosmetic levels such as the degree of decoration, amount of expensive materials used, and variations in size. There were no standard plans for Islamic palaces and the most obvious way of indicating power or social importance was to use towers, façades, domes and other architectural components seen in all Islamic architecture. Only in Ottoman or Safavid times can one clearly identify the pavilion in a garden, for instance, as a consistent feature of palace complexes, a motif whose earlier history is still impossible to delineate properly. Even in decoration, if one excepts the explicit themes of Umayyad paintings, mosaics and sculpture, there is little in the arts immediately associated with architecture that can be compared to the royal imagery found in almost all forms of Islamic art. Occasional symbols such as the animals and personages found on the fortresses, walls, and gates of the Fertile Crescent in the 12th and 13th centuries have not yet been fully explained and it is uncertain whether they reflect power or whether they belong to a more fundamental folk tradition of apotropaic images.

Although the same range of forms is used in Islamic architecture to express power as is employed for monuments of trade or for pious buildings, it would probably be a mistake to conclude that no ways existed to express the functions of power. It is nevertheless difficult to distinguish between Islamic caravanserais, palaces and *ribāts* or Safavid royal pavilions and mausolea. For it is unlikely that any culture would be unable to identify the uses or purposes of the monuments that surrounded it; and, even if one can argue the validity of ambiguity in certain kinds of sophisticated artistic endeavours, it is hardly likely to apply to a social art such as architecture.

In other words, means must have existed whereby power, wealth, and authority were identified within a common language of forms. One such means was certainly the symbolism of decoration. This is still a very little-explored area of Islamic art, because of the difficulties inherent to the exploration of non-representational motifs. A very standard, although qualitatively superior, *muqarnas* composition on the ceiling of the Hall of the Two Sisters in the Alhambra can, thanks to the poetic inscriptions surrounding it, be interpreted as a rotating dome of heaven, a motif going back many centuries before Islam. Inscriptions and probably other hitherto undiscovered visual signs served to identify otherwise unspecified forms as symbolic of power. It is probable, for instance, that the relief of a person subduing two dragons on the Talisman Gate in Baghdad symbolized the power of the caliphate, while sculptures in northern Mesopotamia that seem related may have been simply ornamental, because Baghdad was the capital of a revived caliphate.

Another manner of identification was context, or setting. A characteristic peculiar to the architecture of power and wealth in the Muslim world was that its order and sense appear less in formal compositions than in the presence (or absence) of certain, sometimes minor, features or in the relationship of the monument of power to other monuments and especially to contemporary life. For instance, water in the shape of streams, a pool, or fountains or fancy gardens around or within buildings serve to identify it as a palatial setting rather than a sanctuary. But the most consistent identification of a function or power lay in human uses and associations, in the ways in which official ceremonies or ordinary living habits determined the quality of otherwise unspecified forms as forms of power. It is a ceremonial and living routine that really created the Topkapi palace complex, just as the daily life of a Cairene street identified the respective importance of the patrons of façades, domes, and minarets. If this contextual definition of an architecture of power proves acceptable, it would explain several curious aspects of the culture as a whole. It would be precisely because of this unusual relationship of forms to users that the architecture of power in the Muslim world so easily penetrated into imaginative literature, whereas mosques and sanctuaries did not. For the very imprecision of the forms transformed the men who served them – chamberlains, guards, slaves, eunuchs – into magicians who could open secret doors and knew their way in mazes of tortuous passages. The 'open Sesame' which uncovered caves full of treasures is the result of an aura of mystery around the purposes of architectural forms. Then there is the peculiarity that so many descriptions of ceremonies tend to emphasize the things brought to the ceremony or used in it rather than its architectural setting. It is rugs, chandeliers, clothes, gifts, treasures which made a palace and not its shape. And finally, on a more archaeological level, whereas mosques and sanctuaries tended to remain in constant use over the centuries, monuments of power changed in function as the surrounding life changed. A 15-century palace in Diyarbakir's citadel could become a prison, and the walls of Cairo became city landmarks.

The originality of Islamic architecture of power would thus be less in its forms than in the breadth of its uses. Quite unique among pre-Renaissance cultures, except Imperial Rome, the Islamic architecture of power appeared in a wide spectrum, ranging from the totally secret world of the prince to the public announcement of the rich city patrician. It demonstrated an extravagance both visible and invisible. The range of Islamic buildings from extremely private to totally public ones has been usually well preserved, and it lends itself to fundamental questions about the uses of architecture in pre-modern society.

3 Trade and Travel: Markets and Caravanserais

ELEANOR SIMS

Muslim civilization has always been mobile. Both the Arabs and the various non-Arab conquerors from Central Asia were originally nomadic and inherited a tradition of travel. Large armies were constantly on the move. Students and scholars undertook long journeys to sit at the feet of famous masters. The wealth of cities depended upon the transport of goods over vast distances. And the Faith of Islam imposed upon the Faithful the most powerful of all motives for travel, performance of the *hajj*, or pilgrimage.

In the harsh conditions and inhospitable countryside of most Islamic countries, these two last classes of traveller – merchants and pilgrims – needed more frequent places of rest and shelter than the widely spaced towns and cities could provide. This led to the construction of caravanserais along all the main routes – places where men and their animals would be safe for the night, and where they could be sure of food and water. They were often prestige buildings, paid for by the ruler, the state or a rich patron. Most resplendent of a splendid class are the two Sultan Hans (*han* is Turkish for caravanserai) erected outside Konya by 'Alā ad-Dīn Kayqubād in the early 13th century. That between Konya and Aksaray in Anatolia dates from 1229 and is the largest caravanserai on that road, where there are many. The elaborate decoration and the contrast between the deeply cut stonework and the plain ashlar are typical of Seljuq art at its most sophisticated. Yet the portal (*opposite*) with its pointed opening containing the *muqarnas* vault suggestively recalls the shape of a tent, the ancestral dwelling of the Seljuq tribes in their Central Asian homelands. (1)

On the road

Caravans were a form of mutual protection, like convoys of ships in wartime. It was therefore necessary that all the ancillary services – the caravanserais themselves, their urban equivalent, the *khāns*, and the markets – should be built on a correspondingly communal scale, and features such as watch-towers and marker posts could be developed to a degree without parallel in the West. *Left:* an 18th-century view showing members of an Ottoman baggage-train setting up tents for the night after the day's journey. *Right:* two Iranian towers built to direct travellers. The first, dating from the 11th or 12th century, stands completely alone in the deserts of south-east Iran, and seems to have served as a beacon, like a land-bound lighthouse. The second, at Dombi, had a similar purpose but is attached to one corner of a caravanserai dating from Mongol times. (2, 5, 6)

The tent is a form of shelter found throughout Islamic history and is still used today in many areas. Even to the Ottoman Turks, who excelled in solid stone architecture, it remained a natural form of dwelling. The tents of the sultans are comparable to their palaces – the Topkapi is, in a sense, an encampment of glorified tents. *Left:* a miniature of 1582 showing Lala Mustafā Paşa campaigning in Georgia, with the ordinary troops' tents in foreground and background. Many of these men would have been nomads, a way of life that survives all over the Muslim world. *Above:* nomads' tents in the High Atlas, Morocco. The *hajj*, too, still depends largely on tents to house the pilgrims. The camp at Arafat, near Mecca (*right*), is a veritable tent-city, with pilgrims from different countries living in demarcated areas of their own, like the quarters of an Islamic town. (3, 4, 7)

Bridges

Muslim roads often followed pre-Islamic routes, and Muslim bridge-building techniques are based on Roman or Sasanian precedents. Primitive structures can be seen today in remote areas like Afghanistan (*left*). Among the most impressive are those of Seljuq Anatolia, where the Roman prototype is modified by raising and widening the central arch. *Below:* the stone bridge over the Köprüçay River, between Antalya and Alanya in Turkey. Other functions tended to congregate near bridges; the building to the left is a caravanserai. When the bridge at Jaunpur (*bottom*) was built, between 1564 and 1574, pavilions were added for tea-houses, and in time it became the venue for a market. (8, 9, 10)

A **high point** of Islamic bridge-building is reached in the famous Khwajū bridge at Isfahan, where functional and aesthetic considerations are effortlessly combined. The central roadway is flanked by arcaded galleries for walking or standing and chatting. When the water is low, people can also sit and picnic on the stepped cut-waters. (11)

At Dezful, in Iran (*right*), the road ran across the top of a dam built on Sasanian stone foundations. Behind it an artificial lake fed irrigation channels. (12)

Caravanserais

Still in use after 250 years is the magnificent caravanserai of the *madrasa* of the Māder-i Shāh in Isfahan. This engraving shows the courtyard in the middle of the 19th century; it has recently been modernized as the Shāh 'Abbās Hotel. The superb entrance portal of another Safavid caravanserai (*right*), at Chāh-i Sīyāh, 1687, has the same monumental quality as the gate of the bazaar in the Maydān-i Shāh. (13, 14)

Abandoned and alone, the ruins of the Siahkuh caravanserai in Iran clearly display the standard plan and construction. The courtyard is entered by a single gate on the right. There are two rows of internal rooms, both covered by vaults, the outer one probably with an upper storey. Stables would have been in the round corner towers, not directly connected with the living rooms. (15)

By the 19th century, caravanserais were often ill maintained but were still used. This scene, published in 1851, shows merchants resting and smoking after the day's journey. Stables are to the left. Light comes through a hole in the roof. On the racks behind are blankets and saddles, and in the foreground bales of merchandise. (16)

Today caravanserais may be used as animal pens. *Above:* at Yunesi, Iran. *Right:* looking along one aisle of the great vaulted hall of the Sultan Han shown overleaf. (17,18)

Caravanserais

Between Kayseri and Sivas, in Anatolia, stands the second of 'Alā al-Dīn Kayqubād's two Royal Caravanserais, at Palas (*left*). Built between 1232 and 1236, it comprises a large open courtyard and a great covered hall opening from the side opposite the entrance. Here we are looking across the courtyard, with arcades on the right housing stables, towards the hall's splendidly decorated portal. Behind it rises the high central dome of the hall. The free-standing structure on the left was a mosque, raised on arches and reached by stairs. (19)

Within the city the caravanserai is known as a *khān*, and it required less fortification but more space for storage and commercial transactions. A 19th-century view of a *han* at ▷ Güzel Hisar, in Anatolia (*right*), shows that it was a social centre as well. (21)

The battered mud walls and cresting of the caravanserai near Tash Kurghan, in Afghanistan (*below*), contrast with the repeated niches on the exterior of that near Gaz, in Iran (*below right*), although their plans are essentially the same. (20, 22)

Khāns

The urban caravanserai, or *khān,* is essentially a warehouse, often with stabling and shops as well. Few of them are as splendid as the best of the country ones, but they can be of considerable size and complexity. The *khān* Özdemür in Aleppo has a finely decorated portal on the street (*left*). The doors would have been closed at night. (23)

Five storeys high, the great *khān* of Qānsūh ▷ al-Ghūrī in Cairo marks a high tide of Mamlūk prosperity. The two lower floors were for storage. The upper floors were apartments, arranged in vertical units and reached by separate inner staircases. (26)

In North Africa the *khān* is called a *funduq,* but structure and purpose remain the same throughout Islam. *Above:* an example in Tripoli, its columns recalling Byzantine and Hafsid models. (24)

Mustafā III endowed the 'Great New Khān' (Büyük Yeni Han) in Istanbul in 1764 (*left*). It has the standard ground-floor arcade for storage, with living quarters above. It is interesting to see that even in its dilapidated state trade and light industry still find a place there today. (25)

Markets

A **settled hierarchy** governs the layout of Muslim markets, and is surprisingly constant from North Africa to India. Food-stuffs are generally sold in the open air, as in this example at Rissani, Morocco. (27)

The cloth market: detail from a Mughal miniature of the 17th century. (28)

The standard bazaar plan is a network of streets (*sūqs*) covered with vaults and domes, often with higher domed or open areas at the crossing-points. In Central Asia, the market may be enclosed by a wall, as in Bukhara (*below*), where the wall was recently rebuilt. (29)

The bazaar is one of the classic defining features of an Islamic town, the commercial 'spine' of the urban fabric linking mosques, *hammāms*, *khāns* and schools – a city in miniature, consisting of dozens of streets, sometimes intersecting at right angles. Shops selling the same goods are always grouped together, so that there will be a spice bazaar, a leather bazaar, a metalwork bazaar. The plan of Aleppo market is reproduced and explained on p. 108. Where the main streets cross, the large spaces are either domed or open to the sky. One such crossing in Aleppo (*right*) is given elaborate *muqarnas* decoration. (31)

Each shop occupies one compartment in the *sūq*. This part of the carpet section is in the bazaar at Tripoli, Libya. Every available wall surface is used for displaying goods. (30)

The vaulted streets are lit by apertures in the centre of each bay, creating a cool and well ventilated space that is ideal for hot climates. Essentially the same architectural form prevails over the whole Islamic world; a typical interior, such as that of the Aleppo bazaar (*right*), is roofed in a procession of domes. (32)

Bazaar and bath

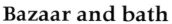

Bazaar and mosque grew together, the twin poles of Islamic urban life, separate but in harmony. This remains true even at a local level, as in this small bazaar at Qazvin, Iran (*above left*). *Above right:* books and spices for sale in the *sūq* at Kashan. Grandest of all the Ottoman bazaars is that of Istanbul (*below*), at whose centre rise the two multi-domed sections of the *bedesten*, where the most precious goods were sold. (33, 34, 35)

The bath (*hammām*) was an institution inherited by the Muslims from the Classical world. A 19th-century engraving of the 18th-century Çağaloğlu Hammām in Istanbul (*above*) shows the hot stone in the centre and the stone benches where bathers stretched out and steamed. *Below left:* the disrobing room of a Mughal bath, depicted in 1603, showing bathers undressing and preparing to enter the hot rooms. *Below right:* part of the baths of Ganj 'Alī Khān at Kerman, recently restored. (36, 37, 38)

The bazaar of the silk merchants: one of David Roberts's evocative lithographs of Cairo in 1849. The bazaar has grown up in the space between the early 16th-century collegiate mosque (left) and tomb (right) of Sultan Qānsūh al-Ghūrī. Many such bazaars in Cairo were located in streets and passages that could be closed at night by wooden doors and chains. Mamluk windows, placed at least two metres above the ground, enabled stalls to be pitched against them without difficulty. The wooden roof is substantial but is not a permanent structure, and the shopkeepers stand on a kind of dais some feet above the road. (39)

ONE OF THE MORE underestimated characteristics of Muslim culture is the extraordinary mobility of its people, their matter-of-fact traversing of distances that even today daunt the traveller in the Middle East. Islam, however, was born in a land with many centuries' experience of trading on the land-routes between the Yemen and the Mediterranean; and the revelation of Islam was entrusted to a man from a trading family, who had himself been to Syria at least once by camel-caravan. By the middle of the 7th century the armies of Islam controlled territory from the Pyrenees to the marches of Central Asia, and these peripheral areas were kept within the *dār al-Islām* as much by the constant provisioning by caravan as by military garrisons and governors. Islam's secondary, mainly peaceful expansion along the coastal regions of India, South-East Asia and Africa also followed in the wake of routes opened by traders; and accessibility, whether for commercial or for military communication, was always to be a significant factor in the choice of sites for the many new cities founded by Islam.

In addition to a long established commercial tradition, Islam imposed upon its followers the supreme reason to travel: the performance of the *hajj*, the pilgrimage to Mecca and the other holy places in the Arabian Peninsula. The Qur'ān commands the Muslim: 'Pilgrimage to the House is a duty to Allah for all who can make the journey' (Sūra iii, 97–8). Religious and commercial activities were by no means mutually exclusive, however: 'It shall be no offence for you to seek the bounty of your Lord by trading' (Sūra ii, 199). From early Islamic times, therefore, Muslims who made the *hajj* carried goods with them on their return from Mecca to defray the costs of travel. By the 9th century appeared the practice of visiting the places in lower Iraq where 'Alī, the fourth caliph, and his sons, Hasan and Husayn, had been martyred, while shrines of saints in other parts of the Islamic world increasingly attracted pilgrims in search of blessing, *baraka*. Thus it was, that for commercial, religious or educational reasons much of Islam was constantly on the road.

Merchant, pilgrim and student alike needed protection from robbery and from weather, both in the cities and in the inhospitable deserts or semi-arid lands that comprise so much of the Muslim world. An assured source of water was needed for drinking, bathing and ritual ablution, as was a place in which to perform daily prayers. Ways of crossing were needed at rivers, while in less inhabited areas road-markers and watch-towers were necessary. In towns, the corresponding source of shelter, security and water and equally the mercantile focus of so many journeys was the market area, usually at the heart of the Muslim city. Markets were also manufacturing centres for goods of all kinds, especially for small and precious wares; although goods produced by offensive methods – tanned skins for example – were produced on the outskirts of towns.

The financial basis providing for the amenities of the road, and also for the urban shelters, schools, baths and markets, was more broadly spread throughout the Islamic community than elsewhere in the medieval world, and as early as the 9th century private revenues were being used to erect facilities for pilgrims all over Arabia. Such funds were made available as a *waqf*, an inalienable gift of money, property or other valuable object, to be used only for the purpose specified in the deed of endowment and administered in perpetuity, according to religious law. As regards trade and travel in the Islamic world, a *waqf* could operate in two ways: funds maintained shelters, caravanserais, for travellers to stay gratis for a specified number of days and to receive food for themselves and their beasts during that period; or the caravanserai, the *khān* or the *hammām* could be turned into the revenue-producing instrument. Thus, both on the road and in cities, caravanserais and their urban equivalent, the *khāns*, provided facilities for the storage and sale of foods whose revenues in turn supported not only the markets but mosques, *madrasas* and convents in the city, and the caravanserais of the road.

The sources contributing to our knowledge of Islam's architectural response to the needs of its travelling citizenry are several. The most obvious source would seem to be the buildings themselves, although caravanserais, *khāns*, baths (*hammāms*) and bridges survive unevenly distributed across the entire

Islamic world and in widely varying states of preservation. A few caravanserais, like that built by an Ottoman grand vizier in Edirne, about 1560, are still in use as hotels today; some are empty monuments marking a trade or pilgrimage route, while others are in ruin and reveal little more than a stone or mud-brick ground-plan. Furthermore, the very nature of Islamic travel architecture, linked as it always was to geographical factors and to political policy, meant that many caravanserais and bridges were never intended as major architectural monuments but rather as facilities en route, more noticeable by their absence than by their presence. Indeed, caravanserais in certain parts of the Muslim world – in Egypt, Ifrikiyah and North Africa, in southern Iraq, in parts of Afghanistan – were never a major architectural expression and, even in the Arabian Peninsula, caravanserais of early date are known almost entirely from literary references. The Islamic caravanserai has often been likened to the American motel, where shelter, water, food and a place for one's vehicle are combined in one structure. An even better modern equivalent might be the petrol station, occurring at regular intervals – ubiquitous, unremarkable and unremarked – along the motor roads of the entire world. Markets, *khāns* and baths, on the other hand, are primary focal points of the urban landscape and tended to remain relatively fixed in location, but the original structures are hardly ever extant, owing to the ravages of war, fire and other natural disasters, and the upgrading of market facilities over the centuries, not to speak of the destruction wrought by modern town-planning.

Literary sources of many kinds are, therefore, of signal importance to a study of Islamic trade and travel architecture. There exists a vast literature in Arabic and Persian and, at a later date, Turkish: the 'route-books', lists of roads, settlements and cities by which the extent of the Muslim world was calculated and its taxes computed; geographical writing, a genre that flourished from the 9th century onwards; local historians; references in belles-lettres; and the travellers who wrote so copiously about their journeys. Nāsir-i Khusraw, for example, visited Egypt in 1046, leaving an invaluable picture of Fātimid Cairo; Ibn Battūta left his native town of Fez in 1325 to traverse the length and breadth of the Islamic world and even beyond, to China, performing the *hajj* four times and each time approaching the holy cities by a different route. To such accounts may also be added, from the 13th century, the writings of Europeans travelling for religious, commercial, diplomatic, scientific or military reasons.

Origins and characteristics of trade and travel architecture

Islam inherited a world with a material apparatus of military and commercial routes and trading centres, all of which continued to function under Islam in essentially the same way as they had before these areas were brought within the *dār al-Islām*.

The institution of the safe road with protected stations along its length was established, as Herodotus writes, under the Achaemenid Great King Cyrus:

The whole idea is a Persian invention, and works like this . . . At intervals all along the road are recognized stations, with excellent inns, and the road is safe to travel by, as it never leaves inhabited country . . . the total number of stations, or posthouses, on the road from Sardis to Susa is 111.

About the architecture of these inns, however, we have virtually no information, although they were probably built of beaten earth or mud-brick, materials that are highly perishable and now difficult to distinguish from the earth in which their remains have long been buried. We have equally sparse information about the network of roads by which, in the six centuries between Herodotus and the Romans, silk came overland from China through Sasanian Persia to the upper Euphrates where it was transhipped to Rome, or by which spices and perfumes travelled from India and the Yemen through the oases of western Arabia and thence to the caravan cities of Petra, Palmyra and Dura Europos for transfer to Rome – and, later, to Constantinople.

From the 1st century AD, Rome responded to the necessity of defending its Syrian frontier, the *limes arabicus*, with a line of solid stone forts, doubtless providing one of the models for later Islamic caravanserais with their open courts, strong enclosure walls and large single portals. There are other prototypes, however, for a caravanserai such as the Seljuq Ribāt-i Māhī, which resembles the castles in Soghdia in the middle centuries of the 1st millennium BC as much as it does the Roman frontier forts in the 3rd century AD. These Soghdian castles were probably descended from still more ancient communal dwellings in Central Asia and Iran, whose plans are also characterized by a rectangular outline surrounding an open space in the centre for animals to graze in, high walls with fortified corner towers and a single large gateway dominated by a watch-tower. This simple plan has remarkable longevity and can be seen not only in the 5th-century BC castle of ancient Khwarazm, but in almost any Islamic caravanserai; whether in the stone remains of Kunar-i Siyah in Iran; in the 13th-century Evdɪr Han in southern Anatolia; or in the grand Qājār complex of Aliabad, built north of Qum less than a century ago, in 1886. Nor can analogous structures from cultures further east of Islam be ignored, such as the stone-built Buddhist monasteries found along the trade routes leading westward from China through Central Asia. Like later Islamic caravanserais, they served travellers and merchants as well as pilgrims. A continuous line of Chinese military posts, small square forts, and watch-towers was in existence by late in the 2nd century BC to protect China's frontier on the west, just as the *limes arabicus* protected Rome's eastern frontier. Thus the institution of a line of shelters with water, erected at fixed intervals on routes throughout vast uninhabited areas, was long established in the Ancient World and was simply continued by Islam, though both the institution and the architectural form were shaped to Islam's specific needs.

Much the same can be said of the origins of bridges. Those that rank as major architectural monuments clearly continued to use Roman engineering techniques and methods of construction, although their basic forms were filtered through Sasanian Iran, or subsidiary structures such as toll-gates, pavilions and caravanserais were grafted to them. Even boat bridges, pontoons lashed together over which roads were laid, such as were always used in Baghdad, derived from Roman usage, especially over the Euphrates in Syria.

The origins of the minaret, in its guise as an aid to travellers, are far more various and complex, for not only is its pre-Islamic history harder to trace, but its function within Islam is by no means uniform. In central Islam, especially Syria, the bell-towers of Christian churches have long been considered the formal and functional prototypes of minarets; in specific cases in Iraq, Egypt and North Africa, older oriental forms have been suggested, such as the ziggurats of Mesopotamia or, more recently, the Sasanian fire-temple. Yet many minarets are quite strikingly different from any of these models: most conspicuously, the cylindrical Iranian brick minaret, and especially those of the Seljuq period with their tall slender tapering forms. The facts that many Seljuq minarets are free-standing and that some, with exceptional decoration, have been found in places where there was not, nor ever could have been, a mosque, suggest that their functions were not limited to the purely liturgical. Instead, minarets seem to have taken over the functions and certain aspects of the following forms: lighthouses (especially those of Classical Antiquity on the North African coastline running west from Alexandria, with its famed Pharos); watch- or signal-towers (such as those of the Roman *limes arabicus* or along the Chinese frontier with Central Asia); towers for fire signals, spoken of in Islamic Central Asia by Mahmūd of Kāshghar, in the

11th century; and commemorative columns in India, known from at least the 3rd century BC. The important point here is that the Islamic minaret served as a beacon for travellers on the trade and pilgrimage routes. A great number of single minarets dating from the 11th and 12th centuries are known on the Khurasan Road, on the routes west of the central Iranian desert and between Kerman and the Isfahan region, such as that at the Masjid-i Malik in Kerman, and the minarets at Kirat and Golpayegan. Such minarets usually have interior staircases giving access not only to the balcony, where the muezzin would call the Faithful to prayer, but to the very top of the tower, where the beacon itself, probably a bituminous substance, could be lit.

According to the historians and geographers of Islam, the market, along with the congregational mosque and, occasionally, the *hammām*, defined the very essence of the Islamic city. The Classical precedents for Islamic markets are obvious; but Soviet archaeologists have demonstrated that, because Central Asia as early as the Achaemenid period was probably as urbanized as the Mediterranean littoral, the market structures and practices in eastern towns in what are now the provinces of Soviet Central Asia are also of significance in the development of Islamic markets, although the exact sequence of influences is usually difficult to assess.

Three specific kinds of structures contribute to the typical Islamic market: a network of covered streets, a securely gated and covered edifice in its midst, and *khāns*, the urban equivalent of the caravanserai. Any Muslim settlement with a market also had a number of *hammāms*, since Islamic law demanded complete immersion on certain occasions, and at least one bath – and very often more – was always found in the market district. It is important to realize that, while all towns of any pretension had a central market with covered streets, *khāns*, the secured structure and a *hammām* clustered around the congregational mosque, capital cities and larger towns were composed of many quarters, each containing the cardinal elements of a town – mosque, bazaar and *hammām* – on a small scale and without the specialized structures of the central market. Like the central market, these elements were often grouped at the crossing of roads, at the *chahār-sūq* (literally 'four sides' or 'roads'), and this concept is expressed in the most common names for markets in Islamic countries: the Arabic *sūq*, for the covered streets of the market, and, by extension, the market itself; the Persian *chahār-sūq*, or *chahār-sū*, for the major intersections within the covered network of market streets; and the Turkish *çarşı*, the whole market complex.

In the lands that had been part of the Classical world

and its Byzantine successor, markets were usually located around the congregational mosque in precisely the same arrangement and serving the same functions as had the Classical agora with its surrounding public buildings and colonnaded market streets. A much paraphrased passage describes the hierarchy by which wares tended to be grouped around the congregational mosque. Purveyors of candles and incense were directly next to the mosque, in the company of booksellers, stationers, bookbinders and the vendors of other small leather goods. These were followed by the general clothing and textile markets, although precious textiles and furs, with other valuables, would have their own enclosed market. The hierarchy descended through furniture, household goods and utensils until, with the most mundane of goods, the edge of the city – or its walls and gates – was reached. Nearest to city perimeters, where the caravans often assembled, were the ironmongers and smiths, and the other vendors and craftsmen serving the caravan trade: workers of large leather goods with metal finishings, such as saddles and bridles, the suppliers of sacking and string, tents and whatever else the long-distance traveller needed for his journey.

As in the Classical world, Islamic *sūqs* were normally covered, and if a statement applicable to the entire Islamic world can be made, it is that beaten earth, mud and wood tended to be replaced by brick and stone vaults or domes, whose most permanent expressions do not commonly survive from before the 15th century. Canvas awnings or tents, however, were the more usual protection for the markets that sold food-stuffs and livestock in open areas, transforming these areas into temporary but regularly occurring markets. Important exceptions were the horse markets of Mamlūk Cairo and Aleppo, for horses were prestige wares in the Mamlūk military aristocracy and were sold at the foot of the citadel inside the city walls. The stone façades of certain buildings in Mamlūk Cairo, the *madrasa* of Sultan Hasan, for example, display a permanent reminder of these temporary markets: the fenestration on the side of the building facing the *maydān*, an open area, does not begin for some metres from the ground, leaving a blank wall against which awnings could be pitched on market days.

The segregation of goods and trades, so characteristic of Islamic markets, is also of Classical origin and was paralleled in medieval Byzantium: Ibn Battūta, visiting Constantinople in 1331, notices that its spacious paved bazaars were organized strictly according to what was being sold. He also remarks that each bazaar had gates that were closed at night. This is a feature of a specific Islamic market structure usually called the *qaysāriyya*, an oblong hall, roofed and colonnaded, often (and always in Ottoman Turkey)

domed, with a door at one or both of the short sides that was securely locked at night. Its form is derived from the Classical basilica; its name is said to commemorate a covered market built in Antioch by Julius Caesar, and called *kesária* by the Byzantines. Security was its most important feature, as security had been the most evident feature of the large rooms carved out of living rock at Petra, with their single openings and their small recesses for the deposit of relatively small objects or parcels of value. The Ottoman *qaysāriyya*, the *bedesten*, was a similar internal strong-room, always located at the heart of the market area. It housed the trade in valuable objects just as London's Burlington Arcade does today: precious metals, gems, and the richest textiles. Gold and silver were naturally linked to other financial activities: coinage, taxation, and money-changing. Thus *qaysāriyyas* often became the fiscal centre of government, where taxes and duty were collected and funds distributed for the upkeep of municipal institutions. It is no coincidence that the mint of Shāh 'Abbās I was included in the *qaysāriyya* he erected at one end of the Maydān-ī Shāh. The same structure also housed his Royal Caravanserai, with its decorated galleries that looked out over the *maydān*, and the shops where were sold the valuable silk textiles that were part of his planned economy. The Islamic silk trade, both raw silk and finished fabrics, was almost always a state monopoly closely controlled by the central government, and its vending locales were equally closely supervised, whether in the *alcaicería* of Granada or in the Sandal Bedesten in the Kapalı Çarşı (the Great Covered Market) of Istanbul.

After the *sūqs*, fanning out from the congregational mosque, and the *qaysāriyya*, or monumental strong-room, warehouses are the third basic element of the Islamic market. Known by a variety of names, of which *khān* is the most common, warehouses were generally two or three storeys high and rectangular or square in plan, with a single portal. On the upper floors, galleries gave access to small rooms of approximately the same size, with windows, and chimneys if the climate required, while historical and regional differences dictated innumerable variations in roofing and the disposition of other details. The chambers for merchants, where their merchandise could also be deposited, were usually on the upper floors, and the ground floor was originally used for stables and shops, together with large-scale storage, although with time the stables tended to be removed elsewhere in the market. Clearly, the standard form of most warehouses is related to the caravanserai, but both form and function continue to be modified by the urban setting of the structure and its specific purpose.

In the early Islamic centuries, if we may judge from

the warehouses excavated in the important Gulf port of Siraf, shops were not an architectural component of *khāns*, as they were later to become. Siraf had, instead, a warehouse with an entrance hall that opened onto an oblong courtyard surrounded by rooms of various sizes. The areas excavated to date in Siraf that might have served as shops appear to be rudimentary in the extreme, many almost as small as the compartments in the Petra warehouses and, therefore, not much larger than the lockers of modern bus stations. At the other end of the scale are the *samsara*, the *khāns* of Sanʿaʾ in the Yemen, sometimes six or seven storeys high. Throughout Islamic history, the complement of *khāns* built in a city at a given time provides a good index to its commercial prosperity. In Aleppo in the 14th, 16th and 17th centuries, in Bursa in the mid-14th century, in Istanbul from the middle of the 15th century, and in Damascus and Cairo as late as the 18th century, the ruler and his family, as well as wealthy officials and private citizens, built warehouses in what was originally a fruitful use of surplus capital, but was to become increasingly a conservative and unproductive one. In most Muslim cities *khāns* in the midst of the central market are still used today for storage, if no longer for merchants' lodgings or for manufacture. Others, especially those in Aleppo built for European merchants, remained a focal point of commercial, political and social life abroad, as exemplified by that which became the French consulate.

Warehouses were also built by officials and private individuals as pious works, made *waqf* for the benefit of a particular quarter or a specific monument – a mosque, *madrasa* or a convent – in the same way that *hammāms* were so endowed. The Hammām al-Bzouria in the grain *sūq* in Damascus, for example, was built by the Zangid ruler Nūr ad-Dīn Mahmūd some time between 1154 and 1172 to provide income for his *madrasa*, erected in 1172 in the same quarter of the market. The accumulated practice of centuries came to ordain that the Muslim patron include a *hammām* in an architectural complex he endowed, whether strictly commercial or religious, as in the 14th-century necropolis of the Marīnid dynasty at Chella, on the outskirts of Rabat.

Caravanserais

Leaving Cairo for Damascus in July of 1326, Ibn Battūta travelled on the main road connecting Egypt with Palestine and Syria, staying not in the colleges and convents, as had been his custom in North Africa and Egypt, but in caravanserais: 'At each of these stations between Cairo and Gaza there is a hostelry which they call a *khān*, where travellers alight with their beast, and outside each *khān* is a public watering-place and a shop at which he may buy what he requires

for himself and his beast.' Ibn Battūta's statement perfectly summarizes the function of the classic Islamic caravanserai, though certain aspects, the exterior shops and watering-place, may be unique to Syria in the 14th century. But almost any Islamic caravanserai presents to the traveller a square or rectangular walled exterior, with a single portal wide enough to permit large or heavily laden beasts such as camels to enter. The courtyard is almost always open to the sky, and along the inside walls of the enclosure are ranged a number of identical stalls, bays, niches or chambers to accommodate merchants and their servants, their animals and their merchandise. Water is provided in some way, for washing and for ritual ablution, and some later caravanserais have elaborate baths. From the earliest period fodder for the animals and the stables were separated from the lodgings for travellers. Later and larger caravanserais might have special rooms or suites in the entrance block for important guests, and a resident staff of caretakers might be permanently housed in small rooms in the portal block. Shops for travellers to replenish their supplies and for merchants to dispose of some of their wares are often found, from the 14th century onwards, and some of the later caravanserais were so well provided for, with mills, bakeries and tea-shops, that they came to resemble small villages.

Among the earliest surviving Islamic caravanserais are the Syrian remains of Qasr al-Hayr, East and West, the former only recently identified as such. Here, recent excavations have disclosed a paved courtyard with a portal; a series of twenty-eight tunnel-vaulted rooms; two rooms at opposite corners almost certainly destined for storage, to judge from their internal disposition; half-round towers, which seem to have had no function except to house latrines; and a small *mihrāb*-like niche on the south side of the entrance. These features, with the probable absence of a reception hall on the upper storey, proclaim the Lesser Enclosure of Qasr al-Hayr East to be a caravanserai, and not a palace, as had been formerly thought. The same plan and basic components are found, though in less elaborate fashion, at Chah-i Siyah (Chaleh Siah), near Isfahan, which can probably be dated between 770 and 785. Chah-i Siyah is particularly notable because the monotony of its interior walls, with identical small rooms opening onto the courtyard from under a portico, is interrupted on the axes by four *īwāns*, larger arched rooms open to the court. This neutral and flexible plan will thereafter characterize almost all Iranian caravanserais, as well as Iranian religious buildings, mosques and *madrasas*; although, at an early stage, the plans of early caravanserais most closely resemble forts, or *ribāts* (already described in Chapter 2). Indeed, it is often difficult to distinguish caravanserais from *ribāts* by plan alone. The *ribāt* of Sousse, in Tunisia, probably constructed between 771 and 788, is a square two-storey building with corner towers, a single fortified entrance and an open courtyard with small cells opening off it, differing only from the standard carvanserai plan in its hypostyle mosque, located above the portal on the first floor.

Essentially the same plan occurs again in the fortified caravanserais on the Tigris in Iraq, in the Jazira (the lands lying between the upper reaches of the Tigris and the Euphrates) during the Artuqid and Zangid periods and in Ayyūbid Syria, as well as in the splendid brick caravanserais of Seljuq Iran and Central Asia. By the second half of the 10th century, the refinements that distinguish the Iranian royal caravanserais are already apparent at Ribāt-i Kirim, about thirty miles from Saveh: a projecting portal flanked by larger domed chambers, with an entry passage leading into a courtyard, domed stables in the corners opening directly onto the court; smaller rooms for travellers, ranged around the court; and in the centre, a two-storey building that was possibly a refuge from the summer heat, intense in that part of Iran.

Ribāt-i Malik, built approximately a century later on the road between Bukhara and Samarqand, has the appearance of a fortress and is so named in its building inscription. Yet its impressively niched façade recalls earlier palatial buildings in the same district, its corner towers and half-round piers are hardly military fortifications, and its internal disposition, with many rooms opening onto a central courtyard, shows that it is actually a caravanserai whose plan was already quite standardized and recognizable for what it is, despite the elaborate decoration of its façade.

At this stage three general points suggest themselves. The first is that, as early as the 8th century, functional distinctions between basic Islamic architectural forms were becoming blurred, so that essentially the same plan could be utilized for frontier fortresses, for caravanserais, and – with modifications – for *madrasas* and mosques. The second is that the actual function of the *ribāt* was being superseded, at least in the central Islamic lands, by the caravanserai: civilian institutions in the interior of the realm came to replace frontier military posts as that which had to be defended.

The third point is suggested by the finest of all surviving Seljuq Iranian brick caravanserais, Ribāt-i Sharaf, dated 1114. From the exterior it still appears as a fortress; inside, its highly elaborate plan, unusual double courtyard and luxurious brick and stucco decoration suggest instead a palatial edifice. The same is true of the Anatolian Seljuq royal caravanserais of the 13th century. They are unique among Islamic hostelries in having magnificent covered halls instead of, or in addition to, an open courtyard. Normally built of rubble faced with ashlar, they display a mastery of stone masonry comparable to that of neighbouring Syria and the Jazira but virtually unknown outside this region except in India. Anatolian Seljuq caravanserais exist almost exclusively west of Malatya and the Euphrates and east of Denizli, on an axis running roughly south-west to north-east, of interest because the line appears to veer away conspicuously from the Islamic lands with which Anatolia shares its borders: Syria, the Jazira and Iran. This may be simply because Anatolia was a newer member of the *dar al-Islām* than its neighbours east of the Euphrates and did not yet possess a network of caravanserais and the apparatus of travel and communication. On the other hand, a recent study has shown that the great majority of Anatolian caravanserais not only follow the trade routes used by Roman and Byzantine merchants, but are very often located on the same sites and were even made of the very stones of earlier hostelries.

Anatolian *hans* offer the same facilities to the traveller as other Islamic caravanserais, but they demonstrate such a different conception of interior organization, resulting in such different architectonic forms and spaces, that purely practical explanations like the severity of the winter climate seem inadequate.

The typical Anatolian *han* consists of two parts: an open courtyard, entered by a high wide portal, behind which is a covered hall entered by a second portal. Both areas almost always have a single storey, whose flat roof was used for comfortable sleeping in the summer. On this basic theme a number of permutations occur. The long covered hall may be as wide as the court or narrower; its roofing system may consist of barrel vaults running parallel to the side walls, or of transverse arches forming side aisles lower than the central barrel-vaulted 'nave'; the court may or may not be provided with arcades for shelter or storage along the back and side walls leading to the covered hall. A few examples, usually non-royal establishments, have no courtyards, while six notable *hans*, all in the southern part of Turkey, have no covered hall at all but follow the more usual Islamic arrangement of rooms around a central courtyard. The ordinary place for the storage of goods and fodder, the stabling of animals, the lodging of travellers and the facilities for washing is in the arcades of the courtyard and the covered hall. In the two Sultan Hans, or Royal Caravanserais, of 1229 and in those modelled after them, such as the Ağizkara Han (1231–7), a *masjid* is prominently placed in the centre of the courtyard on a raised platform, reached by stairs, sometimes with an ablution fountain at a lower level under the *masjid*.

It is not easy to convey the extraordinary architectural impression of these Anatolian caravanserais at their most grandiose. The vast covered halls, with massive stone supports, and dim light coming from a single aperture in the central dome, suggest the spatial effect of French Romanesque churches such as St Sernin in Toulouse and St Front in Périgueux, rather than the mundane utility of a staging-post, and it is hard to avoid feeling that some greater significance was intended by 'Alā'ad-Dīn Kayqubād's Sultan Hans, for example. This feeling is intensified by a consideration of the decoration of both royal and non-royal Anatolian caravanserais. Usually found only on the entrance portals, it is nevertheless often spectacularly elaborate, with deeply recessed *muqarnas* forming an overhanging canopy of stone. This portal decoration has aptly been compared to the tents in which Turkish rulers traditionally dwelt and might well be seen as more permanently and palatially rendered versions of the ancestral tent – an observation that parallels the palatial effect of the slightly earlier Iranian royal caravanserais. It is perhaps also pertinent to recall that the patron of the Sultan Hans in Anatolia is remembered by no religious foundations whatsoever, but by numerous secular edifices: more than thirty *hans* located between Sivas and Denizli, two cities, a sugar factory, shipyards at Alanya and one of the earliest of surviving Islamic palace complexes, on the shores of Lake Beyşehir. This suggests again two of the points raised earlier: the blurring of formal differences between military, commercial and religious architectural types, and the replacement of frontiers by routes and markets in the civilian interior as that which had to be defended.

After 1260, when Baybars I, the Mamlūk sultan, revived the *barīd*, or postal service, to permit regular and relatively swift communication – four days – between the Mamlūk capitals of Cairo and Damascus and the more distant cities of his realm, the sturdy stone caravanserais of Syria and Palestine were given yet another role to play beyond offering transit amenities. Because the primary purpose of the *barīd* was the relaying of official messages, the routes by which its courtiers often travelled differed from the caravan and pilgrimage routes. Just as the Pony Express operated in the western United States in the 19th century, the solitary Mamlūk *barīd* riders usually took ways that were more direct but more arduous and with fewer amenities. Like the caravans, however, the *barīd* required stations for rest, water and stabling, and thus, especially at its inception, it made use of existing caravanserais wherever possible. One such example is at Qara Khān, midway between Damascus and Homs, where Baybars carved his emblem, a running panther, on its entrance corridor. More often, however, relay-stations were specially constructed for the *barīd*. They were smaller in scale, cruder in quality and far less

uniform in the disposition of rooms than the caravanserais, and most are now in ruins. *Barīd* stations were usually rectangular in plan, although the court could be aligned in either direction, with the stables, living quarters, latrines, cistern and storerooms arranged around it in no easily discernible order. Some had mosques, others an *īwān* with a *mihrāb* to serve as a place for prayer. Some were built around an earlier defence post, a Roman watch-tower or a disused enclosure of the Umayyad period. Others, particularly of the 14th century, are architecturally ambitious and far more carefully constructed, such as the *khān* called as-Sabīl, or Khān Manjak, near Inqirata in Syria, which was built in 1371 and is comparable in every respect except size to an actual caravanserai. The Mamlūk *barīd* posts, then, can be seen as a specialized kind of travel architecture of the 13th to the 15th centuries, although they are not unique. Certain details of the postal reorganization of Baybars I have been shown to be derived partly from the practices of the Mongol invaders of the Middle East, despite the fact that not a single building originally intended for postal or communications service in Iran or Iraq can actually be identified.

One of the ramifications of the Ottoman conquest of Syria, Egypt and the Arabian Peninsula, in 1516–17, was the opening of a major pilgrimage route through Syria to the holy cities of Arabia and the Red Sea. From the Anatolian border the Syrian Hajj Route passed through the cities of Payas, Iskenderun, Antakya (Antioch), Hama, Homs and Damascus, and thence south to the Arabian Peninsula. Between Payas and Damascus lay about a dozen staging-posts, nine marked by Ottoman caravanserais of the 16th and 17th centuries. Some were totally new buildings; others occupied the sites of older hostelries. The Ottoman section of Khān Hasye, built in the reign of Süleyman the Magnificent, is merely attached to an older and smaller *khān*; Khān Tuman is actually two caravanserais, one Ottoman and one late 12th century. Khān ar-Rastān, constructed in the late 16th or early 17th century, is exceedingly similar in plan to southern Anatolian Seljuq *hans*, as is the smaller one at Baylan. At Payas, the caravanserai of Selīm II, built in 1574, comprises the usual sleeping and stabling quarters, as well as more luxurious chambers for high-ranking guests, and a kitchen, garden and shops. Still others, for instance Khān al-Qutayfa, include such a variety of amenities that they constitute communities in themselves.

In this, al-Qutayfa recalls the Ottoman *külliye*, or endowed complex of religious and charitable structures surrounding the mosque and including the tomb of the founder, which the Ottomans built from the middle of the 14th century onwards. The travellers' amenities at the *külliye* of Çobanmustafa Paşa, in Gebze, at the eastern end of the Sea of Marmara, include a caravanserai with vizier's apartments, kitchen, shops, bakery, fountain and bath, and are thus rather similar to those offered by al-Qutayfa, with its large caravanserai, a mosque with rooms for religious itinerants, a bath, kitchen, bakery and shops, all enclosed within a vast stone wall.

The most ambitious and monumental complex of the whole Syrian Hajj Route, however, is the Tekkiye, or rest-house for pilgrims, beside the Barada River in Damascus, designed by Sinān for Süleyman in the mid-1550s and completed by his son Selīm II. Even before the Ottoman conquest, Damascus had been the major staging-point for the departure of pilgrims to Arabia, and it was also the place where they were joyously welcomed on their return. Inside a huge enclosed meadow by the river, a small mosque faces an immense courtyard surrounded by double porticoes, from which opened chambers for important visitors. The majority of the pilgrims, however, pitched tents in the enclosure, as caravans had done in the courtyard of the mid-15th-century mosque of Mehmet Fātih in Istanbul, and as they were still doing in Damascus in the 19th century. Opposite the mosque and the porticoed courtyard were the kitchens and refectories for pilgrims, and the necessary service areas, while a small bazaar, composed of rows of vaulted shops facing each other across a walkway, allowed for the purchase of necessities for the journey. In its plan, its spatial relationships and the massing of its many domes, the Tekkiye is a very Ottoman complex; in its fine decoration of alternating white plaster and dark stone courses, it is very Syrian. But in its concept – as a building ministering to the material comfort of the Mecca pilgrims at the threshold of a profound religious experience – the Tekkiye in Damascus is a supremely Islamic architectural phenomenon.

A number of brick caravanserais were erected by the Safavid shāhs of Iran to facilitate travel on the pilgrimage route to Mashhad and the Shrine of the Imām Riza. Although they are both socially and architecturally less significant than the Tekkiye in Damascus, these buildings and their Qājār successors testify to the importance attached to the re-establishment of trade and travel routes throughout Iran in this late period. The Iranian pilgrimage route, following the northern and western fringes of the Central Iranian Desert by way of Semnan and Shahrud, ran parallel to the trade and military routes of Khurasan and Central Asia; and common lore would have the traveller believe that every caravanserai on that route was built by Shāh 'Abbās I. Many actually were, especially those on the north-south trade and diplomatic routes between the Caspian Sea and the capital of Isfahan. The

most impressive of these Iranian hostelries display such a masterly hand in the sophisticated details of shelter and stabling, storage and facilities for cooking and bathing that they surpass even the Ottoman *hajj* caravanserais in comfort and luxury. Three Safavid examples, all on the road from Isfahan to Shiraz, are octagonal; for the most part, however, Iranian caravanserais of the 17th to the 19th centuries, whether of the rudest brick or the most elaborate royal foundations, are square or rectangular, with a monumental projecting single portal and an open courtyard. Inside the portal, the imaginative disposition of the amenities suggests a very long experience with the building-type.

Certain Safavid caravanserais were built not for the use of the ordinary trade caravan or for pilgrims, but for the peripatetic court as it moved between Isfahan and the Caspian coast or the mountains. Three such caravanserais survive from the reigns of the last two effective Safavid shāhs: the Māder-i Shāh at Murcheh Khvort, near Natanz, built between 1687 and 1694; that at Chah-i Siyah, 1687; and the Māder-i Shāh at Dhur, 1701. The caravanserai at Murcheh Khvort was actually an official extension of the court in Isfahan, for it was the last major halt for anyone arriving from the north, and from it an escort of honour was provided for ambassadors as they made their way into Isfahan. It had a particularly fine projecting portal, with two-storey niches in its angled sides, and a domed entry hall. Chah-i Siyah was the most sophisticated of the three; and both it and the caravanserai at Dhur were distinguished by interior courts for the ladies of the harem, and large and elaborate dome-chambers in the entrance block, from which the various smaller rooms and suites were reached.

The relationship between these Safavid caravanserais of the road and the ceremonial buildings of the capital is strikingly evident. An ambassador who had been met and welcomed at Murcheh Khvort would have been lodged in the Royal Caravanserai in Isfahan, located just to the left of the bazaar portal leading into its main street; he would have had access to the portal, with its decorated niches looking out onto the Maydān-i Shāh, by a covered passageway above the second storey of the caravanserai. Seated there, he could have heard the shāh's musicians and drummers performing at sunset from their niches, which looked out over the *maydān* from either side of the portal. A similar connection between the ruler's musicians playing at fixed hours or on ceremonial occasions, and their customary location at the bazaar gate, seems to have been made by the Mughal emperors of India; for at Fatehpur Sikri a walled enclosure inside the Agra Gate, and past a now-ruined stone caravanserai, is called both the *naqqār-khāna*, the drum or music place,

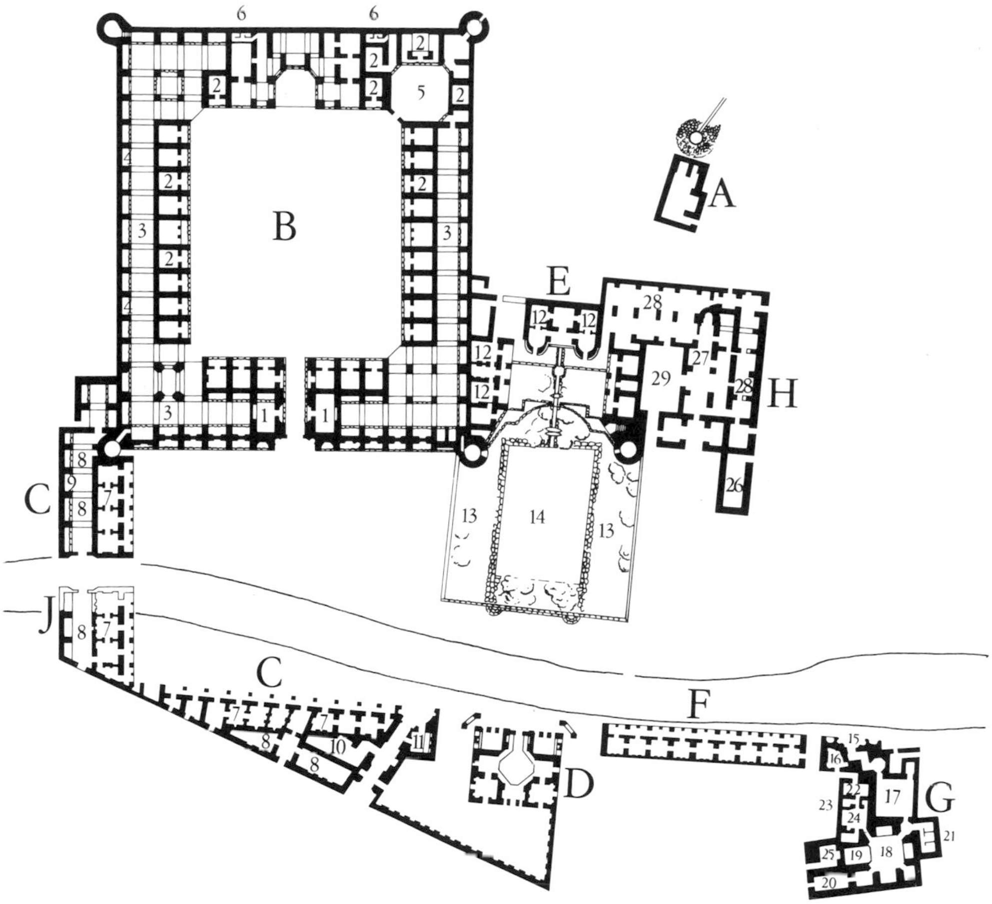

A *Mill*
B *Caravanserai*
  1 guards
  2 sleeping rooms
  3 stables for camels
  4 stores for merchandise
  5 private house
  6 latrines
C *Muletiers' quarters*
  7 sleeping rooms
  8 stables for asses
  9 stores
  10 fodder
  11 bakery
D *Tea-house*
E *Hostelry*
  12 bedrooms
  13 garden
  14 pool
F *Extra rooms for travellers*
G *Bath (hammām)*
  15 entrance
  16 tea-room
  17 men's disrobing room
  18 men's massage
  19 hot pool
  20 cold pool
  21 latrines
  22 women's disrobing room
  23 women's latrines
  24 women's massage
  25 furnace
H *Food depot*
  26 cattle
  27 bakery
  28 shops (corn, etc.)
  29 courtyard
J *Old main gateway, now partially demolished to make way for traffic*

The 19th-century caravanserai of Aliabad, between Teheran and Qum, represents a high point in elaborate planning, with so many ancillary buildings that it becomes practically a self-contained village. The caravanserai proper (B) resembles the classic type, but with certain differences. Three of the corners form hypostyle halls, the fourth is a private dwelling house with rooms opening off a small courtyard. The traditional īwāns are replaced by a single recess opposite the entrance forming an approach to the main reception hall. There is an elegantly planned tea-house (D) and extra accommodation of a high standard at a separate hostelry (E) where the rooms overlook a garden and a large pool. The bath (G) has complete duplicate facilities for the two sexes. (1)

and the *chahār-sūq*. Less ceremonial and more practical is the caravanserai of the Māder-i Shāh, finished in the reign of Shāh Sultān Husayn in 1714 as part of a larger complex that includes a *madrasa* supported by both revenues from the caravanserai and the income derived from a row of shops attached to the rear of the *madrasa*. The caravanserai has recently been refurbished as a grand luxury hotel, and on the occasions when the Shāhanshāh and his family come to Isfahan it still serves as an imperial hostelry.

Other Safavid and Qājār caravanserais were still in use by the Mashhad pilgrims in the early years of the 20th century, and handsome new rest-houses were built before about 1905 in eastern Iraqi towns – in Miqdadiyah and Ba'qubah, to serve pilgrims to the Shī'ī shrines in Najaf and Karbalah, for the Shī'ī pilgrimage may be performed throughout the year, unlike the *hajj*. In plan, however, these late caravanserais adhered to the general plan we have traced throughout this survey and, like them, were often funded by *waqfs*, as caravanserais had so often been during the history of Islam.

Bridges

Whether of stone, as Turkish bridges tend to be, or of brick, as Iranian and southern Mesopotamian bridges sometimes are, or even of mud-brick, as are those in Afghanistan, Islamic bridges are usually built to take careful advantage of their sites. Sometimes they twist and turn to utilize a natural stone piling, as at Shushtar, in Iran. Buttressing was provided where conditions dictated, as with the bridge of Sultan Baybars I near Lod (Lydda), in Israel. Where the river to be spanned flowed in a natural gorge, the bridge might be combined with a dam, as at Shushtar and Dezful (in Iran), both Būyid brick constructions on Sasanian foundations of well cut stone. Where there was danger of flooding, the Roman system of secondary piers with chambers to relieve the pressure of water on the main piers was employed; the piers might also be buttressed by cut-waters, as at the Altın Köprü in Iraq, spanning the Lesser Zab on the way to Irbil.

In Iran and southern Mesopotamia, bridges are usually combined with water-works, as their Sasanian predecessors had habitually been. More typical of Syria and the Jazira is the bridge complex of crossing, toll-gate and guard-house, with the caravanserai close by, since it was naturally at frontiers – often marked by rivers – where goods were unloaded and tolls computed and paid.

The most visually impressive of Islamic bridges are, again, those of Anatolia and the Jazira. The Roman prototype with its uniform semicircular arches had been modified by the pointing of the central arch, which also widens it, thereby creating a central span of much greater size than the flanking arches and producing a distinctively humped silhouette. Such are the many bridges of cut stone that span the rivers of Anatolia and the Jazira; for example, at Eski Mosul, Jazirat ibn 'Umar (Cizre) and Hisn Kayfa, and the Seljuq bridge over the Kızıl Irmak, between Sivas and Kırşehir. This humped form is sometimes retained by the Ottomans, as in the single stone span over the Narenta at Mostar, in Yugoslavia, built in 1566. The quadruple stone bridge at Büyükçekmece, erected by Sinān for Selīm II in 1567, shows only a slight humping, however, especially in comparison with the slightly later Persian bridge at Amol, built by Shāh 'Abbās I.

The most elaborate combinations of bridges with subsidiary structures, like the most elaborate caravanserai buildings, are found in Safavid Iran and Mughal India. Where the Gumti River flows through Jaunpur (in northern India), a bridge whose roadway was carried on ten arches was begun in 1564; when it was finished, four years later, its massive piers supported twenty-eight pillared and screened pavilions at road level, the pavilions projecting well out over the water on decorated brackets. Similar in conception and only slightly later are the celebrated Safavid brick bridges that span the Zayandeh River in Isfahan: at once, bridges, weirs, tea-houses, belvederes and promenades.

The market: fabled emporia, bedestens, khāns, hammāms and the waqf

Monumental caravanserais and well organized routes of trade in Islam were complemented in the cities by extensive markets, of which those in Isfahan and Tehran, Aleppo and Damascus, Bursa and Istanbul, Baghdad and Cairo and Fez represent their brilliant

apogee. The functional and architectural form these markets would assume was already apparent in the early centuries of Islam. The renowned commercial centres of 'Abbāsid Baghdad, of Umayyad Spain, of Fātimid Cairo and of Sāmānid Bukhara are justly celebrated in Islamic literature, both in belles-lettres and in the writings of the more prosaic historians and geographers. The teeming *sūqs* of Baghdad, and particularly the luxurious textiles they produced, were famed – and imitated – throughout the Islamic world. Cordoba was the important Western emporium for all kinds of goods from the East, including singers, dancers and courtesans; and the modern names of the ancient streets between the Great Mosque and the Eastern Gate still indicate the goods that were sold in the *sūqs*: Los Pergamineros, parchment; Las Perfumistas, perfumes; Los Zapateros, slippers. The immense fortified oasis of Bukhara occupied a highly strategic position on the trade routes between India and the Far East, and northern Europe and Scandinavia. The geographer, Yāqūt, provides a perfect vignette when he speaks of a prosperous 12th-century merchant who owned three warehouses: one on the Volga River, one in the Bukhara oasis, and one in Gujerat, in western India. Nevertheless, for each of these famous commercial centres, and indeed for most other market-cities of early Islamic times, our knowledge of the architectural disposition of the markets is sketchy. Only a combined reading of the historians and geographers discloses the importance of the markets and their associated workshops to the life of 'Abbāsid Baghdad, for example, and even then it is the wares made and sold in the *sūqs*, rather than the architectural features of the market, that are endlessly and lovingly described.

We are better informed about the markets of Cairo throughout its history. As early as 690, Marwān I, the Umayyad caliph, had built covered markets on a site on the Nile that was to become the city of Fustat. During the next four centuries Fustat grew, establishing itself as the chief emporium not only of Egypt but of the entire Fātimid Empire, rapidly replacing Alexandria as its primary entrepot and leaving only the silk trade to the once-great maritime city. Fortunately, Fustat's cultural brilliance and the wealth of its markets are described by such travellers as al-Maqdisī (writing in 985) and Nāsir-i Khusraw (in 1047), for Fustat was put to the torch in the mid-12th century as a defensive measure on the part of the governor of the newer city of Cairo. Al-Maqdisī writes that goods from al-Andalus, from the Turkish lands and from China were all to be found there, stored or being sold in an immense commercial district of long narrow streets that were permanently covered and artificially lit. The tall houses that lined the streets, variously described as between four and fourteen storeys high, seem to have functioned as both dwellings and warehouses for the storage of goods of all kinds – from precious gems and textiles to fruit and food-stuffs. Both wholesale and retail commerce, not to speak of manufacturing, was carried out in the *khāns*, under the colonnades of the *sūqs* or in the open markets of Fustat. In Nāsir-i Khusraw's opinion, the open market fronting the mosque of 'Amr ibn al-'Ās, the Sūq al-Qanādīl, could claim to be the richest market in the entire world.

Five centuries later the most precious of goods found in the markets of Cairo would have been concentrated in its *qaysāriyya*, the Khān al-Khalīlī, built early in the 16th century. In Syria, Spain and North Africa during those centuries, *qaysāriyyas* were predominantly places for the sale of silk; in Aleppo and Damascus, as in Turkey and the Balkans, *qaysāriyyas* housed the trade in furs, in all other precious textiles and in gold and silver. Unlike the Ottoman countries, where a town would normally have a single *bedesten*, the commercial quarters of Aleppo and Damascus were studded with *qaysāriyyas*. As an architectural institution with a specific form, however, the most important secure market structures are found in the Ottoman Empire. Ottoman Turkey built more of these interior market strong-rooms, *bedestens*, with many-domed ceilings and heavy bolted doors, than any other Islamic country, a fact that may not be unconnected to the proximity of Armenia to Anatolia (although this has not yet been fully demonstrated). Mardin, in the Jazira and therefore open to equally strong influences from Syria, appears to be the first documented Anatolian *bedesten*; the first fully developed Ottoman example to survive, however, is that built in Bursa by the second Ottoman sultan, Orkhān, some time after 1326 (although a recent study has suggested that in its present form it represents a rebuilding of about a century later). Bursa's *bedesten* occupies the heart of an enormous market district, and in the 15th century it served as the town's treasury. In plan it is rectangular, measuring 70 × 35 metres, and is covered by 14 small cupolas over the 14 interior bays, sheltering 32 shops in its interior and 56 in its exterior walls, with enormous doors at either end. This plan is essentially that of the Seljuq congregational mosque, or *ulu cami*, whose flexible components – a number of small domed units carried on piers or pillars – ensured that, although it was to die out in Anatolia as the ideal plan for a mosque, it was still perfectly suited to the architectural demands of the *bedesten*. From the grandest, Istanbul's Yeni Bedesten, to the comparatively modest, such as those at Gallipoli or Sarajevo, *bedestens* housed the trade in valuable textiles and precious metals. As the foremost civil structures of the

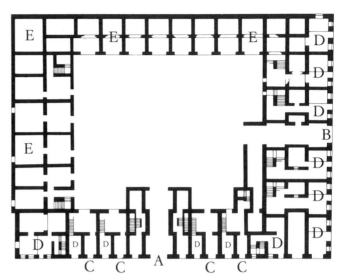

The island town of Suakin, on the Sudanese coast of the Red Sea, was a major port for five hundred years, but was abandoned in the early 20th century after the building of Port Sudan. By 1922 it was deserted and has now practically disappeared. In its heyday it was a splendid example of a complete trading town, with rich merchants' houses, khāns and warehouses in the Turkish style. This very large khān, situated just off the island at the end of a causeway on the mainland, was built as late as 1881. It could accommodate caravans of up to a hundred camels. There were two main entrances (A,B) but pedestrians had access to the courtyard via four smaller passages (C). The building also incorporated separate three-storey houses of which only the entrance halls (D) were on the ground floor. Two whole sides (E) were given over to warehouses and stores. (2)

Ottoman Empire, after the provincial fortresses and citadels, the Ottoman *bedestens* have rightly been called 'true fortresses of trade and commerce'.

Such 'fortresses' did not stand alone in the market, of course. Rather, they formed its nucleus. Around them were grouped long vaulted or domed streets that intersected at right angles (like their Classical prototypes) and enclosed *hans* for the manufacture, deposit and warehousing of various goods; the entire covered complex, the *kapalı çarşı*, was closed by gates and locked at night or on holidays, whereas in Iran only the shops are locked and shuttered. The long streets of the bazaar are still open and empty on Fridays, for example, when their characterisic brick vaulting can be seen clearly without the usual frenetic activity. Brick is the material of which the seemingly endless pointed domes are constructed, and it is laid in imaginative and sometimes highly intricate patterns, especially where streets cross and a higher dome crowns the intersection, the *chahār-sūq*. These interior streets are a major focus of commercial activity in a

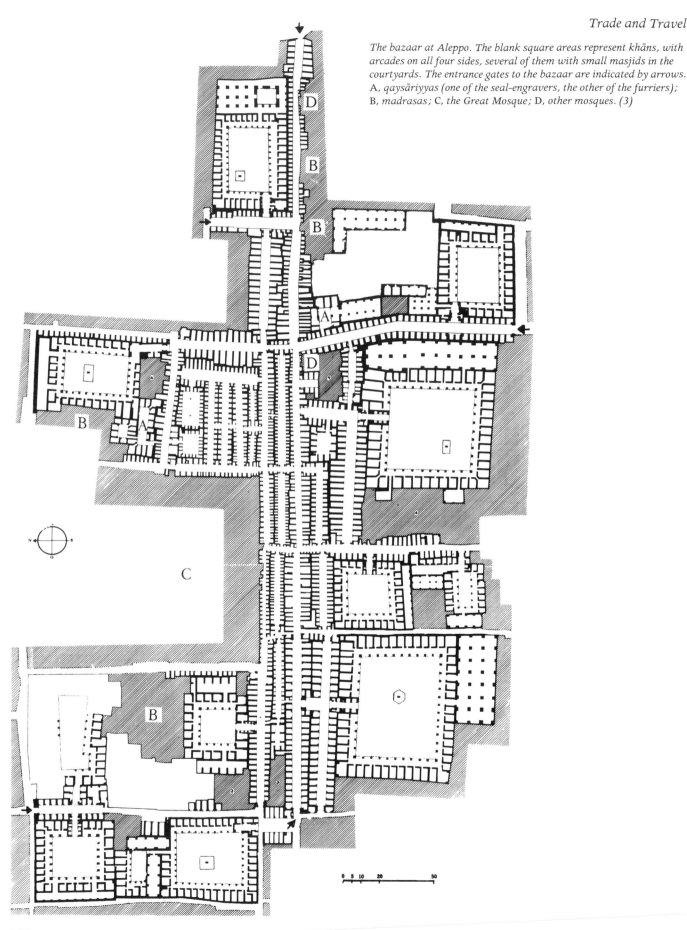

The bazaar at Aleppo. The blank square areas represent khāns, with arcades on all four sides, several of them with small masjids in the courtyards. The entrance gates to the bazaar are indicated by arrows. A, qaysāriyyas (one of the seal-engravers, the other of the furriers); B, madrasas; C, the Great Mosque; D, other mosques. (3)

land where many façades are interior rather than exterior; they are as significant an expression of commercial architecture as the highly developed Ottoman *bedesten*, the Syrian *qaysāriyya* or the splendid stone-vaulted *sūqs* of Damascus. The market district of Damascus was also celebrated for its numerous *khāns*, in which many of the famed workshops of Mamlūk Damascus had been located. From an architectural point of view, however, the greatest *khāns* of Damascus were built after the Ottoman conquest of 1516, when all of Syria experienced a renewed commercial – and religious – life owing in large part to the opening of the Syrian Hajj Route.

The markets of such cities are virtually cities in their own right. Istanbul's Kapalı Çarşı offers the irresistible pleasure of numbers. One list includes a *maydān*, 61 streets, 3,300 shops, 21 *hans*, a mosque, 5 *masjids*, 7 fountains as well as a *şadırvan* for ritual ablution, a school, 18 gates and 2 *bedestens*. In this it is unusual; because the earlier *bedesten*, erected in the mid-15th century and covered by fifteen domes, could not handle the volume of precious fabric traded in the markets of the new capital, a second had to be built in the 16th century during the reign of Süleyman the Magnificent. Larger, and roofed by twenty domes, it was reserved exclusively for the sale of silk. The two *bedestens* were solidly constructed of brick and stone, as befits their strong-room function, and they are said to be the only two buildings in the Kapalı Çarşı to have escaped the fire of 1546.

Another familiar aspect of any market complex is the *hammām*, whether identified by only its smoking chimney and a low glass-studded dome or by the most splendid of domed structures rising above the level of the surrounding *sūqs*. Despite bathing procedures that have remained virtually unchanged over the centuries, the baths of Islam show an extremely wide variety of plans, with greater or less emphasis on certain rooms and a corresponding external emphasis. Variations notwithstanding, the Muslim *hammām* is directly descended from the Classical bath, although from the evidence of the earliest, urban, public heated *hammāms* – the only type considered here – it is also clear that Islam altered the emphasis of the Classical bath and substituted for its social and sporting purposes the Muslim concern with both ritual and actual cleanliness. In view of the role the *hammām* came to play in urban Muslim life, especially in the social life of women and before weddings, it is worth recalling that as late as the 10th century certain Muslim authors expressed a distrust of the *hammām* as a foreign practice and a place of unseemly decoration; while at the same time other geographers listed *hammāms* in every city and village, often in improbably great numbers.

The Hammām al-Bzouria, in many ways a typical *hammām*, is entered from the *sūq* by an inconsequential doorway interrupting the row of shops in the *sūq*. Once inside, however, the hall widened and gave access to a spacious domed disrobing room lit by a

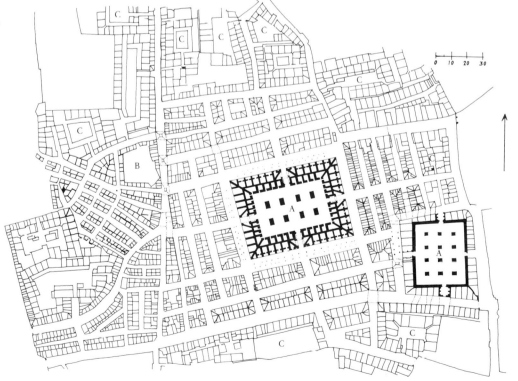

The great bazaar of Istanbul, with its warren of sūqs, each devoted to a separate trade. The two bedestens (A,A,) visible in pl. 35 are shown in heavy black lines; B is a mosque; C, hans. (4)

109

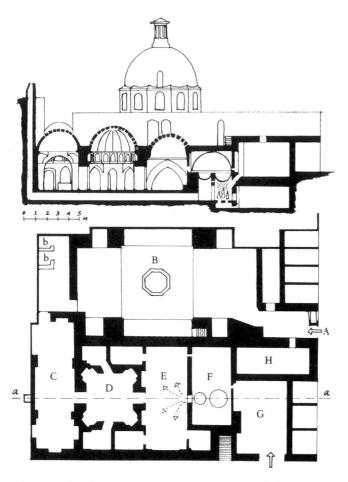

The Hammām al-Bzouria, Damascus. A, entrance with shops on each side; B, disrobing room, with fountain in the middle; b,b, lavatories; C, cold room; D, warm room; E, hot room; F, steam room; G, fuel; H, water-tank. The section is taken on the line a–a, and behind it can be seen the great dome of the disrobing room. (5)

sat or lay in the hot steaming atmosphere to work up a sweat before returning to the elaborate warm room, where he would be cleansed and massaged, soaped and shampooed and rinsed by the bath attendants. He would then return to the disrobing room through the 'cold room' and lie down to rest on the couches or benches provided for a period of restoration – when coffee, tea or sherbet would be served to him.

As the earliest known public *hammāns* date from not much before the middle of the 12th century, it is difficult to know for certain whether the changes made in the Classical bath, as seen in the plans of such a bath as the middle to late 14th-century Hammān al-Sultan in Damascus, were already made by Islam in its earliest centuries or whether they represent alterations that emerged over the course of several centuries. If the plans and the essential features of some of the earliest surviving Islamic baths, the desert baths of the Umayyad period, can be used to gauge the extent of the changes, it would seem that Islam adopted the notion of the Classical bath as a means of achieving ritual cleanliness, but subordinated the lavish size and elaborate ornamentation of the *frigidarium* to either the disrobing-and-resting room, the warm room, or the hot (or steam) room, depending on the century and the period. Certain aspects of the Classical prototype, mostly in the service arrangements, could not be altered, however, since the Islamic bath required an assured and continuous supply of water, fuel, soap and linen if it was to serve the community and thus generate the income for either the patron or the institution to which its revenues were endowed.

The methods by which Islam endowed its charitable and religious institutions for their upkeep in perpetuity has been briefly touched upon earlier: *waqf* revenues deriving from commercial enterprises. The hospital of the Mamlūk sultan, Qalā'ūn, for example, was supported by the income from all of his commercial properties, including each of his warehouses (locally known as *fundūq*). The second of the two *khāns* built by Sultan Qāyitbāy in 1480–1, after the sultan had made the *hajj*, was endowed for the benefit of the poorer inhabitants of Medina. The revenues of the Tiryakı Çarşı (originally a drug dispensary) in Istanbul, across the avenue from its parent mosque, the Süleymaniye, and the Mısır Çarşı (the Egyptian or Spice Bazaar), part of the foundation of the Yeni Valide on the Golden Horn, were both permanently attached to the *külliyes* of which each formed part. In Bursa the Geyve Han was founded by Mehmet I as a *waqf* to support his great mosque, the Yeşil Cami (the Green Mosque); while the Birinc (Rice) and Koza (Cocoon) Hans were founded by Beyazit II to furnish revenues for his mosque in Istanbul. The latter endowment involved a particularly complicated

lantern in the dome directly over the pool in the centre of the room. At either end, the room was lengthened by deep wide *īwāns* with lower ceilings. Leaving his clothes and wrapping himself in a towel or a loin-cloth, the bather left the disrobing room and turned left, proceeding to a long room covered by three domes, the so-called 'cold room'; cold in relation to the succeeding rooms because it lay furthest from the source of heat. Accustoming himself to the temperature and the humidity, and the dim light from the ceiling, which filtered in through thick round plugs of glass-like bottle-ends, the bather again turned left and entered the warm room, far more elaborately constructed and decorated than the 'cold room', and larger, with niches in the four corners of the chamber where the bather could rest on stone benches. The hot (or steam) room was arranged on an axis with the 'cold room' and the warm room, had a lower domed ceiling and was far simpler in construction; and it was here that the bather transfer of land to the benefit of the mosque of Orkhān, in Bursa, because the land on which Koza Han was constructed was already *waqf* to the mosque of Beyazit's ancestor, Orkhān.

Another variety of 'built in' financial support for a parent institution was known in Ottoman Turkey as the *arasta*, the row of shops attached to a religious structure, as we have already noted in the shops along the back of the Māder-i Shāh, in Isfahan. The classic example is the Kavaflar Arasta, the Cobblers' Market, on the lower level of the hill on which the mosque of Selīm II, Sinān's masterpiece, stands in Edirne. Although the *arasta* was built in the 1580s, several years after the mosque was completed, both institutionally and architecturally it forms an integral part of Selīm's *külliye*. It consists of a double row of twenty-four shops, 255 metres long, arranged on either side of a central corridor lit by cupolas. Slightly earlier is the *arasta* of the *külliye* of Sokollu Mehmet Paşa in Luleburgaz (1569), a seemingly insignificant town that owned its development in the 16th century to the fact that it lay on the main road from Istanbul to Edirne, the gathering-point for the European campaigns of the 16th century. In Istanbul, the Laleli Külliye, built by Mustafā III between 1759 and 1763, was endowed not only with an *arasta* in the basement of the precinct under the prayer hall of the mosque, but a *han* as well, to provide larger revenues for the sultan's foundation.

Functioning in much the same manner, and architecturally also part of the structure for which their revenues are intended, are the shops built into the ground floor of the *khāns* of Ottoman Aleppo. They serve the merchants lodging in the *khān* as an assured locale for the sale of goods carried from foreign cities, and at the same time they ensure a permanent income for the upkeep of the *khān* itself. Other Ottoman *khāns* of Aleppo, with *sūqs* that were part of the same enormous endowment in the market district, are paralleled in some ways by the viziers' foundations in Anatolia. A good example is the Khān al-Gumruk, the Customs Khān, in Aleppo: built by Ibrāhīm Khān-zade Mehmet Paşa in 1574, the foundation comprises a monumental entry, 2 fountains, a mosque, 52 stores and 77 chambers in the *khān* itself, while beautifully vaulted two-storey *sūqs* of stone, each lit by 5 cupolas, added an additional 344 shops to the total number.

The income from *khāns*, *sūqs* and the *arastas* attached to *külliyes* or other endowed building complexes was always available for the benefit of religious and charitable institutions – if such a stipulation had been written into the original deed of endowment; while the income from the specialized *qaysāriyya*, or the Ottoman *bedesten*, was not. Yet just as its architectural features gave rise to the notion that the *bedesten*, or the *qaysāriyya*, is the true fortress of the Islamic market, so the trade it guaranteed – the most valuable of goods and the safe-guarding of currency and exchange – was, in turn, the guarantee of all the transactions in the market-place.

If the types of the architectural forms taken over by Islam and developed for its specific purposes of trade and travel are few, these have proven to be flexible and adaptable for many purposes, whether apparently secular and non-religious, such as the caravanserai and the *khān*, or religious, such as the *ribāt* of early Islamic times and the *madrasa*. The hypothesis invoked earlier – that Islam was content to utilize a comparatively small number of architectural forms for a fairly large number of functions – would thus seem to be confirmed. But it is also true that during the course of more than twelve centuries the architectural settings for the specific needs of Islam's different commercial activities were greatly refined, even in those places where caravanserais and market structures were never so highly developed and articulated as they were in Aleppo, Istanbul, and Isfahan.

It is also clear that the notion of sacred and secular does not operate in Islam as it does in the West, even in areas so apparently mundane as the market-place and the caravan route. We have seen that even on the *hajj*, trade was encouraged. Furthermore, the architectural settings for much of Islamic trade and travel have formal and functional parallels in Islamic religious architecture, especially edifices in what might be termed the minor mode: *ribāts*, *khānaqāhs*, *tekkes* and *tabhanes* for caravanserais and *khāns*; minarets for beacons. The revenues from commercial enterprises provided the financial underpinning for many of these religious institutions, as well as for major edifices – mosques, *madrasas* and tombs – as *waqf*, the disposal of which was very strictly regulated by religious law. Thus, on many levels, it proves to be difficult to separate the secular from the religious aspect of Islamic life.

Finally, two building-types usually associated with notions of power in Islam, the palace and the fortress, are also highly relevant in assessing the significance of the most spectacular of Islam's trade and travel structures. The Seljuq caravanserais of Iran, Central Asia and Anatolia, and their later Safavid and Qājār versions, are truly palaces of the road; *qaysāriyyas*, and especially Ottoman *bedestens*, are fortresses of trade and commerce and, by extension, the commercial support of the entire realm. And that the form of the Ottoman *bedesten* perpetuates the plan of the Anatolian congregational mosque of Seljuq times is yet one more indication of the inseparability of sacred and secular in the life of Islam.

4 Architects, Craftsmen and Builders: Materials and Techniques

RONALD LEWCOCK

The men who built the mosques, caravanserais, palaces and baths were for the most part anonymous craftsmen using techniques that go back to before the Islamic era. These techniques are still alive today, and by studying them we can gain insight into the construction methods of the past. The pictures reproduced opposite are from a record of crafts prepared in Kashmir in the 1850s. *Top left:* hewing stone, loading it into baskets and taking it away in a boat. *Top right:* a brick-kiln – again sited outside the city and needing river transport. *Bottom left:* preparing a rammed-earth wall. The earth is puddled by two men with spades at the bottom, placed between wooden shuttering and pressed down hard. *Bottom right:* wood-turning and the tools of the carpenter; the man is using a drill operated by moving a bow backwards and forwards, a technique for drilling and turning wood found universally in the Islamic world. (1–4)

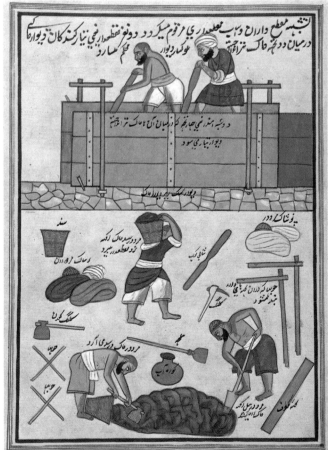

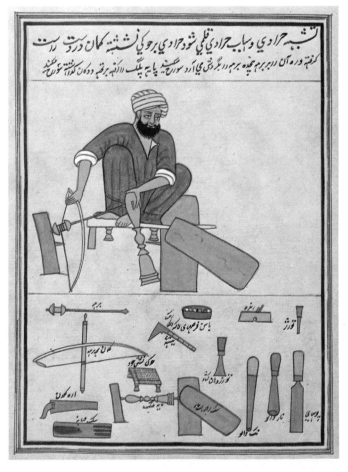

Building methods

A 15th-century miniature from Herat (*below*) shows the building of a portal. The wooden scaffolding is of particular interest; the beams supporting the planks on which the workmen stand rest on one side on a framework bound together with rope, and on the other on the wall itself. Mortar is being prepared and bricks shaped near by. (5)

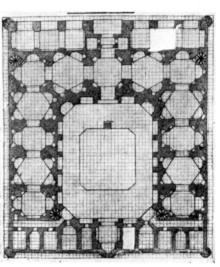

Plans were drawn on squared paper whose module corresponded to the ancient cubit. In the top picture the architect of the Mughal emperor Bābur is seen holding such a plan, and a few actual examples have survived from Uzbekistan (*above*). The module, which determines the dimensions of walls, windows, doors, etc., usually related to brick-sizes in simple ratios. (6,7)

Building a dome without centring (*right*): a detail from a Mughal miniature showing Akbar's construction of the Red Fort at Agra. (8)

Shaping stone: the man works by eye, checking with a straight-edge. The stone will be smooth on the outer face, rough on the inner. (9)

Making a tracery window: the pattern is carved free-hand on semi-dry gypsum (plaster of Paris) laid on a wooden board, and installed as a complete unit. (10)

Repairing: the workman here, suspended on a cradle in the traditional manner, is preparing the wall for the application of a layer of paint. (11)

Mud walling: the new layer – showing dark in the photograph – is composed of balls of clay compacted by beating. (12)

Brick-kilns (*right*): in the foreground are sun-dried bricks awaiting firing. (13)

Shaped blocks of stone – made in the way shown above (pl. 9) – form the face of the wall, leaving the rough sides to be buried behind the central filling of rubble. (15)

Quadripartite vaults made without centring (*left*) belong to a type unique to Iran; see diagram on p. 140. (14)

Decorative brickwork and tiles

The apogee of this technique is reached in the tomb of the Sāmānids at Bukhara (*above*), where both exterior and interior surfaces are covered in fine brick patterns. In the 'Abbāsid 'palace' at Baghdad (*below:* one of the aisles in the audience court), exposed baked bricks form *muqarnas* vaults. (17,18)

Bricks had been used decoratively from early Islamic times, laid in different planes to create dramatic effects of light and shade on the façades of buildings. An 11th-century Seljuq tomb at Qarraqan in Iran (*above*) shows a variety of patterns, including a band of calligraphy near the top made with specially shaped bricks. At the bottom, part of the decorative veneer has fallen away, revealing the structural brick core. (16)

Glazed tiles, used as veneer over a brick core, were common from 'Abbāsid times onwards, and came to full flower in Iran and Turkey during the 16th and 17th centuries. These two examples display their rich colour and sophisticated finish. *Right:* the 15th-century Yeşil Türbe at Bursa. Here, the tiles are relatively plain and the effect is one of restraint. *Above:* the dome of the Madrasa-i Shāh at Isfahan – Safavid tilework at its most brilliant. On parts of the dome, and especially on the minarets, the tiles are curved to fit the forms of the architecture. (19,20)

Stone

Good building stone is available in many Islamic countries, and was used both constructively and decoratively. As we shall see in the next chapter, Islamic artists made no distinction between different materials, and the same motifs occur in stone, stucco, wood and tile. *Right:* portal of the mosque of Sultan Baybars, Cairo, 1269. The zigzag goes back to ancient Arabia, and the circles flanking the arch were probably battle-shields in origin. *Below:* the Büyük Karatay Madrasa, Konya, outstanding for its polychrome decoration. Note the joggled lintel in two colours of stone below the stalactite arch. (21,22)

A **web** of intersecting lobes covers the minaret of the mosque of Hasan at Rabat, Morocco, a 12th-century example of the luxuriant Hispano-Moorish style. (23)

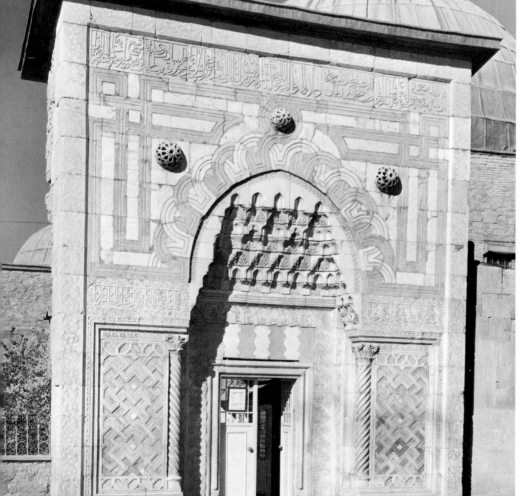

Red sandstone and white marble of the 'Alā'ī Darwāza, Delhi, 1305, were to become typical of the later Mughal architecture in India. (24)

Striped masonry and paving employed by ▷ builders in Syria influenced Seljuq and Ottoman architects in Turkey. *Opposite:* the Great Mosque of Homs, Syria. (25)

Metalwork and wood

Metal has a subordinate place in Islamic architecture, but where it occurs is often richly decorated. Much of it is concentrated on and around doors. Hinges and locks are executed in a variety of metals – iron, brass, silver and even gold. More elaborate work also incorporates pull-rings, knockers, doorplates and bosses. Rows of bosses often cover the heads of bolts holding together the massive wooden members of the door. *Below:* a door of the Gulf type at Bushire, Iran, which was made in Kuwait, showing a typical row of knobs and door-pulls. (27)

A door-plate (*right*) of the Madrasa-i Shāh, Isfahan, is in a shape often found in the other arts, such as miniature painting, in Iran. (26)

Lion door-knocker in Kerman, Iran. Probably 19th-century in date, it follows a form that goes far back into Iranian history. (28)

Wood was an integral part of buildings, even when the structure was of other materials. In relief carving, in marquetry and in lattices made of intricately jointed turned wood, Islamic craftsmen produced work that has few parallels in the West. In the porch of the 'Alī Qapu palace (*above*), timber columns support a patterned ceiling executed in precious woods of several colours inlaid with mirrors. (29)

The transparent screens so characteristic of Islamic houses are due partly to the need to create through-draughts and partly to the practice of segregating the women's quarters. These views (*above and left*) show the interior and exterior of similar Mamlūk windows in Cairo. The screens, which display a wide variety of ingenious patterns, consist of small pieces of turned wood socketed together. Projecting boxes in the upper storeys allow the women to look out and down without being seen, and also serve to hold cooling earthenware vessels of water or aromatic plants. (30, 31)

121

Brick, clay walling and stucco

At Sa'dah, in the Yemen, the houses are built up from layered clay in courses about fifty centimetres high. The technique used is that shown in pl. 12. (33)

San'a', the capital of the Yemen (*above*), is a spectacular city consisting of tall houses of baked brick above stonework, often rising to eight storeys. The way these houses function internally is described in Chapter 6. On the outside they are given colourful variety by bands of whitewashed brick decoration across the walls and round the windows. At Skoura, in Morocco (*right*), the lower part of the house is made of layered clay, the upper part of dried brick arranged to form decorative surface patterns. (32, 34)

Stucco reliefs imitate the effects of stone but with a greater freedom and complexity. The *mihrāb* of the Friday Mosque at Reza'iyeh, Iran (*above*), dating from 1277, contains a whole repertoire of ornamental designs, deeply undercut interlacings, circular bosses, stylized foliage and a foliated band of calligraphy. (35)

Window grilles several metres in height were made of stucco and have proved almost as durable and as crisp as stone. *Left:* a detail of the Mamlūk mosque of Sunkur Sa'dī in Cairo, built in 1315. It is covered with a wealth of stucco ornament. Here, Qur'ānic quotations are incorporated into the frieze around the drum of the dome. (36)

123

The dome

Domes became increasingly characteristic features of Islamic architecture after Seljuq times. More or less structurally stable themselves, they are difficult to place over the square base resulting from rectilinear planning. A safe structural transition has to be made between the square and the circle, and Islamic architects evolved a number of ingenious and beautiful solutions. The simplest was to use corner squinches, creating an octagon which could merge easily into the circle. In a dome of the Great Mosque at Damascus (*left*), built in the 8th century, reconstructed in the 19th, the surface within the squinch is shaped into a small semi-dome, and is load-bearing. Above, an octagonal drum supports the dome. By the 10th century, Islamic architects had developed a technique for bridging the corners by using tiers of superimposed arches. Eventually these arches were organized according to a complex interlocking geometry to produce a stalactite, or *muqarnas*, vault. *Below left:* the *khānaqāh* and mosque of Sultan Barqūq in Cairo. (37, 38)

An alternative to the squinch was the pendentive, a triangle of masonry filling the same space. This became the commonest solution in Ottoman mosques, which adapted the standard Byzantine curved pendentive. The Seljuq Büyük Karatay Madrasa at Konya (*above*) employs a variant faceted form consisting of a simple radiating fan of plain surfaces. (39)

The ribbed dome over the bay in front of the *mihrāb* in the 10th-century mosque of Cordoba (*above*) is one of many brilliant technical improvisations created by the Muslim builders in Spain. The lobed arches bridging the corners alternate with identical arches containing clerestory windows. The lines of the colonnettes framing these arches are continued upwards to form slender semicircular ribs linking each arch to its neighbours on either side, and combining to form an octagon supporting the dome. (40)

In the Alhambra (*left*), the last great work of Muslim Spain, the octagon is transformed into a sixteen-pointed star containing windows, above which the *muqarnas* vault resolves the star into a hemisphere. Dazzling as the display is, ornament has here become largely divorced from structure. (41)

125

Structural form

Where a Gothic master mason openly exposed the structural skeleton of his building, the Islamic builder sometimes chose to conceal it behind smooth surfaces and abstractly proportioned façades. This rear view (*left*) shows the reinforced brickwork of one of the *īwāns* of the Masjid-i Shāh at Isfahan. The spectator on the ground sees only the scintillating tilework planes of the façade screens and the recessed porch with its lavish stalactite vault. (42)

Pointed arches had the same function as in Gothic architecture, but for the Islamic architect they are not associated with soaring verticality. These four-centred 18th-century brick arches are in the Vakīl Mosque, at Shiraz. (44)

The play of domes gave obvious delight to Ottoman architects. In this hospital of the Beyazit II complex at Edirne, a dome on a twelve-sided drum is surrounded by a six-sided ambulatory, one small ambulatory dome corresponding to each side of the drum. The ambulatory certainly acts as a buttress for the central dome, but this is not given external visual expression. (43)

126

The classic minaret began square, changed to an octagon, then into a cylinder and was finally capped by a miniature dome. This example is in the southern cemetery, Cairo. (45)

Variations on the basic theme are numerous. *Above:* minaret of the al-Azhar Mosque, Cairo – first a square, then a sixteen-sided shaft and then, above the balcony, an octagon. (46)

The continuous cylinder, rising from a square base, gave opportunities for rich polychrome brickwork in areas where stone was scarce. This is at Natanz, in Iran. (47)

Horseshoe arches rest on reused Classical columns in the 8th-century Cordoba mosque. Additional height is achieved by doubling the arches. (48)

In front of the mihrāb at Cordoba, part of the 10th-century enlargement, interlocking arches take a lobed form, executed in two colours of stone. (49)

Wooden tie-beams act as two-way reinforcements to the arches in the mosque of 'Amr in Cairo; originally 7th-century, but much rebuilt. (50)

127

The genius of Islamic architecture arises out of a sensitive handling of materials – the perfect realization of their decorative and tonal qualities. Here, chiselled stucco and carved timber in the courtyard of the al-'Attārīn Madrasa at Fez combine different designs in subtle relief. Not only do the different surfaces of the building, the spaces beneath the arches and the projecting bands, permit a play of light and shade, but the patterns themselves are conceived in overlapping planes. Here, techniques, material and design are perfectly unified. (51)

Materials and Techniques

RONALD LEWCOCK

In the month of Rabī' II, 665 [1267], the Sultan [Baybars] occupied himself with building a mosque in the Husayniyya [of Cairo]. He sent for the Atābek Fāris ... and a number of architects [muhandis] to look for a suitable place for building the mosque.... The Sultan mounted on horseback, in company with his favourite retainers, and the Wazīr al-Sāhib Bahā' ... and went down to the ground of Qarāqush and spoke about the question of the mosque. He had measurements made and settled matters concerning it and details relative to its building ... the plan of the mosque was drawn out in his presence. He intimated that its door should be like that of the Madrasa al-Zāhiriyya, and that a dome should be built over its mihrāb of the same size as the dome of ash-Shāfi'ī. He wrote letters at the same time to different places requiring marble columns to be sent from every place, also that camels, buffaloes, kine and other beasts of burden should be sent from every province. He wrote likewise for iron appliances and good timber for the doors and ceilings.... He appointed officers to supervise the building of the mosque.... The building was begun in the middle of Jumādā II 665 [1267] and on 1 Jumādā II 666 [1268] the Sultan left Egypt for Syria. He stopped at Jaffa and took the town from the Franks.... He took a quantity of wood found in the Citadel and slabs of marble, and put them in one of the ships at Jaffa and sent the ship to Cairo. He ordered that the screened enclosure in the Mosque ... should be made of this wood, and the mihrāb should be made of the marble. The wood and marble were used accordingly. When the Sultan was back in Egypt ... the mosque was finished in Shawwāl of that year 667 [1269] he went to the mosque on horseback and viewed it. He found it as beautiful as could be and was pleased with its having been finished in so short a time and with so much care. He gave robes of honour to those who had carried out the work.

THIS ACCOUNT by the 15th-century historian, al-Maqrīzī (*Khitat*, II), is one of the rare descriptions of the initiation of a work of architecture and its course to completion. It is still difficult to write with certainty about the architects, the craftsmen and the organization of the building industry in Islam. This is principally due to two factors. Firstly, the situation within Islam varied much more from country to country, and from one century to another, than is generally recognized. Early Muslim authors themselves acknowledged this. At-Tawhīdī, who lived in the latter half of the 10th century, wrote: 'With each century people acquire new habits and a mentality which they had not possessed before.'

Secondly, documentation of Islamic buildings is much poorer than one might expect. Accepting that the great periods of Islamic architecture almost all predate the recorded observations of European visitors, we are forced to rely on scanty Islamic sources and inscriptions. Although buildings might have been admired, architecture was seldom considered a subject worthy the concern of the literati, the historians and poets; the architects themselves do not seem to have recorded much about their work, with the rare exception of Sinān at the height of the Ottoman period, and most of the craftsmen could not write more than their signatures and a few words. The records of building – the drawings, the estimates and accounts, if they ever existed – have not come down to us, except in one or two cases. There are some architectural models in semiprecious materials, but they may be miniature replicas of buildings made after their completion; in any case, they are late, dating from the last centuries of the Ottoman Empire.

These difficulties are mitigated to some extent by our ability to extrapolate backwards in time in certain areas where building techniques and social structures have changed less than in most, and by the painstaking search for clues hidden in the fragmentary surviving evidence. The position, role and techniques of the craftsmen are the easiest to reconstruct, but the role of the architects, the designers of the famous buildings, is more difficult, for documentation is rather scarce. It is possible to surmise a marked change in their position at the Ottoman court, but in earlier centuries of Islam we can only obtain brief glimpses of the architects at work.

The architects

Islamic architects varied from highly trained specialists in calculation and design, capable of imaginative leaps in conception and structural achievement, to successful craftsmen who, through a steady growth in their practical knowledge, became large-scale building contractor-designers. Professional architects seem to have been found only in cities, and in periods of great building activity; they sometimes found it expedient to move from one major centre to another and even on occasion to travel to remote areas to design particular monuments. Contractor-designers

129

must have executed the great bulk of building in Islam. More readily than most, Islamic architecture lent itself to the unskilled designer, since the forms and plan formulas were simple, and could be repeated with only slight variation; originality could be provided in the applied decoration, which was, in any case, in the hands of inventive craftsmen.

We know very little about the formal training of architects in Islam at any period. Ottoman architects were sent to train in the West in the 18th century, which seems reason to assume that the idea of a formal training was current at that time and probably had been for several centuries. Indeed, it is hard to believe that the great masterpieces of Islamic architecture could have been achieved without the disciplined cultivation of design skills over a long period, together with training in geometry, mathematics, applied mechanics and drawing. Yet the great Sinān was a fighting Janissary for most of his early life; he may indeed have combined this with a love for, and a part-time study of, engineering and architecture, but he appears to have begun his architectural career only when he was forty-six.

Other architects were the sons or nephews of established architects, following the traditional Islamic custom of the heredity of occupations. Sometimes the profession of architect existed in a family for some generations, as in the al-Munīf family of Sfax, in Tunisia, who are first heard of in 1630–1, and last, several generations and four well-known architects later, in 1748. In such cases it seems reasonable to assume that training in the art and science of architecture existed for young sons within the family. Indeed, architectural training was probably of this apprenticeship type in most periods and places. Whether it was also common for an aspiring young architect to be apprenticed in a craft is not clear. We know of a number of men bearing titles that can reasonably be identified with 'architect' (rather than just 'master' of a craft), who are also described as workers in a craft. For example, Muhammad ibn al-Husayn ibn Abī Tālib, *al-muhandis al-bannā'*, 'the architect', who finished the Kāshāna tower in Bistam (1301), signed a stucco *īwān* in the mosque of Shaykh Bāyazīd, in the same city, as *jassās*, 'plaster decorator'.

There are, however, a large number of references in inscriptions and texts to 'masters' *designated* with the name of a craft, who erected buildings; these probably belonged to the second category of building contractor-designers. Two of the most important were master (*ustādh*) Muhammad Ghadīr, 'the bricklayer' (*ājurr-tarrāsh*), who in 1715 erected the portal of the Darb-i Imam at Isfahan, and master Niyāruk, 'the carpenter', who in 1712 rebuilt the mausoleum of Imāmzāda Qāsim at Kharāba-Shahr. Qiwām ad-Dīn

Shīrāzī, 'the mason' (*at-tayyān*), designed three important buildings in north-eastern Iran and Afghanistan in the first half of the 15th century.

There are also clear references in some texts to building supervisors, who may have varied in function from clerk of works to the role of supervising architect. Such was probably the case with Ahmad ibn Jamīl, who was both superintendent (*al-wakīl*) and an architect-engineer (*al-muhandis*) of part of the city wall and two gates of Diyarbakir in 909–10.

Builders or contractors who built according to the designs of others are also mentioned; the term *al-bannā'* is often used for them, as in the case of Abu'l-Faraj, who erected part of the walls of Diyarbakir in 1236–7 'following designs made by Ja'far ibn Mahmūd al-Halabī. Similarly, Yahyā ibn Ibrāhīm erected a tower of the same city wall to a design by the Artuqid sultan himself (1208–9).

Other architects rose from among the artist-craftsmen. One of Sinān's successors as chief architect, Dalghich, was trained as an artisan in mother-of-pearl. His successor, Muhammad Āghā, who was likewise trained in the same craft, designed the Great Mosque of Sultan Ahmet I in Istanbul, 1606–17.

Architects often achieved a high social standing, as in the case of the at-Tūlūnī family in Cairo in the 14th and 15th centuries, two of whose daughters married, successively, Sultan Barqūq. The younger generations, at least, were highly educated. Hasan at-Tūlūnī was given a scholar's education, being a pupil of the historian as-Sakhāwī, who praised his learning. His career as chief architect in Egypt was almost unbroken from 1453 until 1517.

The great Sinān, according to tradition, became a close friend of Sultan Süleyman; and other architects are known to have been amirs.

The association of the profession of architect-engineer with mathematics is naturally strong. Ahmad ibn Muhammad al-Hāsib, who was employed to restore the Nilometer at Roda in 861, and who acted as architect for various buildings in Iraq, was called in his inscriptions 'the mathematician' (*al-hāsib*), but in texts 'the engineer' (*al-muhandis*). Shaykh 'Alam ad-Dīn Qaysar was an architect who, at the same time, was a famous astronomer and mathematician; and Maslama ibn 'Abdallāh, who was an architect at the Umayyad court of Cordoba, was also a geometrician.

Other architects were members of the ruling class who apparently designed buildings for pleasure. An example is the governor Aydemür, who was the architect (*mi'māruhu*) of the Ulu Mosque in Sandıklı, built in 1379. Another is 'Iwad ibn Akhī Bāyazīd who, as vizier of the Ottoman Mehmet I, specified on the door inscription of the Yeşil Cami in Bursa that he 'designed, arranged and fixed its proportions' (*c.* 1414–23). Scholar-architects included Fath ibn Ibrāhīm, who reputedly built mosques in Cordoba and Toledo in the 10th century.

The terms used for 'architect' varied according to place and time, but it is clear that there *was* such a term, distinct from 'headman of a craft' or 'qualified builder'. Certain men are known by the term 'architect' from a given date onwards, suggesting that they were not entitled to use it before, although it is unlikely that there was any formal qualification or point at which legal recognition was given (except in the case of appointments to official posts, and these were rare).

The movement of architects between different areas of the Islamic world has often been commented upon, but, because there were often wars, with accompanying looting and pillaging, it is not surprising to find many architects travelling as refugees. Then, too, there was the planned seizure of leading architects and craftsmen from captured towns so that their skill could be used in adorning distant cities. The three Christian architects from Urfa (formerly Edessa, in Greater Syria), who built the fortifications and the three surviving gates of Fātimid Cairo after 1087, had probably fled before the Seljuq armies captured Urfa in 1086. Tīmūr carried off masons from Turkey to embellish Samarqand, and Sultan Selīm brought as a prisoner to Istanbul from Iran in 1515 the architect, 'Alī, who afterwards became chief architect of the Ottoman sultanate. Sometimes architects who had travelled great distances executed work that was much admired for its unusual style. The architect of the minarets of the Qusūn Mosque in Cairo came from Tabriz, and based the design of the minarets on those in Tabriz of the mosque of the vizier, 'Alī Shāh.

On the whole, architects' names seldom appear on their buildings, even when there are inscriptions recording the name of the patron and other officials. This must have been largely a matter of fashion, however; Sinān's name does not appear on any of his buildings in Istanbul, but in some earlier periods (the Seljuq period in Anatolia, the Tīmūrid period in Samarqand and the Umayyad period in Spain) it was customary to single out the architect's name in a prominent place in the building. This practice is certainly evidence of the high status held by leading architects, though its absence in the Ottoman Empire during Sinān's lifetime is no evidence that his status was inferior.

An important advantage enjoyed by Islamic architects was that even the biggest mosques and tombs were usually erected during an amazingly short time. Islamic architects were proud of their ability to build quickly, and sometimes such feats were recorded in the inscriptions. The autocratic Muslim ruler could

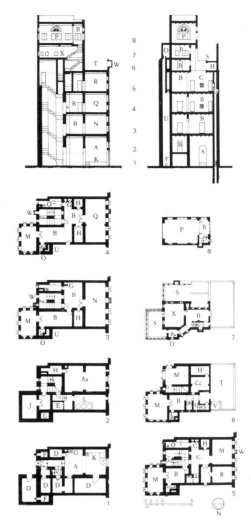

Plans and sections showing the typical organization of a San'a' tower-house. The plans are taken at each of the eight floors; the sections are taken at right angles to each other. A, entrance hall; Aa, entrance hall upper level; B, lobby; C, court; Cc, court upper level; D, animal stall; E, sheep pens; F, excrement room; G, well; H, store; J, grain and fruit store; K, loading; L, grinding rooms; M, personal room; N, living room; O, lavatory; P, mafraj; Q, dīwān; R, kitchen; S, terrace; T, laundry terrace; U, shaft; V, rain-water; W, water cooling box; X, women's room and wardrobe. (1)

assemble vast numbers of workers and quantities of material from his widespread domains, and thus it was frequently possible for a large building to be conceived, planned and completed by the same architect – a phenomenon which was much rarer in the West.

Architectural drawings and design techniques

There is ample evidence for us to be certain that most Islamic monuments were designed in drawing form before they were erected. Islamic architects inherited the drawing techniques of the Ancient World, which, from the delicate geometrical drawing instruments that have been found in archeological excavation, as

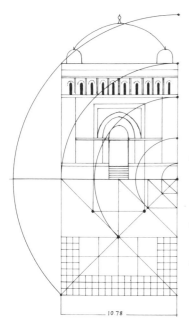

Systems of proportion governing the elevation of a building, based on the tomb of the Sāmānids, Bukhara. Dimensions such as those of the dado, the door, the doorframe, and the row of upper windows are all governed by simple divisions of the basic grid. The walls form a perfect cube, while the height of the dome corresponds to the diagonal of the generating square (see pl. 17). (2)

well as from fragmentary drawings, we know to have been highly refined. The account of al-Balawī, the historian, of the building of the mosque of Ibn Tūlūn in Cairo (876–9) confirms that parchment was used until the introduction of paper from China in the 9th century. 'Ahmad had [the prisoner] brought and said: "Come, what is it you say about building the mosque?" The Christian replied: "I will draw it out for the Prince, for him to see with his eyes, without a column but the two for the *mihrāb*." Ahmad ordered the skins to be brought to him ... and he drew the mosque.'

The oldest surviving Islamic architectural drawings so far identified are probably those of the 16th-century Uzbek master described below. But artists' drawings and miniature paintings from a much earlier period depict buildings drawn in pure elevation and plan, showing every detail and decorative pattern with great skill and precision. So we need have no doubt of the ability of architectural draughtsmen to create on paper the asesthetic images they wished to build and to convey them to the craftsmen.

A well known 16th-century miniature shows the Mughal conqueror, Bābur, discussing the setting-out of a formal garden in Afghanistan with his architect, who is seen to be holding a large plan that is apparently mounted on a board. The artist has taken the trouble to draw a close grid of fine lines across the architect's plan, presumably because this was a common feature of architects' drawings. This conclusion seems to be confirmed by a collection of architectural drawings by an Uzbek master of the 16th century, which are preserved in the archives of the Institute of the Oriental Academy of Science of the Uzbek SSR. The

plans are drawn on paper of very good quality, of Samarqand manufacture, from the 15th and 16th centuries. All the drawings are executed across a grid of squares (42–62 mm), which represent the structural modules of the plan. The Soviet scholar K. S. Kpyukov has analyzed a number of surviving Central Asian buildings from the 9th century onwards in terms of such grids, and found that their design conforms so exactly to them, even in detail, that there seems no doubt that this was the method by which the buildings were drawn, designed and set out. He has been able to establish from these grids the varying sizes of the 'cubits', or modules, used in designing, which tend to vary from building to building – not surprising when it is observed that the sizes of brick used also vary a great deal from site to site.

The use of a grid does not preclude the use of other co-ordinating systems of design. It is hardly surprising that these should be derived from geometry, for Ibn Khaldūn (1332–1406), among other early Islamic authors, refers to the use of geometry in architecture: 'It requires either a general or a specialized knowledge of proportion and measurement, in order to bring the forms [of things] from potentiality into actuality in the proper manner, and for the knowledge of proportions one must have recourse to the geometrician.'

Proportioning seems to have been primarily based on arcs drawn from the diagonals of squares to give ratios of $1 : \sqrt{2}$. Convincing analyses have been done by a number of art historians, notably M. S. Bulatov, to demonstrate the universality in Islam of this simple method of establishing a commensurate system of proportions throughout a building. This system had the advantage of deriving its ratios from the perfect square, which appears a favoured shape in Islamic buildings century after century.

According to several Islamic writers, the design of a work of architecture was sometimes tested in small wooden models before construction commenced. Such models are recorded in 'Abbāsid Baghdad, and as part of the design stage of the Tāj Mahal at Agra. The surviving inlaid models of Ottoman buildings may not be of this type, but are possibly miniature replicas executed at the time of the completion of the buildings.

Expenditure on buildings

Islamic writers often refer with awe to the great cost of a famous building work, partly because good appearance was popularly identified with expensive construction. L. A. Mayer cites a Turkish legend in which, to do justice to the beauty of the Süleymaniye Mosque, it is told that the stones of its minaret were mixed with jewels. Important buildings were expected to cost fabulous amounts, and for this reason the figures quoted in the histories must always be regarded as suspect. On the other hand, the buildings themselves are evidence that vast sums were often spent over short periods. And considerable expenditure was certainly involved in feeding the master craftsmen and sometimes all the workmen. Al-Walīd I is said to have taken seven years of the land tax of Syria for the Great Mosque of Damascus. With caliphs spending so lavishly on building, it is no wonder that one of the succeeding caliphs promised, in the first speech after he ascended the throne, not 'to lay one brick upon the other'. The Mughal, Shāh Jihān, eventually deposed partly for the excessive sums he devoted to building, used the revenues of thirty towns near Agra, on whom the burden must have fallen heavily, to finance the erection of the Tāj Mahal.

Most Islamic building was more restrained. In fact, Islamic religious literature even censured lavish expenditure on mosques. The reason was not the one sometimes given of the distaste of the bedouin for town life, but an awareness of the suffering inflicted on the poorer classes by forced labour and taxation.

Writing on architecture and the building crafts

No books devoted solely or primarily to architecture are known earlier than the 13th century. The architectural treatise of Vitruvius was probably not translated into Arabic in the early centuries, as was the case with so many other Greek and Latin authors. Books for determining the direction of the *qibla* were available from the 10th century (e.g. those of Abu'l-'Abbās Fadl and Abu'l-Wafā), but the first text that could be said to include a manual of architecture seems to have been Rashīd ad-Dīn's *Book of Living Things and Monuments*, written by the prime minister of the Il-Khanid rulers of Iran at the end of the 13th century. No copy of this work appears to have survived, but the table of contents included a chapter on the rules to be followed in building houses, religious buildings and fortresses, and information on the construction of tombs. In the early 17th century Safar Efendī wrote a treatise on architecture for the Turkish chief architect, Muhammad Āghā, which set out in detail the approach of the contemporary architect to his work.

Texts on the application of mathematics to practical architecture may have been more common. We know of one by the Iranian writer, Ghiyāth ad-Dīn Kāshī (*c.* 1423), which included tables for setting out arches. At least two handbooks on carpentry survive, an early example from Iraq and a later one from Tunis; both exist only in single manuscript copies.

Craftsmen

The extent of specialization in building trades and crafts in Islam depended on the needs of the local community. In large urban communities craftsmen were highly specialized, and each type of finished article seems to have warranted a special craft to make it. Recent research suggests that more than 265 manual occupations existed as separate crafts in the Cairo of Fātimid and Ayyūbid times. Some idea of the extent of specialization may be gleaned from the division of woodworking into at least five different crafts: sawyers, who prepared the rough timber to the correct dimensions; carpenters, who did most of the woodwork in buildings; the makers of wooden door locks, on whom depended 'the safety of property and the guarding of women'; the turners, who manufactured, among other things, the wooden screens for windows; and the makers of chests for clothes and chests for money and valuables. It seems likely that there were, at various times, at least two other woodworking crafts: the carver or decorator, and the incruster, who worked in precious woods, ivory and mother-of-pearl. Each craft had its separate identity, and its workers were frequently grouped together in the same locality or street. The effect of specialization was to reduce the need for technical knowledge to a minimum, but it also gave an opportunity for reaching the highest possible perfection.

These craftsmen were not organized into guilds of medieval European type; they were loosely affiliated, with one or two of their most respected members acting as spokesmen and as arbitrators in disputes. The selection of these leaders was done by tacit agreement, seldom with any formality. Training and the organization of work, which likewise followed custom, varied somewhat with time and place, and was rarely structured according to any fixed practice. There was sometimes division into master, pupil or boy apprentice, journeyman and unskilled assistant or labourer, but the evidence of the considerable number of market-law documents suggests that there was seldom any standard apprenticeship or legal agreement between the various workers. The aim of all craftsmen seems to have been, above all, their independence, so that once the apprenticeship was over craftsmen became self-supporting, working only with their own apprentices and unskilled assistants, or in brief partnerships with other craftsmen for the execution of big commissions. The only exceptions are found in Iran, Iraq, Egypt and Turkey after the 12th century, when the existence of mystical Islamic brotherhoods seems to have extended to the crafts, giving them a greater cohesion. In general, however, such movements did not last more than a hundred years.

Although many urban Muslims could at least read the formal script of the Qur'ān, it was probably unusual for craftsmen to be able to write the cursive script of everyday affairs. This undoubtedly limited the scope of work most craftsmen could undertake, and acted as a brake to prevent many of them from becoming supervisors of large buildings, or architects.

Craftsmen travelled throughout the Islamic world to an extraordinary extent, undoubtedly encouraged by the demand that existed, especially in the big centres, for variety and richness. In Fātimid Cairo there were craftsmen·from Spain, Morocco, Byzantium, Palestine, Lebanon, Syria, Iraq and Georgia. But often techniques spread because craftsmen were deliberately shifted by autocratic rulers or conquerors, or fled in the face of an enemy. The spread of a unique type of north Syrian wooden marquetry, for example, is explained by the advance of Mongol armies threatening the populations of Aleppo, Konya and Cairo. Large quantities of conscript labour were commonly used, and in the building of the ʿAbbāsid capital, Samarra, workers were brought from Syria, southern Iraq, 'and from other countries artists of every type and artisans of every craft,' according to Yaʿqūbī, the historian.

The general absence of guilds permitted great occupational freedom. Jews, Christians and other non-Muslims took part in almost every craft, and some crafts were largely in the hands of non-Muslims. These were mainly precious metal and jewellery crafts, and, as a rule, not crafts related to building.

The craft and market laws, which were included in the *hisba* laws, were administered by the head of the market and played a major role in maintaining the quality of artistic and craft production. A number of *hisba* documents survive containing regulations for fixing rates of pay, governing standards of workmanship and prohibiting the use of inadequate or cheap materials. For example, a 14th-century *hisba* document states: '[Workmen] must not combine together against the public. Masons must swear not to take bribes or gifts from lime-burners or makers of gypsum who wish to secure their acquiescence when the lime is insufficiently burnt or of bad quality.'

The size of bricks, wooden floor joists, flooring boards and timber beams was likewise meant to be regulated, as was the quality of the glazed surface on tiles. The 9th-century *hisba* manual of al-Nāsir li-Dīn Allāh recommended: 'Makers of baked bricks are to use a standard size of mould.' While the 12th-century *hisba* manual of Ibn ʿAbdūn urged: 'The bricks ought to be thick and of the width of the wall which is going to be constructed. A series of form-types which are designed to establish the thickness of the bricks, the surface of the tiles, the width and thickness of the joists, the thickness of the beams and that of the flooring boards ought to be kept by the headman of the market or should be hung in the Friday mosque. These forms should be in hard wood, not susceptible to damage [by weather or insects].'

From *hisba* documents we also learn something of building practice. Ibn al-Ukhuwwa states that builders were to be equipped with 'angles, weights and lines to ensure that the building will be true and without any departure from the perpendicular'. These simple aids to alignment remain the few essential tools of master builders in many Islamic countries today.

Masonry techniques – stonework

There was no one single craft of stonemason, as has already been explained, but a number of different specialist crafts. Besides the quarry men, there were on the building site the shapers of the separate stones, often divided into men preparing roughly shaped blocks for inner walls and foundations, men preparing finished plain ashlar blocks and the most skilled carvers. Usually the builders were similarly divided into men building fine smooth outer walls, the masons of the rougher stonework on the inner faces of walls (which were later to be plastered), and, most unskilled of all, the masons of the rough rubble cores between the outer and the inner faces of walls. The wages for all these occupations were fixed by the head of the market in consultation with the senior men of the craft along the guidelines of the *hisba* regulations. Most of the workers were paid per block shaped or laid.

The speed of work of these men repeating the same limited task all day long was amazingly fast. In recent restoration work Western architects have been astonished by the short time in which complicated carving could be copied flawlessly. This specialization and speed of work enabled skilled craftsmen, masons in particular, to earn salaries that were high compared to those of most of the community.

Except in the regions where stone was so rare as to be prohibitively expensive, walls had stone foundations reaching up to about fifty centimetres above ground level, or higher if there was likely to be flooding. They were of rough rubble or river boulders in the cheapest work, roughly shaped coursed stonework in most circumstances and smooth ashlar only in the largest and finest building. The hardest stone available was chosen, often granite or basalt. Foundations were almost always sunk below ground level, varying in depth from fifty centimetres in poor work, to as much as eleven metres in the case of the Gunbad-i Qābūs near Gorgan (1007).

Although it is not always easy to distinguish whether 'gypsum' or 'lime' is meant in the records, gypsum was the more easily prepared, and was a common bonding agent for mortar in the Ancient World, continuing to be used in much of the Islamic world throughout the medieval period. There is some evidence, however, that mortar manufactured from lime, wherever available, was preferred for the foundations and the corners of buildings. Gypsum mortar was then used for pointing the joints of face stonework or brickwork, in which case the mortar of the inner faces and cores of walls was seldom more than a local clay grout, occasionally mixed with chaff or straw.

One record (961–2) tells of the deep foundations of a palace in Baghdad being 'filled with lime and clay up to a cubit (about 40 cm) above the surface'. As the rest of the building was in brick, this was clearly a technique that made it possible to avoid the use of expensive stonework for foundations.

In many parts of the Islamic world it seems to have long been the practice to build the ground storey in stonework, and sometimes the floor above, and then change the system of construction of the upper floors to brickwork. This was the case in Qasr al-Hayr ash-Sharqī (East, 728), in Syria, where it is probably derived from a common Byzantine practice. Such construction is still used in areas where traditions are strong and stone is available, such as in the highlands of southern Arabia. It was also a common technique in building minarets, such as that of the Great Mosque of Harran, probably built in 744–50.

The curious fact that there are few known instances of early Islamic architects employing newly quarried stone columns in their buildings is probably explained by the growth of a fashion for reusing richly carved columns and capitals, or shafts of precious marbles, from earlier buildings, rather than by any inability of the craftsmen to handle the excavation and carving of large stones, as K. A. C. Creswell suggests. It is significant that original pre-Islamic capitals, shafts and bases were almost never incorporated into Islamic buildings in their correct combinations; instead, they were often separated or built in upside down. Sometimes an inverted capital serves as the base for a shaft of a different size, taken from a different building. The intention seems to have been to enrich the new building, while at the same time making a gesture of unconcern with preceding architectural styles and pretensions. Most of the reused columns came from earlier religious buildings, as we know from a number of sources, and therefore the symbolism of the triumph of Islam over older religions may have been involved as well.

The use of stones of ill-assorted sizes, together with the great height of columns in the early flat-roofed columned mosques, frequently led to the introduction of iron rods as reinforcement up the centres of columns, or to poured-lead shafts being made within them; al-Walīd I's rebuilding of the mosque at Medina (707–9) had the former, and the latter practice is testified to by Ibn Jubayr, who further says that the exteriors of columns, presumably those of poorer stone, were coated with gypsum which was polished until the columns resembled white marble. The practice of reusing old material for columns disappeared with the growth of 'Abbāsid architecture, by which time the supply had been largely exhausted, and from then on finely carved column shafts and capitals were newly made.

Also during the 'Abbāsid period we hear of various forms of 'concrete', such as the walls of Huwaysilat in Iraq, which were monolithic, a mixture of gypsum and pebbles, rather than brick. They were finished in stone veneer, ornamented stucco or plaster, perhaps in imitation of Roman concrete.

Stonework was patterned in alternating bands from an early date. Several Umayyad buildings, such as the mosque in Hama, and parts of the Great Mosque at Cordoba, were built using this technique, which was first used in Assyrian and Achaemenid architecture, and was taken up in some Early Christian and Byzantine buildings before Islam. Later, it became characteristic of Mamlūk and Ottoman stonework. A variation was the alternation of courses of stonework and brickwork, a Roman constructional technique which was exposed for decorative effect in some Byzantine buildings; it was adopted in Anatolia in Ottoman architecture, as in the mosques of Murād I (1363) and Murād Paşa (1466) at Bursa.

A more precise use of differences in stone colour was the outlining of architectural shapes and forms in stone of a much lighter or darker tone. The practice was introduced, it seems, in Seljuq times, and was taken up in India in the 14th century, where it afterwards became one of the most telling characteristics of Indian Islamic architecture.

Polychrome panelling in stones and marbles for dados and floor patterns was especially popular in Hellenistic, Roman and Byzantine buildings. Its use was adopted for the earliest Umayyad buildings, the Dome of the Rock in Jerusalem and the Great Mosque at Damascus. Originally square, rectangular, polygonal and circular, the panels became more intricate in shape, eventually developing into the star-like, cut stone patterns and fretted curvilinear ornament of Seljuq Anatolia and Mamlūk Egypt, and the *pietra dura* inlays in floral patterns of the Mughals in India. Related to this use of stone panelling is stone mosaic-work.

Openings in stonework in early Islamic architecture often employed lintels, sometimes with stone relieving arches above them, following Roman and Byzantine practice. Lintels made up of voussoirs, from the same origins, appear at Qasr al-Hayr ash-Sharqī and in the Great Mosque at Cordoba. The voussoirs of these 'flat arches' are sometimes built up of interlocking shapes, in which case the lintel is called 'joggled'. Several

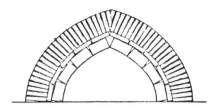

The construction of a typical Islamic pointed arch in an area which is short of wood. The bottom layer is constructed first, with light centring. This supports a thinner layer of flat bricks: when the mortar has hardened these two layers of brickwork act as permanent shuttering for the arch of radiating brick voissoirs above. (3)

Roman examples survive, including that of the Golden Gate of the palace of Diocletian (303–5), at Spalato (Split), and a gate at Antioch, both with relieving arches above. The Muslims early adopted the joggled lintel, using it in the same way in another enclosure gateway at Qasr al-Hayr ash-Sharqī. In later centuries the patterns of the joggled voussoirs became more elaborate, serving decorative rather than functional purposes; they were frequently further accentuated by being executed in alternating stone colours.

Arches were, at first, predominantly semicircular, like those of Rome and Byzantium; but in their desire for rich and varied effects, Islamic architects were quick to seize on other arch shapes, the first and most durable of which was the pointed arch, used in the palace of Mshattā (744) in Jordan, and increasingly thereafter, becoming common in the early 8th century. Horseshoe arches, anticipated in Byzantine architecture in Syria from the 3rd to the 6th centuries, were used in the extensive building programme of al-Walīd I, for example in the Great Mosque at Damascus and the Aqsā Mosque (705–15), in Jerusalem. From there, they probably travelled to North Africa and Spain, eventually becoming one of the main features of the Islamic architecture of those regions. Horseshoe arches of both semicircular and pointed form were found, the latter more commonly in Egypt, Syria and Arabia.

Other shapes of arches that made an early appearance in Islamic architecture were trefoil, multifoil (or cusped), two-centred and four-centred arches. A blind trefoil arch occurs in Qasr al-Hayr ash-Sharqī (727). Multifoil arches occur in 'Abbāsid architecture in the mid-8th century, at first as frames to pointed arches. Two-centred pointed arches appeared slowly at first, almost indistinguishable from round arches, then grew bolder until they reached their full form in the Dome of the Rock (688–91). Here they were used in a minor position, however, and it was another hundred years before the form became popular. Four-centred pointed arches appeared last, such as those in the Baghdad Gate of Raqqa (789), in northern Syria.

Stilted arches were developed in Byzantium, and were introduced in Islamic architecture from the 7th century onwards, in both semicircular and pointed forms of arches. Corbelled stone arches were built in the earliest surviving Islamic buildings of India, some with notched or ogee heads. It may be from these that ogee arches in the European architecture were derived. Corbelled arches with both notched and ogee heads were also characteristic of the East African coast, apparently having spread there from India on the monsoon trade routes.

Early arches were frequently built with wooden tie-rods, as though the architects were unsure of the strength of their construction. Such a practice may have been simply the logical extension of a system of timber reinforcement, common in pre-Islamic times in Mesopotamia and Arabia; even in stone structures it served to strengthen high buildings and to resist settlement due to poor foundations and earthquakes. Such timber tie-rods were built across the arches in the mosque of 'Amr, Cairo (673), in the Dome of the Rock (where they were encased in sheets of bronze), in the Great Mosques of San'a' (c. 750) and Qairouan (836) and in the restoration of the mosque of al-Azhar, Cairo, (1130).

Window grilles of marble or alabaster were adopted by Islamic architects from Byzantine practice, and were employed in all phases of Islamic architecture, ranging from the fine geometrical grilles of the Great Mosque of Damascus (705–15), to the magnificent stone grille screens of Mughal India in the 16th and 17th centuries.

Brickwork

The separate crafts of brickmaker, bricklayer, brick-cutter and layer of ornamental brick were found only in large urban centres. In rural areas and small towns unbaked bricks were made and laid by a single man. Though baked bricks were regarded as necessary for permanent buildings in the large urban communities, unbaked bricks for many purposes were widespread in all parts of the Islamic world. The sizes of the unbaked bricks did not need to be standardized beyond the job in hand, as they were made from the clay on the site, allowing the builder to choose the most convenient size. Great variations took place, even in neighbouring sites, from as small as 10 cm square by 3 cm thick, to 50 cm by 25 cm and 20 cm thick.

Islamic architects in the early centuries, and for long thereafter, used types of baked bricks inherited from the Roman and Sasanian worlds. According to Vitruvius, the Roman bricks were of three kinds: two taken from the Greeks, 'five or four palms every way', approximately 50 cm and 40 cm square; and the third of Etruscan origin, oblong, approximately 41 cm by 27 cm and 14 cm thick. But larger baked bricks have been found in both Sasanian and Roman buildings, frequently as much as 60 cm square. The square Roman, Byzantine and Islamic bricks were all of roughly the same thickness: 4 cm. Sasanian bricks were up to 10 cm thick. In many areas of the later Byzantine and Iranian lands bricks were smaller, and it is common to find early Islamic builders using bricks as small as 20 cm or 17 cm square, sizes which persisted throughout later periods, although larger bricks were also in use.

Unbaked brick is made from earth taken on or near the building site, which is wet thoroughly and mixed with straw and chaff by treading it with bare feet. The bricks are moulded on a bed of chaff using an open wooden frame, until rows of bricks have been made and closely ranged side by side. They are dried for half a day before being turned on their sides, to dry for a further day. They are normally used immediately after being made. After laying, they are often rendered with a mud-straw mix, which can be renewed after heavy rains. Burnt bricks are made in the same way, using more carefully chosen clay and clean sand, which is soaked for twenty-four hours before moulding. The moulded bricks are made on a grey sand bed, and dried for twice as long as the sun-dried bricks before being packed into a large brick-kiln and fired for three days, using fuel that varies from dried dung to small shrubs and sticks. A ramp usually leads up to the top of the kiln, allowing most of the bricks to be packed and unpacked from above.

The mortars commonly used in laying bricks are a mud-straw mixture in the case of sun-dried bricks, and gypsum for baked bricks, except in exposed or damp conditions, when a lime-sand mortar is employed. String-courses were made by corbelling out bricks, often placing them diagonally so that the corbelling was decorative when seen from underneath. By corbelling several times, a narrow corridor could be spanned completely by bricks laid in flat courses.

The Islamic use of decorative patterned brickwork bonds is first known in the 8th-century desert palace of Ukhaydir, and the city gate of Raqqa (772). It reached its apogee in the tomb of the Sāmānids, rulers in Bukhara (913–43), and continued as a popular technique in many areas until modern times. Its inspiration seems to have been patterned brickwork from ancient Rome. Seljuq brickwork introduced projecting and receding bricks to cause shadow effects, especially useful in creating calligraphic inscriptions in brick. Plaster joints were sometimes carved, or moulded or carved plugs were introduced between the bricks.

Glazed brick faces had been used in Babylonian and Achaemenid times, and were revived under the 'Abbāsid caliphs, so that the Great Mosque of Baghdad, in 903, was wholly ornamented with bricks glazed in lapis-lazuli, according to the writer, Ibn Rusta; and in the same century al-Yaʿqūbī speaks of the green minaret of Bukhara. Sometimes the glazed bricks did not cover the entire surface, but were inserted at spaced intervals in a wall of common, ornamentally arranged, bricks.

Brick-cutting was a specialized craft utilized for the production of brick-mosaic panels. Bricks were cut into polygonal, triangular or star shapes with a bolster and then the faces were ground smooth on a coarse hard stone. The cut bricks were laid face downwards and combined to form geometrical patterns, then cast into a panel by laying gypsum plaster across them. The edges of the panel were stiffened by a wooden frame, which was removed once the dried panel was lifted into position on the building.

Clay walling

A number of different techniques survive in various parts of the Islamic world for building coursed, earth walling without the use of bricks. At the beginning of the 15th century, Ibn Khaldūn described earth walling techniques with moulding boards or shuttering.

One builds walls with it [earth] by using two wooden boards, the measurements of which vary according to [local custom]. The average measurements are four cubits by two [approximately 1.7 m by 85 cm]. They are set upon a foundation. The distance between them depends on the width of foundation the builder considers appropriate. They are joined together with pieces of wood fastened with ropes and twine. Then, one puts earth mixed with quicklime into [this frame]. The earth and quicklime are pounded with special mixers... until everything is well mixed throughout. Earth is then added a second and third time, until the space between the two boards is filled. [Then] the earth and quicklime have combined and become one surface. Then, two other boards are set up in the same fashion, and [all] is treated in the same manner... and then piece by piece, until the whole wall is set up and joined together as tightly as if it were of one piece.

Another technique of clay walling uses no moulding boards; instead, the packed clay is laid in high courses, each of which is allowed to dry before the next is superimposed. A typical course, 40 to 50 cm high, is wider at the bottom, so that it slightly overhangs the one below, creating a visual separation between the courses, which is frequently accentuated by weathering. The stone foundation, of rubble, usually extends to a height of 30 or 40 cm above ground. The composition of this type of walling includes small proportions of sand, straw and chaff. It is mixed with large quantities of water and left to mature for two days before being made into mudballs, which are thrown up to the workmen on the walls. There, the balls of clay mixture are pummelled into a homogeneous mass the width of the wall, which dries after two further days in warm weather. Openings are braced with stone slabs or with rough timber reinforcing built into the clay. Each course is slightly curved upwards from the centre. At the corner it steps up in an even more pronounced way. The walls batter slightly inwards as they rise, becoming thinner at the top. As a result of these precautions, cracking due to weathering or earthquakes does not result in the corners falling outwards; rather, the building tends to consolidate itself with age. It is a technique that seems clearly related to construction in ancient Egypt. Walls are waterproofed at the top by limewashing, sometimes over a layer of poles to prevent the clay cracking at the exposed upper surface.

Carpentry

It is often claimed that wood was scarce in most of the lands of Islam, and that this resulted in the special character of Islamic woodwork. However, this is only partially true. In earlier centuries, many regions were frequently less barren than they are today, and countries even pursued active afforestation policies, as, for example, Egypt did under the Fātimids and Ayyūbids. Owing to irrigation, Damascus and other cities had forests, and half-timbered construction was common in many areas. Even in later centuries, when wood certainly became scarcer and more expensive in Egypt and Syria, small and relatively poor mosques were still provided with the usual wooden furniture, such as the *minbar*, *dikka*, tomb screens, lecterns and chests. The ceilings were mostly in wood, often richly carved (as were those of even moderately sized houses), and wooden grille windows remained a standard feature of domestic architecture. Indeed, the use of timber in Egyptian architecture almost seems to develop in inverse proportion to its availability; just as in Asia Minor, where wood was never scarce, important constructions and Mosque furniture were of stone.

The reuse of old timbers was probably motivated by their original associations or because they had acquired a certain sanctity, rather than because of great shortage. We know that mosque doors and *minbars* were often reused, as happened to the original door of the Sultan Hasan Madrasa in Cairo, reused in the mosque of al-Malik al-Mu'ayyad Shaykh.

Of course the very preciousness of some woods made their use desirable, and may have encouraged the development of compositions in small panels — although the latter is, in any case, a characteristic of all rich Islamic decoration.

Woodcarving was a specialized craft, its techniques varying from relief carving and sunk carving to various types of drilled and pierced lattice-work. The wood-turner used a simple lathe worked with the left hand, while the right hand held the chisel. Like the carpenter's drill, the lathe was turned by running a taut string held in a bow backwards and forwards, the string being looped once around the drill or the piece of wood being turned. Turned pieces joined together made up the intricate lattices of the screened window openings in many areas, especially in Egypt.

That carpenters' work was often highly respected is clear from the number of works that carry their signatures. An example is the richly carved pair of doors from Afushteh in Iran, 'done by the master Husayn ibn 'Alī, joiner and cabinet maker of Abadeh'. As with architects, a certain number of highly placed amateur woodcarvers were also mentioned in Islamic texts: the Turkish sultan, Beyazit II, and amirs of the Tanūkhī dynasty of Lebanon, such as 'Izz ad-Dīn Jawād ibn 'Alam ad-Dīn Sulaymān (1357).

Ironmongery

Building ironmongery was done by a general blacksmith in small communities, but in larger towns the manufacture of nails and bolts, hinges and catches, knockers and locks was in the hands of specialist craftsmen.

Hinges were of two types. In the areas of Iranian influence, pivot hinges were common; in the remainder of the Islamic world, hooked strap-hinges operating in ringed sockets fastened to the door or window frames were used. The latter had the great advantage that they allowed the door leaves and sashes to be taken away and replaced by simply unhooking them. Catches often closely resembled the hinges, and hooked into a ringed socket. Alternatively, sliding bolts with drilled holes to take padlocks were used.

Plastering

In most areas of the Islamic world gypsum was the common cementing material of plasters and mortars. Gypsum, found in many parts of the Middle East and in Iran, could be fired at a much lower temperature than lime, an important factor in areas where wood was scarce or other fuels expensive. Lime plaster was reserved for waterproofing roofs, canals and drains, and for special marble plasters, and had a wider use only in areas near the sea, when it was burned from sea shells, and in regions under strong, late Roman influence. It is generally true that gypsum ('plaster of Paris') was preferred for precise and highly finished stucco-work, and lime for mortar in damp conditions, for roofing plaster, and for marble plasters.

The burning of gypsum and lime were separate crafts, except in rural districts when they might be done by the same man, who generally combined them with brick-burning. Kilns consisted of a low masonry oven with a perforated top, on which were piled small broken pieces of quarried gypsum rock, limestone or shells. An intense fire was maintained, from twelve to twenty-four hours, the longer and slower the better; then the material was packed with earth and allowed to cool slowly. Lime was sold as it was to the builder, for slaking, preparatory to use; whereas the gypsum rock had to be crushed in a vertical stone-mill before it was ready for use.

Gypsum stucco was in universal use throughout the Islamic world as a medium for decorative ornament and applied colour. It was cheap and easily worked. Over many centuries plasterers developed mixtures and techniques of application; some, employing lime, provided plasters of amazing hardness and durability, while others, of extraordinary smoothness, took the high polish of precious marbles and alabasters. Making the special polished lime plaster required great skill. It was used in various countries for ornamental dados around walls, for decorated columns and capitals, and for the roofs of important mosques and palaces. In the Yemen, where the craft has survived unaltered, the sand is specially ground, very fine, from marble. It is mixed with lime and fermented for a week before being applied layer upon layer, each layer being beaten in place with a large rock for three days (in Ibn Khaldūn's time it was 'rubbed in until it sticks'). Two or three layers are laid, depending on the exposure, then the plaster is limewashed three times, and finally polished three times with pumice. After a further week has elapsed, it is brushed with water using a fine soft brush, and the surface changes in colour from white to pale cream. This brushing proceeds laboriously, the surface being worked over again and again, only six square metres being finished in one day. Bone marrow is then applied with a cloth or by hand and worked into the surface to complete its polish and its richness of colour, giving it the appearance of fine cream marble.

Similarly, the use of gypsum plaster is laborious and demanding, requiring one labourer to sift, and another to stir the wet mixture for long periods so that its rapid-setting powers are 'killed' and it becomes possible to mould and carve it over several days. The master plasterer lays the gypsum in several layers, each being allowed to set, and ornaments the top layer with a moulding board or by cutting it away with a knife. The surface is finished by rubbing it with a wet cloth and a fine brush, or by dusting it with a fine powder of mixed gypsum and talcum and then polishing it to a high gloss.

The carver of plaster windows works away from the building site. He lays a thick layer of gypsum plaster on a large flat board and traces the ornamental pattern by eye, cutting out the openings with a sharp knife. After the screen has dried for two or three days the board is turned over and the screen panel removed.

Often the outer tracery of a window is unglazed, and there is another layer of tracery on the inside face of the wall, which contains coloured glass. The inner glazing is made by laying small pieces of glass, thin sheets of semiprecious stones, or alabaster over a dry tracery panel, then casting another sheet of gypsum across the top. The greatest skill has to be used by the window-carver in matching the pattern he now cuts out to that on the other side, which he can no longer see. It is a matter of pride among carvers that they do not repeat the same pattern in another window until many months have passed.

Tiling

The use of tiles on walls and floors was common in the Middle East and Iran before Hellenistic times and had been revived by the Sāsānids. The Islamic use of tiles begins in earnest in 'Abbāsid times, at Samarra, where the application of a metallic sheen was developed. From there, it spread to Fātimid Egypt and Spain, and subsequently, in the 13th century, hexagonal and star-shaped lustre tiles were in widespread use in Iran. In addition, mosaic tiles that could be cut into small pieces and reassembled into rich and complex designs were evolved in Iran. The first complete covering of a building with this material was the Sirçali Madrasa at Konya, in 1242. The use of painted tiles reached unprecedented richness in Iran and Turkey in the 16th and 17th centuries.

Tiles sometimes need to be trimmed by the tiler before they are placed, using a straight-edge and a stone-chisel. The tiles are then laid in gypsum plaster, either directly on the wall, or after preassembly in large panels backed with gypsum. Tile-mosaic is preassembled face downwards in plaster panels after the pieces have been cut to shape using paper stencils. If the tile surface has to be curved to fit a vault or dome this is done by casting the panel to this shape on a matching curved surface.

Building regulations and arbitration

Islamic law assumed that the open space around a building could not be built on or otherwise infringed without the owner's agreement. What is more, because of this the owner often felt that he was entitled to build out in any direction, even into the thoroughfare in front of the building. The headman of a town quarter, or the ruler of a city, was responsible for ensuring that the passage along a thoroughfare was not constricted by new buildings. Another of his duties was to settle the innumerable disputes that arose between the owners of adjoining properties about new buildings, about the common space between them, about party walls and about the problems of the exclusion of light and air.

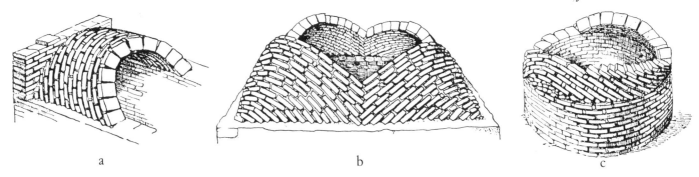

a   b   c

Traditional methods of building stone or brick vaults without centring: (a) Brick barrel vault of a type excavated at Khorsabad, 8th century BC. Layers of brick 'lean' against the end wall until a complete arch can be formed, whose slope provides the necessary support for the next layer. (b) Covering a square space by bridging the corners until the edges meet in the middle: in other words, a diagonal groined vault. Pl. 14, p. 115, shows a vault being constructed in this way today. (c) Domed roof to a pit excavated at Khafaje, going back to about 2000 BC; this again uses sloping bricks, which rise in two vaults to meet at the centre. (4)

Customary law in particular places, sometimes supplemented by edicts of the autocratic ruler, established certain controls. These usually related to water rights and taxes, drainage, building heights and the good construction and maintenance of buildings to ensure their safety. But all these aspects were by no means regulated universally throughout the Islamic world. The zoning of animal stockyards, slaughteryards, tanneries and mills away from houses was also sometimes determined by customary law.

Ash-Shayzarī in the *Nihāyat ar-Rutba* includes this description of regulations for a market: 'The height and extent of the *sūqs* must be according to what the Byzantines laid down anciently [an interesting reference to the inheritance of building regulations from an earlier society], and there should on the sides be two raised platforms on which the people walk in time of rain if the street is not paved. And it is not permitted to put up a counter beyond the corner piers supporting the roof, to enter the essential place of passing because it would be a nuisance to the passerby. . . . Each craft has to have a special *sūq*. And those who need fire, the blacksmith and the potter, their streets shall be remote from those such as the spice merchant because of their not being of the same kind.'

One method of height control had the advantage of increasing revenue. R. B. Serjeant, referring to Wadi 'Amd, in southern Arabia, observed that a single-storey house was untaxed, but multi-storeyed dwellings were taxed according to their height.

Water supply and drainage regulations were necessary to ensure that there was not a mixing of the sewage with fresh water supplies. Where channels or streams led fresh water into the towns, sometimes to the houses themselves, they were to be designed and regulated so that they could not be used for ablution purposes until the channel had passed the point beyond which fresh water could not be drawn, and from there the water continued on its way carrying off the sewage led into it. Where houses depended on wells, it was usually left to the inhabitants to ensure that sewage pits were not built in such a way as to foul the wells – a cause of dispute between neighbours in dense urban communities.

Building equipment and machinery

Ibn Khaldūn, writing in the late 14th century, said that architects 'must know how to move heavy loads with the help of machines. Big blocks of large stones cannot be lifted into place on a wall by the unaided strength of workmen alone. Therefore, the architect must contrive to multiply the strength of the rope by passing it through holes, constructed according to geometrical porportions, of the attachment called *mīkhāl* [pulleys]. . . . They multiply the power and strength needed to carry the loads required in building.'

The use of cranes in building was mentioned by Aristotle, and several Classical authors state that Archimedes was the inventor of both the triple and the compound pulley. Archimedes also used a windlass with an endless screw. Vitruvius describes in detail a number of kinds of crane, and illustrations of some of them survive from ancient times. Essentially, they use one, two or more masts carrying a triple pulley or a compound pulley of five sheaves. A windlass at the bottom was slowly turned, raising the loads to which a second compound pulley was attached. In the case of very large cranes, a treadmill was added to provide enough power to turn the windlass. The crane was raised by means of a backstay or stays attached to its own windlass. Sometimes the windlass was turned by animals.

Hero, who wrote *c*. 70 AD, and whose work was early translated into Arabic, describes five simple means of increasing power: the windlass, the lever, the pulley, the wedge and the screw. These five mechanical clements permit a small force acting over a long distance to be transformed into a large force acting over a short distance. Hero recommended that no nails or bolts should be used in cranes; the heavier the burden the more important it was that only rope lashings should be used to assemble the parts of the crane. Hero also describes the use of 'crayfish' hooks inserted into the stones that have to be raised; and other kinds of 'hangers', the use of counterbalanced carts for lifting weights up steep inclines, the counterbalance being filled with loose stones. Canted walls were righted by placing a wooden beam along the sunken edge, then hauling it up from the other side of the wall by means of a windlass with a pulley. All these mechanical building devices were the common heritage of the Byzantine and early Islamic worlds. Although some of them were forgotten with the decline of Islam, there is no reason to doubt that they formed the basis of the building machines still in use at the time of Ibn Khaldūn.

Special types of construction: vaults, domes and minarets

In areas with little timber, alternative methods of spanning between walls had to be adopted from the preceding civilizations. The tradition of brick building in Mesopotamia and Iran, which had reached new heights of achievement under the Sāsānids, was the main source of the brick constructional techniques of early Islamic times.

Stone had some tensile strength and could therefore be used in the form of slabs to span short distances between walls, or as cross-ribs as was common in Syrian construction; but the brick of the flood plains and semi-deserts did not possess this tensile strength, and was further weakened by the need for frequent mortar joints. Forms had to be adopted that utilized brick in compression, therefore, and of these the arch, the vault and the dome were the most simple.

The shortage of timber introduced another difficulty; vaults and domes had to be built without shuttering, and with as little centring as possible. For this reason the form of vault most commonly adopted was a special type of barrel vault, which required no shuttering or centring at all. This was built by laying an arch of bricks on edge leaning at an angle against an end wall. Subsequent arches were laid parallel and cemented with mortar to the flat brick faces of the previous arch until a long barrel vault was constructed. To utilize whatever tensile strength was available, a course of bricks was then laid flat above the first barrel vault, and third and fourth courses of bricks were laid on edge, running in the long axis of the vault, and so on, until a sufficient thickness to take the superimposed loads had been created.

Besides barrel vaults, groined vaults – intersecting barrel vaults – were built. A variation on these

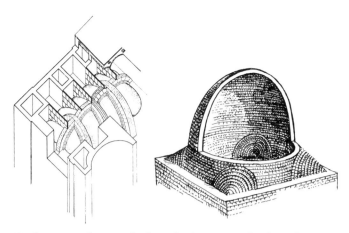

Roofs or upper floors are built on slender cross-walls above the vaults or domes to cut down weight; these rest not only on the ribs but even on the cells between them. (5)

Type of Iranian dome, showing how the brick coursing is used constructionally: four squinches consisting of radiating semi-circles produce a circular base for the dome. The constructional technique of the squinches is close to that used in example (b), *opposite. (6)*

involved the intersection of four sloping barrel vaults, still using the sloping arch construction, which rose from corners of a square plan. On a circular plan, the construction of a dome using sloping arches was also possible, so that, again, shuttering and centring of wood could be avoided.

In all these cases, the creation of a flat floor above the vault or dome introduced another problem. Where wood was scarce, it was economical to create a masonry floor; however, by filling up the space on either side of the vault to make a level surface heavy loads on the vault were introduced. The solution was to build light parallel walls on top of the surface of the vault or dome, and the spaces between these were then spanned by small, brick vaults under the floor surface, leaving most of the volume below as void.

Methods of effecting the transition from square room plans to circular domes had been exercising the ingenuity of Byzantine and Sasanian architects for several centuries before Islamic designers began to consider them. The problem was what to do in the corner spaces, especially as the dome demanded continuous support at its lower edge, and these loads had to be transferred to the square plan above head-height. From the Sāsānids, Islamic architects learned the principle of converting the square plan into a polygon by the use of squinch arches across the corners. These arches might have groined vaults behind them, possibly of the sloping type described above, which then appeared as semi-cones, or small semi-domes, or a series of concentric squinch arches corbelling from one another. The final transition from the polygon thus formed to the circular base of the dome could be easily achieved by further slight corbelling across the corners of the polygon.

141

The Islamic method of bridging the gap between square base and circular dome combines the advantages of both squinch and pendentive. In the mausoleum of Umm Qulthūm, Cairo, a series of squinches rests upon one another, resulting in a pattern that prefigures the muqarnas vault. (7)

A muqarnas vault section. Instead of being supported from underneath, the stucco vault is actually suspended from above by means of a complicated system of timber hangers attached with lumps of gypsum mortar to the brick or stone structural arches – and to each other. (8)

An important Islamic development from the squinch arch was the concept of a small squinch arch in each corner flanked by two further arches, the heads of which corbelled outwards to form the springing of a superimposed squinch arch set in the diagonal wall of the polygon. The effect was of a series of niches superimposed in two tiers. This was the origin of the so-called 'stalactite pendentive', the *muqarnas* vault, which appears almost simultaneously in Iran (Great Mosque of Isfahan, 1088) and in Egypt (mosque of Sayyida 'Ātiqa *c.* 1100). Soon afterwards we find stalactite pendentives of three, four, five and even more tiers of niches, which begin to be a major decorative feature in the architecture, although their origin and function was essentially structural. Eventually the stalactite pendentives grew to cover the whole surface of the dome or semi-dome, and, in their final form, they were often merely decorative skins suspended on wooden hangers from the structural arches and vaults behind them. Some amazingly daring constructions of their kind have recently been disclosed in Isfahan.

In Syrian pre-Islamic architecture the transition from the square plan to the circular dome had been simply effected by spanning the corner with stone slabs. Where the room was large, a series of superimposed beams across the corners, each corbelled slightly above the one below, produced a sloping triangle of stonework (Tetrapylon of Latakia *c.* 300 AD). This feature developed in Islamic architecture in two ways: it became a field for the decorative application of tiers of superimposed arches (mosque at Ramla 1267–8); or, alternatively, it was used alone (mosque at Bursa 1136) or in a series of adjacent triangles (Maqām Ibrāhīm and Madrasa Shād-Bakht, both at Aleppo, 1168 and 1193 respectively). The latter reched its finest form in the Karatay Madrasa at Konya, in Anatolia (1252).

The use of spherical pendentives of the Byzantine type was again anticipated in Syria by the Roman use of the so-called 'simple dome'. This form of roofing, though necessarily limited to small spans, later became popular in Islamic buildings. The transition from the square plan to the dome was here effected by beginning the semicircular curve of the dome from the corners of the square. This meant that the dome intersected each of the four walls in a semicircular arch, and the resulting dome was rather flat and structurally weak. From the shape of the parts of the dome that extended downwards in the corners, the Byzantines evolved the idea of the 'spherical pendentive', which, for large domes, acted as a strong, structural transition element between the springing of the dome and the square plan. Spherical pendentives were copied from Byzantine examples in a number of

Islamic buildings, beginning with those of the bath in the Umayyad ruins of Qusayr 'Amra, *c.* 712–15. The period of their greatest popularity came with the revival of Byzantine-inspired architecture in Seljuq and Ottoman times.

Two inherent structural weaknesses were likely to lead to the instability of domes. The first was the change in shape from a smooth contour that occurred under the springing of the dome in the corners of the square plan, where squinch arches or spherical pendentives were used; this caused the thrusts from the dome to spread outwards, a tendency that could be partially corrected by adding dead weight above the corners. The second weakness was the tension force needed to contain the circular foot of the dome, which otherwise cracked and spread; neither stonework nor brickwork had enough tensile strength to resist this, unaided, except in small domes. Islamic architects resorted to the use of timber reinforcement rings at the foot of the dome, and used iron cramps between the stones, after the example of the Hagia Sophia in Constantinople. In later Ottoman mosques in Istanbul, straight wooden ties were introduced across semi-domes to perform the same purpose. Another alternative was to lighten the dome by use of two distinct shells for the outer and inner surfaces, separated by radiating rib walls within the void between them. This had the advantage of creating great depth to aid in spanning the room below, as well as raising the external dome so that it might be more imposing. These double domes may have been modelled on earlier timber examples such as that of the Dome of the Rock. The finest of them was the dome of the mausoleum of Öljeytu at Soltaniyeh, which had a span of twenty-six metres.

The Romans introduced brick ribs into the construction of vaults and domes, to act as integral centring before the pouring of massive weights of concrete – only a relatively light timber centring was necessary for the construction of the ribs. While adopting this technique, Islamic architects used the ribs even more for decoration than for structural purposes, allowing them to project on the face of the domes or vaults to create complex patterns of intersecting lines. A simple form of ribbed dome was the so-called 'melon dome', derived from Roman practice, in which the surface of the dome was constructed as a series of small barrel vaults focused on the crown. Decorative ribbed vaulting was a fully developed art form by the time of the building of the Great Mosque at Cordoba, in 961–5. Its continued use in Spain is seen in the mosque of Bāb Mardum (1000). Ribbed vaulting, both structural and purely decorative, was used in the Friday Mosque at Isfahan, after 1121, and later appeared in Seljuq buildings in Anatolia.

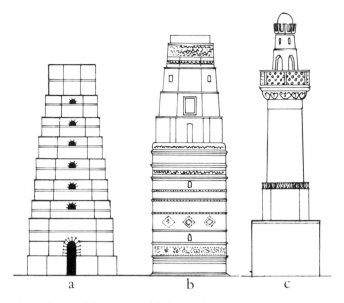

The evolution of the minaret: (a) the standard Roman lighthouse (in this case a reconstruction of the pharos of Dover); (b) west minaret of the mosque of al-Hākim, Cairo; (c) a characteristic later type, incorporating square base, octagonal centre and cylindrical top. (9)

Minarets

Minarets began as low, square masonry towers on the pattern of pre-Islamic Syrian towers, which had been built for both pagan and Christian purposes. As soon as Islamic architects desired to make them higher, however, they resorted to the stepped storeyed construction typical of Roman lighthouses. The minaret of the Great Mosque at Qairouan (724) is one example, and that of the mosque of al-Hākim, in Cairo (1002–13) is another. From there it was but a short step to the introduction of varied shapes on different storeys. Eventually a common form of minaret developed, which began as a square, changed in the next storey to a polygon and then to the cylindrical main shaft. The balcony was constructed of light wood, or cantilevered on brackets or superimposed niches. The top of the minaret formed another storey, frequently contrasting in shape, and it was then crowned by a dome or a conical roof.

The stability of high minarets was assured, not merely by the system of superimposed storeys of decreasing size, but also by the use of the staircase construction to tie the outer skin of each minaret to its central core. With stone treads the tie was simple and strong, with brick it was created by building an arch under each tread, or a sloping barrel vault under each flight. Minarets of square plan were further strengthened by introducing arches under the landings. In this way the whole height of the minaret was constructed as a hollow screw of greater strength than its slender appearance suggested. Using this technique, Ottoman minarets rose to heights of more than seventy metres.

5 The Elements of Decoration: Surface, Pattern and Light

DALU JONES

Islamic decoration covers buildings like a mantle; its purpose is to conceal the structure rather than reveal it. The elements of decoration are mostly limited to calligraphy, geometry and foliation, but their manipulation results in a rich and sumptuous effect. The wall shown opposite is the base of the Friday Mosque at Herat in Afghanistan. It is covered with areas of pattern, as a wall or floor would be covered with hangings or carpets. Each area has its own logic, and there is a larger logic that relates them all together. The same logic, the same principles, apply to any medium – textiles, ceramics, woodwork, metalwork, books – and on any scale. Without the figure of the man it would be hard to tell whether the subject of this photograph were very large or very small. Flexibility of scale is matched by the interchangeability of the designs, which can contract or expand to fit different areas. The wall shown here is divided into a number of panels, each with its own distinctive pattern. The effect of richness or complexity is heightened by the use of ceramic inlays, which introduce the dimension of colour. The reflecting quality of the ceramic permits the play of light on the surface of the building, giving it a glossy effect, changing subtly as the sun moves. Despite the fact that this building surface is flat, not sculptured, its decoration, through contrasts of colour and complexity of design, has three-dimensional implications. (1)

The frame

Islamic architectural decoration does not run into mere overall richness and complexity. It is tightly controlled by the discipline of primary and secondary grids, which create frames by which building façades are organized. The Tāj Mahal at Agra, for example, when carefully analyzed, shows a strict and rigorous consistency in its organization. The primary unit is an arch within a rectangle – a motif recurrent throughout the history of Islamic architecture. Here it occurs in a magnified form as the portal in the centre of each side, and in a reduced form as the flanking niches on two levels (*opposite and below left*). In a further diminution of scale it appears as the windows and doors within the larger portal and niches. Reduced even further and multiplied, the same motif fills the upper parts of the niches as *muqarnas* decoration. The walls and the platforms in turn bear the same motif as a flat design. As a trilobed arch within a rectangle, it is found on the base of the building and in the kiosks that surround the main dome, and also as a pattern on the drum of the main dome itself. Each appearance of the arch within the rectangle repeats the fundamental conception in the subsidiary buildings of the tomb complex. (2,3,5)

Windows repeat the same motif on a smaller scale within the deep shadows of the great niches. The same principles of reduction and repetition apply to the foliated panels and calligraphic bands. (4)

Geometry

Islam transformed geometry into a major art form, using the circle as the basis for the generation of patterns and applying the principles of repetition, symmetry and change of scale to create a bewildering variety of effects. *Below*: detail from the tomb of I'timād ad-Dawla, Agra. (6)

Surfaces, curved or flat, in brick or stucco, are covered by designs that are infinitely expandable. Patterns are rendered visible from a distance by contrasts of plane which permit the play of light and shade. *Left*: the curved outline of the minaret of the Great Mosque at Damghan, Iran. *Above*: part of a stucco panel from the *madrasa* of al-Mustansir, Baghdad. (7,8)

Optical effects achieved by negative and positive areas are created in different coloured stones. On the tomb of Akbar at Sikandra, India, it is applied on a huge scale, yet would be unchanged if the object were a small inlaid box. (9)

Different textures and materials are unified by the geometric principles that govern their design. At the Bū-'Ināniyya Madrasa, Fez, stucco, ceramic mosaic and the wood of beam and screen share a common decorative conception. (10)

The star, six, eight, sixteen or more points, is one of the fundamental and ubiquitous shapes of Islamic geometrical design. It can be used equally in two dimensions or in three, to transform a dome into a complex net

of interlinked surfaces or to decorate timber and bronze fittings inside the buildings. *Above*: ceiling of the tomb of Hāfiz at Shiraz. *Left*: detail from a door in the *madrasa* of Sultan Ḥasan, Cairo. (11,12)

Calligraphy

Inscriptions are found incorporated in the
decoration of almost every Islamic building,
and in that of a large number of objects as
well. Arabic lettering was brought to a high
level of artistic sophistication and scripts can
vary from the flowing cursive styles (*naskhī*
and *thuluth*) to the angular *kūfī*. Often
different styles appear on the same building,
some of them so complicated as to be barely
legible. On the tomb of Tīmūr at Samarqand
(*right*) the drum of the dome has a continous
inscription, whereas on the wall beneath an
extremely stylized writing is set in irregular
panels defined by darker coloured tiles. (15)

Stone calligraphic bands, both linear and
circular, proclaim the word of God on the
façade of the mosque of al-Aqmar, Cairo.
Such inscriptions are Qur'ānic and give
meaning to the building by clarifying its
function. (13,14)

Undulating bands of carving carry the
Qur'ānic message around the base of the
Qutb Minār, Delhi. Characteristic of Islamic
art is the way in which geometric and foliated
designs mingle with calligraphy; in this
example the letters themselves are set against
a floriated background. (16)

Side by side, cursive script imitating the strokes of the pen and the heavy monumental *kūfī* climb the façade of the monastery, *khānaqāh*, at Natanz in Iran. Arabic reads from right to left, but in architecture is frequently placed vertically. Different styles of lettering are found in different materials, as in the ceramic and inlaid marble of the pier from the Bū-ʿInāniyya Madrasa, Fez. (17, 18)

A dazzling display of calligraphic ingenuity is shown on the façade of the Ince Minare Madrasa at Konya, Turkey. Here the decoration consists almost entirely of bands of inscription that frame the portal and cross in a knot above the door as if they were banners. (19)

Play of light

Reflected light: the development and multiplication of *muqarnas* cells beneath the domes can be understood by their function in reflecting and refracting light. To accentuate their play of light, shining ceramic tiles and even mirrors are utilized, as in the Shāh-Hamza ʿAlī mausoleum at Shiraz. *Right:* a similar effect achieved in the Shaykh Lutfallāh Mosque in Isfahan. *Opposite:* sunlight reflects upwards from a window of the Alhambra, Granada, to be diffused in the *muqarnas* vault. (20, 21, 24)

Light penetrating through glass or transparent screens projects patterns onto the already patterned interior surfaces and dissolves the boundaries between solid and void. *Above:* a window in the Süleymaniye Mosque, in Istanbul. *Right:* a screen at Fatehpur Sikri, India. (22, 23)

Foliation

The Classical vine and scroll motifs provided Islam with a starting point for a whole repertoire of lithe, living forms, ranging from almost scientific naturalism to the completely abstract art of the arabesque.

Contrasts in early Islam: the Umayyad wooden panel (*far left*) is clearly based on the Classical vine emerging from a vase. Wholly stylized forms (*left*) appear on a stucco dado from Samarra, of the 'Abbāsid period. (25,26)

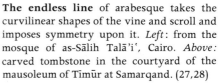

The endless line of arabesque takes the curvilinear shapes of the vine and scroll and imposes symmetry upon it. *Left*: from the mosque of as-Sālih Talā'i', Cairo. *Above*: carved tombstone in the courtyard of the mausoleum of Tīmūr at Samarqand. (27,28)

Phases of naturalism: *(from left to right)* spandrel in the Great Mosque at Damascus, dado from the Tāj Mahal, Agra, and Iznik tiles from the harem of the Topkapi palace, Istanbul. (29,30,31)

Curling tendrils, leaves and flowers form the exquisite stone screen of a window in the mosque of Sīdī Saʿīd, Ahmadabad, India. From the trunk of the tree grow twisting curved stems, forming shapes that from a distance seem abstract but are in fact organic and asymmetrical. (33)

A repertoire of foliated designs was used on the voussoirs of the *mihrāb* arch in the Great Mosque at Cordoba. The mosaic panels of arabesque do not correspond to the joints of the stones underneath. (32)

Arabesque in three dimensions: like other types of Islamic decoration, the arabesque may be applied to curved surfaces. Here, a subtle geometry underlies the carved luxuriant pattern on the dome of the tomb of Aqsunqur, Cairo. (34)

Water

Wealth, fertility and coolness are all associated with water, which is an essential part of Islamic architecture. Channels and pools are the most important elements of Islamic gardens. Originally necessary for irrigation, they were developed for their visual beauty and incorporated into elaborate architectural schemes. *Above*: a private garden near Mahan, Iran. The trees produce a sense of enclosure from the landscape. (35)

Pools gave a sense of repose and openness to the enclosed courtyard. In the Court of the Myrtles, in the Alhambra at Granada, water becomes part of a formal, rectilinear composition. (36)

Water enters buildings. In some of the most opulent Islamic palaces, water flows through marble channels from room to room, here and there expanding to fill basins and descending in cascades from one level to another. In the Red Fort at Delhi, water originally covered this inlaid and carved marble lotus, creating soothing sounds and continuously shifting patterns through its transparent motion. (37)

In the Alhambra, too, water emphasized the axes of the buildings, linking the various spaces in a directional sequence. Here we look through a series of arcades into the Court of the Lions. (38)

Sheets of still water act as mirrors, multiplying patterns and extending them beyond the limitations of the physical. This effect holds good whether the setting is open or confined. The reflection of the Hārūn Minār, near Lahore (*above*), is essential for creating a monumental impression. By contrast, in the courtyard of the Yūsuf Madrasa at Marrakesh (*below*) the reflected decoration enlarges the space, which is confined. (39,40)

Figures and animals

Despite the fact that figural and animal art was at all times discouraged, there existed a vigorous representational tradition in many Islamic countries. Figural sculpture in architecture is nevertheless extremely rare. The stucco decoration of the ruined Khirbat al-Mafjar (*below*), near Jericho, is exceptional: caryatid figures in the pendentives appear to support the dome. The horses (*right*) of a carved panel from Cairo have become almost abstract designs – a typical example of the Islamic tendency towards symmetrical pattern-making. (41, 42)

Heraldic animals (*above*) on fountains, gates or portals probably had a protective function. These are from Erzurum, Turkey. (44)

Courtly ritual is reflected in these figures from Qusayr ʿAmra, an Umayyad hunting lodge in the Jordan desert. (43)

Secular rulers could often patronize a figural art that would have been unthinkable in a religious context. *Below*: painted Iranian tiles showing a courtier. *Right*: stone angel from a building in Konya. *Below right*: warriors fighting, a tile panel from the Lahore Fort. (45,46,47)

Surface, Pattern and Light

DALU JONES

THE ROLE OF DECORATION is central to any analysis of Islamic art; it is one of the unifying factors that, for thirteen centuries, have linked buildings and objects from all over the Islamic world across an enormous geographic span, from Spain to China and Indonesia.

Islamic art is an art not so much of form as of decorative themes that occur both in architecture and in the applied arts, independently of material, scale and technique. There is never one type of decoration for one type of building or object; on the contrary, there are decorative principles which are pan-Islamic and applicable to all types of buildings and objects at all times (whence comes the intimate relationship in Islam between all the applied arts and architecture). Islamic art must therefore be considered in its entirety because each building and each object embodies to some extent identical principles. Though objects and buildings differ in quality of execution and style, the same ideas, forms and designs constantly recur.

If in their choice of forms the artists and architects of Islam were rarely innovatory, their preoccupation with surface decoration was highly original. They perfected a type of decoration whose purpose was first and foremost that of providing buildings and objects with an intricate and complex overlay, covering their structural cores (often of a different material) as with an outer skin or a 'mantle'. The textile metaphor is apt as there is a close interdependence between Islamic architectural decoration and textiles. Walls are reduced to borders, to enclosing curtains, and in turn are literally covered with textiles – hangings, carpets, curtains – so that the demarcation between the permanent parts of the buildings (the solid walls) in masonry, and temporary ones (tents, awnings or screens) in cloth, is very subtle.

In Islamic architecture decorated surfaces have a physical reality as well as a visual impact – an independence of their own, which gives them an importance at least equal to their architectural forms.

The fact that little furniture is needed for daily life in Islam – trays for food and mattresses for sleep are all moveable – also helps to create the sense of continuous space and decorative coherence that are characteristic of Islamic architecture. The layers of surface dec-oration are increased and the complexity of visual effects enriched by the use of carpets and cushions, which often reflect the same decorative schemes as those found on walls and ceilings. Floors and ceilings contribute to the fluidity of space by the nature of their decoration, since they are often patterned in the same manner as the walls; sometimes, in the case of floors, the decoration actually reproduces carpets. The tomb of I'timād ad-Dawla in Agra, for example, has an inlaid marble floor that exactly reproduces the designs of Mughal carpets.

There is a common misconception in the West: that Islamic art is an art severely restricted to two dimensions. Admittedly there are few examples of Islamic sculpture in the round, but the very character of Islamic decoration implies three-dimensional possibilities. One purpose of interlacing designs, for example, is to create the illusion of different planes, often accompanied by variations in colour and texture. Equally, the mastery of negative and positive contrasts is evident just as much in the minor arts as in the inlay and carved stone and tilework on a larger scale. Surfaces of buildings are provided with a series of interwoven layers of different textures and depths. This preoccupation with textured surfaces explains the presence of stucco and tilework in places where alternative materials exist. Even ceramic tiles, which generally make their impact by smoothness of plane, are not only animated by colour contrasts and intricacy of design but also appear counterposed to rougher materials like brick, or are themselves moulded in relief so as to produce maximum effects of translucency and glossiness and also of depth and thickness. Brick and stucco, in particular in Iran when applied to such buildings as the Qarraqan tomb towers or the minaret of Ardestan, demonstrate the virtuosity of Islamic craftsmen in the handling of materials to produce three-dimensional effects. Bricks are laid at an angle to cast maximum shadow and therefore increase depth of plane. Stuccoed bands of calligraphy bulge and recede or are incised so deeply as to appear to pulse and float against an equally patterned background. Masterpieces like the *mihrāb* of Pīr-i Bakrān near Isfahan and the *mihrāb* of Öljeytu in the Friday

161

Mosque of Isfahan itself are common in Iran and Central Asia, but there are also remarkable examples of three-dimensional stucco decoration in Egypt (Fāṭimid and later) and in North Africa and Spain. There again, *mihrāb* niches are filled with high rounded reliefs where three-dimensional, profusely foliated arabesques expand into hollowed bosses punched with different designs.

The development of artistic techniques throughout the range of Islamic art is always geared to creating increasingly intricate surface decoration by the use of reflecting and shining materials and glazes, the repetition of designs, the deliberate contrasting of textures and the manipulation of planes. However, despite this tendency towards effects of decorative richness and intricacy, there is always an ultimate sense of sobriety in Islamic art, surprising as this may seem in an art renowned for its sumptuousness and complexity.

Islamic art is an art of repose, intellectual rather than emotional, where tensions are resolved. It is a conceptual art where questions and answers are finely balanced. Absence of tension is achieved mainly through the subtlety of surface decoration in which patterns are limited to well defined areas but are at the same time infinite in the sense that they have unlimited possibilities of extension. The principles are of repetition and the continuous permutation of motifs and designs. Like water itself, which plays such a unique role in Islamic architecture, the decoration continually reflects and multiplies patterns to provide a 'cool' refuge for the eye and the mind, creating an art which is dynamic and yet unchanging.

This concept of decoration – flexible in nature, independent of form, material and scale – employs a limited number of basic formulae: calligraphy, geometry and, in architecture, the repetition and multiplication of elements based on the arch. Allied with and parallel to these are floral and figural motifs. Water and light are also of paramount importance to Islamic architectural decoration as they generate additional layers of patterns and – just as happens with surface decoration – they transform space.

Surface and space

Decoration in Islamic architecture is not limited to the covering of surfaces, it also helps to transform space.

Islamic buildings cannot always be clearly identified by their form because each form is not restricted to any one purpose; on the contrary, each form implies multiplicity of purpose and flexibility of space. The same structural combinations, the arcades, the domes, the vaulted *īwāns*, the high portals, can be applied to buildings as diverse as a palace, a stable, a school or a mosque. The same is true of the themes of their decoration, which can be entirely interchangeable.

Space is defined by surface and, since surface is articulated by decoration, there is an intimate connection in Islamic architecture between space and decoration. It is the variety and richness of the decoration, with its endless permutations, that characterizes the buildings rather than their structural elements, which are often disguised. Many devices typical of Islamic architectural decoration – for example, the *muqarnas* – are explained by a desire to dissolve the barriers between those elements of the buildings that are structural (load-bearing) and those that are ornamental (non-load-bearing).

The decoration underlines not so much the structures of buildings and the forms of objects as the interplay between forms and surfaces. The tendency is for surfaces to be fluid: decoration helps to make the transition, imperceptibly, from one plane to another. No sharp divisions are allowed. Light is filtered, water reflects, unifies and cools.

Another way of blurring the distinction between structure and surface is to use elements out of their normal structural context, for example by placing niches in ceilings (as is the case in Safavid buildings like the 'Alī Qapu palace in Isfahan, where niches, which would normally contain objects or pots, are cut out from the shell of the ceilings); the niched walls curve into the domed ceilings, thus changing the normal spatial order of domestic interiors. Similarly, *muqarnas* that are painted, tiled or lined with mirrors deny the association their shape might have with a structural purpose. Ambivalence is also clear in the decoration of the *mihrāb* of the Great Mosque at Cordoba where the voussoirs decorated with mosaic of different background colours do not correspond to the real arch blocks.

There is, too, an inherent ambivalence in Islamic designs. An abstract curving shape can be read as a bird; calligraphy is decorative as well as being a message conveying a precise meaning. The lines in a primary grid of a façade, as in certain arabesques or in 'Abbāsid woodcarving, transform a decorative element into the contour of a form. The same designs are reproduced side by side in different materials and for different purposes. For example, pierced screens are set in a façade next to blind arches identical in their shape and decoration to the screens, thereby disguising both the solid structure and the light openings. Changes of plane are often blurred by the use of dazzling optical effects created by related geometric designs along diverse but linked surfaces delimiting spaces of different shape.

Not only are structural elements such as the arch and column transformed on one plane as motifs for surface decoration or designs exchanged with the minor arts, but certain techniques and materials used to simulate others are applied, confusing the eye. Ceramic glazes, like lustre, which were originally used on pottery to imitate metalwork, are also used for wall tiles; bricks are interwoven; plaster imitates wood and even bricks.

The multiplication of a given pattern or architectural element on a different scale in one plane also helps to avoid sharp contrast and clear definition of scale and surface. Endless cadences of arches and columns, the multiplication of domes – the elements most typical of Islamic architecture – all create a feeling of continuous space. A square building with a dome – that is, a cube with a hemisphere – has no directional axes. A dome is a rotated arch; in a circular domed space there are no corners, edges or axes. The focus is inward towards the centre. The decoration supports this focusing inwards by inviting contemplation with its challenging but resolved complexity. A curve implies dynamism, the concept of change, of expansion. It extends the meaning of the form that is drawn or built by suggesting a change into the dimension of time. The builders of Islamic buildings very soon realized the dynamic possibilities of the arch as a form combining structural and decorative implications. Just as there were geometric patterns within geometric patterns in surface decoration, so the structural elements deriving from the arch, such as niches, squinches, pendentives, were multiplied, magnified or reduced, exploded and reconstructed endlessly in three-dimensional forms. Arches, squinches and niches occur both in a simple, straightforward way with a totally visible function or meaning, and in a multiplied form, complicated at times beyond recognition into meaninglessness, at least from the point of view of the element's original purpose. The squinch in particular occurs widely as an ornamental feature outside its functional use as a transitional element supporting the dome: magnified, it becomes a portal which in turn contains in its upper part multiples of itself – the *muqarnas*, the honeycomb decoration so characteristic of Islamic architecture.

The Tāj Mahal perfectly exemplifies this combination in a building of arches and squinches of different types and scale for structural and decorative purposes. Dominated by the main dome, each façade of the building has two tiers of three arched niches hollowed out of the principal mass. The portals in the centre of each side are but a magnification of these niches. They are in their turn each filled by miniatures of themselves, the *muqarnas*. The smaller-domed pavilions on the upper part of the building rest on open arches that echo the blind arches of the platforms on which the whole building rests. Each element of the decoration therefore reproduces a structural element.

The same arrangement of niches and arches is repeated in all the peripheral buildings within the Tāj complex – the gateway, the mosque, the guest house. There is a very close relationship between the main structural lines of the building and its decoration, which in its design not only follows the same proportions but echoes their repeated shape. A secondary grid controls the lines of the surface decoration proper – in this case the inlaid calligraphic bands and foliated designs.

A good example of the ambivalence of form and the flexibility of surface treatment in architectural decoration is given by the requirements set for the planting of flower beds in Islamic gardens. These are sunk so as to be seen from above like a carpet. At the same time, carpets must look like gardens. The 'garden' carpets, especially, reproduce the formal arrangements of gardens, their geometrical divisions, their water courses. If one imagines such types of carpets with their intricate floral designs laid on a patterned floor in a garden pavilion, it is possible to come closer to the idea fundamental to Islamic architecture of a continuity of space suggested by surface decoration.

Another example of the conceptual basis of much Islamic decoration is given by the floor decoration of the Tāj Mahal which, with its rippled effect, suggests that the tomb is set in a tank of water. The decoration, as in the case of garden carpets, does not imitate the water or the garden in precise details, but it conveys the idea of water or garden: it creates a situation, a 'landscape of the mind', a subtler environment than any naturalistic rendering.

General principles

While various strains can be detected in the decorative repertoire of Islamic architecture, several fundamental underlying principles are immediately apparent. One is the ubiquity of patterns in time and space, the interchangeability of the same design from one medium to another and the repetition of the same design on different scales, often within the same buildings. This can be explained by the fact that in Islamic decoration – whether applied to objects or buildings – each motif is merely part of an overall patterning of surface, achieved by the counterposition and superimposition of a variety of different designs and materials, each of which retains its identity within the whole composition. No single design or pattern need therefore be given significance or pre-eminence over others, and all can be reused at will in new yet familiar combinations.

Another constant feature of Islamic decoration is the expanding or diminishing property of each pattern, its capacity to be symmetrically repeated *ad infinitum*. Just as the volumes, the forms and the structural elements may be multiplied, so it is with their decoration. Each part of the design answers every other part and is capable of extension to infinity because the structure of the design is such that it can go on multiplying itself forever as a metaphor of eternity. Thus façades and wall surfaces are mostly decorated with symmetrical repetitions of units which in turn are made up of smaller repeated units.

There is, for example, an endless permutation of the *mihrāb* motif – an arched niche, either deeply recessed or shallow, contained in a rectangular frame. This motif is used indifferently in secular and religious buildings in western and eastern Islam. Façades, walls, even ceilings, are punctuated by rows of arched niches of various depth and scale. Striking examples of the use of this motif are found in Iran and India.

While individual components of the overall decoration of a building, a façade or a portal can be taken away or added to (as was literally the case with the addition of a hanging or the layering of carpets at certain times of the day and on certain special occasions), each of these individual components (or a substitute) is needed for the balance of the overall composition.

Another principle is that, however far from the viewer and however intricate the patterns within it, the design of each surface can always be discerned. Often the patterns are so intricate that they are only distinguishable by the rhythm they set up when they are repeated – still, the framework of the designs is always visible even when the details are not.

Wall surfaces in Islamic architecture are subdivided into several layers of designs, each one echoing elements of the other. Although sometimes difficult to detect because of the intricacy of pattern, the overlay of design is far from haphazard. The layering can vary but not the overall organization, where primary and secondary grids echo each other.

Primary grids indicate the principal elements of the decorative scheme. They control the calligraphic bands and the arches, niches, squares and rectangles by which each overall surface is subdivided. Patterns are mostly contained in rectangular or square panels, which are themselves strongly framed by horizontal and vertical bands. The framing bands of course produce a primary grid of their own, which reflects and underlines the contours of the building. This is frequently the case with the calligraphic bands which link façades with portals, secondary openings with the main portals and windows, or different patterned or textured surfaces. Their function is to hold these elements together visually, as if with a belt. For instance, in the architecture of Egypt, in particular, and in that of Norman Sicily of Islamic inspiration, calligraphic bands run continuously along the upper part of the exterior of buildings, terminating their walls with a secondary cornice and divide the lower parts of the walls into carefully proportioned areas.

Secondary grids control the patterning within each of the elements of the primary grid. Here are found the counterposition of designs and the contrasts of texture, materials, colours and patterns which produce the decoration of an inscription, a *mihrāb* or a portal. Within these secondary grids are also found the qualities of repetition which unify each element with the other and each surface with the rest of the building. These common elements within a decorative scheme harmonize and bring together the different designs and patterns that are found near each other but are visually different or contrasting.

Primary and secondary grids in Islamic decorative surfaces demand to be 'read' – literally in the case of calligraphy, which by its nature is directional. Calligraphic bands run across buildings, and the viewer, by reading their texts, also participates in a continuous recomposition of the elements of the decoration. Here again the analogy is with the applied arts, manuscript painting in particular, where the same principles are applied to the balance between decoration and calligraphy as on a façade.

Although at certain periods and in certain regions there are differences between the type of surface decoration chosen for the interior and exterior of buildings and where on the building it is applied, nevertheless there is always a correspondence of designs and materials between the two, and the same compositional principles are applied. Sometimes it is the same material or the same pattern that gives the key to the harmony of certain compositions, as they provide its common element. This is the case, for example, in the Madrasa al-ʿAttārīn in Fez, in Morocco, where rectangular stucco panels filled with a net of intersecting arches are repeated along the façades of a courtyard otherwise decorated with wood and tiles. At other times, as in the Court of the Lions in the Alhambra, at Granada, it is the odd discordant unit within a regular repetition of elements (the columns) that provides the link with an adjacent repeat, also regular but based on another mathematical progression.

Historical development

The story of decoration applied to Islamic monumental architecture falls into three broad chronological phases, although the impulses determining these phases sometimes run concurrently and overlap in different parts of the Islamic world, or recur at later periods. All three may be found operating at the same time, in the same country, on the same building or even the same object.

The Classical heritage: The first phase comprises the early centuries of Islam when, under the Umayyad dynasty in the 7th to 8th centuries, the techniques and the motifs are inspired by and follow logically from the inheritance of the late Classical world. Early Islamic monuments such as the Dome of the Rock in Jerusalem, the Great Mosque in Damascus or the palace of Khirbat al-Mafjar in Jericho show in plan, and even more in their decoration, how close was the art of early Islam to that of the civilizations preceding it, so much so that it is sometimes difficult to differentiate non-Islamic from Islamic buildings and objects. The old building techniques were still alive and probably much of the work continued to be carried out by craftsmen working in the Syrio-Byzantine and Sasanian imperial traditions. In buildings in various parts of the Umayyad empire, in Syria and Palestine in particular, but also as far south as Medina and Mecca in Arabia, wall and floor surfaces were decorated with mosaics, which in their subject-matter and technique are almost indistinguishable from those found in earlier Christian buildings. Mosaics were still being used in Spain in the interior decoration of the Great Mosque of Cordoba, in the 10th century, but, despite apparently short-lived manifestations under the Seljuqs, the Zangids and the Mamlūks in Syria and Egypt between the 11th and 14th centuries, this form of decoration gradually disappeared from the repertoire of Islamic art.

Wall- and floor-paintings are further examples of the survival of an ancient Classical technique into Islamic times. Again, as in the case of mosaics, the subject-matter, composition, technique and colour range of such paintings as those in the baths of Qusayr 'Amra in Jordan, with their nudes, signs of the Zodiac and hunting scenes, are a direct continuation of the Classical repertoire. Few early wall-paintings survive outside Syria and Jordan; fragments from the 9th century have been found at Samarra in Iraq, and others of the 10th century come from as far apart as North Africa and Afghanistan.

In Umayyad palaces, the decoration seems to make no particular differentiation between interior and exterior. Doorways and windows are framed with the type of continuous band that had been one of the striking and unifying elements of the Christian architecture of Syria. The stucco figures decorating façades and interiors have the prominent eyes and flesh folds of some of the Coptic sculptures from the convents and churches of Egypt.

A preference for overall patterning, repetition of elements, and intricacy is already clear in the stucco and stone decorations of the façades of the 7th-century palaces of Qasr al-Hayr al-Gharbī and Mshattā, with their regular diaper patterns contained in triangular, square or rectangular frames. The repetition of the same motif in different media – the row of birds in the paintings of Qusayr 'Amra, for example, transposed from painting into sculpture in Khirbat al-Mafjar – also shows this preference. At the same time the Classical repertoire of figures and floral motifs is interspersed, for instance on the screens of Qasr al-Hayr al-Gharbī (West), with diminutive architectural motifs such as the intersecting arches, columns and capitals. This successful eclectic fusion between the different cultural strains, the diverse legacy of the Classical world in the eastern Mediterranean – a compound of Graeco-Roman elements mingled with more Eastern influences – is immediately apparent in Umayyad buildings and forms a basis for the development of Islamic decoration. The same legacy is still apparent in 'Abbāsid buildings, although here the tendency is towards gigantic monumental architecture where the decoration had to be applied fast, cheaply, and on enormous surfaces. This explains the use of stucco on an unprecedented scale as a material for decoration, and its popularity, with tiles and brick, throughout the centuries in Islam. These three materials became in time the materials par excellence of Islamic decoration.

The various phases in the evolution of the 'Abbāsid style found in 9th-century Samarra punctuate the development of Classical motifs – the vine scroll, for example – into more abstract compact compositions where strong contrasts of light and shade are sought through deep bevelled carving. With the introduction of moulds it became possible to apply stucco panelling to even greater surfaces in a repetitive manner, principally as dados, giving 'Abbāsid interiors a continuous, sumptuous, monumental and plastic revetment. The similarity in design and treatment between stucco and wooden decorative elements is another factor in the coherence of 'Abbāsid decoration. Often motifs found in diaper patterns, deeply and smoothly carved in wood, are the same ones that give the stuccoed, compartmented dados their wavy, rippling effect. This type of overall stucco treatment for interior and exterior surfaces travelled far in the Islamic world; it is found, for example, in a mosque in Balkh in Afghanistan and at Nayin in Iran. By the 13th century a subtle difference between the mouldings suitable for interiors and exteriors was evolved in regions such as Khurasan although the repertoire of motifs remains virtually the same for both – an abstracted version of Classical designs including the vines and palmettes.

In the Fātimid buildings of North Africa and Egypt, the shell niche of Classical inspiration finds a new life through its Islamic 12-century interpretation. It becomes narrower and elongated and terminates in a rather rigid, fluted but angular head niche decorating the outer and inner walls of buildings – the mosque of as-Sālih Talā'i' (1160) in Cairo, for example – with rows of tall blind niches. The tendency to articulate façades with tall blind niches continues in Ayyūbid architecture and becomes one of the characteristics of Mamlūk architecture, when they run almost through the whole height of buildings.

Meanwhile Spain, almost up to the fall of its last Islamic dynasty in the 15th century, preserved the decorative schemes it inherited from the local Classical tradition (as it had survived mainly through Visigothic art) and from Umayyad Syria. These were to create an architectural decoration in marble and stucco which uses Classical elements such as the acanthus leaf and the palmette, but in compositions on one plane and in increasingly intricate combinations. The range of motifs used in Spanish architectural decoration remains limited throughout, probably because of the political and geographical isolation of the Peninsula from the rest of the Islamic world. Because of these limitations in range and in choice, there is also an increasing tendency towards virtuosity in the elaboration, permutation and repetition of motifs such as the intersecting arch, which appears in a simplified version on one scale and at the same time in a complicated version – as in the Great Mosque of Cordoba, where the arches are multilobed when structural – or appears applied serially in compartments to façades or to minaret towers.

Eastern influences: The second phase in the development of Islamic decoration derives from the non-Hellenized elements of the art of Persia and even further East. It is characterized by strong contrasts of plane and texture using stone, brick and stucco in various combinations.

From a tentative start in Mesopotamia, of which we see evidence at Raqqa, Ukhaydir and at Balis on the Euphrates, through to the fully achieved development in Iran, Afghanistan and Turkestan, remarkable decorative effects are obtained by a subtle use of geometric brick and terracotta patterns, sometimes combined with stucco and later with coloured glazed tiles. Particularly in the Iranian plateau at certain periods (the Seljuq especially), richness of effect is conveyed not by the richness of material but by the manner in which simpler and cheaper materials like stucco and brick are used. The decoration of the mosque of Ibn Tūlūn in Cairo, the older parts of the Great Mosque of Isfahan or the minaret of Jam all show monumental variations of the sophisticated use of these readily available materials. The tomb of Ismā'īl the Sāmānid in Bukhara (10th century) and the minaret of Mas'ūd in Ghazni (12th century) both show how imaginatively brick in different layers and contrasting shapes was used by Muslim craftsmen to create textured effects of striking monumentality. A similar effect was achieved in India in the Quwwat al-Islām Mosque complex at Delhi (12th century), but in carved sandstone. The materials are different, but the deep carving and the luxuriance and complexity of the designs are akin, as well as the general effect of a woven and brocaded covering.

From the 10th century onwards, the decoration of portals and *mihrābs* – the way into an actual or mental space – is increasingly emphasized, while the rest of the building is left relatively plain or is decorated with individual panels, inscription bands or rows of niches. The exuberant decoration found almost exclusively around portals and windows in the Seljuq stone buildings of Turkey is exceptional. Strong contrasts of plane, deeply recessed *muqarnas*, carved framing bands with geometric and plaited designs, heraldic figures – all produce an effect of engraving and at the same time of encrustation, of gigantic growth superimposed on otherwise rather plain façades. Thanks to their depth and tiered decoration these Seljuq doorways and windows become like caverns filled with stalactites.

By the 14th century, glazed tiles no longer appear sporadically as they had in Samarra or in Tunisia in the *mihrāb* of the Great Mosque of Qairouan and in palace architecture, but are combined with bricks or else used by themselves as a means to cover large architectural surfaces.

Colour: The universal application of glazed tiles marks the third phase of Islamic architectural decoration, together with an emphasis on colour rather than on texture. In the western Islamic world of Spain and North Africa, tiles are generally confined to the lower parts of walls and are mostly geometric in design. Sharp contrasts of dark and light colours – in the Alhambra, for example – are counterposed to produce star-shaped and chequered patterns of great visual complexity. Alternatively, harmonically related colours are used to define the geometric patterns of tile-mosaic panels and dados.

In Spain and North Africa, tiles and stucco are combined with carved wooden elements in very sober, geometrically and symmetrically determined schemes whereby the dados, windows and doors are underlined and framed and often set in plain or stuccoed walls. The Madrasa Bū-'Ināniyya in Fez and the interiors of the Alhambra exemplify this type of combination.

In later centuries floral designs and representations of imaginary or real buildings like mosques, tombs, *mihrābs* or the Ka'ba – compositions favoured in Istanbul and other parts of the Ottoman Empire – were introduced with overwhelming success in the North

African tile repertoire, particularly in Algeria, Tunisia and Libya.

In Iran and Central Asia, brick and tile often cover the whole surface of buildings as with a continuous wallpaper, the one textured, the other glossy and smooth. The tomb of Ismāʿīl the Sāmānid in Bukhara and the Friday Mosque in Isfahan best exemplify this almost excessive use of brick and ceramic in architecture. Contrary to the North African and Spanish custom, the dados in major Persian buildings are generally in marble. The palette for ceramic tiles is dominated by shades of blue and turquoise, punctuated by white, black and green as well as yellow and pink, in the later Safavid and Qājār periods especially.

This tendency towards an overall covering of the whole building whereby all inner and outer surfaces are decorated with ceramic, first with meticulously assembled tile inlays and later with individually patterned tiles, culminates in the Tīmūrid buildings of Iran, Afghanistan and Central Asia and the Safavid and Qājār buildings of Iran. Buildings such as the Masjid-i Shāh in Isfahan achieve their visual impact from the smoothness and 'coolness' of their tile decoration, which vividly contrasts with the plain brick colour of the surrounding buildings and the landscape, and through the subtlety of colour combinations and fluidity of designs combining floral scrolls and calligraphy.

The decoration of Ottoman architecture stands somewhat apart from that of contemporary architecture in other parts of the Islamic world in that it combines great sobriety in its exteriors, mostly in stone (discreet masonry *muqarnas* in corners, calligraphic inscriptions in stone or ceramic insets, marble screens and delicately carved stone panels) with lavish interiors, often almost entirely covered with tiles. There, a colour scheme of predominantly blues and greens, sometimes enriched by a very deep tomato-red, is characteristic.

Mughal buildings in India, although they rarely have tile decoration, reflect the same principles of decoration as those in Iran: they too aim at an overall effect, at total impact where there are no sharp contrasts of texture and the same type of design covers the whole building. In India, the effect is achieved with more precious materials, marble inlaid with hard and semiprecious stones. The result, however, is more sober than in Iran because the range of colour is limited, and the general effect sought is monochromatic, with an emphasis on white marble or red sandstone backgrounds. The Tāj Mahal appears almost translucent as if made of mother-of-pearl, though in fact it has a rich inlaid polychrome decoration inset in the white marble.

It is in this type of decoration that the relationship between architecture and the minor arts is closest. The designs of contemporary carpets, bookbindings and miniatures were probably devised by the same court artists and appear at the same time on precious objects as well as on a monumental scale on buildings.

Stone is superbly worked in India and in countries like Turkey, Egypt and Syria, which all have a long established tradition of stone-carving. But the boldness of the stone-carved decoration of Muslim India (the screen of the Quwwat al-Islām Mosque in Delhi, for example) or its delicacy when applied to marble reliefs (as in the tomb of Shaykh Salīm Chishtī in Fatehpur Sikri) are probably unparalleled in the Muslim world.

In Egypt, Palestine and Syria a sophisticated technique of stone-cutting is used to achieve effects of texturing which are not sculptural but are akin to marquetry in woodcarving. Joggled voussoirs of extraordinary complexity and inlaid panels of different stones are particularly characteristic of Ayyūbid and Mamlūk buildings. Immense skill is also used to achieve effects of inlay and contrasts of colour by alternating stone courses of different colours, a device preferred in Syria; or by mixing brick and stone, as in the arcading of the Great Mosque of Cordoba; or by contrasting different stones like red sandstone and white marble, the typical combination of many Indian buildings of various periods, for example, the ʿAlāʾī Darwāza and Humāyūn's tomb in Delhi or the mosque attached to the Tāj Mahal complex. The main volumes and the primary grids of these Indian buildings, the domes and the decoration of the portals, can be lined in white marble alone while the rest of the walls are in red sandstone. Marble articulates the façades: its role in this case is essentially that of definition. Elsewhere, as in Akbar's tomb in Sikandra near Agra, it is part of the building which is all in marble – in this case, the upper pavilion – while the lower storeys are in red sandstone punctuated by white marble insets.

Marble and stone carved in low relief of great beauty are also found at all periods in Spain and Egypt. In Cairo there are particularly delicate examples of this craft. In the Ottoman Empire, marble fountains and tombstones were gracefully carved with low-relief floral decoration.

Wood is used for screens, balconies, doors, ceilings and for the niched cupboards found in Ottoman domestic interiors. Perfect craftsmanship is displayed in the assembly of small pieces of wood fitted together in complicated inlaid combinations often in conjunction with ivory or mother-of-pearl. Most ceilings are made of carved wood, inlaid and often painted; lacquered panels and doors are occasionally combined with painted wood for the decoration of reception rooms. Striking effects are sometimes achieved with pieces of mirrors used in mosaic inlays. These were particularly popular in Qājār times in Iran and in Mughal India where a whole series of *shish mahalls* (palaces of mirrors) has survived.

The elements of decoration

Calligraphy: In the Islamic world, calligraphy is considered the most important of the arts because of its role in recording the word of God in the Qur'ān. Despite stylistic differences and local variations in script, the use of calligraphy in architecture is the element of decoration that has at all times done most to unify different types of buildings throughout the Islamic world. There are very few Islamic buildings, or indeed objects, which do not have somewhere on their surface an inscription – in Arabic if Qur'ānic, or in the vernacular if meant to record the names of donors, foundation dates, repairs or additions, or lines of poetry.

Calligraphy, like all Islamic decoration, is closely linked to geometry. In Arabic it is referred to as 'the geometry of line', implying that the proportions of the letters including the curved strokes are all governed by mathematical proportions. Inscriptions on buildings are generally written in an angular, sober and monumental script, *kūfī*, or in later more cursive styles, *naskhī* and *thuluth*. The range of variations between these basic types is immense, varying from century to century and from region to region. *Naskhī*, *thuluth* and *kūfī* bands can also be found in the same inscription, interwoven one within the other or superimposed, perhaps set out in different materials or colours.

In combination with late Classical floral decoration, as it evolved in the Muslim states of the Mediterranean after the first centuries of the Arab Conquest, calligraphy is applied to all parts of buildings in a variety of materials – stone, stucco, marble, mosaic and painting. Capitals in Spanish Muslim buildings, for instance, have calligraphic inscriptions as part of their decoration, sometimes against a background of tightly organized leaves.

The earliest Islamic buildings, such as the Dome of the Rock, already contained important inscription bands. The script at this time is a simple, well spaced, rather squat *kūfī*, in which Arabic letters have an angular regularity. By the 10th century calligraphy shares with other elements of Islamic decoration a multiplicity of planes and an emphasis on textured effects. Calligraphy then often becomes part of arabesque compositions, and letters themselves become floriated and foliated, appearing against a background of vegetal scroll. In a later development the vertical shafts of individual letters are plaited so as

to form a type of linear band decoration that has regular rhythmic and symmetrical proportions.

In the early periods, polychrome effects are achieved by painting or mosaic or by differences in materials, while after the 14th century tile-mosaic and marble inlay allow for thinness of line, subtle colour combinations, and sudden shifts of emphasis from one inscription to another. The mastery of the inlaid mosaic technique allowed calligraphers to display their skill on a very large scale, and designs that originated in the delicate pages of manuscripts are often found reproduced in architectural decoration.

Inscriptions are mostly used as a frame along and around the main elements of the buildings they decorate, portals and cornices in particular, although they are also found as part of an overall design in a diaper pattern arrangement on the whole of a façade, or alternatively they may be contained within a single panel. Single words are also repeated and arranged into patterns over the entire surface of walls or are contained in square, round or rectangular panels as well as in bands on minarets. The script generally used in this case is a very angular *kūfī*, called 'square' or 'sealed' *kūfī*. The words used in this manner are mostly the names of Allah and Muhammad, as well as those of ʿAlī and Husayn in Shīʿī buildings. Another favourite text for calligraphic compositions is the *bismillāh*, the habitual introductory formula to prayer. This type of calligraphy is mostly used in tile decoration in Persia after the 13th century but occurs also in Egypt, in Mamlūk buildings, in North Africa and in Anatolia. Sometimes calligraphic texts appear in pierced cartouches, providing a pattern for light filtering through windows. On minaret shafts inscription bands are clearly separated by bands of geometric or floral decoration, each band of inscription differing from the other in texture, calligraphic style and scale.

Religious inscriptions make visible the word of God. As such they are not only a powerful visual sign containing a specific religious message, but they also act as a sort of talisman for the whole building or object upon which they are inscribed. It has often been pointed out that many Islamic inscriptions are so positioned on the building or are so intricate as to be barely legible. This argument does not take into consideration the function of the inscriptions as a sort of badge or 'identity card', sometimes a talisman, immediately recognized by literate and illiterate alike, which by their presence immediately proclaim the cultural and religious affiliation of the building they decorate.

By lending itself to two simultaneous and partly contradictory functions – the iconographic and the ornamental – and by providing at the same time a legible message and a decorative motif, calligraphy solves, to some extent, a tension always latent in Islamic art between representation and abstraction; it gives an identifiable content to abstract patterns and thereby provides a substitute for the figural decorative repertoire of pre-Islamic and non-Islamic cultures.

Inscriptions have only recently come to be considered an essential element for the study of the iconographic content of Islamic architectural decoration. Scholars have shown that calligraphy in Islam not only identifies a building or its builder or patron but also identifies, clarifies and subdivides the functions of the building by emphasizing certain parts rather than others, thus in many ways acting as the abstract equivalent of the figural decoration in Christian buildings.

Inscriptions also link parts of buildings apparently different in purpose and decoration, unifying them through the symbolic associations contained in their text. The decoration of the exterior façade of the mosque of al-Aqmar in Cairo, for example, is better understood if one knows that the inscriptions on this façade are of the same type as those on the *qibla* wall inside the mosque, both being related to the 'Sūra of the light', which speaks of the light of God shining in a *mihrāb*. It becomes clearer, then, that the façade can be regarded as an exterior *qibla* wall, the portal functioning as a *mihrāb* for the man in the street. The inscriptions also explain that the window in the façade, really a pierced niche with a hanging lamp, is another version of the *mihrāb*. Similarly, the type of decoration applied in certain buildings to the background of some (but not all) calligraphic bands underlines the symbolic content of their text and its relevance to the design of the whole building. In the courtyard of Sultan Hasan's *madrasa* in Cairo, by virtue of the floral decoration in the continuous inscription band that runs along its walls – itself of large and monumental proportions – and of a text that uses metaphors for paradisic associations, the whole courtyard becomes a Paradise Garden. It is the place of repose, the symbol of the unity in God of the four religious schools that were meant to share the building.

Another dimension was later added to the already complex layering of designs found in the interior of buildings such as the Alhambra or the palaces and tombs of Mughal India. This was the introduction of verses of poetry, with their implied music, into the calligraphic and decorative repertoire. The type of calligraphy used, either *ta'līq* or *nasta'līq*, and its placing in the decorative scheme of each interior, would echo the rhythm of the verses themselves. Calligraphic architectural decoration in this case is perceived not only visually but also intellectually and musically.

Geometry: Abstract forms of geometric shape are found

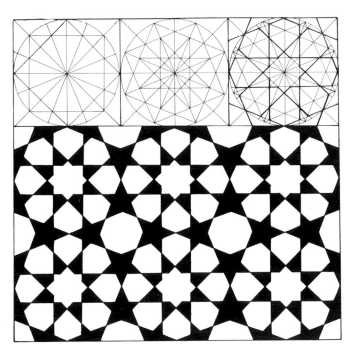

The making of a typical Islamic pattern. The circle generates an eight-pointed star. By filling in certain areas and leaving others blank, a pattern suitable for tile-making is evolved. (1)

throughout Islamic art and architecture in a bewildering variety of combinations at all periods.

Islamic art inherited the geometric patterns common to the later Classical world, but developed these to a degree of complexity and sophistication previously unknown, transforming decorative geometry into a major art form. These patterns clearly demonstrate the fascination of Islamic artists with the visual principles of repetition, symmetry, and continuous generation of pattern. Clearly the art of geometry is related to the study of mathematics and the other sciences (also derived from Classical sources), which were keenly pursued by the scientists and philosophers of Islam. Here also is found the close link that relates the visual arts in Islam to music and poetry through the same subtle manipulation of rhythms in controlled mathematical sequences.

The superb assurance of the Islamic designers is demonstrated by their masterful integration of geometry with such optical effects as the balancing of positive and negative areas, interlacing with fluid overlapping and underpassing strapwork, and a skilful use of colour and tone values.

Geometric patterns also form the basis for organizing the other decorative elements, being independent of scale and applicable to any material. More than any other type of design they permitted an interrelationship between the parts and the whole of a building complex, the exterior and the interior spaces and their furnishings.

The generating source of much Islamic design is the circle, with the radius functioning as a basic linear unit, and divisions of the circumference determining the system of proportion. The basic unit may be developed into a square, a triangle or a polygon. Squares, pentagons, hexagons and octagons, frequently star-shaped, are in turn often contained in circles. These forms are then elaborated by multiplication and subdivision, by rotation and by symmetrical arrangements. Designs can be subdivided and sections of the overall pattern can be given prominence to decorate borders or special sections within or around the main design.

One of the most common geometric patterns found in Islamic architecture is the star, which occurs in countless variations, with six to sixteen points, and in every material, scale and variety of application, from pierced window screens and woodwork to tile panels and embroidery. Frequently an overall pattern is imposed on a counterchange of patterns and is expressed in colours and materials that reverse those in the background pattern as it passes over them. This is particularly evident in Mamlūk inlaid marble decoration in Egypt, where striking optical effects are achieved by counterchanges and positive and negative patterning with inlay marbles of contrasted colours, combined with shiny materials such as mother-of-pearl or hard stones. Diagonal sequences in counterchange patterns are produced by the addition of yet another colour or texture to create a triple counterchange. Particular attention is paid to the principles of repetition and continuous permutation of design so that objects and their decoration seem to reflect only a fleeting impression, being but a portion of a design which can extend itself beyond the form it decorates and by implication beyond the world of reality. In the Islamic context these infinitely extensible designs have been interpreted as visual demonstrations of the singleness of God and His presence everywhere. They represent 'unity in multiplicity' and 'multiplicity in unity'.

Floral patterns: The artists of the Islamic world often observed nature faithfully, reproducing and interpreting it with a great deal of accuracy. A particular taste for naturalism was cultivated in the arts of the three great late Islamic empires, the Ottoman, the Safavid and, above all, the Mughal. Flowers and trees were depicted in manuscripts as botanical exemplars, or as motifs for the decoration of textiles, objects and buildings. This taste coincided with a similar contemporary trend in European art and architecture, and much borrowing took place between Europe and the East, especially India. In Mughal architectural decoration a curiously hybrid type of floral design emerged out of a combination of European botanical drawings, late Renaissance floral scrolls and acanthus leaves and local and Persian traditional flora. These designs were applied with supreme taste: monochrome panels of white marble, with rows of flowering plants exquisitely carved in low relief, alternate with delicately tinted polychrome inlays of precious and hard stones, set in marble or stone, which trace the outline of the same design or that of more intricate, abstract floral scrolls.

However careful the naturalistic reproduction of each plant, in the 16th century and later, plants and flowers occur in symmetrical and repetitive schemes. Isolated, they become the repeat element in diaper patterns on Indian, Persian and Turkish textiles, ivories, manuscript borders and architectural decoration. This overall floral patterning is applied indifferently to large-scale, monumental decorative compositions and to small objects. It is found on the tile revetments of Ottoman mosques like that of Rüstem Paşa and the royal apartments at the Topkapi palace in Istanbul, as well as on glass hukka bowls in India or silk textiles in Iran.

The sophisticated asymmetry of the floral repertoire of China had already disappeared when motifs such as that of the lotus were transposed from China and Central Asia into an Islamic context after the Mongol invasions of the 13th century. Equally, the freely composed vine and scroll motifs of the Classical world had evolved by the beginning of Islam into the strictly confined, regular and symmetrical overall designs found in the stucco decoration of the Umayyads and 'Abbāsids.

The arabesque: The possibility of scrolling or interlacing plant forms, already found in a naturalistic rendering in the Hellenistic art of the Near East and beyond (even as far as T'ang China) as well as the more abstract vegetal ribbons of the art of the Steppes, had given the artists of Islam the impulse to evolve more and more complicated designs. These designs are disposed symmetrically over the entire surface of objects or domes, or contained in bands or panels. From a motif originally centred on a stem, dividing surfaces regularly into recognizable abstract versions of the alternation of leaves and grapes, the vine motif of Classical times becomes, thanks to overlapping and interlacing, an overall pattern capable of unfolding in every direction. The ultimate extension of this tendency towards the denaturalization of natural forms is the arabesque.

The arabesque is characterized by a continuous stem which splits regularly, producing a series of counterpoised, leafy, secondary stems which can in turn split again or return to be reintegrated into the main stem.

This limitless, rhythmical alternation of movement, conveyed by the reciprocal repetition of curved lines, produces a design that is balanced and free from tension. In the arabesque, perhaps more than in any other design associated with Islam, it is clear how the line defines space, and how sophisticated three-dimensional effects are achieved by differences in width, colour and texture. Shapes left in the background contribute to this effect, as in geometric patterns, adding another dimension to the overall design.

The underlying geometric grids governing arabesque designs are based on the same mathematical principles that determine wholly geometric patterns. This explains why a certain type of Islamic geometrical decoration has sometimes been called 'geometric arabesque', although it does not always represent foliated designs. The term describes a specifically geometric architectural decoration based on the same principles of repetition and continuous self-multiplication as the arabesque.

The development of the arabesque from Classical vine tendril to extreme stylization happened very early in the Islamic world. The stone carvings on the façade of the 8th-century Umayyad palace of Mshattā consist of repeated triangular compartments enclosing curving vegetal scrolls; the motif here has already the greater intricacy, the denser ingrowing quality, and the symmetrical arrangement associated with the arabesque proper rather than with its immediate antecedents in Coptic Egypt, Greater Syria and Sasanian Mesopotamia.

With the fully developed arabesque, the Classical appurtenances of vases and cornucopias from which scrolls and acanthus leaves emerge in the Classical and early Islamic prototypes (like those in the mosaics in the spandrels of the Dome of the Rock) often become abstract designs; they are transformed into leaves and entwining stems. Leaves represent a direct prolongation of the main stem; stalks grow through leaves, and leaves develop into new stems in an endless process of self-multiplication.

By the 10th century, the continuous arabesque with ogee motifs, half-palmettes and overlapping stems was well established in the stucco, marble and mosaic decoration of the Great Mosque of Cordoba. By the 11th century, mature arabesque decoration was widely used on architecture in both Spain and Egypt. The classic arabesque of this period is that used in square panels on the façade of the Great Mosque of al-Hākim in Cairo, where interlacings are built up on geometric principles. By the 13th century, examples of arabesque are known in India in the Quwwat al-Islām in Delhi, combined with motifs from the Hindu tradition, the lotus scroll in particular.

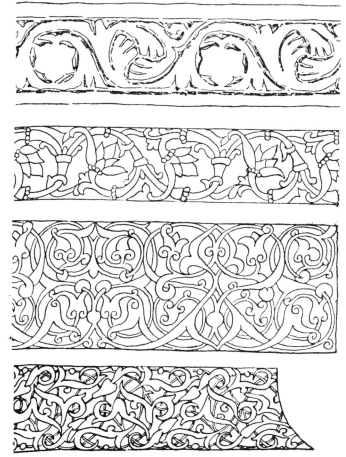

Four stages in the evolution of the arabesque. The decoration of the mosque of 'Amr at Fustat (top) is still close to the classical running spiral. A 13th-century panel of woodcarving from Egypt and a detail from the mosque of Sīdī 'Ukba at Qairouan show the basic pattern developing into the free and more serpentine forms. In the last example, a 15th-century Qur'ān from Granada, it has become a mass of writhing lines in a complex arrangement of overlapping layers. (2)

It was in the 14th century that different superimposed planes of arabesque designs became more clearly differentiated and, in the eastern part of the Islamic world, Iran and Central Asia in particular, were used on a large scale to provide overall monumental decoration for the outer surface of domes and great façade panels. This use of the arabesque in a magnified version does not appear in western Islam, with the exception of the monochrome stone-carved decoration of some Mamlūk domes in Cairo; these, however, cannot compare in dimension and polychrome complexity of tilework with eastern examples. It was in these regions too, that Chinese motifs were introduced into arabesque designs, perhaps copied from pottery or textile originals. Cloud bands, lotuses and peonies were inserted along the continuous line of stems. Masks and protomes of animals were combined with arabesques in compositions not unlike the grotesques of European architectural decoration.

The arabesque long fascinated Europe and the term has come to be synonymous with complex foliated designs. Already in 1480 Vasari had described a type of decoration very akin to the arabesque as being *alla damaschina*, that is, from Damascus and the Levant. Elsewhere, such designs were described as *à la façon arabicque*. The 'Moresques', collected in pattern books, were the designs inspired by these Damascene prototypes. Immensely successful, engraved in countless editions and used widely all over Europe by architects and craftsmen, the 'Moresques' and the 'knots' of the 16th century inspired a whole series of exotic designs and stimulated the imagination of many artists, in Italy, France and Northern Europe. The notebooks of Leonardo da Vinci show his interest in this sort of design, particularly in the linear interlacing, which he would have known from the metalworkers established in Venice.

In 16th-century Europe the term 'Moresque' was used to describe any intricate pattern inspired by the East, even arabesque proper, as in the case of those used by Dürer for the decoration of a celebrated ewer. A little later 'arabesque' became the term used for exotic designs in interior decoration, where figures were dressed in fanciful Eastern clothes and background and furniture were Easternized in a manner very similar to that found in the more famous *Chinoiseries* of the time.

Figures and animals: Like the iconoclasts who from time to time dominated early Christianity and Buddhism, the lawyers of Islam tended to discourage the depiction of figures, whether human or animal. Nevertheless, a vivid figural art is found at all times throughout much of the Islamic world, though admittedly mostly confined to miniature painting and the decoration of objects and secular buildings. Much of Islamic figural art belongs to the private world of the patron, both royal and mercantile, and in painting it is mostly devoted to the illustration of scientific treatises, heroic epics, romances, biographical accounts and erotica.

The iconography for the representation of Islamic rulers and the glorification of their princely life remains, on the whole, predominantly figural. In the Middle Ages, it derived its motifs from the international repertoire of royal attributes common to Islam, Christian Europe and Byzantium at the time. These were used in the decoration of buildings, princely and otherwise, and on objects. In the architectural context, most figural decoration is found in wall-paintings, on tilework and in sculpture.

The Umayyad was the first Islamic imperial dynasty and as such it adopted much of the imperial iconography of the Christian and Sasanian dynasties that had immediately preceded it. It often expressed its role as a world power by employing a sumptuous

figural imagery, painted and sculpted, in its palaces. Umayyad wall-painting is best preserved in the baths of Qusayr 'Amra. The subject-matter of these wall-paintings, however, is still not entirely understood. There are scenes of daily life, a zodiac, hunting and kingly scenes with the ruler enthroned and surrounded by attendants. There are also the fragments of paintings with figures and architectural landscapes from the palace of Khirbat al-Mafjar, which are clearly in the Classical tradition and are akin in subject-matter to the famous architectural landscapes in the mosaics of the Great Mosque of Damascus.

Figural sculpture is very rare in Islam, but fragmentary examples are known, again from Khirbat al-Mafjar, where stucco figures function as decorative caryatids in the spandrels of the pendentives of a domed chamber. There are also traditional effigies of the ruler and his courtiers on the main façade of Khirbat al-Mafjar and on the walls of another Umayyad palace, Qasr al-Hayr al-Gharbī, as well as lively representations of animals and birds. At the other end of the Muslim Empire, in Lashkari Bāzār, in the 10th century, hieratic figures painted in profile decorate the walls of the palace, and sculpted reliefs in stucco and stone have been found in Iran and Turkey. Sculpted animals also become integral parts of fountains, as base supports, as in the Court of the Lions in the Alhambra, or as decoration, as on a Spanish marble ablution basin in Marrakesh. Most Islamic palaces were similarly decorated with paintings and occasionally with sculpted figures or reliefs in wood or stone. These were generally stereotyped images of the ruler and his attributes, and of the courtly life. During the 13th century, and occasionally before, a great number of lustre-painted tiles were individually decorated with figural and animal designs. Sometimes they were framed by calligraphic bands containing proverbs and good wishes. These tiles were cross- and star-shaped and would fit one with the other into a regular geometric pattern, running as a dado along palace and house walls. In North Africa there were round and square wall tiles with figural designs also fitting together to form a continuous pattern. Another form of princely figural or animal decoration is the use of stone reliefs for heraldic devices, particularly in Seljuq Turkey, Iraq, Syria and Egypt. These devices, when they were not just personal emblems, might have had a protective function as well as indicating tribal and totemic affiliations. Heraldic eagles, lions and symbols of the zodiac, dragons and angels, often decorate and protect the façades of religious complexes as well as city walls, gates and bridges.

Towards the 16th century in Safavid Iran a new style of wall- and tile-painting evolved, partly under

European influence. These paintings represent court and battles scenes, courtiers banqueting, and stereotyped portraits of individuals. Their style, however, is not that of murals but of miniature painting. The images are merely extended to fit the larger scale.

In Qājār Iran a curious neo-Sasanian style was current for stone sculptures and tile panels in which the rigour of European neo-Classicism was blended with reminiscences of the imperial style of the large stone reliefs carved in Iran under Sasanian royal patronage.

Light: A mystical symbolism has been attributed by some authors to the careful control of the sources and play of light in Islamic architecture. For those writers, light is the symbol of divine unity, and they believe that 'the Muslim artist seeks to transform the very stuff he is fashioning into a vibration of light'. In addition to having a religious dimension, light has in Islamic architecture a decorative function which is twofold: it modifies other elements of decoration and it originates patterns.

Architectural elements in Islamic buildings and the materials chosen for their decoration are often shaped so as to reflect, refract and be transformed by light and shade. There is a subtle use of glossy floor and wall surfaces to catch light and often to throw it over the facets of diamond-shaped ceilings, which in turn reflect it back. The *muqarnas* trap light and refract it; ribbed domes appear to rotate according to the time of day. Façades appear to be made of lace-like materials and become transparent screens when the sun strikes their stucco decoration – deliberately pierced and fashioned to create this effect of disembodiment. Mirrors, lustre tiles, gilt wood and polished marble all shine, glitter and reflect in the strong, harsh light of the Islamic countries.

In this sense light, like water, contributes a dynamic quality to Islamic architectural decoration. It extends the patterns, forms and designs, into the dimension of time. As the day progresses, so the forms change according to the angles of light and shade, as in a kaleidoscope. Light and shade create strong contrasts of planes and give texture to sculpted stone and stuccoed or brick surfaces. Water and light, alone and combined, provide a mobile projection of patterns. As light filters through wooden *masharabiyyas*, stucco and marble screens and patterned coloured glass windows, it projects further patterns on the surfaces behind and beneath, an evanescent and everchanging overlay of colours and shadows. The effect is sometimes intensified by the artificial lighting system used. Hanging glass lamps, decorated with painted calligraphy and geometric and floral patterns and often held in perforated and patterned metal containers,

were intended to cast not a clear beam but a patterned projection on to already patterned surfaces, creating extra layers of design. The patterns on the lamp would be of the same type as those on the walls and ceiling and therefore would produce a harmonious environment both dynamic and restful.

The range of effects in Islamic architecture achieved through the variation of light screens is extraordinary. These effects seem to have been consciously pursued from the earliest centuries of Islam, for already in Umayyad times there are geometrically patterned stone or stucco windows – monumental examples exist from Khirbat al-Mafjar – that indicate a preoccupation with patterned light effects. The impetus might have been given by similar devices common in the late Classical world, where windows and screens which carried geometric designs were used. But the effect of one design superimposed on another by light projection is peculiarly and ubiquitously Islamic.

The most sophisticated application of pierced screens is found in Mughal buildings in India. There, walls are often completely replaced by sandstone or marble screens so as to provide privacy and at the same time allow cool breezes to run through the interiors. The designs on the screens are geometric or floral and contained in compartments. A particularly subtle example is found in the tomb of Shaykh Salīm Chishtī at Fatehpur Sikri where the outline of a *mihrāb* niche is part of the design, so that structure, decoration and symbolism are one.

Water: Water is an essential complement to and an illustration of the nature of Islamic architectural decoration. Its use for decoration as well as for coolness is best seen in house and palace architecture rather than in religious buildings, where the paramount function of water is for ritual purposes – although the pools and fountains in the courtyards of Iranian or Moroccan mosques and *madrasas* are an important complement to the architecture. But it is in the gardens and the palace and tomb architecture of Mughal India and Spain that are found the best surviving examples of the sophisticated and combined uses of water for symbolic, decorative and practical purposes. There, water is not only a mirror to reflect the architecture and multiply its decorative themes, but a means of emphasizing its visual axes. The straight-sided pools and the channels that feed them make a set of controlled and geometrically defined frames which provide a counterpoint for the grids of the architectural scheme, and subtly divide space into the right mathematical proportions. Pools of water also multiply the images they contain, and distort their reality; like the decoration they mirror, they are immutable, yet constantly changing; fluid and dynamic, yet static.

Sheets of water, strictly defined and geometrically organized, are found not only in the open spaces surrounding buildings, as in the gardens of the Tāj Mahal or the Chihil Sutūn, but also in more confined spaces, at the centre of courtyards, as in the Alhambra in Granada or the Bū-'Ināniyya Madrasa in Fez. Here, water helps to convey a sense of repose and coolness and, more importantly, by its mirror effect, openness and breadth to spaces that are often small and always enclosed.

But water also enters buildings – it is part of the internal decoration of certain Islamic buildings, palaces in particular. Fountains, channels and the *shādurwān* (weir) are all integral parts of the furnishing of Islamic interiors. Rooms are often divided by a central pool or channel, which provides both coolness and the pleasing sound of trickling water. Here, too, not only does water reflect the decoration but it gives it another, more opulent dimension, because of the natural association in the Islamic world among wealth, fertility and water.

A beautiful example of interplay of light and shade filtered through marble screens and projected on a stream of water is found in the interior of the Rang Mahall, a pavilion in the palace complex of Shāh Jihān in the Red Fort in Delhi. There, water is channelled in an open canal that runs through the whole length of the building, in and out of rooms, under screens and platforms, cutting through the floor which it decorates and of which it forms a part. It also unifies the entire layout of the palace, linking all the pavilions in a directional sequence. On a more modest scale, domestic fountains in reception rooms were very common, certainly in Sicily, Egypt, Syria and Turkey. Generally it was the *shādurwān*, a slab of decorated marble, monochrome or inlaid, tilted at an angle to permit a gentle flow of water over its surfaces, which provided the opportunity for a clever interplay of patterns between the running water and the textured surface underneath it and their reflections on ceilings and walls.

A spectacular combination of the functional and decorative uses of water allied to architecture is found, of course, in Islamic gardens, those of the Mughals in particular, where it is true to say that water, more than soil and vegetation, is their most important element. Here again, as in the terraced garden of Amber resting in its artificial lake, the whole decorative repertoire of Islamic art is found harmoniously combined, although the palace was built for a ruler who in fact was not a Muslim. The beds are patterned in a geometric combination of stars and polygons that was widely adopted elsewhere throughout the centuries, in endless permutations, for tile revetments, on metal and pottery objects, and on costumes. The pavilions have pat-terned screens with similar or contrasting designs. The whole complex is mirrored and framed by the sheet of water that surrounds it. And the garden is but a part of the great palace which towers above it and which in turn has in its interior a sequence of pavilions, courtyards, fountains and pools and channels of water decorated with variations of the same designs.

Islamic sources

The writings of the great Islamic travellers of the past include accurate descriptions of buildings, their dimensions and materials, the time needed for their construction, as well as their cost, their patrons and sometimes the astrological signs connected with their foundation. But the descriptions are mostly lacking in technical terms and in detail of building methods, design and decoration, even when the buildings were spectacular or unusual. However, the occasional references to the richness of material used and to its polish and glitter give a precious clue to what were considered, throughout the centuries of Islam, the requirements for a successful and pleasing building.

The Sūfī interpretations – mostly by European scholars – of the geometric patterns reflect a general mystical approach to Islamic art, rather than a knowledge of specific texts giving exact instruction to decorators of buildings and objects. Although an oral tradition obviously existed, so far as we are aware, no documentation, pattern books or theoretical treatises have survived from the Islamic world, with a few untypical exceptions from Spain, as they have from the European world, to tell us what aesthetic criteria the builders used as guidelines for the decoration of buildings. There is no Islamic equivalent to Vitruvius's famous three orders. A paper fragment, probably of the 12th century, shows an arch and a roundel with calligraphic decoration, of the type that can be seen on a 12th-century Egyptian façade. Although by no means certain, this might be an indication of how motifs for architectural decoration were transmitted on paper in the early centuries of Islam; probably groups of craftsmen specialized in certain techniques and motifs and brought their unrecorded repertoire with them from one job to another. This is not surprising as Islamic art was the art of a community, not of individual artistic personalities, and the situation was akin to that of Europe in the Middle Ages, where pattern books were used by more or less gifted craftsmen.

Russian scholars have found in Central Asia later paper fragments with geometric designs. These might have been transferred from paper to plaster to indicate the guidelines for the main pattern. Alternatively, it seems that designs were incised in the wet plaster. These, however, are indications of the existence of a system of transmission of techniques, not criteria for aesthetic choices.

In later centuries, however, and in particular in the Ottoman, Safavid and Mughal empires, individual calligraphers and illuminators are known; they designed the decoration of buildings and signed their work. The mosque of Rüstem Paşa (1561) in Istanbul is a particularly sumptuous example of close collaboration between the artists of the same imperial atelier working in different media. Here, the tiles that decorate the interior of the mosque – a masterpiece of Sinān – constitute a sort of pattern book of the best designs available at the Ottoman court at the time. The tiles with inscriptions were designed by master calligraphers and made to fit closely within the architectural scheme devised by Sinān for the mosque. Similarly, the floral tiles display the whole repertoire of designs available to the court painters. Other examples exist, from India and Iran. European designs were introduced to the Islamic world through pattern books and also through engravings and textiles. But the part played by European craftsmen themselves working at Islamic courts (in the decoration of Mūghal buildings in particular) is still not clear.

It is the minor arts that provide the evidence missing for the architecture of certain periods and give a clue to its aesthetics. Miniatures in manuscripts, for example, accurately portray the decoration of buildings and their use. A famous miniature by the great Persian painter Bihzad, for instance, shows a mosque being built in Iran, and it is clear from this painting that the decoration of the building was a separate, second phase in its construction. Similarly, another masterpiece of Persian painting – a miniature of a building in ruin – shows how a mosaic of tiles forms a thin layer of covering over a coarse structural core of bricks.

The western view of islamic decoration

Since the great studies of Owen Jones (1842–5), Prisse d'Avennes (1877), Bourgoin (1899) and others of the last century, rare attempts have been made at a comprehensive study of the role played by decoration in Islamic architecture and art. Geometric Islamic patterns have been much discussed and their mathematical principles studied, but seldom with a view to identifying the historical development and the geographical spread of the patterns or – more importantly – to investigating the nature of their relationship with the architectural elements of the buildings they decorate.

Many of the books on Islamic geometric design share with Jones's *The Grammar of Ornament* a desire to stimulate new creativity in pattern-making and in architectural design. In origin, these books were didactic, aimed at improving the aesthetic standards of Western architecture. Today, the same trend can be observed though the same geometric patterns of Islam are now asked to provide not merely aesthetic but also moral and philosophical guidelines. The bias is towards mystical interpretation rather than art historical research.

On the whole, there has been a tendency among writers to dismiss all Islamic decoration as stultifying or as excessive in its richness. Many books on Islamic art and architecture still talk of an art obsessed almost hysterically with a compulsive *horror vacui*, in which individual objects or buildings may be admired but most are 'over-decorated'. The image of the over-rich quality of Islamic decoration was encouraged by travellers' tales from Herbert (16th century) to the great Victorians, all of whom shared a fascination with and a puritanical dislike for the decorative excesses of the East.

They contrasted the apparent rigour of European neo-Classicism, or the symbolic content of Gothic, with what appeared to be a clutter of different but always 'rich' materials and designs, useful only when copied discreetly and used out of context in 'tasteful' interiors. Yet the clutter was Rococo or Victorian rather than Islamic. Admittedly, few Europeans were acquainted until recently with Islamic architecture at its best and *in situ*. Mostly they knew drawings and objects, particularly those seen at the great exhibitions in London and Paris, which tended to show commercial exports rather than works of art. This confusion still exists to a certain extent between the European idea of clutter, excess and richness, and the careful superimposition and layering of textures and designs that characterize Islamic decoration.

One exception was Owen Jones, who saw in the Alhambra the perfect embodiment of the principles of decoration he wanted to sponsor and revive. His articles in *The Grammar of Ornament* state this clearly:

> The Moors ever regarded what we hold to be the first principle in architecture – to *decorate construction, never to construct decoration*: in Moorish architecture not only does the decoration arise naturally from the construction, but the constructive idea is carried out in every detail of the ornamentation of the surface.

> We believe that true beauty in architecture results from that *repose which the mind feels when the eye, the intellect, and the affections are satisfied, from the absence of any want*. When an object is constructed falsely, appearing to derive or give support without doing either the one or the other, it fails to afford this response, and therefore can never pretend to true beauty, however harmonious it may be in itself: the Mohammedan races, and Moors especially, have constantly regarded this rule; we never find a useless or superfluous ornament; every ornament arises quietly and naturally from the surface decorated.

6 Vernacular Architecture: The House and Society

GUY T. PETHERBRIDGE

A rich heritage of vernacular systems of building has developed in the various environments which make up the Islamic world. Informed interest in these constructions is still relatively recent, but they must certainly claim a place in any comprehensive survey of Islamic architecture. It was from vernacular building technologies, with their intimate knowledge of local materials, that the better known monumental constructions were derived. Indeed, in expressiveness, vigour and virtuosity, popular architecture often rivals the grander metropolitan creations.

This massive portal is from the Wadi Halfa district of Sudanese Nubia, now flooded by the Aswân Dam. Made in 1944, its coloured mud-relief decorations include a water-wheel between two trees above the lintel. Invasion of domestic privacy in Islam is discouraged by a formidable system of religious, legal and social prohibitions so that the house entrance – the vulnerable threshold between the household and the public – is accorded particular symbolic importance. (1)

Records of an architectural past

The transient architecture of past centuries is evoked for us by the depictions of European travellers and occasional fragmentary remains of cities and dwellings. *Above left:* a town on the lower Nile, painted by a Venetian artist about 1565; the tall spire-like structures are pigeon towers. *Above right:* Timbuktu in 1830, after a watercolour by the French explorer Caillie showing the rectangular mud-brick style introduced by Islam co-existing with indigenous African shelters. *Below:* the ruins of the old city of Bam, south-eastern Iran, preserve an almost complete record of a historic Islamic urban environment. (2, 3, 4)

Cairo (*right*) impressed travellers by its multi-storeyed houses on the banks of the Nile, with their projecting screened balconies and wind-scoops rising from the roofs to channel the prevailing north breezes into the rooms beneath. (6)

An Egyptian village in 1802 (*right centre*). Low blank walls enclose courtyards; next to them stand pigeon towers used to collect fertilizer, similar in function to the Iranian examples shown in pl. 36. (7)

The shores of the Bosphorus were once lined with waterside pleasure villas. These *yalıs* represent the most sophisticated development of a style of wooden-frame construction typical of Turkish building in the Balkans and Anatolia. Upper storeys are cantilevered out to gain additional space as well as to exploit the view, a constant preoccupation in Ottoman domestic architecture, as reflected in legal ordnances. (5)

The men's reception room, where guests can be entertained without interfering with the life of the *haram* (or *harem*), is a necessary feature of the Islamic house. This engraving, dated 1782, after a drawing by the French traveller Count Choiseul Gouffier shows the summer reception room of a wealthy Turkish house, with the host and most important guests seated on the upper level. (8)

179

Regional styles

The **inventiveness** of the village builder – both structural and plastic – transforms the elementary building materials of stone and mud into an astonishing variety of regional house-types. An Afghan village (*below left*) consists of houses with domed mud-brick chambers grouped around courtyards, in which are pitched the tents of nomadic relatives, constructed of felts tied around collapsable wooden frames. On the border of Turkey and northern Syria (*below centre*), houses consist of clusters of beehive domed chambers. The same type of construction is used for ovens and granaries. (9, 10)

Around the mosque and its tall minaret cluster the whitewashed houses of a Kharijite community in the M'zab in Algeria, one of five adjacent similar walled towns. The purist principles of this fundamentalist sect are reflected in the austere undecorated architecture. (12)

◁ **Tower-houses** are characteristic of the upland areas of the western Arabian Peninsula, such as these in the city of Marib, central Yemen (*left*) built on its ancient *tel*. The settlement is unprotected by walls, each house becoming a fortress in times of trouble. The whitewashed reception room (*mafraj*) is visible on the upper storeys of some of the buildings. (11)

In southern Tunisia (*right*) and neighbouring Libya, the houses use vaulting systems going back to Roman times. This village, Takrouna, has courtyards flanked by longitudinal and cross barrel-vaulted rooms. The houses are whitewashed to consolidate their plastered walls and protect them from the winter rains. (13)

The Islamic house: the public face

Niger: where vegetation permits, nomadic shelters may be built of plant materials. In this Tuareg encampment, grasses are woven into a framework of bent branches; the compound is protected by a wattle fence. (14)

Yugoslavia: in colder and rainier areas like the Balkans, activities that in the central areas of Islam would take place out of doors have to be under cover. Hence the survival of closed structures with high pitched roofs, as in these village shops and houses in Herzegovina, Yugoslavia. The half-timbered construction, with mud-brick and wattle-and-daub infill, is plastered over and whitewashed. (15)

Saudi Arabia: in Abha, houses have successive mud courses separated by bands of downward projecting stones, to prevent the frequent rains from eroding the walls. (16)

Nigeria: the old city of Kano demonstrates the decorative expressiveness of much sub-Saharan architecture. Corner pinnacles on the houses have an apotropaic function, and the principal chambers are given prominence by elaborate external reliefs, characteristic of the Hausa culture. The main building material is cob (puddled mud). (17)

Egypt and Iran: folk-painting illustrating local life and customs in the Nile Delta (*above*), and (*right*) thatch-roofed farmsteads of the rice-growing region of Ghilan. (18, 19)

In Mecca, the holy city (*left*), the façades of tall multi-storeyed houses are embellished with a multiplicity of screened openings of brick or wood. (20)

West Anatolia: in the town of Sivrihisar, the brick infill of the half-timbered building is left exposed in decorative patterns. (22)

Cappadocia: only occasionally in Islam has a vernacular tradition of fine stone masonry developed. In central Anatolia the local volcanic tufa is easily dressed and carved into a variety of fine decorative and structural elements. (23)

Tunisia: the blank walls of Tozeur are unrelieved except by fine burned brick decoration, and exemplify the way the Islamic house turns its back upon the world. (21)

183

The Islamic house: the private core

Public and private life are strictly demarcated in Islamic society, and even within the house degrees of privacy are expressed architecturally, the most fundamental division being between male reception areas and the *harem*, the family sanctum. The interior courtyard house is the ideal expression of these concepts. Although an austere façade is presented to the outside world, the interior courtyard is a place where the family is free to work and relax.

A room where guests can be entertained and major family occasions celebrated is included in the Islamic house wherever economically possible. It is usually the most decorated room in the house, in which the family's most precious possessions are displayed. In this winter room in a house at Çavus In, Cappadocia, carved decoration is concentrated on the fireplace and window arches. (25)

A townhouse in Isfahan, Iran, has all the elements of the ideal Islamic domestic environment: a sheltered courtyard with trees, a pool, outdoor furniture and a shady *īwān*. (24)

Flat roofs serve a variety of purposes in the hot areas of Islam: storing and drying foodstuffs and, as in this house in Rajasthan (*right*), as a sleeping area. The roof's status as a normal living and working area is clearly indicated by the permanent staircase leading to it. (26)

The shady courtyard of a fine Mamlūk house in Cairo epitomizes the elegant wealthy townhouse architecture of the large commercial centres of the Near East. Constructed in fine stone ashlar, this verdant courtyard repeats many of the elements of the Isfahan house opposite. (27)

The earliest detailed depictions of the interior of the Islamic house are the miniatures from the *Maqāmāt* of al-Harīrī, painted in Iraq about 1230 A.D. This illustration depicts the visit of Abu Zayd to a house in Kufa. He knocks at the exterior door on the right and is admitted into an interior with a galleried upper floor. The structure on the roof is a ventilating tower enclosed in reed mats which can be opened to the prevailing breeze. (28)

Rural strongholds

An isolated watch-tower (*left*) in the Jafarah plain of northern Libya guards the approaches to the populated plateau of the Jabal Nafusa. This type of fortified tower, usually with machicolations, is extremely widespread and can be considered the prototype of the defensive tower-house. (29)

Fortified ksars of Ait Benn Haddu, south of the Atlas Mountains in Morocco. In parts of Islam where topographical conditions precluded strong central administrative control, fortified houses and communal structures were necessary for tribal security. These forms have persisted as the regional architectural type even when the need for defence is no longer paramount. (30)

The **tower-house** may preserve its defensive characteristics even in walled urban areas, as in this example at Sa'dah, north Yemen. Note the impenetrable aspect of the lower floors, and the machicolation high above the entrance door. (31)

The Islamic legacy in the Balkans survives in fortified tower-houses like this one in the mountain village of Rozago, Montenegro. The lower storeys are of stone, with a cantilevered wooden upper storey containing the living quarters. (32)

Communal fortified storehouses are characteristic of North Africa: a circular enclosing wall, with a single guarded entrance, is made up of superimposed barrel-vaulted storage chambers. (33,34)

Industrial vernacular

The versatility and the depth of knowledge of practical technology possessed by traditional Islamic craftsmen is best evidenced in utilitarian structures serving the highly specialized needs of environmental control, industry and agriculture. Although these buildings are realized within the formal limitations of local bulding traditions, their special requirements have sometimes led to spectacular architectural expression.

Weavers' huts (*above*), on the island of Djerba, southern Tunisia, are semi-excavated so as to take the lateral thrust of the transverse-arched vaults of the roof. (35)

Pigeon towers (*above*) near Isfahan. Groupings of cylindrical towers, decorated with bands of folk-motifs, house the pigeons, who enter through the central turrets. (36)

Rows of windmills (*below*) with apertures open to the prevailing winds are found in Sistan, eastern Iran. Vertical vanes of reeds power the millstones below. (37)

Water-mill (*below*) at Jajce, Bosnia. The water is channelled to gush against a horizontal paddle, which turns the mill-stone, here mounted in the wooden super-structure. (39)

Wind-towers (*above*), used in Iran to ventilate houses, are also constructed to cool underground cisterns, as in this example in Yazd, its dome of patterned brick projecting above ground level. (38)

Ice-house (*below*) at Kerman, Iran. Ice, formed during frosty winter nights in shallow channels protected from the sun's rays by the high wall, is packed between layers of straw in the mud-brick dome. (40)

Popular worship

The basic architectural requirements of Islamic worship are few and can be supplied by the simplest vernacular resources. *Left:* mosque and minaret on Djerba. (41)

Contrasting means, identical ends. ▷ Mosques at Travnik, in Bosnia (*below*), and Zaria, northern Nigeria (*opposite*). The mosque at Travnik is directly related to the indigenous dwellings of the area, differing principally in scale – as does the Zaria mosque, which utilizes the indigenous Hausa vault of arched mud-plastered palm trunks to support the roof. (42, 45)

Cities of the dead. *Above:* the tomb of Shaykh Ammi Saʿīd, Mʾzab, Algeria. *Left:* necropolis of Minieh, Egypt. In many areas of Islam, funerary architecture has taken the form of a dome set upon a square chamber. In these examples, the smallness of scale of the tombs and the plasticity of the mud medium has allowed the builder to sculpt free shapes, untrammelled by structural considerations. (43, 44)

A nomad tent next to a fortified farm exemplifies the range of Islamic vernacular architecture – from light mobile shelters of perishable materials to massive domestic defensive structures. The scene is Bamiyan, Afghanistan. (46)

The House and Society

GUY T. PETHERBRIDGE

In 1854, a French observer of colonialism in Algeria, wrote: 'The Muslim Algiers that we found in 1830 is falling to pieces under the indifferent eyes of the European crowd. The imposition of regular street plans is ripping it apart and legal injunctions in the interests of public security are causing it to be pulled down. The invading fleet of our population with its antipathetic attitudes to the indigenous architecture is obliterating it, or at least altering it profoundly, everywhere it reaches. Within a quarter of a century, a Moorish construction will be as much a curiosity to the inhabitants of Algiers as to the European tourists.' Half a century later, in 1911, Ernest Richmond, Director of Public Buildings for Egypt, addressed the Royal Institute of British Architects on the subject of indigenous Egyptian building techniques: 'If . . . local methods do not provide all that is needed in an age of change and activity, they are at any rate, though perhaps curiously, adapted to the physical conditions of the country; and an architect will lose nothing by studying them respectfully.'

This acknowledgment of the significance of Islamic popular building traditions is atypical. Those interested in Islamic architecture have been primarily concerned with monumental structures, both extant and documented in written sources, and with the personages responsible for their conception, construction and decoration. Such buildings are characterized by their uniqueness, permanence and luxury of construction, and were built to impress God and the populace with the piety and power of the patron and his lineage. Monuments and public buildings do not, however, exist in isolation but play a particular symbolic role in a total spatial and hierarchic system of building and decorative forms, serving to reinforce political and social structure and religious belief. Because of their status and massiveness of construction, such buildings tend to survive while associated domestic and utilitarian complexes of a contemporary date are destroyed. To consider monumental architecture without these associated complexes is to create an unbalanced and perhaps erroneous impression of the nature and development of Islamic architecture and its relationship to the society that formed it.

Islamic society, in which every member is acknowledged as being equal in the eyes of Allah, is actually divided into two broad social groupings; the *khāssa*, the educated wealthy stratum, usually of respected lineage, occupying positions of temporal and spiritual authority; and the *ʿāmma*, the majority of urban and rural humanity. It was the *khāssa* who were responsible for the building of the major mosques, mausolea, palaces, *hammāms*, caravanserais, bridges and other civil engineering works, but these technical and artistic achievements represent only a minor proportion of total building activity at any period. The neglected architecture and the traditional building techniques of the *ʿāmma*, the vernacular matrix, is the concern of this chapter.

The historical background

The scale and rapidity of the initial Arab invasions of the 7th and 8th centuries by a numerical minority made it inevitable that existing buildings were taken over, that local craftsmen were employed to construct new domestic quarters, and that these builders would be instrumental in giving architectural form to the germinal concepts of the new religion. Ibn Khaldūn, the well-travelled 14th-century historian and social philosopher, writes in his *Muqaddima* ('Introduction to History') of building activities in the areas newly conquered by Islamic forces: 'The Arabs are quite firmly rooted in the desert and quite unfamiliar with the crafts. Furthermore, before Islam, the Arabs had been strangers to the realms of which they took possession. When they came to rule them, there was not time enough for all the institutions of sedentary culture to develop fully. Moreover, the buildings of others, which they found in existence, were sufficient for them. Furthermore, at the beginning, their religion forbade them to do any excessive building or to waste too much money on building activities for no purpose.' The gradual absorption and interchange of indigenous culture traits, ideas of authority and administrative systems (together with their architectural expression), and intermarriage by the hierarchy of the invading minority (whose control was sometimes usurped by native Islamicized dynasties) helped to ratify the continued use of indigenous regional forms. Vernacular techniques, adapted as they were to the dictates of climate, the suitability of local materials and the exigencies of their availability and cost, continued to be used under Islamic rule in the domestic architecture of the majority of the population – in the noble houses of the bourgeoisie and the ruling elite, as well as in the majority of religious buildings.

However, the Arab conquerors were not all nomadic tent-dwelling tribesmen, contrary to the popular Western view and the implications of the Arab pastoral-warrior tradition, which was idealized in early texts and perpetuated in Islamic literature and oral poetry, and Western academic research. The bulk of the Arab armies recruited from the west and south-west Arabian Peninsula were heirs to an established regional building tradition, which continues to the present time. Although some of the population were agriculturalists and nomads, many lived in urban commercial centres such as Mecca, Medina, Ta'if and San'a'. Apart from the well known contemporary descriptions of Muhammad's house in Medina and those of his associates, and the successive rebuildings of the Ka'ba at Mecca, there are references to multi-storeyed constructions in the Yemen from both pre- and early Islamic sources. A Himyaritic inscription in Ta'izz Museum from pre-Islamic times mentions the construction of a house with 'six floors and six ceilings'. Many Islamic histories refer to the tall palace of Ghumdān in San'a', in the Yemen, which was destroyed on the orders of the Caliph 'Uthmān in the 7th century. The 10th-century commentators, Ibn Rusta and al-Hamdānī, both refer to the tall houses of San'a'. Multi-storeyed houses of defensive aspect continue to be characteristic of the mountainous areas of western and south-western Arabia and the Red Sea littoral.

Generally, however, there is little contemporary documentation enabling us to reconstruct earlier Islamic vernacular architecture in satisfactory detail. Depictions of dwellings in manuscript illuminations tend to be schematic and largely uninformative; written material mainly derives from courtly circles and does not reflect the life of the majority of the population. The 13th-century illustrated manuscripts of the *Maqāmāt* ('Assemblies') of al-Harīrī, as Oleg Grabar has perceptively demonstrated, are exceptional in their portrayal of a characteristic Mesopotamian townhouse of the period as a setting for many of the anecdotes. This house, sometimes depicted with a second storey, has a large central area covered with a wooden-frame conical ventilator, which can be opened by rolling a section of folding mats to one side. An internal staircase, used as a cooling place for water jars, and a heavy entrance door are common features. There are, unfortunately, few other details of internal arrangements.

Geographers and travellers, such as Ibn Battūta (1304–77), al-Maqrīzī (1364–1442) and Leo Africanus (writing *c.* 1526), briefly comment on the domestic, commercial and utilitarian architecture of the areas through which they travelled, and help us to establish a very broad pattern of regional building types. Ibn Khaldūn is exceptional in the considered attention he gives to building and society. He comments on the nature of monumental architecture and on the early contacts between the Arab conquerors of the Middle East and the indigenous building traditions and urban cultures of the sedentary peoples dwelling there. He analyzes the craft of architecture and carpentry with knowledge and sophistication; he also describes the effect of climate on the form of dwellings, and the need for insulation against heat and cold. He contrasts the way of life of the rural people, the bedouin, and their unornamented mud architecture with the complex social organization and craft specialization, characteristic of urban civilization, and the resulting building techniques, structure and decoration of urban housing.

Building regulations often provide useful evidence about vernacular forms and techniques. However, in Islamic law, the stress on the juridical rights of the individual and the inviolability of the domestic unit means that building codes (such as that compiled by the 14th-century Tunisian, Ibn ar-Rāmī) rarely deal with aspects of individual structures, except in circumstances where these infringe on the freedom and social inviolability of other individuals – and even here the legal bias can be difficult to determine. The *Mukhtasar*, the 14th-century compilation of Mālikī law by Sīdī Khalīl, for instance, states: 'The law does not prohibit the interception of a neighbour's light by new buildings and works; nor the interception of the sun or wind, unless the intended site is to be used for threshing on . . . nor will it intervene in the case of noises produced by many voices. . . .'

Archaeological excavations have tended to concentrate on building complexes in the grand design tradition. Because of the involved and subtle relationship among all aspects of the Islamic building tradition, however, such excavations may furnish information relevant to the history of vernacular structures. Of particular interest are the remains of domestic complexes at Fustat, the early Islamic capital of Egypt, established near Cairo in the 7th century, and the recent discoveries in Sistan, on the borders of western Afghanistan and eastern Iran. Valuable information can be gathered from the occasional survival of abandoned cities, such as Bam in south-eastern Iran, where the dry climate has preserved the original mud-brick buildings. Alternatively, an analysis of extant vernacular architecture may provide clues to the appearance and structure of a monumental and urban architecture that has now disappeared. Thus, although historical texts tell of the power and importance of Sijilmassa, the second largest Muslim city established in North Africa, it was in ruins by the end of the 14th century, its architecture irretrievably lost. The people of the city, however, took refuge in the surrounding area of the Tāfilālt, and from the evidence of surviving *ksars*, built of pisé (rammed earth) with sun-dried mud-brick decoration, it has been possible broadly to reconstruct the building techniques of the ancient capital.

Vernacular styles and building traditions are not necessarily static, unchanging and thus non-historical, as is frequently supposed. There is evidence to suggest, for example, that brick building technology was introduced into the sub-Saharan savannah by Arab merchant communities from North Africa, and was then spread by Islamic traders; it created radical changes in building: from round puddled-mud constructions to rectangular flat-roofed structures. A lengthy sequence of change in domestic architecture has been well documented in Nubia, northern Sudan.

In the present century, when not only building styles, but techniques and materials thoughout the Islamic world are increasingly drawn from alien cultural and technological traditions, it is essential to understand what traditional Islamic society itself sees as significant in its architecture, domestic or otherwise; to learn what its priorities may be in the function of its built forms and their symbolic and social connotations.

The urban setting

Islamic villages, towns and cities rarely conform to the geometric symmetry of urban planning that is characteristic of cultures who conceive their settlements as images of an ordered cosmos, a cosmological diagram (notable exceptions are al-Mansūr's round city of Baghdad and the fortified hamlets of southern Morocco). However, Islamic settlements are neither fortuitous nor amorphous in their organization, and reveal a consistent underlying order of hierarchical sequences of access and enclosure responding to patterns of social intercourse and allegiance particular to Islamic society.

Islamic urban organization is the physical manifestation of the equilibrium between social homogeneity and heterogeneity, in a social system requiring both segregation of domestic life and participation in the economic and religious life of the community. The city characteristically comprises a tripartite system of public, semi-public and private spaces, varying in degree of accessibility and enclosure.

The main public areas of the town are those of the central bazaars, lined with open booths and workshops, with associated major mosques, caravanserais, cafés and *hammāms*. This is the domain of men, with the emphasis on accessibility and unrestricted contact. Off the wider bazaar street, usually bordered by relatively low buildings, branch the central streets of the different quarters, bordered by buildings taller than those of the commercial centre; off these streets, in turn, branch the narrow, blank-walled alleys and culs-de-sac onto which open the doorways of individual dwellings.

Town and city quarters, perhaps occupying just a single street, are formed by relatively small, usually homogeneous communities bound by common religious, ethnic or occupational ties (jewellers, tanners, weavers, potters, etc.) and have a strong feeling of group solidarity with reciprocal duties and obligations. Migrants sharing common village or regional origins might also occupy or even build their own distinct quarter, as has happened recently in the *bidonvilles* of the Moroccan cities. City quarters are an ancient and ubiquitous phenomenon in Islam; the 8th-century plans of al-Mansūr for Baghdad included provisions for individual quarters, each of which was to have a bazaar and workshops for its needs. Quarters were not divided according to status; each was a microcosm with rich and poor living alongside one another and sharing mosques, fountains, *hammāms*, ovens, markets; or, in rural towns, mills and threshing floors. The quarter was traditionally considered by the state authorities as an administrative and taxation unit, and had a headman, a council and, in periods of social tension, its own defence unit.

Although the quarter is a closely knit group, providing consciousness of social identity and security, there is always a balance maintained between this social self-sufficiency and isolation and the quarter's participation in the communal and economic affairs of the city as a whole. Though its entrance might be guarded at night and in times of civil unrest, each quarter is not usually architecturally emphasized and is physically linked with the neighbouring buildings of the adjacent quarter. The residents of a quarter sometimes extend their contacts in all directions to include their back-to-back neighbours.

However closely the individual is associated with the life of his quarter, he also belongs to another unit: the family, the basic and irreducible unit of social life. The right and obligation of the family to live enclosed in its house has led to a clear separation between public and private life, perhaps the most significant social characteristic of Islamic culture.

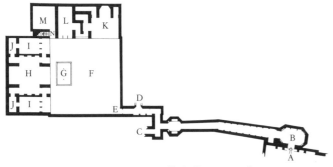

Entry into an Islamic house is usually indirect – nowhere more so than in a house such as this in Isfahan. Coming from the public square (A), the visitor finds himself first in a small entrance hall (B) but then has to traverse a long corridor, passing two other doors to the outer world (C,D), before arriving at the entrance (E) to the main courtyard of the house (F), with its pool (G). From here the rooms are reached: H, main vaulted room; I, side rooms; J, small rooms or stores; K, main room of 'service' house; L, side room of 'service' houses; N, stair to upper floor; M, store room. (1)

Social aspects of the Islamic house

John Jackson, an 18th-century traveller in Iraq, vividly describes the houses he saw on his journeys:

'The roofs are flat and surrounded by a parapet. Here the inhabitants sleep during the summer season, in the open air. To a European every house appears like a prison, as it can receive no light from the street, because it has no windows. Every house forms a square, and the inhabitants have no communication with their neighbours. Within the square are various offices; some under ground, where the people retire during the heat of the day. The kitchen, the water, and not unfrequently the horses, are kept on the ground floor. The hall, where they receive company, the harem, and many other offices, are on the second, which has generally a gallery supported by pillars continued nearly round the inside of the whole building. They have generally two flights of steps; one leading to the hall, where alone strangers are admitted; the other leading to the harem, to which none but the family can have access. Women of the higher class are seldom seen out of doors; but when they do go out, they are always veiled. Many of the Arab women, particularly of the lower class, expose their faces.'

Islam embraces a host of underlying cultures in its vast spatial and temporal span, and its interactions with them are varied and complex. While diverse historical antecendents and a multiplicity of regional economies, geographical conditions, building materials and techniques mean that no single Muslim house-type has developed, commonly held beliefs about the nature of the family and its social role have created typical Islamic attitudes regarding the functions of the house.

In Islamic culture it is both the explicit and the implicit Qur'ānic prohibitions that are the primary determining factors in the formation of a domestic unit, for these define what is socially unacceptable. For example, in the 'Sūra of the Confederate Tribes' it is stated: 'Wives of the Prophet you are not like other women. If you fear Allah, do not be too complaisant in your speech, lest the lecherous-hearted should lust after you. Show discretion in what you say. Stay in your homes and do not display your finery as women used to do in the days of ignorance . . .' (Sūra xxxiii, 32–3); and the 'Sūra of the Light' says: 'Believers, do not enter the dwellings of other men until you have asked their owners' permission and wished them peace . . .' (Sūra xxiv, 27). In early Islam, the wife was *muhsana* (literally 'under ward', 'woman to be guarded'), and was entirely in the keeping of her husband, the responsibility devolving on him, rather than her, to see that her honour was not violated. As a contemporary Lebanese proverb says: 'Girls are the cause of disgrace and reviling. They cause the enemy to have access to one's house.'

The dominant emphasis, therefore, is on domestic privacy and the seclusion and segregation of women. The Arabic name, *sakan*, to denote the house is related to the word *sakīna*, 'peaceful and holy', and the word for woman, *harim*, is in turn related to *haram* (harem), 'sacred area', which denotes the family living quarters. The harem, or domestic area of the house, is primarily the women's domain, the husband usually having his own room near the boundary of this area.

Seclusion of women: Although the outside world is not permitted, or is certainly discouraged, access to the harem, the womenfolk, if suitably protected, may observe public life and under certain conditions may have access to it. In village communities, composed of closely related kinship groups, where interference from strangers is infrequent, seclusion of females is not always as strictly observed as in urban communities. The segregation of women is physically manifested in various forms of barriers, through which woman can see but not be seen. Costume and veiling are designed to detract the eye from the lines of the face and body, and in certain regions of Islam become elaborately fashioned structures. The veil performs many of the functions of seclusion and introversion as expressed in Islamic domestic architecture, whose nomadic form, the tent, is itself a framed or suspended textile. Closer to architecture are the camel-borne palanquins used by nomadic tribes throughout much of the Islamic world, which also veil and protect women who are moving in public. Elaborately decorated palanquins are used by sedentary peoples as bridal litters. In house architecture, the screened balcony allows the female occupants to view the outside world without being seen – it also performs the important function of modifying the climate in the hot areas of the Islamic world. In the interiors of houses, screens may be built opening from the harem onto the reception rooms so that men's gatherings and festivities can be observed from safety.

The Islamic house, therefore, is an *introverted* form, conceived from the inside outwards, with emphasis on the decoration of interior elements, such as the courtyard façade, while the street façade is usually a plain wall (unless it contains shops), and the only opening is the entrance portal. External house walls must be built to a height that ensures that the domestic interior cannot be overlooked, and that intruders are discouraged. Any openings in the ground floor are small, grilled and above the line of vision of passers-by. The windows of upper storeys are generally larger and may project considerably; though admitting light and air, they must not overlook neighbouring courtyards or terraces. A minor ordinance of the *Mukhtasar* of Sīdī Khalīl demonstrates the force of this customary prohibition: 'Anyone may, if necessary, climb up his date palm, provided he previously informs the neighbour into whose house he might obtain a view.'

The house entrance: The symbolic importance of the house entrance – the vulnerable threshold between the household and the public – is often emphasized by the construction of a monumental and sometimes highly decorated doorway, frequently utilizing symbols and colours of an apotropaic or auspicious nature. For example, the doorways of those who have returned from the *hajj*, the pilgrimage to Mecca, are brightly decorated with an abundance of inscriptions, folk motifs and images of places and things seen on the journey. In Muslim East Africa, the elaborate wooden doors of Swahili houses, with their heavy brass locks and chains, are considered such an important feature that the construction of a new house begins with the door. In Salalah, in southern Oman, the first stage in house building is the erection of a perimeter wall and the establishment of a formal entrance way. At Harar, in Ethiopia, the door is an important indication of a man's status. The great 19th-century British traveller, Richard Burton, who visited Harar, observed that a man's door was used as a security for good behaviour during litigation, and that 'when a man rejects a summons, his door is removed to the royal courtyard on the first day; and on the second it is confiscated'. A Lebanese proverb states: 'A house whose door has been removed becomes an asylum for dogs.'

The Islamic house usually has only a single entrance, but a second entrance may be used exclusively by the womenfolk, as in the houses of the Bastakia quarter of Dubai, on the Gulf, and the old port of Suakin, on the Red Sea. Occasionally the upper floors of houses communicate, and in some instances there is even a bridge across the street for members of neighbouring harems to meet without going outside. The main gateway of the house usually does not give immediate access to the domestic quarters, but leads into a vestibule (often with another door opening into the harem) or passage with a right-angle turn so that it is impossible to see into the court from outside. This protective entrance is sometimes extremely exaggerated, as in a number of houses in Isfahan, which contain long entrance passages with multiple turnings and five or more entrance doors.

Rights of wives: In the tribal society of pre-Islamic Arabia, women occupied a subordinate and subjugated position within a patriarchal and patrilinear tribal group. If a man married a woman from another tribe, she and her children then belonged to his tribe. Though marriage was preferentially to a father's brother's daughter (as it has continued to be in Islamic society), the accepted possibility of exogamy meant that women were denied inheritance and rights of succession in order to preserve the power and possessions of the tribal unit. The universal truth of Islam transcended tribal ties, and Islamic law reformed earlier Arabic law emphasizing the more immediate tie existing between a husband and his wife or wives (he is permitted four), and elevated the status of women *within* the tribal group. The legal position of women is not unfavourable, though they are considered inferior to men and have fewer rights and duties, from a religious point of view.

The common Arabic phrase for the consummation of marriage is *banā 'alayhā*, 'he built [a tent] over his wife', for the nomad husband provides a special tent for the first night of marriage. In sedentary Muslim society, the canopied bridal bed, to which the bridegroom is ritually brought, may represent the wife's wedding tent. Though the bride customarily dwells in the house of her husband's father, the survival of the common ancient Semitic concept to 'go to' the bride, to express marriage, may reflect an earlier matrilocal system. In Muhammad's time, the tent or house was called the bride's; the jurist, al-Bukhārī (810–70), states that the Prophet's wives continued to lodge with the Prophet, each wife with her children constituting a separate group. By traditional law, in taking a wife a man is obliged to maintain her and to pay her a dowry, which is unalienable. For example, one of the four major Muslim schools of law, the Hanafī, states: 'After payment of the prompt portion of the dower, the husband has the right to forbid his wife to leave the house without permission, while respecting her right to visit her father and mother, and relations within the prohibited degrees at fixed periods; to forbid her to visit and mix with strange women; and to prevent her attending festivals and social gatherings, even with her relations within the prohibited degrees.' The husband, however, has a reciprocal legal obligation to provide his wives (who must have equal access to him and equal status among themselves) with separate apartments. The same code dictates: 'Where a woman can claim to be removed to another dwelling: . . . the lodging of a co-wife in the same house gives the wife a right to demand a separate lodging elsewhere. The same rule applies where a co-wife or one of the husband's relations is lodged in the same apartment with the wife. Where a husband must provide his wife with a separate dwelling: where husband and wife are both wealthy, the husband must provide a separate house for his wife's residence; where they are not wealthy, the husband must provide a separate apartment according to his means, which must possess the necessary conveniences and must be isolated.'

The combination of both the obligation to supply each wife with a separate apartment and the usual custom (at least in the Islamic heartlands) of patrilocal residence of the married and unmarried sons and other relatives, creates needs that find spatial expression basic to the form of the Islamic house. The rural courtyard houses, *menzels*, of the island of Djerba, off the coast of southern Tunisia, show this aspect of the Islamic house in an elementary form. Rigidly square or rectangular in plan, each side of these low houses is made up of one separate apartment, usually with a corner defensive and storage tower and domed sleeping area. These apartments do not communicate directly with one another, but share the central courtyard and entrance vestibule. In the complex urban houses in the port of Suakin, the harem consists of a series of suites called *majlis*, each of which often has an adjoining smaller room, independent cooking and washing areas, storehouses and a latrine. This spatial organization is characteristic of townhouses throughout the Islamic world. This strict organization, deriving from the ideals of seclusion and wife equality, however, is not economically accessible to everyone; for the poor, physical barriers may be impossible to maintain.

The accretive nature of the Islamic house

Proverbially, the Arab house is never complete; as each extended family grows, so does the house, thereby reflecting the history, accumulated growth and family structure of a number of generations. The accretive nature of the individual Islamic dwelling can be clearly seen in the construction of modern houses at Salalah, Oman.

In this region, as elsewhere in modern Islam, the traditional patriarchal social and economic structure is being transformed, as individual members of the family become economically independent and reside as nuclear families in individual dwellings. These modern structures, however, still provide for future family growth in a form very similar to the indigenous courtyard house. Initially, one or two rooms at ground level are built to accommodate the nuclear family; but these are purposely constructed in a way that will support future rooms above, as in the older houses. Here, as elsewhere in the Islamic world, the courtyard perimeter defines the potential area of the future extended family home, and house construction usually starts by building a boundary wall around the plot. The family head divides this plot into different sections to fulfil particular functions, keeping in mind future expansion. Family extension in dense urban areas may mean that an adjacent house may be taken over and an internal passage constructed to join them into a single unit.

Male quarters and reception rooms

The traditional need to entertain male guests, while at the same time bar them access to the females of the household, has given rise to additional complexities of design particular to Islamic domestic architecture, which therefore must accommodate a double circulation system. The men's reception (or guest) room tends to be located adjacent to, or directly accessible from, the entrance lobby of the house so that visitors do not meet or converse with the female household or violate the harem. The simplest form of separation of male and female areas is found in the tent of the nomad, where there is no permanent structural division. A screen or cloth is hung across the centre of the tent and along one half of the front when unrelated male visitors are present. A basic requirement of the bedouin tent is that it be large enough to entertain visitors. In poorer houses there may be no separate guest room, but the father's room, often located near the entrance, serves as such; however, if he grows more prosperous, the construction of a reception room is considered a priority. The men's guest room is a symbol of the economic status of the household and is furnished with the precious possessions of the family; therefore it is generally the most decorated room of the house. Within it, or adjacent to it, are facilities for preparing traditional refreshments for the guests. Apart from being a place for relaxation and recreation, the guest room is used for religious discussion and instruction. A village leader or a council may construct a community reception room as in the halls, *mudhifs*, of the notables in the Marsh Arab communities in the delta of the Tigris and the Euphrates. It is the custom in some villages of Upper Egypt that anyone returning from Cairo stays the first night in the mayor's reception room, or *madyafa*, to give out his news.

In wealthy establishments, the male and female quarters may be housed in separate buildings. Excavations at Fustat have revealed two basic house-types; one with a single interior courtyard and another with two courtyards. In the latter form, one courtyard was probably for male visitors and the other for the private life of the family. A similar division is found in wealthy townhouses of Damascus and Sarajevo, and in the rural houses of the Mahas Nubians in the northern Sudan. The *menzels* of the Djerba countryside often have a separate men's guest house constructed outside the dwelling itself.

The celebration of important family occasions, such as births, weddings (the giving of a wedding feast is a duty established by the Prophet's own example) and annual religious feasts, is usually centred on the courtyard; but a family reception room (separate from the men's reception room) is often provided, particularly in houses that have no internal court such as the tower-houses of south-western Arabia and the wealthier urban houses of the Balkans and Anatolia. The floor of the guest room is often divided into two levels; that into which one enters and slips off one's shoes is lower than the level used for seating. This division of the guest room can lead to a hierarchical sequence of seating levels, reflecting the relative social positions of the male residents and visitors, a feature that is particularly emphasized in the main rooms of Harari houses in Ethiopia, where more than half the floor space consists of a series of raised platforms. The position and level of these platforms clearly defines relative social status.

Use of interior space

While rooms in European houses are usually allotted to a specific activity, such as bedroom or dining room, the significant divisions in Muslim houses are those of social accessibility, both public and private. In the harem most interior spaces are functionally polyvalent and non-specific; rooms can be used interchangeably for eating, sleeping, recreation and domestic tasks. This flexible use of living space is reflected in the absence of the cumbersome furniture (cupboards, tables and chairs) that is characteristic of cultures whose buildings have rigidly defined interior patterns of use. Chests are commonly used, and constructed beds or divans are found in certain areas, especially in Arabia, Turkey and Egypt. The large straw houses of the semi-nomadic Shoa Arabs of the Lake Chad area contain a separate raised and canopied bed structure, a sort of miniature house within a house. The inhabitants of most Islamic houses sit and eat on the floor – on carpets, rugs, mats and cushions, which can be rolled up and stored away when not wanted. Storage cupboards or open niches, built into the walls and often decorated, are a characteristic feature all over the Islamic world.

Interiors are also characterized by changing diurnal and seasonal patterns of use. For example, in the traditional houses of Iraq most of the day is spent in the galleried courtyard; the siesta is taken in the cool basement, or *sirdāb*, during the hottest part of the day; and at night the roof terrace is used as a sleeping area – a widespread practice in the hot arid areas of Islam. In climates where there is a substantial seasonal change, certain areas of a house may be inhabited only in summer or winter. This practice of seasonal migration within the house is reflected in the common institution of both a summer and a winter reception room. In the Ottoman Balkans and Anatolia, the summer reception room, or *çardak*, is usually a prominent room on the top floor, with large windowed balconies cantilevered beyond the lower façade. The winter guest room is on a lower level, insulated against winter cold and containing an elaborately carved marble or stucco firehood over the hearth.

The courtyard house

Islam accepted the two basic ancient courtyard house-types of the Middle East and Mediterranean periphery: the interior courtyard house, where the house encloses a courtyard, characteristic of urban areas; and the exterior courtyard house, where the courtyard borders on the house, providing a protected area contiguous with the dwelling units, but not enclosed by them. This latter type tends to be associated with rural areas, where there is less pressure on building space and less need for the protective introversion the interior courtyard house provides.

The interior courtyard performs an important function as a modifier of climate in hot arid areas. It allows outdoor activities with protection from the wind, dust and sun. Interior courtyards serve both as light-wells, in a building-type that restricts exterior window area, and as air-wells into which the cool, dense night air sinks. Because it is protected by walls, or surrounding *īwāns*, loggias and galleries, the sun's rays do not heat the courtyard until later in the day. When the sun does reach the interior court, and heated air rises, convection currents set up an air-flow that ventilates the house and keeps it cool. The deep narrow streets of Islamic cities are cooled similarly – façades are relatively unexposed to the sun's rays, and cool air collects at night. In dense urban complexes, the massing of multi-storeyed structures sharing party walls reduces the surface area exposed to the sun. Traditional building materials such as earth, stone and wood, because of a capillary effect, absorb water which can then evaporate from their surfaces and thus hinder the interior air from being rewarmed by convection. In certain Moroccan houses, convection currents are particularly exploited by piercing the floors of successive storeys along a vertical line to

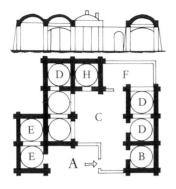

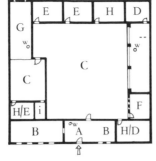

Courtyard house in the Souf, Algeria. (2)

Courtyard house at Qustul, Nubia. (3)

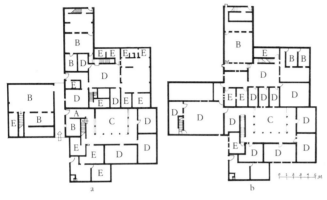

Courtyard house at Al-Majma'ah, Saudi Arabia, showing the ground floor (a) *and upper storey* (b). *(4)*

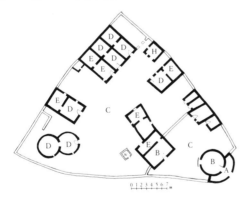

Compound of a West African family house in Zaria, Nigeria. (5)

These plans of interior and exterior courtyard houses are from widely separated areas of the Islamic world; nevertheless, they share common principles of planning, which reflect patterns of social organization. A, entrance placed so that the passerby cannot see directly into the harem; B, men's reception room/s situated on the periphery of the family quarters; C, courtyard; D, living/sleeping area; E, storage/service area; F, stable; G, room for celebration of major family occasions; H, kitchen; I, latrine; W, well. In the case of the West African house, no male strangers are allowed beyond the first reception room, but there is a second (also lettered B), used for meetings, through which one has to pass to get from outer to inner courtyard. The two rooms next to this belong to the household head. The women's quarters are in the far corner, round the kitchen (H). The two circular rooms on the left (D,D) are those of the widowed mother of the household head.

encourage the free circulation of air within the interior.

The spacious courtyards of wealthy townhouses may contain interior gardens. These are usually richly paved with stone or tiles, and lushly planted. Walkways, often raised above ground level, divide the planted areas. Where water is available, a fountain or pool is situated in the courtyard – even those of poor houses may contain some tree, plant or a modest tank. The evaporation of water and the presence of plants both raises the humidity in unpleasantly dry climates and helps to keep the air cool. In moderately humid climates such as in Algiers, on the other hand, houses do not contain courtyard pools because any increase in the already high relative humidity would cause discomfort. In more humid climates with abundant natural vegetation the micro-climatic value of the interior courtyard house-type is reduced, but in many areas, such as northern India and the central Balkans, the imported Islamic form persists because of its social and symbolic function.

There are, however, a number of more temperate or inaccessible areas where the courtyard house has not become ubiquitous. In these regions, more compact house-types have persisted for a variety of climatic and cultural reasons. Excessive seasonal cold and precipitation severely restrict outdoor domestic activities and render an open-air courtyard impractical. Along the Caspian coast of north-western Iran and in the upland valleys of Bosnia-Herzegovina in Yugoslavia we find a house-type ideally suited to the climate: cubic, timber buildings with a central hearth and a steeply pitched roof of thatch or shingle. In the Aurès Mountains of Algeria, the greater social freedom of women in traditional Berber society, together with the geographical isolation of most villages, has influenced the retention of a simply organized house, with the living area opening directly onto the street. In the mountain ranges of Lebanon and the Kabylie region of northern Algeria, the courtyard house is equally uncommon, though the individual dwellings of an extended family or clan may be grouped to enclose a common court with a single entrance.

In urban settings, the courtyard house is often multi-storeyed. The courtyard may even be located on an upper floor, the lower floors being lit by skylights. Where the courtyard house is greatly reduced in size or not in an open-air form, the role of the courtyard is taken over by a large central hall lit from the roof, such as the *qā'a* of the townhouses of Cairo. The importance of the courtyard and the relationship between its area and height differs according to the region and the degree of affluence of its builders; but despite these variations, the plan of the courtyard is basically square or rectangular – triangular or polygonal courtyards being very unusual. The four-side plan with an interior space covered by the dome of the sky may have a symbolic value as a microcosmic image of the order of the universe.

Although uneven terrain, pressure on building space and pre-existing streets may mean that the sites of houses in cities and towns are confined and irregular, Islamic builders are able to compose symmetrical, rectangular interiors. This spatial organization is achieved in upper floors by projecting rooms over the street to create more internal space and right-angle corners. These cantilevered upper rooms are supported on wooden, brick or stone corbels, often elaborately decorated. Such projecting structures shade the street that they overhang, and in the Balkans and Turkey they protect passers-by from the rain; on the other hand, the proximity of overhanging wooden structures on both sides of a street meant that fire could spread rapidly and engulf a whole quarter. In Istanbul and Cairo (where the large, intricately worked, wooden *masharabiyya* constructions were a particular fire hazard) this danger resulted in municipal ordinances restricting their construction.

Semi-permanent shelters

Despite the introverted aspect of Islamic family life, and housing in general, many domestic activities are carried out in the open air. This is primarily a function of climate, but also in many cases a residue of a nomadic ancestral tradition, and has resulted in the creation of a diversity of lightweight temporary or semi-permanent shelters built from vegetable materials, such as reeds, palm-fronds and light branches. The usual form of nomadic shelter, however, is the tent of woven goat hair, camel hair or of felt. Where vegetation permits, portable dwellings of plant material are built as an alternative to tents.

Near the south-western Arabian coast, in the area of Shuqaiq, the village dwellings are circular huts of thatch, weed and rope, mud-plastered on the interior with conical roofs, grouped within thatched enclosure walls. The *nouala*, a complex typical of the agricultural

The houses of the Marsh Arabs of Iraq are built entirely of reeds, but achieve forms of considerable scale and sophistication. This is the reception hall of a shaykh. (6)

plains of western Morocco, consists of a rectangular plot surrounded by a protective mound with thatched-roof huts built on stone foundations. In the Maghrib, dwellings of plant material similar to these, may have been the usual nomadic shelter before the intrusion of camel-herders from the East, with their woven tents of animal hair.

Perhaps the most striking architectural achievements in non-durable materials are the reed houses of the Marsh Arabs of the lower Tigris and Euphrates Valley. A series of transverse arches made from tied bundles of giant reeds provides the framework for these buildings, to which are lashed further, thinner, horizontal reed bundles on the exterior. The structure is then covered with reed mats, as is the floor. The entrance always faces Mecca, and is framed by reed pillars.

Control of the environment

Ibn Khaldūn, in his *Muqaddima*, describes the architecture he knew in this way: 'The craft of architecture is the first and oldest craft of sedentary civilization. It is the knowledge of how to go about using houses and mansions for cover and shelter. This is because man has the natural disposition to reflect upon the outcome of things. Thus, it is unavoidable that he must reflect upon how to avert the harm arising from heat and cold by using houses which have walls and roofs to intervene between him and those things on all sides.'

In both the hot and dry, and the hot and humid areas of the Islamic world, architecture is a means of controlling the environment by the creation of domestic micro-climates, of which the courtyard house is the most common example. In Islamic popular architecture, the insulation properties of many natural materials have been exploited and a range of ventilation systems developed, some very sophisticated in conception and design.

Orientation: A simple and ubiquitous response to local climate is found in the orientation of dwellings. In Egypt, the orientation of buildings tends to be constant: courtyards are open to the north to receive the cool prevailing breeze of the evening. Houses in Salalah, Oman, are situated in a relationship to one another that encourages the maximum circulation of air, with care being taken that each house is built well beyond the 'wind shadow' of the neighbouring house.

While most natural materials, such as mud, brick and stone, are efficient insulators, certain materials may be consciously selected for use in specifically orientated parts of the construction. Thus in the exposed Beqa'a Valley of central Lebanon, all village houses have their windowless southern wall built of stone as protection against the cold south-blowing wind, although the rest of the structure is of mud-brick. In Lebanese coastal cities, the porous and friable sandstone walls of the houses are usually rendered only on the south-west side to resist the penetration of rain-water. In the eastern regions of Iran, such as Mazandaran, houses have wide porches and over-hanging eaves as protection against the heat; walls on the south side are often massively thick, absorbing heat without transmitting it to the interior – in effect, storing up heat against the short cold spells of winter.

Factors other than the climate may also influence the orientation of buildings. In the houses of the Lebanon mountains, the view of the sea is as important a factor as the direction of the prevailing winds in determining house orientation. The Ottomans had a particular love of a view and their urban regulations frequently protected against obstruction; thus, their houses were often sited according to the best aspect. Orientation may be religiously or socially prescribed. For example, the tents of the shaykh of the Sudanese Kabābish nomads all face towards Mecca, in an alignment that also reflects the group's social hierarchy. The tents of the shaykh's wives, for instance, are placed in a straight line, so that no one wife takes precedence over another; and the important social position of the shaykh's mother is indicated by positioning her tent at the end of the main line and some way forward of it.

In Muslim dwellings in Bosnia, in central Yugo-slavia, doors are ideally placed so that the back of the person entering should not be turned to the south-east, that is, towards Mecca. Even the positioning of toilets is influenced by religious injunctions relating to pollution and the sanctity of the *qibla* orientation. The 9th-century jurist, ash-Shāfiʿī, in a text considered to be one of the foundations of Islamic jurisprudence, the *Risāla*, quotes the Prophet as saying: 'Let him who eases nature or makes water not face the *qibla* or turn his back to it; but turn either eastward or westward.'

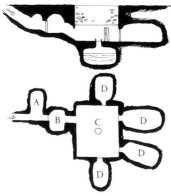

Plan and section of an underground house in southern Tunisia. The sloping tunnel entrance is on the left. A, visitors' room; B, stable or storehouse; C, courtyard open to the sky, with cistern in the centre; D, living rooms. (7)

Underground dwellings: In most areas of the Muslim world where geological and climatic conditions permit, the natural insulation properties of the earth are used to great advantage, either by excavating underground chambers or using natural caves for dwellings, stables, storage areas and cisterns. Many houses in hot areas contain an excavated basement room, as in the townhouses of Baghdad where the excavated room is ventilated by air-scoops. These basement rooms are found in many houses in Iraq and Iran and were certainly in use as early as the 9th century (by the time Samarra was built) and are also described in the 10th-century city of Qum, in Iran. Houses may also be semi-excavated. Ibn al-Balkhī describes 12th-century houses in Iran that were partly excavated and partly constructed of pisé; and similar buildings in the same area were in use in about 1900. In the Egyptian oasis of Siwa, a necropolis of underground tombs was converted into dwellings.

In design and construction, the most complex Islamic underground dwellings are those of the mountain belt between Matmata in southern Tunisia and Garian in western Libya (excavations have revealed that the houses of Bulla Regia, in Roman Tunisia, had both underground and ground-level rooms). The Tunisian and Libyan dwellings are essentially interior courtyard houses, each consisting of a deep, open pit courtyard excavated out of the dry sandstone, from which are tunnelled living, work and storage spaces, often on two levels. A cistern for collecting rain-water is usually excavated below the courtyard. The central open courtyard is square or rectangular, whereas the tunnelled chambers are longitudinal vaults with rounded corners. There may be underground passages leading to other courts in the complex of the extended family. Door and window openings are often reinforced with stone arches, and the central court may be faced with ashlar. The pit is approached by a sloping excavated ramp, which can be closed off in times of danger. Near its entrance there is usually an underground chamber for livestock, and there may also be a guest room. Such excavated houses mirror in reverse the structures built above the ground in this area, both in their spatial organization and their defensive aspect. When the entrance is sealed, the excavated dwelling is virtually impregnable. In these houses every room is under a layer of bedrock at least seven to ten metres thick; it is thus better insulated than anything that could be built on the surface and affords protection from the desert windstorms. Not only houses but underground and semi-underground mosques, which serve the troglo-dyte communities, occur in this region, such as those of Abu Zakariya, near Tmizda, and that of Thumayat – both in Libya and dating from the 12th century.

Wind-towers: While underground dwellings, such as those of Matmata, are effective solutions in hot, arid climates with extreme diurnal or seasonal temperature ranges, they are not as effective in hot, humid climates where ventilation rather than insulation is of prime importance. A range of structures was devised to deflect selectively the outside air-flow into building interiors to create a flexible artificial ventilation system. The earliest known reference to this use of ventilators to convey cooling breezes down into a room is an 8th-century BC Assyrian inscription.

There are two basic categories of wind-ventilation structures: the unidirectional wind-scoop and the multidirectional wind-tower. In both types the inlets are placed high above the roof terraces where wind velocity is greatest and the air cleaner and less laden with dust – the wind-towers of southern Iran and the Gulf often rise to fifteen metres above the ground.

The unidirectional wind-scoop, or wind-catcher, in its simplest form is seen in Baghdad, in the lower Sind district of Pakistan, where traditionally every building had one, and in Herat in Afghanistan, where almost every room contains one. The wind-catcher consists of a fixed inlet made of brick, timber or metal, and inclined at about 45° to the prevailing wind, which it deflects into a channel built in the wall of the building. The conduits are preferably interior walls, not subject to direct solar radiation. After passing through the rooms, the air disperses into the courtyard, pushing warm air upwards. In the Baghdad houses, each room, depending on its size or function, may have two or more independent scoops. In the old townhouses of Cairo, wind-catchers, *malqaf*, are used to ventilate the principal reception halls and living rooms. The inlet of the wind-catcher faces north into the evening breeze and communicates through a large opening in the ceiling, and is the only ventilation inlet for these inner chambers. 'Abd al-Latīf, a 13th-century historian, mentions the tall ventilators of the houses of Fustat as being 'open to every wind', probably the forerunners of those in Cairo.

A very simple form of wall wind-scoop, or ventilating screen, is found in southern Iran, and in those areas of the Gulf settled by immigrants from the Iranian coast. These are blank-façaded screens, double-walled with an interior cavity, which form part of the exterior or courtyard wall. Outside air enters at the top, passes down through the cavity wall and enters the room at the level of people sitting on the floor.

In some areas the prevailing wind changes direction seasonally or diurnally, necessitating a multidirectional wind-scoop or wind-tower. The simplest solution to this problem is to incorporate a sail- or fin-like projection into a scoop rotating on a pivot, in the

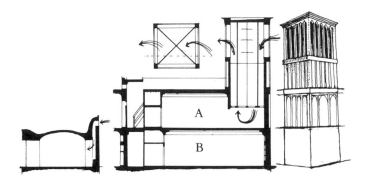

A common form of wind-tower, characteristic of Iran and the Gulf and neighboring areas, consists of a tall structure with vertical openings in all directions, and with internal walls arranged diagonally (see plan to the left of the tower; the section is taken along the dotted line), so that any breeze entering it is forced downwards and up again before it can escape. This creates a circulation of air in room A, which is used in summer. Room B is used in winter. The section on the left shows a simple form of wind-scoop ventilating a ground-floor room at Herat, Afghanistan. (8)

manner of a wind-vane, so that it always faces into the wind. In central and southern Iran and the Gulf, high multidirectional wind-towers, or *bādgīr*, are a characteristic architectural feature, and are often sculpted and decorated. Marco Polo, who visited the city of Hormoz in the late 13th century, commented: 'The climate is excessively hot – so hot that the houses are fitted with ventilators to catch the wind. The ventilators are set to face the quarter from which the wind blows and let it blow into the house. This they do because they cannot endure the overpowering heat.'

These wind-towers are square in plan, showing an X configuration of interior planes. They are built around an armature of wooden poles, which stabilize and reinforce the structure, and whose projecting ends are usually left to serve as scaffolding for cleaning and maintenance. The top half of the wind-tower is an enclosed funnel that accelerates the descending air into a room below – in such torrid areas as Kashan and Yazd the air is channeled into sub-basement chambers. The inward flow of air is matched by a strong updraught in the opposite side of the wind-tower, and it is immediately beneath the wind-tower that people sit or sleep during sultry weather.

In some rural areas of the Gulf, for example the Batinah coast of Oman, where much of the housing is of light palm-frond and wood construction, cloth wind-catchers, designed on the same principles as the masonry wind-towers, ventilate the houses, and can be easily dismantled during cool winters. Neither type of wind-catcher depends solely on the force of the prevailing wind to propel air through the building: the air outlet is as vital as the air inlet. As houses heat up during the day and the hot interior air rises, the change in pressure draws the breeze down through the wind-catcher and sets up a ventilation flow. An additional factor taken into consideration by the builders is that while the wind exerts a high positive pressure on walls facing its flow, an opposite effect is created on the leeward walls. Exhaust openings, therefore, are placed in these areas to cause the air to be sucked through the building. Incoming air is cooled by contact with interior surfaces of conduits within the house walls; it may be further cooled by placing porous water jars or damp matting in its path. Evaporation cools both the air and the water in the jars, which is used for drinking. Similarly, throughout the hot areas of Islam, window screens are built with holes or niches for water jugs. This principle of evaporative cooling is documented in Iranian palaces from the 10th century onwards, where fans and curtains of scented felt were saturated by a steady drip from overhead pipes.

Heating: In the colder regions of the Islamic world much attention is paid to insulation and to heating systems. In many Turkish houses the winters are spent on the ground floor, which is built of stone, while summers are spent on the upper floors, which are of wood. Some of the wealthy townhouses of Kabul, in Afghanistan, have radiant-heating systems under the pavement of the ground floor. A fire is built in the basement at one end of the house and hot air is circulated by means of flues under the floor. In Syria, where winters can be very cold, certain upper-storey rooms are used as solariums. Alternatively, in many areas the winter and summer rooms may be on the same floor, but are situated, respectively, on the south and north sides of the house.

Defensive structures

In the isolated mountainous regions of western Arabia, Morocco, the Balkans, Afghanistan and Pakistan, where the terrain hinders policing by a centralized political authority and where communication is difficult, tribal tensions, internecine feuds and banditry have always been features of life. In these areas the basic form of individual dwellings and house complexes is determined by defensive requirements. These structures range from the simple rural watch-tower, similar in form over a wide geographical area, to complex tower-houses and fortified hamlets.

Tall tower-houses without a central courtyard are characteristic of the western and south-western Arabian Peninsula, and early Yemeni texts and inscriptions, together with archaeological evidence from southern Arabia, indicate their existence there in pre-Islamic times. In rural areas such houses may occur singly, but are more usually grouped for mutual protection in strategic positions dominating access routes or on the sides of arable wadis. Similarly, the townhouses of major cities such as San'a', Shibam and Mecca perpetuate the archaic defensive house-type, while at the same time adapting well to urban pressure on building space and high land values – though in the cities of San'a' and Sa'dah the density of housing is balanced by cultivated areas within the walls.

The problems of stability in structures of such height have given rise to a number of ingenious engineering solutions. In the houses at San'a', for example, stone or brick walls are strengthened horizontally at regular intervals by exposed timbers parallel to the face of the walls, held in place by short wooden cross-pieces. These timbers take up stresses caused by unequal settlement or earthquake shocks. This system of building is of very ancient ancestry in south-western Arabia and Ethiopia. The lower parts of tower-house walls are of more massive construction than the upper storeys, being of stone or having stone foundations. The ground floor, which in rural areas is used for stabling animals, but which in cities mainly serves for storage, has a single entrance; there are no other openings that might jeopardize the structural strength of the building or its defensive aspect. Upper storeys are of burned or sun-dried brick or cob, becoming progressively thinner with each floor. In the Sa'dah region of northern Yemen, walls of tower-houses are constructed of horizontal courses of puddled clay raised at the corners, a system also intended to accommodate settling in the building.

In the mountainous areas of Wallachia, Bulgaria and the south-west Balkans, a distinctive form of defensive tower-dwelling, the *kula*, developed among both the Christian and the Muslim communities during the insecure period of the decline of Ottoman authority from the 17th century onwards. *Kulas* are characteristically of three or four storeys, square or rectangular in plan; their lower floors are massively walled with stone, and have a single entrance and no windows except for defensive loopholes or very small openings for light and ventilation. The staircase is internal and each floor is essentially a single space with non-load-bearing wooden or wattle-and-daub partitions. The upper storey, the harem, is often cantilevered on wooden consoles beyond the lower walls to give greater living space, and may be constructed completely of wood or made up of a wooden skeleton with an infilling material. A projecting balcony is also common. The roof is pitched and covered with wooden shingles, tiles or schist slates. Except for its defensive features the interior architecture of these towers corresponds largely to that of other Balkan Muslim dwellings. In the town of Girocaster, in Albania, urban tower-houses developed from the 17th century onwards; more massive than rural examples, but with similar external defensive features, they have large windows in the upper floors and luxuriously painted and carved interiors characteristic of the wealthy Turkish Balkan townhouses.

In the Maghrib, domestic defensive complexes have evolved out of topographical and social conditions similar to those in the Arabian Peninsula, if not through actual cultural contacts. In the wadis of Dra, Dades and Ziz on the Saharan fringes of the Morrocan Anti Atlas and High Atlas, communal and individual multi-storeyed defensive complexes have been developed by the indigenous Berber communities. The basic unit and earliest form is the fortified hamet, the *ksar*, which consists of a square or rectangular enclosure wall with square corner towers and a single entrance leading to a median street or alley. The whole space between this street and the external wall is occupied by courtyard houses built contiguously. A mosque and a well are essential elements. As the village grows, more quarters are constructed around this unit with new exterior ramparts and entrances. Separate fortified houses are also found, preserving the same basic courtyard plan with high ramparts and corner towers. Houses and villages are constructed of pisé and have characteristic mud-brick decoration in the upper storeys. Generally, the *ksars* and fortified houses are wider and lower than the tower houses of Arabia, and differ from the latter in having an interior courtyard. Their prototype may have been the fortified towns or border camps of the Roman or Byzantine *limes*, with which the Berbers are known to have been familiar.

One of the most interesting features of the vernacular architecture of the Maghrib is the communal fortified granary or storehouse of the indigenous Berber communities of isolated mountain areas from the Jabal Nafūsa in Libya in the east to Morocco in the west. The need for nomad communities to store grain and dates in one protected place, and for the sedentary agriculturalists of the mountain valleys to amass food reserves and to store arms and valuables safe from decay and the ravages of marauding tribesmen, led to communal building efforts. Walls, fortifications and water-cisterns are built jointly by the whole tribe or clan, while the individual storehouses within are built by each family. They provide a refuge for women and children and livestock in times of battle, and those storehouses situated on trade routes and strategic crossroads may function as market-places and caravanserais in times of peace. The fortified granary embodies in both physical and symbolic terms the power of survival of the group, and its identity; most have a written charter, which the group considers as the respository of customary law. Because the granaries were a potent architectural symbol of community autonomy, they were systemati-

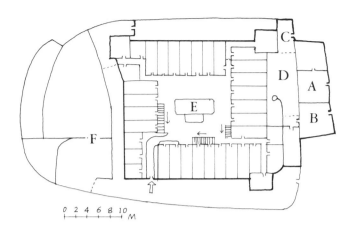

Communal granary in southern Morocco. The high containing wall is entered by a narrow door on the right; the entrance to the granary proper is marked by an arrow. A passage leads to a central courtyard with a cistern (E) in the centre. All around are the narrow rectangular cells belonging to individual families, and there are watch-towers at three corners. A, council chamber; B, room dedicated to the granary's patron saint; C, stable; D, yard for animals, with trough in the centre; F, mosque and religious school. (9)

cally destroyed by the Glaoui overlords during their expansion in southern Morocco in the early years of this century. The collective granary may also include a small mosque (each one is under the protection of a local marabout, or saint), and the granaries of the Anti Atlas and the western High Atlas also contain a council chamber, a reception room and a blacksmith's workshop. The collective granary may be interpreted as a nucleus or intermediate stage of urban organization among the Berbers of the Maghrib, the next evolutionary stage of which may be the *ksar* in its simplest form.

Collective granaries occur in two basic forms: those with an interior courtyard (which seem connected with shepherd communities, for livestock can be sheltered inside); and those where storehouse cells are aligned along either side of a long narrow median alley, more characteristic of agricultural communities of the western High Atlas. Cave granaries are also found in the Central Atlas. In northern Morocco, groups of small wooden granaries with thatched roofs are protected by the nature of their inaccessible mountainous or forest sites.

Though differing in building materials and techniques in various parts of the Maghrib, the citadel granaries all have common features. There are usually two to four tiers of small storage chambers grouped around the central court or alley, which is entered by steps made from protruding stones or beams. In the blank and impregnable exterior façade, there is only one entrance guarded by watchmen. In the Atlas Mountains of Morocco and the Aurès Mountains of Algeria, walls are of dry stone, but in the Saharan fringes walls may be of pisé with flat, earth roofs supported by timber beams. In southern Tunisia and Libya, each of the storage chambers is formed by a small barrel vault of rubble and mortar, giving an organic cellular aspect to the granary

Industrial vernacular

The demands of specialized crafts and agricultural activities in Muslim society have led to the evolution of large-scale machinery and distinctive forms of workshop. This industrial vernacular architecture uses techniques and materials common to domestic architecture and falls into the realm of the folk building trades. Islamic engineers and craftsmen made significant contributions to mechanical technology, and even in court circles, alongside the intricate automata designed to entertain and provoke wonder, there was great emphasis on the design of utilitarian machinery, such as mills and devices for raising water and for irrigation (as may be seen in the illuminated manuscripts of al-Jazarī's *Book of Knowledge of Ingenious Mechanical Devices*, written at the beginning of the 13th century).

Two types of water-mill have been known in Islam since Classical times: the vertical water-wheel that drives the millstones via a pair of gear-wheels, and the horizontal wheel with direct drive to the millstones, mentioned by Strabo in the 1st century (in the southern Balkans and northern Anatolia). From the accounts of geographers and travellers it is known that both types were widely used in the Islamic world for grinding grain and for driving industrial machinery, such as paper-mills. The horizontal water-wheel is still found in the Balkans and Anatolia, Iran and Turkestan. While the basic milling machinery is common to all these areas, the mill houses reflect the varying vernacular architecture of each region. In the steep Balkan mountain valleys of Bosnia-Herzegovina and Montenegro, mills are housed in small wooden structures with pitched wooden-shingle roofs, built on piles over fast-moving streams or specially diverted channels, as at Jajce in Bosnia. The mills are clustered in groups, each one serving the needs of a separate family.

In the long mountain valleys of Azerbaydzhan, in north-western Iran, there is often a series of mills, the water serving one mill after the other as it descends. The mills have rubble and mortar walls supporting flat, mud roofs in the style of the regional domestic architecture. The 14th-century historian and geographer, Hamdallāh Mustawfī, mentions a valley in Khurasan, in eastern Iran, where forty mills operated along the same stream, whose waters were so swift that it took no longer to grind one donkey-load of grain than to sew the heads of two flour-bags. In Iran many mills operate underground in order to gain the necessary head of water. Most of the major rivers of the Islamic world, however, are sluggish and are more suited to driving large, vertical water-wheels such as those of Hama, on the Orontes River in Syria. They may be used to drive grain-mills or machinery or to raise water for irrigational purposes.

The presence of water is a crucial factor determining the pattern of settlement and form of economy in most parts of the Islamic world – in Persian, the word for a human settlement, *ābādī*, means literally 'a place where there is water'. Much imagination is devoted to means of extracting water, regulating its distribution and storing it. There are many types of devices constructed of simple materials by village craftsmen, showing engineering ingenuity. They range from the Archimedean water-screw, still used in the Nile Valley, and the *shadūf*, which consists basically of a long pole balanced on a fulcrum with a rope and bucket at one end and a counterweight on the other, to the animal-powered systems, such as well-head devices used throughout Iran, the Middle East and North Africa and the apparatus driven by an animal walking in a circular path. In the latter system, the rotary movement powers a horizontal gear-wheel which engages a vertical wheel carrying a chain of pottery vessels, which in turn are immersed in the well and then discharge their contents into an irrigation channel or reservoir.

A survival of the magnificent hydraulic systems of the ancient southern Arabian kingdoms is the number of open, stepped cisterns of the Yemeni plateau and the Hadramawt. Some, such as that near the Grand Mosque of Tayyiba near Sanʿaʾ, have been maintained since pre-Islamic times. In Iran, underground circular cisterns are domed above ground level and cooled and aerated by one or more tall wind-towers.

Traditionally, Iranians of all classes have had a passion for drinks and sherbets cooled by snow or ice. In their desert environment, by a method possibly introduced by the Mongols, ice was produced cheaply and in substantial quantities in ice manufactories. During frosty winter nights water was left to freeze in successive shallow layers in a long channel or pond, protected during the day from the sun's rays by a high, massive mud wall. The ice was broken up and stored between layers of insulating straw in a large domed ice-house of mud-brick, from which it was distributed throughout the year. In the Kashan area, it is recorded that a single, salaried individual often had responsibility for the three major service buildings of the village community: the mosque, the cistern and the ice-house.

The traditional Islamic windmill revolves around a vertical axis, and not a horizontal axis as in the Aegean and Western Europe, and seems to have originated in Khurasan and Sistan, in eastern Iran, where it is still extensively used. The 13th-century geographer, al-Qazvini, mentions the mills of Sistan, as does the Syrian cosmographer, ad-Dimashqī, who provided a lengthy illustrated description. A typical wind-wheel is about six metres high and consists of a strong vertical wooden axis with horizontal radiating spokes, to which are attached vertical sails made from bundles of reeds. The axis is pivoted between an upper horizontal beam and a base block in the centre of the millstones. The machinery is supported and buttressed by two opposing solid mud-brick walls parallel to the prevailing wind direction. There is no wall on the leeward side, but on the north, facing the prevailing wind, there is a narrow wing wall leading the wind against one half of the vertical wind-wheel. Villages in this windy region, characteristically, are dominated to the north by long rows of these vertical windmills.

The special spatial requirements of many industrial processes have led to the adaptation of a wide variety of vaulting techniques, as can be seen in the specialized kilns of the lime-burning, brick-making, pottery, glass, resin, chicken-incubating and bread-baking industries. To give a regional example: on the island of Djerba are a number of interesting, vaulted workshop forms, which serve as examples of the unique and specific nature of buildings for artisan and agricultural activities. Weaving, a major local industry, is carried out in distinctive weaving huts, semi-excavated and rectangular in plan (underground or semi-underground buildings are a common feature of southern Tunisian architecture). Their roofs are formed by a series of narrow barrel vaults springing from transverse arches, supported by a sequence of external buttresses. The façade at either end is triangular. The olive-mills of this area are also excavated and are approached by an entrance passage opening into a large, rectangular underground hall. On one side of this chamber are built the storage bins into which olives are poured through holes in the roof; on the other side is the olive press with its long wooden beam. The far end of this hall gives access to the circular mill room, which has a domed roof projecting above ground level.

Another witness to the inventiveness and monumentality of form in Islamic utilitarian architecture is the pigeon tower. These are a noticeable feature of the agricultural landscape of Iran (particularly the Isfahan district), central Afghanistan, Iraq and the Nile Delta. They are erected to collect pigeon droppings for use as fertilizer, and, when full, the structures are dismantled and their contents spread over the fields. In the Isfahan area the pigeon towers are tall, cylindrical structures of mud-brick (constructed so that each brick alternates with a space that can be used as a nesting niche). They are formed by two concentric cylindrical walls, the inner one projecting like a turret. In the Golpayegan district to the north-east of Isfahan, the towers are square in plan. They are mud-plastered and often decorated with bands of popular motifs. In the Nile Delta, pigeon towers are constructed of pottery vessels set in a mud mortar, and are shaped like tall tapering cylinders or rectangular towers with slightly battered walls. They are frequently whitewashed.

Popular shrines and places of worship

The Qur'ān discourages the worship of saints and the commemoration of the dead, and the majority of ordinary Muslims in country and city are buried in simple anonymous graves marked by a stone or wooden pillar at their head and foot; the graves of women may be indicated by a third post at the centre. The graves of rulers of purist orthodox sects, such as the contemporary Wahhābī dynasty of Saudi Arabia, are indistinguishable from those of their brethren. However, the uncanonized veneration of saints and the erection of shrines and memorial structures is a major and widespread feature of Islamic popular religion, doubtless influenced by pre-Islamic and regional religious beliefs and cult practices. These are particularly perpetuated in the closed, conservative domain of women, who tend not to pray in the major mosques but to approach the spiritual world through localized popular cults of saints and seers. The holy persons so venerated may be scholars, eminent jurists, respected tribal leaders and popular heroes as well as religious figures. Although dynastic tombs and shrines of important saints tend to be luxurious, monumental structures, those of holy men of local renown are usually much simpler and follow local variations of style and building methods of the regional vernacular.

These popular shrines may not be tombs, but simply a place associated with some event in the life of the saint, and consequently endowed with his *baraka*, the spiritual power of blessing and protection. In the Skoura region of southern Morocco, for example, the protective power of certain local saints, around whose shrines the communal granaries are erected, is considered so effective that it is not necessary to enclose the complex with fortress walls. Shrines may be very simple: a cairn of stones, or a tiny dome at the head of the tomb-slab of a holy man with a cavity in which offerings of grain or fruit can be placed, and candles, oil lamps or incense burnt. The shrines are usually whitewashed and often hung with coloured cloths, usually green and white, the colour of the garments of the angel of the revelation according to Muhammad.

Although vernacular tombs of saints follow no consistent plan or structure and display a great diversity and individuality of form, they tend to imitate in small scale the shapes of the major monumental mausolea particular to each region. Thus, in Iran, vernacular tombs with a cylindrical base and conical or pyramidal roof are obviously related to such major tombs as the 11th-century Gunbad-i Qābūs. In the Middle East, Arabia and North Africa, the cubical tomb chamber surmounted by a hemispherical dome is the most popular form. Though derived from the geometrically formal metropolitan models of ashlar or burnt-brick construction, the structural principles of the models are often misunderstood and the local builders, working in simple plastic materials such as mud and plaster, imaginatively transform the tomb into votive sculpture. Saints' tombs of the domed type usually have a pointed, triangular or horn shape at each corner of the roof. The horn symbolism is of great antiquity, having an apotropaic function in warding off malevolent influences; it can form the major decorative element in shrines, houses and mosques. Its most developed form is found in the necropolises of the M'zab, in Algeria, the mosques of Oman (where horns are ranged in tiers) and the houses of Ghadames in Libya and Zaria and Kano in northern Nigeria.

Characteristic of the Muslim attitude to the place of prayer is this quotation from the *Masadjid*: 'Wherever the hour of prayer overtakes thee, thou shalt perform the prayer and that is a *masjid*.' Although in the cities and towns of most of the Islamic world the congregational mosque and other major mosques are constructed in the prevailing architectural mode of the ruling élite, the simpler mosques and shrines of the city quarters and rural areas reflect more closely the vernacular building traditions and patterns of religious observances of the populace. In West Africa, where the grand traditions of Islamic architecture did not arrive until the present century, the architecture of mosques and tombs is an exclusively vernacular development.

Ibn Khaldūn relates of the early Arabs: 'At the beginning, religion forbade them to do any excessive building or to waste too much money on building activities for no purpose.' During the first period of Islamic expansion, a schematic *qibla* wall sufficed as a place of prayer and such simple prayer areas – with the *qibla* wall indicated by a line drawn on the ground and a semicircular projection to indicate the *mihrāb* niche, or a line of small stones – are still used by nomadic tribes today. Larger versions of open-air prayer areas, or *musallās*, are found on the fringes of many towns and cities. In the Prophet's time it was the custom on the feast-days of the 'Īd al-Fitr and the 'Īd al-Adhā to pray communally in the *musallā*, a custom that continues today. Schematic prayer areas may contain a *minbar*.

Although it is customary to attend the congregational mosque on Friday for communal prayers, religious observances during the week can take place at home or at work, or in small local oratories connected to a house or to a group of dwellings. These, typically, have neither a minaret, as the Faithful are not called to prayer, nor a *minbar*, as no sermon is given. The local mosque in the old Red Sea port of Suakin is a characteristic example: a simple platform open to the sky enclosed by a low wall with an entrance and *mihrāb* niche. In Isfahan, as elsewhere, such simple structures are transformed during religious festivals by the erection of a canopy, and are furnished with rich textiles, carpets and cushions.

A *mihrāb* niche might occasionally be constructed within the house, or an apartment set aside as a private chapel, such as the *imāmbāra* of Indian and Pakistani houses or the *mescits* of the houses of Kayseri in central Turkey. The Companions of the Prophet, Abū Bakr and Abū Umāma Asad, are both recorded as having had private mosques. Muhammad himself used his courtyard house at Medina for prayer and religious instruction, and, as we have seen in Chapter 1, this may have been one of the factors influencing the adaptation of regional domestic architecture for the construction of mosques. This relationship between house-types and mosque-types can be seen clearly in the two major early mosque-types, the courtyard hypostyle mosque and the Iranian courtyard mosque with axial *iwāns*, as well in the multitude of simpler town and village mosques reflecting localized vernacular building traditions.

Tradition and change: The vernacular mosque might be considered to epitomize Islamic vernacular architecture in its merging of age-old building techniques and structural forms with the devotional requirements of Islam. It accents the often less obvious adaptation of regional indigenous house-types to serve Islamic social needs. Today in the Islamic world, major social changes are affecting the form of domestic architecture. The nuclear family, the decline of polygamy and the reduction in the number of children per couple (in the wealthy and professional classes) have resulted in correspondingly smaller housing units. Existing houses, formerly inhabited by extended families, have become tenements for unrelated groups – or are abandoned. There is increased acceptance of freedom of movement for women, with greater social contact, resulting in less need for fully enclosed environments.

Key Monuments of Islamic Architecture

Arabia

GEOFFREY KING AND
RONALD LEWCOCK

The urban areas of Arabia are separated in the south and west by mountain ranges and, in the rest of the Arabian Peninsula, by broad gravel plains and sand deserts. But neither mountains nor deserts have proven effective obstacles to travellers, and routes in ancient times passed up the western side of Arabia and across the central plains; however, for convenience as well as for security, many travellers preferred to go by ship. From early times merchants and pilgrims to Mecca traditionally have made up the sea-going traffic, the pilgrims being in the majority. During the ʿAbbāsid, Fātimid and Mamlūk periods, vast quantities of goods were brought from the Far East and Africa, through the Gulf and the Red Sea, by Arab ships. The Omanis sailed a succession of fleets which ousted the Portuguese from the area and, until 1856, helped to maintain an Indian Ocean empire encompassing the East African coast including Zanzibar.

The architecture of the Arabian Peninsula can be divided broadly into that of the interior, and that of the coast or coastal influenced areas. The climate of these areas varies from the severe extremes of summer and winter in the interior to the exceedingly hot and uncomfortable humid climate of the coast. Inner Arabian buildings have thick walls, mostly of unfired mud-brick, with only small openings. Decoration is in cut plaster, roofing and doors in wood, and stone replaces mud-brick in some cases. In contrast, coastal houses are normally built of coral aggregate, the interiors decorated with fine plaster relief and pierced screens. In all parts of Arabia doors are highly decorated, and those in coastal houses are carved. The doors of Omani houses are closely related to East African examples. Coastal buildings are relatively open; in order to permit circulation of air various devices are employed, including the wooden screens of the Red Sea and the Gulf, pierced plaster screens, large openings and, in certain Gulf towns, wind-towers.

The forms of Arabian architecture vary considerably: the towered structures of the Yemen appear to preserve a plan of some antiquity, possibly related to the lofty buildings of Mecca, Medina, Taʾif and Jidda and also to the tower-houses of the Hijaz highlands. The decoration of these houses is related to that of the lower buildings of the Gulf, where Iranian, Indian and East African influences may be detected. The great

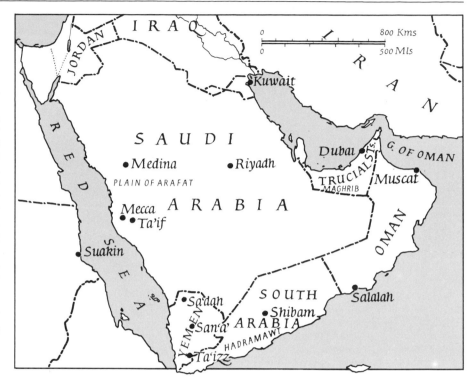

courtyard houses of Oman are rather different to the buildings of the northern Gulf, closer to Zanzibar and other East African forms. The settlements of the interior were originally towns of mud-brick with stone walls within which houses were closely packed.

In the fringe areas between the coast and interior, architectural distinctions are less clear: in inner Oman, mud-brick buildings have fine wooden carved doors like those on the Omani coast; at al-Hasa, inland from the coast, architecture is in the coastal style but of stone rather than coral. Similarly, in Mecca, Medina and Taʾif, the coral aggregate of the Red Sea ports is replaced by cut stone and brick. Finally, certain Arabian buildings do not stem from local traditions but reflect the pious patronage of non-Arab Muslims visiting the holy cities and their sanctuaries. In more recent times, the Ottomans ruled parts of Arabia, erecting a number of monuments in the Turkish style.

Chronology
Prophet Muhammad 622–32
Caliphal period 632–61
Umayyad period 661–750
Rasūlid period 1235–1510
Ottoman period c.1520–c.1630
Yaʿrubid period mid-17th century–1741
Saʿūdī period 1746–
Rashīdī period 1887–1902

Saudi Arabia

MECCA, Mosque of the Haram
Converted into a mosque by the Prophet, 630, with many later additions.

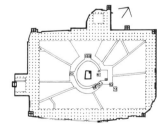

This is the most sacred site in Islam, to which it is incumbent upon all Muslims, insofar as they are able, to make the pilgrimage once in their lifetime. The building consists of a vast irregular colonnade surrounding an open courtyard in the centre of which is the Kaʿba. It is towards the Kaʿba (a cube-shaped chamber measuring 13 m × 11 m, more than

16m high) that all Muslims turn in prayer five times each day. Muslims believe that the prototype of the Ka'ba was designed by the Prophet Ibrāhīm (Abraham). The site was sacred before Islam, and with the Muslim conquest of Mecca, in 630, Muhammad destroyed the numerous idols in the building. In the north-east corner of the Ka'ba is the Black Stone, said to be a meteorite, an object of reverence for the pilgrims who kiss it as they ritually circumambulate the structure. The stone-built Ka'ba has been reconstructed several times but preserves its ancient form: it is entered by a door on the north side, high above ground level, whose frame was sent from Constantinople, after a rebuilding of 1627. The structure is covered with black silk, formerly renewed annually by the reigning caliph. Within the courtyard are several sacred sites, including the burial place of Abraham and the Zamzam well, which sprang up miraculously for Ishma'il and his mother. The mosque was enlarged in the 7th century by the caliphs, 'Umar I and 'Uthmān; then by Ibn az-Zubayr. The Umayyad caliph, al-Walīd I, decorated it with wall mosaics, in the 8th century. In the 9th century the 'Abbāsid caliph, al-Mahdī, built colonnades around the courtyard; but it was the Ottoman sultan, Selīm II, who, in the 16th century, gave this mosque the form it preserved until the recent rebuilding by the Sa'ūdīs.

MEDINA, Mosque of the Prophet
Founded by the Prophet, 622, with later enlargements.

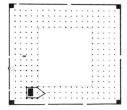

Only the Mosque of the Haram at Mecca is more revered than this mosque. In 622, after reaching Medina, Muhammad laid out a rectangular mosque next to his house; and when he died, the Prophet was buried under the floor of the house. In 707, the Umayyad caliph, al-Walīd I, enlarged the mosque, including within its enclosure the tomb of the Prophet. Christian workmen decorated the mosque with marble and mosaics of gold glass, representing trees and buildings. These covered the walls of the open courtyard and the colonnaded sanctuary against the *qibla* (south) wall. The mosaics, which are now lost, were closely related to those in the Great Mosque at Damascus erected by the same caliph. Subsequently, the mosque was redecorated by the 'Abbāsids, the Mamlūks and the Ottomans. At present, the rectangular mosque enclosure has five minarets and a great green dome before the *qibla* wall; the *mihrābs* are Mamlūk and Ottoman.

RIYADH, Qasr Masmak
Sa'ūdī or Rashīdī period, 19th century

Built of unfired mud-brick, covered with mud plaster, this castle is rectangular in plan, reinforced with round and square towers. The walls are raked, as in all the fortifications of central Arabia, of which this building is typical – although it is more important for its historical associations with the Sa'ūdī royal family. The great wooden door, with a smaller door set in it, enabled the guards inside to compel visitors to pass single file and bow, thus exposing their necks to the sword.

The Yemen
SAN'A', Great Mosque
7th–17th centuries

Early Islamic sources stress that this mosque was laid out at the instruction of the Prophet, and that he indicated the site and the precise limits of the building. Even allowing for later expansion, the original mosque cannot have been less than about 55m square. Until archaeological excavation is undertaken, however, it cannot be established whether parts of the surviving mosque date back to this original foundation. It was extensively enlarged, *c.* 707, by the Umayyad caliph, al-Walīd I, and parts were rebuilt at various times during the next four centuries – particularly the ceilings, which, in their present form, date from the 11th and 12th

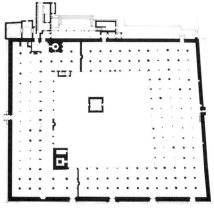

centuries, with the exception of a few preserved earlier fragments. At least one minaret was standing by the early 9th century; both were renovated in the 12th century. The domed treasury in the main court was built by the Ottomans in the early 17th century; it is not yet known whether this replaced an earlier treasury on the same site. The mosque is built of semicircular arches on reused Antique columns; in its final form, the main prayer hall of five aisles on the north is flanked by side halls on either side of the central court, each of which is three aisles wide; to the south is a second prayer hall of four aisles, with tombs to the east and west. In the present century two libraries were built above the south hall.

SAN'A', Mosque of al-Bakīriyya
Ottoman period, 1597

This is the finest surviving monument from the Ottoman occupation of the Yemen, and was built by Hasan Paşa. It is a large and imposing complex comprising a prayer hall, covered by a single dome on flat pendentives, with an extension on the east side containing a tomb and covered by three smaller domes. There is a triple-domed porch on the south, richly decorated with fine stucco-work of Ottoman type. A long courtyard separates the porch from the domed ablution block; on the east is a covered passageway and the towering minaret; and on the west is a fine central-domed portal with two lateral domed chambers, added during the second Turkish occupation in the 19th century. Against the south wall of the prayer hall, a free-standing *dīwān* for the governor is surmounted by a platform (from which to read the Qur'ān) supported on six porphyry columns. The high marble *minbar* and the *mihrāb* are of material imported from Istanbul.

TA'IZZ, Ashrafiyya Mosque
Rasūlid period, 13th and 14th centuries

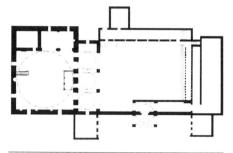

This *madrasa*-mosque was apparently built in two stages; the first by al-Ashraf I (1295–6), the second by al-Ashraf II (1377–1400). In its first stage the mosque had a prayer hall with eight small domes flanking one large central dome. The whole was decorated in stucco and painted ornament of outstanding quality. A square courtyard lay behind, flanked by a royal tomb chamber and rooms for the Qur'ānic school, bringing the plan to an almost perfect square. In the corners of the south side rose a pair of minarets of subtly varied design. The *qibla* wall is decorated externally like the courtyard, with superimposed arcades of diminishing size. The projecting *mihrāb* has, externally, a *muqarnas* decoration motif and is crowned by a domed pavilion, which rises above the roof. About a hundred years later, three royal tombs were introduced into three of the corners of the courtyard; their design and decoration is Cairene work of the finest quality. An open-roofed loggia was added around three sides of the mosque, with arcades on the outside terminating in two domed pavilions in line with the *qibla* wall. Three impressive portals jutted out from the new loggia with teaching rooms flanking the central south portal.

South Arabia
SHIBAM, Mosque
9th century

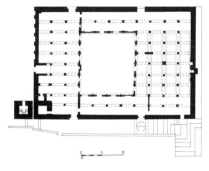

Substantially preserved in its 9th-century form, this mosque gives an impression of the original appearance and character of great South Arabian hypostyle mosques of the early centuries of Islam. Externally, the mosque is surrounded by an immense stone wall, barely interrupted by openings; internally, there is a square court, originally surrounded on all sides by high stone columns carrying flat ceilings on wooden beams. At some date after its original construction the flanking halls were protected from the weather by the erection of screen walls around the courtyard, rising from arcades, with alabaster windows above and a crowning cornice of Sasanian design. The columns of the prayer halls are 8m high and carry capitals of palmette design derived ultimately from Hellenistic prototypes. The north prayer hall has a magnificent ceiling of richly carved and painted woodwork, comprising twenty-four panels of different design, eighteen smaller panels and a number of carved and painted beams. The present minaret was built of brick, probably in the 16th century. It replaced the earlier minaret dating from the foundation of the mosque, a low square structure in the south-east corner of the south prayer hall.

Oman
JABRIN, Palace of Imām Bal'arab ibn Sulṭān
Ya'rubid period, 1675

This palace is a rectangular, stone-built structure with great round towers at the north and south corners. A canal passes through the two courtyards, which are entered by a doorway in the south-east wall. Although built to withstand siege, the scale and decoration of the interior is palatial rather than military. The palace contains the tomb of its founder. Among several highly decorated rooms, the Hall of the Sun and Moon is particularly striking, with a high flat wooden ceiling, reinforced with wooden beams and painted with floral motifs. The plastered walls have high arched recesses around the windows, designed so that the light is excluded but ventilation is encouraged. Fine views of the surrounding countryside are provided. Elsewhere in the building are other painted wooden ceilings and fine stucco. The decoration of the palace reflects the external cultural influences that affected Oman at this time.

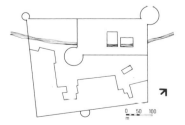

Spain

GEOFFREY KING

Muslim armies began to conquer Visigothic Spain from North Africa in 710 and, within varying territorial limits, Islamic rule continued in the Spanish Peninsula until 1492. Many Muslims also lived in Spain under Christian monarchs and, at least until the 15th century, Islamic artistic and cultural influences flourished in the service of Catholic princes. Despite these centuries of Muslim autonomy and a deeply embedded Islamicizing culture, there are very few extant Islamic monuments. Nevertheless, those which still stand serve to illustrate not only the cultural wealth of the Muslim rulers of Spain but also the architecture of other parts of the Islamic world, where major monuments often have not been preserved. Thus the royal palace and gardens of the Nasrids at Granada, the Alhambra, suggest not only the other lost palaces of Islamic Spain, but the vanished complexes of 'Abbāsid Iraq, Tūlūnid and Fātimid Egypt, Norman Islamic Palermo and many other lesser seats of power.

The Muslim state in Spain began to flourish in the second half of the 8th century, after a member of the Syrian Umayyad royal house escaped from the 'Abbāsids and set himself up in Cordoba with the help of the many Syrian Arabs who had migrated to Spain. Cordoba henceforth became the capital of the Spanish Umayyad princes and, eventually, a new Umayyad caliphate was proclaimed in opposition to the claims of the Fātimids of Cairo and the 'Abbāsids of Baghdad. By the 10th century, Umayyad Spain had achieved a society in which large Christian and Jewish groups were tolerated by the Muslim rulers and non-Muslims could rise to high office. At a time when western Europe consisted of little more than barbarian villages, Muslim Cordoba was compared with Constantinople and Baghdad.

From the first efflorescence of Islamic architecture in Spain, there was a strong preference for elaborate decorative effects. In the earlier period stone and stucco were favoured; later, brick replaced stone and polychrome tiling was also included. Complexity of architectural form and decoration characterizes the Great Mosque at Cordoba at all periods of its enlargement, the delicate Alhambra at Granada and, above all, the luxuriant, even overblown decoration of the Aljaferia at Saragossa. Contrasting with this is the severe simplicity of the Giralda at Seville and related buildings, both in Spain and North Africa. This simplicity was derived from the fundamentalist teachings propagated by the puritanical Almohad movement. However, the Spanish Islamic influence in its more extravagant forms was also felt in North Africa itself and it is there that Spanish architectural and decorative motifs in stucco and tile-mosaic continued to be used long after Muslim Spain had collapsed. Within Spain itself, the type of brick tower and relief in brick, developed by Muslim artists, was subsequently employed by Christians, especially at Toledo, and adapted to Christian architectural needs. As to the origins of Spanish Islamic architecture and its decoration – much was borrowed from the earlier Visigothic tradition, but many of the motifs adopted may also have originated in Syria, whence the Umayyads and their supporters came. In addition to the architectural forms common to the whole Muslim world, Spain also inherited the general artistic repertoire of the pre-Islamic Mediterranean world.

Chronology

Umayyad period, 756–1031

Mulūk at-Tawā'if period 1010–1142

Almoravid period 1056–1147

Almohad period 1130–1269

Nasrid period 1230–1492

CORDOBA, Great Mosque
Umayyad period, 784–6, 961–6, 987–90 and other restorations

This stone structure, with marble columns and some brick, forms a rectangular enclosure within high walls. There is an open courtyard to the north and a covered sanctuary to the south. The original 8th-century mosque of 'Abd ar-Rahmān I had only ten arcades running perpendicular to the *qibla* (south) wall: these were subsequently extended to the south, while at a later date, more arcades were added to the east. The most remarkable aspect of the mosque is the structure of these arcades. Because the available Antique columns were too short to sufficiently raise the roof of the sanctuary, piers were built on each column to support round-headed arches, with alternating stone and brick voussoirs, on which the roof rested. Reinforcing this structure are bracing horseshoe arches. Although the origin of this structural system is uncertain, the design was followed in all later extensions of the Great Mosque. In 961–6, Caliph al-Hakam II extended the mosque to the south and added a series of highly ornate, intersecting, lobed arches and three domes in front of the *qibla* wall. The domes have complex rib patterns, each differing from its neighbour. The *qibla* wall has two later *mihrābs* flanking the central *mihrāb*, which is a deeply recessed polygonal chamber with floral motifs and Qur'ānic inscriptions in marble. The domes are supported by complex rib-systems, each differing, close in form to dome structures in Armenia and Iran, later spreading throughout western Europe. Gold and glass mosaics on the *mihrāb* frames and central dome recall earlier Umayyad mosaics in Syria and Arabia, allegedly introduced into Spain from Constantinople.

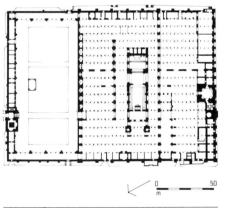

CORDOBA, Minaret of San Juan
Umayyad period, 930

The tower of the church of San Juan was formerly a minaret. It is built of stone and some brick and is rectangular in groundplan. The minaret is not aligned to the cardinal points because of its relationship to the orientation of the mosque to which it belonged, subsequently destroyed (the minaret is now free-standing). It has double horseshoe openings with a central column in each face of the wall, set high up. The

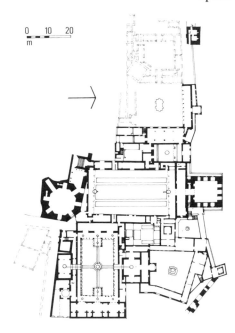

voussoirs of the horseshoe arches are, alternately, stone and brick. The uppermost part of the minaret is of a later date, and restorations were undertaken earlier this century. The building material is typical of Umayyad Spain, while the design is in the Syrian and North African tradition, which greatly influenced Spanish Islamic architecture.

CORDOBA, Madīnat al-Zahrā' Palace
Umayyad period, 936–76

'Abd ar-Rahmān III, the first Spanish Umayyad caliph, built this palace to the north-west of the crowded city of Cordoba,

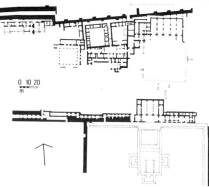

overlooking the Guadalquivir River Valley. Built of stone, brick and plaster, the palace had open courtyards surrounded by reception rooms, with running water, and elegant gardens. It was wrecked by soldiers and slaves in the 11th century and today is in ruins, which have been partly excavated. Numerous fragments of decorative stone remain, as well as some marble reliefs with floral designs. Although built in the style of Umayyad Cordoba, the architects used material and men from North Africa and Constantinople, as well, it seems. The supply of Byzantine craftsmen was a result of friendly relations between Cordoba and Constantinople.

GRANADA, Alhambra (Al-Hamrā') Citadel and Palace
Nasrid period, 13th and 14th centuries

This fortified citadel dominating Granada was founded in the period of Islamic Spain's disintegration into a series of independent states, after the Almohad collapse and withdrawal to Africa. Muhammad I al-Ghālib (1230–72) established his Nasrid dynasty in Granada and built the foundations of the Alhambra as his royal seat. The construction was continued by his son, Muhammad II (1272–1302). The massive walls, reinforced with great rectangular towers, are now entered through the Gate of Justice on the south. The palace was built by Yūsuf I (1333–54) and his successor, Muhammad V (1354–91), and it consisted of residential quarters, mosques and baths. The decoration in carved stucco and tiles includes intricate geometric and floral designs as well as Qur'ānic inscriptions. The palace is in the form of a succession of rectangular courtyards joined by, and giving access to, ornate reception rooms. The private apartments overlooking the more public courts are concealed by wooden grilles. In the Court of the Myrtles and the Court of the Lions, pools and fountains reflect the sunlight, providing a continuity between open and closed spaces.

GRANADA, Generalife Gardens
Nasrid period, early 14th century

Situated on a hill north-east of the Alhambra complex, the Generalife is a series of gardens and pavilions, of which the Court of the Stream adheres most closely to its Arab design. It is a long rectangular garden with a central pool and fountains, fed by streams that run down the hillside. Around the garden are enclosing walls and two-storey pavilions at the north and south ends, both of which are in the same architectural tradition as the Alhambra palace, especially in their stucco decoration.

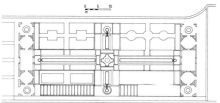

MÉRIDA, Alcazaba Citadel
Umayyad period, completed 835

Built by 'Abd ar-Rahmān II to maintain control of Mérida, whose approaches it dominates, this building is one of a long line of fortresses running from the east to the west across the Muslim frontier with Christian northern Spain. The Alcazaba, on the bank of the Guardia River, is a rectangular fortification approximately orientated towards the cardinal points. It is constructed of well cut stones, some of which appear to be of Roman and Visigothic origin, though the building technique recalls that of Syria. The walls are thick (2.7m) and are reinforced by rectangular towers; the battlements, which once surmounted the walls, have vanished. In the centre of the enclosure is a deep cistern, consisting of a tunnel vault employing Roman stones and ornamented by Visigothic pilasters, giving access to two parallel sloping ramps leading to an underground pool. During the Christian period the Alcazaba became a possession of the Knights of Santiago de Compostella, who restored it. Today it is a museum.

RONDA, Bath
12th–15th centuries (?)

The bath is on the east side of the Ronda citadel, next to the Culebra River. It is one of the best preserved of the Islamic monuments in Spain. Built of baked brick with stone and some marble, it is a rectangular building divided into three barrel-vaulted chambers, the *calidarium*, the *frigidarium* and the *apodyterium*. The central chamber has small openings in the roof, similar to those in the bath in the Alhambra. On the north side is the entrance and a rectangular courtyard with a damaged colonnade around a pool. The water supply for the bath was drawn by a water-wheel from the river and poured into

a system of gulleys. A number of tiles, and marble and wood fragments have been found on the site.

SARAGOSSA, Aljaferia Palace
Mulūk at-Tawā'if period, 1046–81

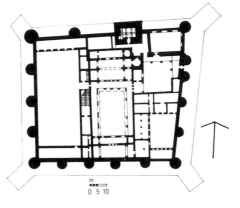

This rectangular walled enclosure of stone and brick, reinforced with towers, is entered from the east. Within the enclosure are the palace and mosque of al-Muqtadir, built of baked brick and decorated with stucco. The palace lies on a north–south axis, and has an open courtyard surrounded by lobed arches with extremely complex decoration of floral motifs, geometrics and attached colonnettes. The courtyard opens onto a throne room with lobed arcades: its upper storey is Christian work of the 16th century. Next to the throne room is a small mosque, whose octagonal interior plan is set within a rectangular building; it is vaulted by a restored ribbed dome. The *mihrāb* is a deep niche in the south-east corner of the mosque, reminiscent of the Great Mosque at Cordoba. The interior of the mosque is entirely decorated with stucco and attached colonnettes; Qur'ānic inscriptions run round the interior and the entrance to the mosque.

SEVILLE, Great Mosque
Almohad period, 1171–6

Although replaced by the 15th-century cathedral, the courtyard of the original mosque survives alongside the north wall of

the cathedral. The enclosure wall is of fired brick and some areas of the inner surface were formerly covered with elegant plaster relief decoration. Two entrances to the enclosure survive to the north and east. The wall is reinforced by rectangular butresses and is surmounted by merlons recalling the earlier enclosure walls of the Great Mosque at Cordoba. Inside the courtyard, slightly pointed horseshoe arches rest on piers and form arcades around two sides (north and east) of the open courtyard. Along the north side of the cathedral are traces of further piers, presumably remnants of the original mosque. The courtyard has several fountains and numerous orange-trees irrigated by channels in the brick floor.

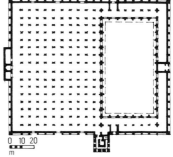

Proposed reconstruction

SEVILLE, Giralda
Almohad period, 1156–98

Today this is the tower of Seville Cathedral, but was formerly the minaret of the Great Mosque, on the site of which the Cathedral now stands. The minaret was begun with reused stone, and was completed, some years later, in fired brick. It is square in plan (about 16m each side) and over 50m high. It is surmounted by a lantern and a belfry, added by the Christians, 1520–68. The minaret is ascended by a ramp built around a series of seven central rooms situated one above the other, lit by windows with lobed and horseshoe arches. The exterior wall surfaces are decorated with a fine, brick, geometric

design set within large rectangular panels. The Giralda is closely related to the minaret of the Kutubiyya Mosque at Marrakesh and the Minaret of the mosque of Hasan at Rabat, both contemporary Almohad buildings.

SEVILLE, Alcázar (Al-Qasr)
Muslim and Christian periods, rebuilt 1364

Though founded in the Mulūk at-Tawā'if period, the earliest parts of this palace are the Almohad walls. The Alcázar was rebuilt by the Christian king, Pedro I ('The Cruel'), in 1364, but is essentially Islamic. It was constructed by Muslim craftsmen provided by the Nasrid sultan of Granada, while the carpenters were from the old Islamic centre, Toledo. Despite subsequent restorations in European style, the Alcázar adheres to its Islamic plan – open courtyards with fountains are surrounded by reception rooms, many lit by reflected sunlight. Stucco and ceramic decoration and light from the pools and fountains break up the solidity of the wall surfaces, giving an effect similar to that of the Alhambra. The cultural fusion between Christian and Islamic Spain by this period is indicated by the Arabic inscriptions, invoking blessings on the Christian 'Sultan' Don Pedro.

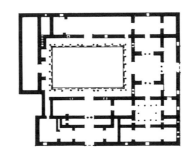

TOLEDO, Mosque of Bāb Mardūm
Umayyad period, 1000

The mosque, now a church, San Cristo de la Luz, was converted after the Christian conquest of Toledo in 1085. A brick apse was added subsequently. The original rectangular mosque is of baked brick, stone and

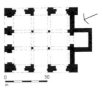

Proposed reconstruction

plaster. The *qibla* (south-east) wall had a large rectangular *mihrāb*, now replaced by a doorway. Two entrances flanked the *mihrāb* (both now sealed) and three entrances were in each of the other walls. The surviving Umayyad entrances are either horseshoe or lobed, and upper areas of the north-west and south-west exterior walls carry blind, horseshoe-arched niches and intersecting arches, all forming part of the decorative repertoire of Umayyad Cordoba. The Arabic foundation inscription is on the south-west wall. Inside, nine ribbed domes in the roof rest on four columns of Visigothic origin. The rib patterns of the domes are coarser versions of the elgant domes in front of the *mihrāb* of the Great Mosque at Cordoba. The purpose of the mosque of Bāb Mardūm is unknown but it is one of a group of similar religious buildings, which appeared throughout the Islamic world in the 9th–10th centuries.

North Africa and Sicily

GEORGE MICHELL

The countries of the Maghrib – Morocco, Algeria, Tunisia and Libya – are here grouped for their historical connections and parallel architectural developments. The earlier monuments, dating from the 9th century, incorporated architectural and decorative elements from both the 'Abbāsid east and Umayyad Spain. After the 11th century, with the devastating invasions of the Hilāl Arab tribes, however, these two traditions became so polarized that such a fusion was no longer possible; thereafter, the Maghrib, especially Morocco, remained

within the same cultural orbit as Muslim Spain. Repeated immigrations from Spain and the political domination there, for a time, of North African dynasties, ensured constant

artistic contact with that country, especially under the Almoravids and Almohads. After the decline of Muslim Spain in the 13th century, the isolation of the Maghrib from the rest of the Islamic world increased despite the coming of the Ottomans; Morocco, cut off by mountains, did not experience the Turkish domination.

The major monuments of the Aghlabids, the first indigenous North African dynasty, especially the mosques at Qairouan, Sousse and Tunis, display a clarity and uniformity of concept – in the disposition of internal arcades, low roofs, courtyards with square multi-storeyed minarets, vast rectangular enclosures – that was to become universal in subsequent centuries. A particular type of fortress, the *ribāt* (Sousse and Monastir), displays a similar forceful simplicity of architectural form. There are also civic hydraulic works (cisterns of Qairouan) and large-scale pleasure palaces (ruins of Raqqāda and al-'Abbāsiya outside Qairouan). Aghlabid buildings are characterized, especially on their exteriors, by large unadorned expanses of masonry or brickwork. Limited decoration is applied in carved stone, stucco and wood, testifying to close artistic contacts with both the eastern Mediterranean and Spain.

In subsequent centuries, North Africa was largely cut off from the stimulus of the east and regional styles evolved under local dynasties. The architecture of the Fātimids, Zīrids and Hammādids is austere and monumental. Mosques (Mahdia, extensions to Qairouan, Sfax and Tunis) and palaces, especially at the *qal'a* of the Banī Hammād, are characterized by recessed arched niches breaking up the wall surfaces. This style is even found in Sicily during the Norman rule.

It was under the patronage of the great Berber dynasties, the Almoravids and Almohads in the western Maghrib, that North African architecture developed its most characteristic expression. There is, in particular, a fascination with different arched shapes and lobed forms to create complex interlacings on a monumental scale – in carved stone for city gateways (Rabat and Marrakesh) and minarets (mosques at Tlemcen, Marrakesh and Rabat), and also in stuccoed brick for the interior arcades of mosques. The characteristic *muqarnas* corbelling also becomes ubiquitous, not only as vaulting but for arches and niches in shallow relief. In general, there is little concern for exterior façades apart from imposing portals and high minarets.

The succeeding Marīnid and Sa'dian dynasties patronized a smaller-scaled architecture, though decoration continued its inevitable course of evolution. There is a preference for exquisitely ornamented *madrasas*, tombs and *zāwiyas* (Fez and Marrakesh), with a sensitive manipulation of chiselled stucco, timber marquetry and glazed tile-mosaic. From Spain come the detached pavilions with green-tiled painted roofs, used in both palace and mosque courtyards, often with pools

of water in attractive garden settings.

During the Turkish period in Algeria, there was a marked impact of Ottoman architecture; in Tunisia and Libya, however, more local traditions were combined with a Europeanized decorative repertory combining tile panels and inlaid stonework with stucco. The great palaces and private houses of Algiers, Tunis and Tripoli are evidence of the sophistication of urban life and artistic patronage that builders and craftsmen enjoyed in more recent centuries.

Chronology

WESTERN MAGHRIB

Idrīsid period 789–926

Rustamid period 777–909

Almoravid period 1056–1147

Almohad period 1130–1269

Marīnid period 1196–1465

Sa'dian period 1511–1659

'Alawid period 1631–

EASTERN MAGHRIB

Aghlabid period 800–909

Fātimid period 909–1171

Zīrid period 972–1148

Hammādid period 1015–1152

Hafsid period 1228–1574

Ottoman period 1516–1830

Morocco
FEZ, Qarawiyyn Mosque
Almoravid and other periods, 859, 956, 1135 and 17th century

Surrounded by a celebrated university, this mosque took on its distinctive dimensions, ornamentation and general appearance in the Almoravid period when the aisles of the original mosque (859) were prolonged. A new minaret was built in 956 and is preserved. In 1135, the mosque was enlarged towards the *qibla* wall by the addition of three transversal arcades; a new *mihrāb* was also added. The fine *minbar*, dated 1144, was probably imported from Cordoba. The central aisle is covered by vaults and domes on ribs and by *muqarnas* cells carried above the green-tiled roofs as a raised pavilion. The rectangular colonnaded courtyard has naves that constitute annexes to the prayer hall.

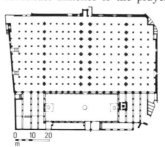

The two pavilions, connected by a fountain and water channel, added in the Sa'dian period, are similar to those at Granada.

FEZ, Bū-'Ināniyya Madrasa
Marīnid period, 1350–5

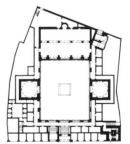

Most monumental of all the *madrasas* of Fez, this example built by Abū'Inān functions not only as a school but also as a Friday mosque, the water-clock on its minaret marking the rhythm of the religious life of the city. The double staircase entry leads to a courtyard paved in marble with an ablution basin and a pool reflecting the subtle and complex decoration of the surrounding façades – piers are clad in glazed tile-mosaic with chiselled stucco panels, windows and *muqarnas*-work sheaths above, supported on carved timber lintels. Marquetry screens and doors separate the courtyard from a corridor giving access to the students' rooms. The prayer hall with five arches creating two lateral aisles is separated from the court by a water channel crossed by two flat bridges, unique among the Fez *madrasas*. In the middle of the lateral sides of the courtyard are two large arches closed by gates giving onto square rooms roofed with timber-ribbed domes.

MARRAKESH, Qubba al Ba'adiyyīn
Almoravid period, *c.* 1120

This rectangular kiosk probably sheltered a fountain in the annexe of the Friday Mosque, erected in 1120 by 'Alī ibn Yūsuf, but now vanished. The luxury of the stucco decoration, limited now to the dome, is outstanding. The exterior of the dome has a chevron pattern above a frieze of interlaced arches; the walls are surmounted by serrated merlons and are pierced with lobed windows of different shapes. Inside, the dome is decorated with deeply carved flutings, the multilobed supporting arches have floral designs punctuated by shell motifs.

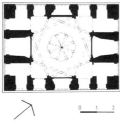

MARRAKESH, Kutubiyya Mosque
Almohad period, 12th century

The Almohad caliph 'Abd al-Mu'min (1130–63) constructed two mosques at several years' interval, the second immediately to the south of the first and a replica of it. The northern (first) mosque has now disappeared though proof of its co-existence with the southern mosque are the portals cut through its *qibla* wall. The sanctuary of the present mosque reproduces the typical T-formation of the aisles. The axial nave is roofed with six cupolas and a further five are positioned over the *qibla* aisle; these consist of decorated *muqarnas*-work vaulting. The aisles of the sanctuary are framed by lobed and festooned arches, harmonizing with the sober scheme of the *mihrāb* surmounted by niches. The court is flanked on its shorter sides by aisles extending from the sanctuary. The minaret, over 60m high, was completed by Ya'qūb al-Mansūr (1184–99), who, probably, only provided the lantern. Its decoration varies on each side – the single or double openings are framed by a variety of lobed, interlaced and festooned arches employing painted, semi-circular and horseshoe shapes.

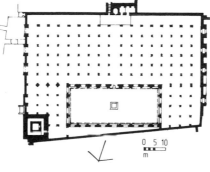

MARRAKESH, Tomb of the Sa'dians
Sa'dian period, late 16th century

This necropolis consists of two pavilions in a garden setting. The earlier structure, containing the tomb of Muhammad ash-Shaykh (who died in 1557), was built by his son (who died in 1574) and is a square chamber open on two sides. This was enlarged in 1590 by Ahmad al-Mansūr, who built for himself another pavilion of three rooms including a central chamber with twelve columns (where the tombs of his family were housed)

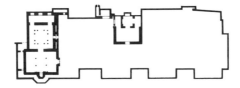

preceded by an ornately decorated sanctuary. Throughout, painted coffered timber ceilings with geometric interlaces, carved columns and capitals, *muqarnas* corbelling and abundant stucco and glazed tile-mosaic enrich these royal tombs.

MEKNÈS, Palace of Maulāy Ismā'īl
'Alawid period, late 17th–early 18th century

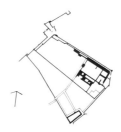

Like the 16th century Badī' palace at Marrakesh, this complex was itself a town – typical of the royal palaces added by the North African rulers to their cities. In a vast space numerous buildings are grouped around rectangular courts. Built partly over colossal substructures, they were used as barracks, stables, olive presses, grain silos and prisons, in addition to the more usual residential and administrative functions. The whole was protected by a triple wall, the outer reinforced with square bastions, the inner defending the palace. Immense reservoirs providing water for the extensive royal gardens were also part of this complex.

RABAT, Gateways
Almohad period, late 12th century

Several gates and fortifications survive from the Almohad period but the most imposing are those at Rabat. The entrance to the Udāya Qasaba, added after 1191, consists of a succession of rooms parallel to the ramparts, roofed with domes and a barrel vault. The interlaced lobed arch surrounding the pointed horseshoe entrance is framed by an epigraphic band; in the spandrels appear shells in stylized vegetation. Bāb Ruwah is more complex in its layout, the rooms being disposed in the more usual bent manner; one room is roofless. The decoration is similar to the Udāya gateway, but the network of lozenges is here replaced by an interlace of horseshoe arches.

RABAT, Mosque of Hasan
Almohad period, end of 12th century

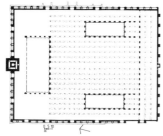

Ya'qūb al-Mansūr founded Rabat in 1191 and at the same time began work on this enormous Friday mosque, left unfinished at

his death in 1199. If completed, the mosque would have constituted one of the largest religious monuments in the Islamic world. The aisles of the sanctuary are multiplied to form a triple transept along the *qibla* wall, and two internal courtyards appear in addition to the more usual long courtyard near the entrance. The columns were composed of cylindrical stone drums. The minaret is partly preserved and probably would have been about 60m high. Each side is covered with decoration similar to that of the Almohad mosques of Marrakesh. The pointed lobed arches on colonnettes in the lower storey become festooned above; the uppermost storey consists of an intersecting net of lobes rising out of a triple arch, a feature that became popular in the minarets of subsequent mosques.

RABAT, Chella Necropolis
Marīnid period, 1310–39

Completed by Abu'l-Hasan on a Roman site, this complex was surrounded by a wall and was extensively fortified. The monumental entrance is in the Almohad tradition, though the arch framing the entrance is distinctly pointed, and the flanking part-octagonal towers are surmounted by unusual square bastions. Within are numerous sepulchral chambers, two mosques and minarets, a *zāwiya* with a central court leading to small cells, a fountain and a bath.

TINMAL, Friday Mosque
Almohad period, completed 1153

Tinmal is a village in the Moroccan High Atlas where Ibn Tūmart organized the first Almohad armies with which he conquered

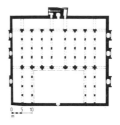

the Maghrib. The walls of this mosque, constructed in a kind of concrete (the piers and arches are in stuccoed brick), form a rectangle containing the sanctuary and courtyard. The two outer and central aisles are larger than the others, the first appearance of this feature, and have *muqarnas* vaults at their intersection with the *qibla* aisle. Three entrances regularly pierce the lateral walls, and the aisles are extended to flank the courtyard. The position of the rectangular minaret above the deeply recessed octagonal *mihrāb* is remarkable. The pointed arches are gracefully embellished with lobes, while the *mihrāb* preserves the more simple horseshoe contour.

Algeria
ALGIERS, Mosque of the Fishery
Ottoman period, 1660

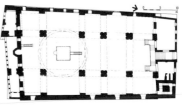

This cruciform building demonstrates some features typical of Algerian mosques in the Turkish period. The sanctuary is covered with barrel vaults and there is a central ovoid dome supported on Ottoman type pendentives and semicircular arches; the drum of the dome is decorated with a frieze of carved stucco niches, evidence of local craftsmanship. The square North African minaret has nonetheless been retained. Turkish-influenced architecture of this period is found also in Tunisia, as may be seen in the Mosque of Sīdī Mahriz at Tunis (1675).

QALʿA OF THE BANĪ HAMMĀD, Palace and Tower
Hammādid period, 11th century

Among the imposing remains of the mountain capital of the first local Algerian dynasty, excavations have revealed a tower and palaces, a mosque with a monumental minaret and extensive fortifications. The Dār al-Bahr (Palace of the Lake) is an extensive complex of monumental entrances, administrative rooms, colonnaded courtyards, residential suites, baths and a circular cistern. Its central feature was a rectangular basin with a state room, flanked by smaller chambers on its north side. The breaking up of the walls into projections and recesses, as well as the various vaulting systems (domes, squinches and *muqarnas*), may be eastern in origin, but the delicately carved marble panels and glazed ceramic marquetry testify to a local, though provincial, artistic tradition. The al-Manār tower is a square edifice whose outer walls are decorated with tall semicylindrical niches. At the centre is a low, dark, vaulted chamber, which probably served as a magazine or prison, surrounded by a ramp giving accesss to an upper room of cruciform plan, roofed by a dome on pendentives.

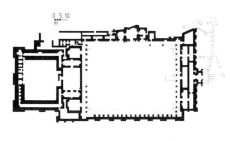

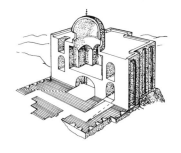

TLEMCEN, Great Mosque
Almoravid period, completed 1136, 13th-century addition

This mosque may be grouped with those at Algiers (1096) and Nedroma. Though begun by Yūsuf ibn Tāshufīn, after he founded Tlemcen in 1082, it was in the reign of ʿAlī that this mosque was enlarged and greatly embellished. The transverse arches are formed into lobes while those that create the naves are horseshoe-shaped; they support beams on delicately carved corbels, above which rise sloping tiled roofs. The two domes are of pierced stucco with vegetal decoration between sinuous brick ribs; each dome is protected by an outer dome with windows. Together with the *mihrāb*, they recall the domes of the Great Mosque at Cordoba. A century later, about 1236, the ʿAbd al-Wādid ruler, Yaghmurāsan ibn Zayyān, added an extension, the awkward shape of which was conditioned by the adjacent castle. The minaret was probably added at this time as well as the new courtyard with flanking arches.

TLEMCEN, Mosque of al-Mansūr
Marīnid period, 1303 and 1306

Work on this barracks-like mosque was begun under Abū Yaʿqūb during the conquest of Tlemcen, and was resumed after the Marīnids returned there some thirty years later. Following earlier Almohad mosques, this example illustrates many of the new characteristics – the axial position of the minaret projecting from the walls, the depth of the sanctuary, the disposition of the three transverse aisles following the *qibla* wall, the use of mud-brick for the walls but stone for

the portals and minaret and, lastly, the regularity of the arrangement and increased scale. Like that of the mosque of Hasan at Rabat, the minaret still stands, though the mosque is otherwise incomplete. The entrance, however, is located in the base of the

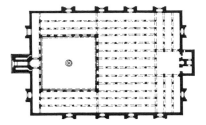

minaret and leads directly into the courtyard. Coloured ceramic pieces were inserted into the carved decoration of the minaret, whose patterns repeated those evolved in the Almohad period.

Tunisia
MAHDIA, Great Mosque
Fātimid period, *c.* 916

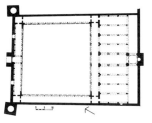

Except for its north façade, this mosque has been destroyed and rebuilt several times; however, it still preserves much of its original scheme. The plan is based on that of the Great Mosque at Qairouan with significant modifications – a projecting entrance porch, no lateral entrances, square or trapezoidal towers at the corners, and a strongly emphasized central aisle of the sanctuary – giving the mosque a military appearance and a strongly processional character. The courtyard is surrounded on four sides by a colonnade. The original *qibla* wall and dome in front of the *mihrāb* have now disappeared. The porch has a semicircular horseshoe-arched entrance flanked by four, narrow, similarly arched niches arranged in two tiers, the upper two being semicylindrical.

QAIROUAN, Great Mosque
Aghlabid, Zīrid and Hafsid periods, 836, 862, early 11th century, 1294

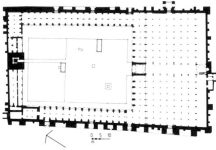

This is the key monument of Aghlabid architecture, dominating the evolution of North African architecture – especially the mosques at Sfax (849), Sousse (850) and Tunis (856–63). Founded on a Romano-Byzantine site at the time of the Arab conquest (670), the mosque was entirely rebuilt by Ziyādat Allāh in 836 – substantially in the same size and shape as the present building. The sanctuary is a hypostyle hall, the arcades emphasized in the characteristic T-formation, with two domes over the central aisle. The semicircular horseshoe arches, braced by wooden tie-beams, rest on carved stone imposts and wooden abacus blocks upon the capitals of reused Antique columns. The sanctuary occupies the end of a great rectangle of buttressed walls opening onto a courtyard entered by eight doorways. The square minaret is a slightly tapering tower of three storeys, which, most likely, belongs to the mosque of 836. The first major refurbish-

ing took place in 862, when additions were made: the marble *mihrāb*, carved with vegetal and floral designs (with hollow spaces behind the pierced panels), surrounded by lustre tiles in part imported from Iraq; and the fluted dome, on lobed squinches and arches in front. The sanctuary was roofed with a painted wooden ceiling, fragments of which have been preserved from the Zīrid period, contempory with the superb timber screen and possibly also the *minbar*. The Hafsids added the porches sheltering the entrances to the mosque, the arcades around the courtyard and probably the upper storey of the minaret.

QAIROUAN, Mosque of the Three Doors
Aghlabid period, 866

The façade of this small mosque erected by Muhammad ibn Khayrūn al-Ma'āfirī of Andalusia, preserves a unique example of early North African Islamic architectural decoration – interesting for its diversity. Before its mutilation in 1440, to make room for an inscription and minaret, the three slightly pointed horseshoe arches were surmounted by three registers. The upper and lower are carved with long *kūfī* inscriptions framing an intermediate band decorated with a floral pattern of alternating designs, limited by the lengths of the stones. The spandrels of the arches are filled with palmette-like leaves set in tendril loops. The interior was much reconstructed in the 15th century.

SFAX, Great Mosque
Aghlabid, Zīrid and Ottoman periods, 849, 988, 1085 and 18th century

Renovated twice during the Zīrid period, little remains of the original mosque, which was modelled on that at Qairouan. The Aghlabid prayer hall was reduced in width creating a narrow sanctuary of five aisles perpendicular to the *qibla* wall, and six aisles parallel to the wall. Two cupolas surmount the extremities of the central aisle. Doubtless originally roofed in timber, the sanctuary was later covered with vaults rising from elongated imposts on the capitals of reused

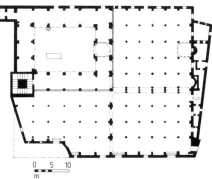

Antique columns. The minaret is richly decorated with arched openings and friezes of dentils, circular bosses and inscriptions. The façade is broken up by slightly pointed horseshoe-arched niches and semicircular recesses linked by dentil mouldings. The sanctuary was enlarged in Ottoman times, the builders restoring the mosque to its original Aghlabid dimensions.

SOUSSE, Ribāt
Aghlabid period, completed 821

It was along their maritime frontier that the Aghlabids concentrated their strategic activities. The small fortified barracks garrisoned with volunteers, the *ribāts*, played an important part in religious and military life – housing the warriors embarking on holy war, providing reinforcement for defences and serving also as an asylum for local inhabitants in times of siege. Of the series of *ribāts* erected at Tripoli, Sfax, Monastir Bizerte and Sousse, the last is the best preserved and most typical. It consists of a square fortified enclosure with semicircular towers at the corners and in the centres of each side, except for the entrance side and that to the

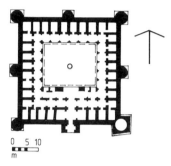

south-east; tunnel-vaulted rooms are positioned around the courtyard. Built in masonry, the style of the architecture is robust and ascetic, suitable presumably for the requirements of the 'Commanders of the Faith'. A staircase in the court leads to the vaulted sanctuary, which stretches over the entrance; the south qibla wall is curiously pierced by loopholes. Recent studies suggest that by the time the south-east bastion was completed, in 821, together with its watchtower or light-tower, the rest of the building was already in existence.

TUNIS, Zaytūna Mosque
Aghlabid, Zīrid and Hafsid periods, 9th, 10th and 15th centuries

Though founded earlier, this monument was rebuilt by Abū Ibrāhīm Ahmad (856–63) in conscious imitation of the Great Mosque at Qairouan. The columns are here coupled at the extremities of each line of arches, which rest on reused Antique columns by means of timber abacuses and stone imposts. The dome in front of the mihrāb was added in 991, during the Zīrid period, contemporary with the dome at Qairouan, but more abundantly decorated. An outside gallery to the west, reached by a monumental flight of steps, and an ablution room, separated from the mosque by a sūq, were added in the middle of the 15th century. The ablution room consists of a corridor leading to a small arcaded courtyard lined in white marble with a central fountain.

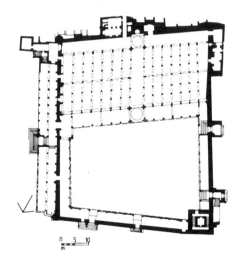

TUNIS, Mosque and Tomb of Hamūda Pasha
Ottoman period, 1655

This mosque is combined with the tomb of the founder and his family. Covered by seven tunnel vaults terminating in arches in front of the qibla wall, the sanctuary opens onto galleries on three sides; even the lateral court to the left, facing a mihrāb in the enclosure wall, is enclosed by galleries. The square tomb has a pointed pyramidal tiled roof. Both mosque and tomb are embellished with finely chiselled stucco with polychrome marbles. The strongly Italianate character of much of the decoration is characteristic of

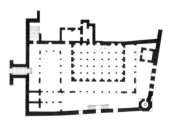

Ottoman and subsequent periods in Tunisia. The slender octagonal minaret with projecting balcony is more typically Turkish.

Libya
AJDABIYA, Palace
Fātimid period, 10th century

Sited at the junction of the coast road and the trans-Saharan route from the Sudan, Ajdabiyah prospered under the Fātimids, and the remains of two important monuments from this period, a mosque and palace, have been recently excavated. The palace is the most important example of Fātimid secular architecture preserved outside Egypt and was possibly built in 972 as a rest-house for the triumphal progress of the caliph, al-Muʿizz, to Cairo. It is a rectangular structure with circular corner towers, a monumental porch with a bent entrance, and an elaborate suite of reception rooms around a court. The central room had a barrel vault; the semi-dome of its apse on corner shell squinches is still standing.

TRIPOLI, Complex of Ahmad Pasha
Qaramānlī period, 1736–7

Ahmad Pasha was the founder of the Qaramānlī dynasty (1711–1835), which took over the rule of Tripoli from the Turks. His complex consists of a mosque, *madrasa* and tombs, surrounded on all sides by *sūqs*. The almost square sanctuary is divided into twenty-five bays, each covered with a dome on pendentives; that in front of the *mihrāb*

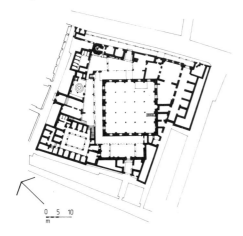

has a higher dome raised on squinches. Tile panels cover the walls, with a frieze of carved stucco above. The domes, supporting arches and blocks of the columns are all enriched with delicate plasterwork. The *mihrāb* and *minbar*, also the doors and windows, are inlaid with differently coloured marbles. This decorative scheme is repeated on the outer walls forming a portico on three sides; above is a raised gallery with a painted flat timber ceiling. In the adjoining tombs are buried Ahmad Pasha together with members of his family. The complex also includes a two-storeyed *madrasa* with rooms opening onto a courtyard, ablution facilities, and an Ottoman style octagonal minaret with projecting balcony.

Sicily
PALERMO, Ziza (al-'Azīza) Palace
Norman, 12th century

Occupied by the Normans from 1061 to 1194, Sicily retained its cosmopolitan population and complex artistic traditions; much of the architecture of this period is typically Islamic, though produced for Christian patrons. In Norman times, an immense park extended to the south-east of Palermo in which palaces, kiosks and fountains were erected, for the most part by local Muslim and North African craftsmen. The palaces were built as high towers and usually included a large central hall. Completed by William II (1166–89), this rectangular palace has outer walls decorated with blind arcades incorporating tiers of windows; a frieze inscription crowns the façade, with merlons above. Large superimposed rooms are flanked by lesser narrow ones. The lower

room has a fountain occupying the niche opposite the entrance. Water was collected in a marble canal and carried across the room. *Muqarnas* corbelling and mosaic decorations are employed throughout.

Egypt

VIKTORIA MEINECKE-BERG

With the Arab conquest in 639 and the foundation in 641 of Fustat, the future Cairo, Egypt received a highly centralized administration and a succession of alien rulers in the new capital. The predominance of Cairo was based on its strategic site, facilitating military and economic control of the Delta and the Nile Valley. Building activities of any artistic importance in Egypt were mainly restricted to Cairo, almost exclusively sponsored by members of the ruling class residing there. Egyptian Islamic architecture is, therefore, more precisely the architecture of Cairo, and its development is closely related to that of the city.

During the course of its changing history the city was gradually expanded to the north, but Fustat, where 'Amr, the first Muslim

conqueror of Egypt, had built his Friday mosque, remained the dwelling place of the common people and the commercial centre up to the Ayyūbid period. Ibn Tūlūn, the first governor to break away from the enfeebled 'Abbāsid caliphate, demonstrated his independence with the foundation of a new garrison city, al-Qatā'i', and a monumental great mosque. In 969, the Shī'ite Fātimid caliphs conquered Egypt from the west, establishing themselves as the major power in the region. Like their predecessors, they extended their domination to Syria, henceforth a source of artistic influx and exchange. Their new foundation, al-Qahira (Cairo), marks the most important step in the history of the city, becoming the nucleus of all further development. At that time, the most significant feature of Cairo – a specific urban architecture determined by existing streets and structures – was already being formulated. The introduction of stone as the

principal building material and the creation of recessed, richly decorated street façades also date back to this period.

The political decline of the Fātimids began in the late 11th century with the loss of the Syrian territories to the Seljuqs and with the invading Crusaders. After the Crusaders reached Cairo in 1168, Salāh ad-Dīn ibn Ayyūb (Saladin), sent by the Zangid ruler of Damascus, seized control of Egypt in 1171; after his master's death, in 1174, he created a new and even stronger Syrian–Egyptian empire. It was under his dynasty that Cairo, a hitherto secluded residential area, was opened for the populace and expanded to the south towards the newly erected citadel. Beside extensive fortification work, the foundation of *madrasas*, serving to promote the re-established Sunnism, was the prime concern of the Ayyūbids. New *iwān*-type buildings, influenced by Syria and Asia Minor, were thus established in Egypt.

The slave dynasty of the Mamlūks, originating in the Turkish bodyguard of the Ayyūbids, usurped the throne in 1250. At once they rose to prime military power in the Near East by halting the Mongol invasion and expelling the Crusaders from their last Syrian strongholds. External peace was accompanied by internal cultural prosperity, which culminated in a boost of building activities in the capital unequalled in any other Islamic city. Above all, the sultans and amirs spent fortunes on the erection of prestigious funerary monuments combined with pious foundations.

In spite of internal struggles, natural catastrophies and economic maladministration, Egypt continuously prospered thanks to the country's monopoly of the Red Sea trade. When this abruptly ended, with the discovery of the new route around the Cape of Good Hope, in 1498, the country quickly fell to the Ottomans. After Sultan Selīm's conquest, in 1517, Cairo was deprived of its royal patrons and, architecturally, degraded to a provincial city. Construction work remained limited up to the 19th century, when a new phase in Cairo's expansion was initiated by Muhammad 'Alī's successors – the creation of a new Europeanized metropolis west of the old city.

Chronology

Caliphal period 639–61

Umayyad period 661–750

'Abbāsid period 750–868

Tūlūnid period 868–906

Ikhshīd period 934–69

Fātimid period 969–1171

Ayyūbid period 1171–1250

Mamlūk period 1250–1517

Ottoman period 1517–1805

Muhammad 'Alī period 1805–1953

CAIRO, Mosque of 'Amr ibn al-'Ās
'Abbāsid period, 827

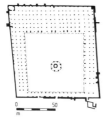

This mosque was originally founded in 641–2, by the conqueror of Egypt, at Fustat, the first settlement of Islamic Cairo. Judging by the rapid growth of the Muslim community there, the mosque was constantly enlarged until it attained its present dimensions, in 827, with the hypostyle construction of the 'Abbāsid governor, 'Abd Allāh ibn Tāhir. From this period some of the carved wooden architraves, which connected the arcades of Antique marble columns on the side walls, are preserved in the qibla wall. As these indicate, the arcades originally ran parallel to the qibla wall. However, following several restorations and a period of deterioration under the Ottomans, the mosque was extensively repaired by Murād Bey, in 1797, who erroneously rebuilt the arcades perpendicular to the qibla wall. The mosque is now undergoing a total renovation.

CAIRO, Nilometer of Roda
'Abbāsid period, 861

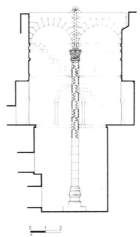

In 715, a Nilometer was erected on the island of Roda, replacing the pharaonic one at Helwan; in turn, it was replaced by this construction, built by the mathematician, Ahmad ibn Muhammad, in the name of the caliph, al-Mutawakkil. The Nilometer consists of a square pit entered by a staircase that descends around the walls, and is connected with the Nile by three tunnels. A graduated octagonal column in the middle of the pit served to measure the level of the river – as soon as a certain height of the rising water indicated the annual inundation of the cultivable land, the government determined the land tax. The importance that this unique monument had for the economy of the country is enhanced by the unusual architectural treatment. Smoothly dressed and profiled masonry was employed instead of brick, which, until the 11th century, remained the principal building material. The recesses in each of the four sides of the pit have pointed arches, the earliest examples in Egypt.

CAIRO, Mosque of Ahmad ibn Tūlūn
Tūlūnid period, 876–9

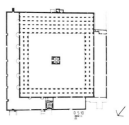

Of Ibn Tūlūn's foundation at al-Qata'i', the new seat of government north of Fustat, only this great Friday Mosque remains. The spacious brick arrangement of arcades of several naves opening onto the courtyard, with additional corridors (ziyādas) surrounding it on three sides, was built under the influence of the mosques at Samarra, in Iraq, where Ibn Tūlūn had received his military training. Like those in the Great Mosque at Samarra, the arcades are based on piers with engaged columns in the corners, a motif that was later repeated in the mosque of al-Hākim, but which did not really become common in Egypt since arcades were preferably built with Antique columns. Likewise, the spiral minaret was unique in Egypt, quite apart from the fact that it was replaced during an early 14th-century restoration by the present stone structure, which recalls the original Iraqi type. As the Samarra style is also represented in the remarkable stucco and woodwork, there can be no doubt that Iraqi craftsmen were employed.

CAIRO, Al-Azhar Mosque
Fātimid period, 970–2

Immediately following the foundation of the new capital, al-Qahira (Cairo), in 969, the Fātimids erected this great Friday Mosque in the centre of the city. A little later, in 989, the mosque also became the nucleus of theological instruction, a position it has maintained – interrupted only by the Ayyūbid reaction against the Shī'a – up to the present day. Because of its importance, the mosque was continuously enlarged. To the original hypostyle construction, which, like the Great Mosque at Damascus, is distinguished

by a transept leading to the central *mihrāb*, the porticoes of the courtyard were added in the time of Caliph al-Hāfiz (1130–49). Of both phases, parts of the important stucco decoration survive. The exterior is totally surrounded by later annexes. The Mamlūk sultans, Qāyitbāy and Qānsūh al-Ghūrī, built two minarets and the former ruler also added a new entrance bay; several amirs attached their *madrasas* to the outer walls. The extension of the colonnades beyond the original *qibla* wall, and most of the present exterior façades, dates back to the 18th and 19th centuries.

CAIRO, Mosque of al-Hākim
Fātimid period, 990–1013

Originally built outside the northern wall, this mosque was included within the city by the construction of the new stone wall in 1087 – the north wall and minaret becoming part of the fortifications. Although the general disposition of the plan – with the transept, the dome in front of the *mihrāb*, and probably also the domes in the corners of the *qibla* wall – follow that of the al-Azhar Mosque, completed only two decades before, the elevation of the arcades with rectangular brick piers and engaged columns is based on

the much earlier mosque of Ibn Tūlūn. Of far-reaching importance, however, are two new features: the entrance and minarets. The great entrance salient in the north-west façade evidently derives from that of the mosque in Mahdia (Tunisia), the first capital of the Fātimids. The monumentalization of this entrance and its embellishment with ornamental recesses leads to the development of the Cairene street façade. Of the two extraordinary walled-in stone minarets, one with a round shaft the other with a square shaft surmounted by several octagonal storeys, the latter anticipates the evolution of the Mamlūk minaret.

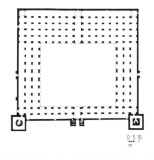

CAIRO, City Walls and Gates
Fātimid and Ayyūbid periods, 1087–92 and 1169–76

In the years 1087 to 1092 the Fātimid vizier, Badr al-Jamālī, replaced the original mud-brick fortifications of the city with stone walls. The splendid monumental gateways, Bāb an-Nasr (Gate of Victory) and Bāb al-Futūh (Gate of Deliverance) in the north, and Bāb Zuwayla in the south, are reported to have been constructed by architects from Urfa (in present-day Turkey); this is confirmed by close similarities, both in construction and in decoration, with the architecture of northern Syria and Iraq. With the possible exception of the citadel of Diyarbakir (Turkey), nothing comparable in scale and

degree of perfection in fortifications has survived from these areas. This connection probably explains the advanced technique of the stone masonry, especially in the superb vaulting systems, which have no precedent in earlier Cairene architecture, brick being the predominant building material hitherto. With the construction of the citadel as the seat of government, the Ayyūbid sultan, Salāh ad-Dīn, began to extend the walls in 1169 in order to connect the Fātimid enclosure with the southern extension of the city, which by then was steadily growing. His plan to integrate Fustat within the fortifications only partly materialized.

CAIRO, Al-Aqmar Mosque
Late Fātimid period, 1125

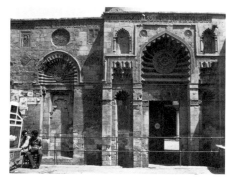

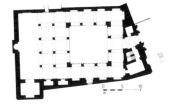

This mosque was built by Ma'mūn al-Batā'ihī, the vizier of Caliph al-Āmir. It is a small hypostyle construction on the main artery, and was of major importance in the development of urban architecture in Cairo, being the earliest building whose façade was adjusted to the line of the street, diverging considerably from the *qibla* orientation of the interior. The façade is also the first to be richly decorated over its full street length and is constructed entirely in stone; previously only the entrance salient, as that of the mosque of al-Hākim, was treated accordingly. Originally, the façade was arranged symmetrically, the three parts consisting of a projecting gateway with lateral wings, each with an elaborate central niche surmounted by a fluted arch.

CAIRO, Madrasa of al-Malik as-Sālih Najm ad-Dīn Ayyūb
Ayyūbid period, 1242–4

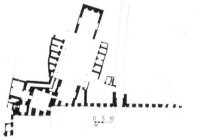

According to the political importance that the Ayyūbids attached to the schools of religious law, the *madrasa* acquired a specific architectural form, which, like the institution itself, was taken over from Syria. The general scheme, as may be reconstructed in the remains of this *madrasa* with two axial *īwāns* and lateral tiers of cells opening into a portico, clearly refers to earlier *madrasas* in Aleppo, which had been developed there under the influence of the Seljuqs from Asia Minor. However, this Cairene *madrasa* was transformed into an impressive construction of urban architecture. In fact, it actually consists of two *madrasas*, probably identical, the first building to unite all four rites in one complex. The two *madrasas* are unified by a long, decorated stone façade on the main artery; the elaborate central gateway being surmounted by the minaret. The mausoleum of the royal patron of this building, incorporated into the *madrasa* complex by his wife, Shajarat ad-Durr, after his death in 1250, is the first example of funerary architecture within the city.

CAIRO, Mosque of az-Zāhir Baybars
Early Mamlūk period, 1266–9

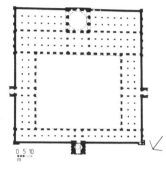

This first Mamlūk Friday Mosque in al-Husainiyya, a suburb outside the north walls of Cairo, was intended to leave no doubt about the political and religious legitimization of the new ruling class. As contemporary historians relate, it was the same size as the mosque of ʿAmr ibn al-ʿĀs, whereas the dome in front of the *mihrāb* recalls that of the mausoleum of Imām ash-Shāfiʿī. Stylistically, Baybars's building owes most to the mosque of al-Hākim (also determined by the dimensions of the ʿAmr Mosque): the external elevation and decoration of the projecting gateways, the piers of the colonnades facing the courtyard and the piers with the engaged columns from the dome in front of the *mihrāb*. The most striking development of this hypostyle mosque is, however, the enlargement of this dome.

CAIRO, Hospital, Mausoleum and Madrasa of Qalāʾūn
Early Mamlūk period, 1284–5

This, the most ambitious architectural project in Mamlūk Cairo, was built by Qalāʾūn on the site of the western Fātimid palace facing the *madrasas* of his predecessors. The hospital (*māristān*), the mausoleum and the *madrasa* were erected successively, united by a long corridor entered by the elaborate main portal which divides the mausoleum and the *madrasa*, leading to the vast complex of the hospital behind. The famous hospital, now almost entirely lost, centred around a four-*īwān* courtyard. The mausoleum and *madrasa* – the latter projecting about 10m –

are lined by an impressive street façade of nearly 70m, including the substructure of the minaret to the north. Both mausoleum and *madrasa* are distinguished by an outstanding and exceptional architectural concept in Cairene architecture. As for the mausoleum, the usual pattern of a square domed chamber is altered ingeniously by the erection of an inner octagon resting alternately on pairs of piers and Antique granite columns. These support the high drum and the dome, raised above the level of the outer flat roof. Significantly, the architectural motif of the inner octagon reflects the most glorious monument of early Muslim history, the Dome of the Rock in Jerusalem. The *madrasa* with two *īwāns* and lateral cells also has interior arcades in the *qibla īwān*, here divided into three naves.

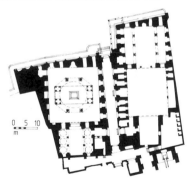

CAIRO, Madrasa and Mausoleum of an-Nāsir Muhammad
Early Mamlūk period, 1295–1303

This four-*īwān madrasa* and the mausoleum attached to it were begun by al-ʿĀdil Kitbughā, who, when deposed in 1296, had raised its façade to the level of the inscription band and, what is most extraordinary, had incorporated into the façade a Gothic portal brought from a Crusader church in Acre (now Akko in Israel), evidently as a symbol of victory over the Crusaders. In 1299, an-Nāsir Muhammad ordered the completion of this *madrasa*, which was situated immediately adjacent to the mausoleum of his father, Qalā'ūn. To this second building phase belongs the minaret with its rich stucco decoration above the Gothic portal, as well as the magnificent, apparently Il-Khanid influenced, stuccos in the *qibla īwān*. Unfortunately, these are now almost the only traces of the formerly rich decoration of the partly ruined interior.

CAIRO, Mausoleums of the Amirs, Salār and Sanjar al-Jāwlī
Early Mamlūk period 1303–4

The twin mausolea of these two amirs are effectively placed on the slope of al-Kabsh, the characteristic ribbed domes of the early Mamlūk period raised on high drums above the tall façade. The accompanying minaret – the first to show the sequence of three differently shaped storeys, later so frequent in Cairo – is associated with the adjoining religious institution, a *madrasa* and *khānqāh*. The arrangement of the remaining part of this annexe, which is neither orientated to the *qibla* nor contains an original *mihrāb*, is rather odd. Its undefined irregular shape may perhaps be due to the steep site, or to the fact that previous secular buildings were adopted for a religious function after the erection of the mausolea. In any case, all the skill of the architectural setting and its decoration was concentrated on the mausolea; also, the rear elevation offers an equally beautiful view. A tunnel-vaulted

corridor serving the mausolea opens into a courtyard, its four pointed open arches filled with exquisite stone screens carved on both sides.

CAIRO, Mosque of an-Nāsir Muhammad
Early Mamlūk period, 1318 and 1335

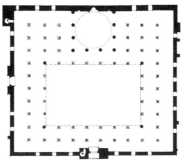

This sultan made prestigious efforts in extending the citadel, especially in the reconstruction of the buildings of his predecessors. Thus, he rebuilt the old mosque, enlarging it again less than two decades later,

in order to raise its height to that of the nearby Great Īwān, the Hall of Justice, which he had also repeatedly reconstructed. Before the erection of the mosque of Muhammad 'Ali in the 19th century, which replaced the Hall of Justice, both the mosque and hall, with their huge domes, were the dominating structures of the citadel. It was also in an-Nāsir Muhammad's time that a great number of Friday mosques, hitherto confined to a few spacious central constructions, were established all over the city. Consequently, the traditional hypostyle mosque-type was considerably limited by the lack of space, and it was necessary to reduce the number of arcades. At the same time, the dome in front of the *mihrāb* continued to be constructed in the extraordinary size it had attained in the earlier mosque of Baybars, thus dominating the *qibla* hall.

CAIRO, Mosque of Amir Altunbughā al-Māridānī
Early Mamlūk period, 1339–40

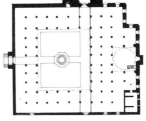

Following in plan the mosque of an-Nāsir Muhammad on the citadel, this mosque is an imperial foundation endowed by the son-in-law of an-Nāsir, Altunbughā. It is prominently located in a street, which, in the course of the sultan's expansive building activities, had developed into a major communication road running from Bāb Zuwayla to the citadel. It is recorded that the sultan took an active interest in the construction of this mosque, providing Altunbughā with building materials and raising funds for the upkeep of the mosque. This building still retains much of its original decoration. Virtually all techniques and materials in use at the time were applied – marble incrustation, stucco, wooden and stone carvings, and even faience for several multicoloured window grilles in the entrance bays, probably the work of Il-Khanid craftsmen. The *qibla* wall was especially lavishly ornamented, including fine stucco-work with unusual tree motifs.

CAIRO, Mosque-Madrasa of Sultan Hasan
Early Mamlūk period, 1356–9

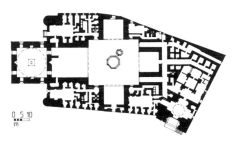

This enormous construction of a four-*īwān* mosque, including *madrasas* for each school in the corners, exceeds all previous buildings with its monumental dimensions. It is reported that the sultan desired to surpass the great *īwān* of the Sasanian palace at Ctesiphon in Iraq, a comment that demonstrates the splendour of the architecture, but does not explain the pretensions of this relatively unimportant patron. The whole complex, also comprising the great mausoleum in the axis of the *qibla īwān*, was raised in a relatively short time owing to a strong influx of foreign artists and craftsmen, mainly from Syria, but also from Iran, whose work can be traced in the wide range of architectural details and ornamentation. Parts of the decoration were left unfinished at the sultan's death. The adoption of the *īwān* structure for the mosque, formerly reserved only for the *madrasa*, had far-reaching consequences, for, with only a few exceptions, it came to supersede the traditional hypostyle mosque, generally in the dual function of mosque-*madrasa*.

CAIRO, Madrasa of the Amir Mithqāl
Early Mamlūk period, between 1361 and 1374

As frequently happened with many pious foundations within the city, the location of this *madraṣa* was chosen near the house of its founder and had, therefore, to be adjusted to rather limited boundaries (about 20m × 20m) on the site of the west Fātimid palace. One problem was to provide access to dwellings behind; this was solved by raising the *madrasa* to the first floor, creating the so-called 'hanging *madrasa*', with a tunnel-vaulted passage beneath. Thus, the façade gains in impressive height accentuated by the vertical recesses containing the doors and windows. The interior, of modest four-*īwān* shape, is beautifully decorated with carved and painted woodwork as well as marble panelling. There is also an interesting feature, common in secular architecture: the lateral *īwāns*, like those of a hall, are divided into two storeys by a wooden ceiling, the upper storey opening onto rooms behind, screened from the *madrasa* by *masharabiyya*-work. As there are no original staircases, the upper rooms were probably reached from the adjoining private quarters of the amir.

CAIRO, Madrasa of Barqūq
Later Mamlūk period, 1384–6

This structure comprises a central *madrasa* of four *īwāns*, also used as a mosque, as well as a family mausoleum and a Sūfī convent. It was built by the court's chief architect, Ahmad al-Tūlūnī, on the main street immediately

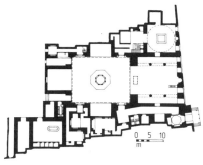

north of the prominent foundations of Qalā'ūn and an-Nāsir Muhammad. By surpassing these neighbouring buildings in height, and especially by citing various significant royal motifs of previous buildings, Barqūq's pretentions to imperial representation are strongly expressed. In general, the *īwān* scheme follows that of the mosque-*madrasa* of Sultan Hasan. In the *qibla īwān* is the unusual feature of the arcades dividing the hall into three naves, repeated from the nearby *madrasa* of Qalā'ūn; yet it is apparent that these arcades of huge reused pharaonic granite columns also refer to the domes supported on similar columns in front of the *mihrābs* in such important Friday mosques as that of an-Nāsir Muhammad.

CAIRO, Khānaqāh and Mausoleum of Barqūq
Late Mamlūk period, 1399–1412

This monumental funerary complex in the northern cemetery outside the city was endowed by Sultan Barqūq, but only begun after his death, by his son Fāraj. Due to political disturbances, the famine of 1403 and subsequent financial difficulties, the decoration of the building was left unfinished

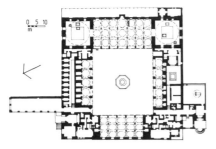

and the intended annexes never materialized. In spite of difficulties, which caused an unusually long building period, this multifunctional structure reveals an outstanding homogeneous architectural conception. The various parts – two mausolea, a convent, a mosque, fountains, etc. – are ingeniously integrated within a hypostyle construction opening into the central courtyard. The prayer hall of three naves at the *qibla* side is flanked by the mausolea. At the north and south sides the Sūfī cells and other areas serving the convent are entered behind a line of arcades. At the entrance side, another smaller hall of three naves is flanked by fountains surmounted by elementary schools, monumental gateways and utility rooms.

CAIRO, Mosque of al-Mu'ayyad Shaykh
Later Mamlūk period, 1415–21

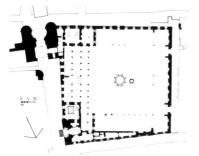

This last Friday Mosque of monumental size in Cairo sums up the traditional hypostyle type with arcades surrounding the courtyard, which, since Sultan Hasan's *īwān* type mosque-*madrasa*, was only rarely used. Two mausolea are incorporated into the mosque flanking the *qibla* arcades, the only ones to have been preserved. For the architectural

disposition of these mausolea, and also for the decorative treatment of their domes, the *khānqāh* of Sultan Faraj ibn Barqūq in the desert outside Cairo, finished about a decade earlier, served as a model. The south-east end of the mosque is built against Bāb Zuwayla. Taking advantage of the urban situation, the two towers of the Fātimid gate were used as substructures for the minarets. Linked with the ablution court west of the mosque, al-Mu'ayyad erected a bath, one of the few pre-Ottoman examples to have survived, although now in ruins.

CAIRO, Funerary Complex of Sultan Ināl
Late Mamlūk period, 1451–60

When still amir, Ināl built a modest mausoleum with an enclosure and a fountain in the northern cemetery outside the city. As happened with many Mamlūk structures, the complex was successively extended according to the rising position of its founder. As soon as he ascended the throne, in 1453, further annexes were added, the prestigious new parts erected in a larger scale. Thus, a Sūfī convent and, probably, the minaret followed in 1454. The richly decorated four-*īwān madrasa*, replacing the original smaller prayer hall beside the mausoleum, was completed in 1455–6. Older funerary monuments on the site were overbuilt or incorporated into the extending complex. Unique in its luxury is the great ablution place with sophisticated water installations.

CAIRO, Funerary Complex of Sultan Qāyitbāy
Late Mamlūk period, 1472–4

Around the central four-*īwān* structure of the mosque-*madrasa*, the mausoleum of the

sultan and adjacent annexes, numerous dependencies are grouped together, including a sumptuous dwelling house for the resident Sūfīs, a great hall and another smaller *madrasa* with the mausoleum of the sultan's sons. Thus, this funerary complex, one of the largest in the northern cemetery, forms a quarter of its own. Of the original surrounding enclosure, only the southern gateway is left. The complex owes its splendour to the high quality decoration, lavishly applied, especially on the central buildings. The masonry dome of the sultan's mausoleum is carved in a sophisticated composition of interlacing arabesques and star patterns – one of the masterpieces of decorated Mamlūk domes. Here, the evolution from simple ribbed constructions to zigzag designs and, finally, to geometric and arabesque ornamentation (probably under the influence of Iranian glazed tiled domes) reaches a peak of technical and artistic refinement.

CAIRO, Mosque-Madrasa and Mausoleum of Qānsūh al-Ghūrī
Late Mamlūk period, 1503–5

With this funerary complex, Mamlūk urban architecture reaches a climax. Built on both sides of the main artery, the mausoleum and mosque-*madrasa* face each other and are raised above the line of shops. There are further extensions of various religious, social and commercial establishments – a *khānqāh*, a fountain and a school above, projecting into the street next to the mausoleum; a loggia behind, opening onto a courtyard; and several tenement houses on either side. The huge mausoleum, which once had a dome with a blue faience coating, is the most prominent part of the complex but in no way dominates it, being harmoniously integrated into the well proportioned monumental setting. The shaping of the large area of townscape into a homogeneous conception is of more significance than the artistic aspect of individual parts of the complex, which consist of rather conventional building-types. Accordingly, the rich decoration has to be valued for its quality as an integral feature of the architecture.

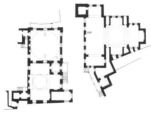

CAIRO, Caravanserai of Qānsūh al-Ghūrī
Late Mamlūk period, 1504–5

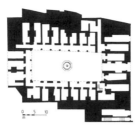

Closely attached to the *madrasa*-mausoleum complex for which it was made *waqf*, this commercial building represents the standard type of caravanserai within the city, as it was in use up to late Ottoman times. The rectangular building is entered by a pretentious portal in the middle of its street façade, leading into a vast courtyard in the centre of which a small prayer hall was originally located. Around the courtyard are two porticoed lower floors containing storage rooms for the goods to be distributed or assigned for export; occasionally they also served as workshops. The upper floors, reached by a separate side entrance, consist of apartments rented by merchants and craftsmen as well as travellers and pilgrims. Each apartment forms a vertical unit, in this case a triplex of rooms placed one above another, linked by inner staircases.

CAIRO, Fountain and School of 'Abd ar-Rahmān Katkhudā
Ottoman period, 1744

The two-storeyed public fountain, surmounted by an elementary school, is a typical Cairene establishment. From early in the 14th century it was generally attached as an annexe to *madrasa*-mausoleum complexes; later, at the end of the Mamlūk period, it was also founded as an autonomous structure, gaining special popularity under the Ottomans. This fountain was erected by an Ottoman official who took a particular interest in building and restoration work.

Exposed with three façades at a street junction facing the main artery, it is one of the most beautiful examples. Mamlūk decorative techniques, always present in post-Mamlūk Cairo, determine the whole arrangement – especially the coloured marble inlay and exquisite stone reliefs at the façades, the *muqarnas* corbelling, above which the loggia of the school is raised, and the carved and painted wooden ceilings of the interior. However, the floral motifs, both carved and painted, are purely Ottoman. In addition, the interior of the fountain possesses a rare and exceptionally preserved tile decoration imitating Iznik patterns.

CAIRO, Mosque of Muhammad 'Alī
Late Ottoman influence, 1830–48.

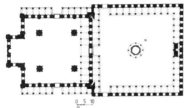

This famous landmark on the citadel of Cairo is regarded as a symbol of the modern Egyptian state founded by Muhammad 'Alī; not accidentally, it supplants the Mamlūk seat of power, the Great Īwān. However, architecturally, this mosque is totally alien to Egypt, deriving from just the cultural background from which Muhammad 'Alī was to gain independence – the Ottoman capital. Adopting the type of the great mosques in Istanbul, the architect, Yūsuf Boşnak (the Bosnian), built a simplified version of the plan first represented in Sinān's complex of Şehzade Mehmet (1544–8), followed by the Yeni Cami (begun 1597) and the mosque of Sultan Ahmet I (1609–17). Thus, the Cairo mosque has a huge central dome supported by four semi-domes and small domed compartments in the corners of the square hall. The spacious porticoed courtyard is in front of the mosque proper. The architectural ornament, especially the alabaster panelled walls, are purely European Classicism. This change of influence indicates the further development of 19th-century Egyptian architecture and its decoration.

Syria, Jordan, Israel, Lebanon

JOHN WARREN

The provinces east of the Mediterranean occupied a privileged position in the late Roman Empire; the architecture of the 4th, 5th and 6th centuries in these lands reflecting a burgeoning independence, prosperity and self-confidence. Its robust Hellenism was exported to Constantinople, Italy and the Adriatic, and on its own rocky hills the limestone took on voluptuous and characteristic forms. In the hands of native architects it reached a height of inventiveness in the Early Christian buildings of the 5th century; subsequently this inventiveness was reduced to a semblance of orthodox Byzantine Classicism under the dominance of Justinian I in the 6th century. Greater changes were to follow. In the 7th century there was a Sasanian invasion, which had a relatively minor influence, leaving only two significant buildings in the area (the castle of Kharāna, near Qusayr 'Amra, and the *qasr* at 'Amman); but the second invasion, the coming of Islam, ushered in a completely new architectural era.

In Syria and Palestine, the Arabs inherited an architecure of impeccable masonry; stonework was so accurate that mortar was often unnecessary, roofs were built of stone slabs, flat 'arches' were stabilized with interlocking voussoirs and windows were fitted with pierced stone tracery. Even doors and windows were closed with leaves of stone. There was also a great tradition of carpentry; basilicas were massively roofed with heavy timber trusses in the Roman manner and major domes were framed in timber. The decorative arts flourished – mosaics covered not only the floors of buildings but also walls, vaults and façades, while carved friezes and painted frescoes enlivened interiors.

Establishing themselves at Damascus, the Umayyads, the first imperial Islamic dynasty, were driven to ambitious building projects by the pressures of their courts; they also felt, to some extent, the need to compete with the Christian monuments of Palestine. Inevitably, they took for their builders native masons and carpenters, and their first great buildings in Jerusalem and Damascus incorporated techniques and styles of their adopted homeland. By 750, when the Umayyad dynasty was destroyed, a distinctively Muslim architecture was evolving, owing, in considerable part, to builders and craftsmen drawn from Egypt, Mesopotamia and elsewhere.

Under the 'Abbāsids, Palestine and Syria (other than the Euphrates province) were architecturally dormant. The same was true

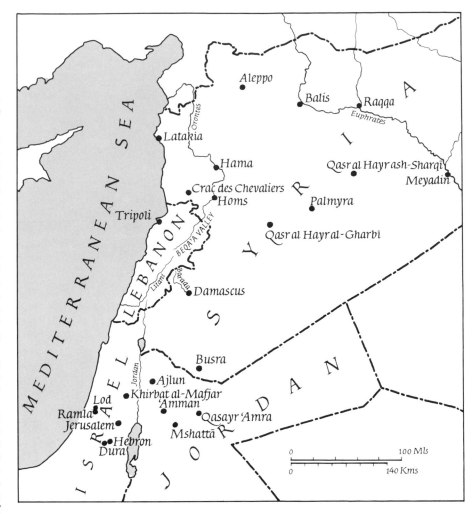

during the Tūlūnid and Fātimid periods, interrupted by Byzantine and Seljuq incursions from the north. It was only under the Ayyūbids and Mamlūks in the 13th century that the great building traditions were revived. The architecture of the Latin Kingdoms of the Crusaders, and the opposed Mamlūk emirates, was as dependent upon native craftsmanship as had been that of the earlier Umayyads. Much of the work was military and often of the most substantial kind. This was a period, too, of charitable and religious foundations and, though Egyptian influences predominated, local and distinctive styles were produced. The political stability that grew with the expansion of the Crusaders, is also reflected in numerous royal *madrasas* and tombs.

A complete reorientation followed in 1517, after the Ottoman sultan, Selīm I, took the provinces and swept on into Egypt. Thenceforward, the eastern Mediterranean looked to Constantinople for political overlordship. The tilework of Damascus imitated that of Iznik, and the new mosques built for the governors appointed by the sultans presented graceful but unfamiliar Ottoman

silhouettes on Syrian skylines. Caravanserais, *khāns* and palaces were also significant aspects of architecture during Turkish rule, with a brief interlude of Egyptian control in the 19th century. In this period, Damascus achieved a distinctive architectural delicacy but the relative unimportance of most buildings and their small number makes this a period of secondary interest. By the beginning of the 20th century, conscious revivalism had affected the area.

Chronology

Umayyad period 661–750

'Abbāsid period 750–878

Various dynasties, including

Byzantine, Tūlūnid and Būyid 878–1075

Seljuq, Zangid and Fātimid dynasties, alternating with Crusader domination 1075–c. 1200

Ayyūbid period 1169–1260

Mamlūk period 1260–1517

Ottoman period 1517–1918

Syria
ALEPPO, Great Mosque
Seljuq to Mamlūk periods, 11th–13th centuries

This mosque, begun in about 715, was built on the cemetery of an earlier Christian church; it was similar in form and size to the Great Mosque at Damascus whose mosaics it rivalled. However, the mosque was destroyed so many times that nothing now remains of the original building. The present structure dates from a total reconstruction by Nūr ad-Dīn in 1158, following a fire, and a partial reconstruction after the Mongol invasion of 1260. Only the tall square stone minaret of 1090, belonging to the Seljuq period, is older. Rising in eight stages to a height of over 50m, it is distinguished by a vigorous interlace in relief on its upper registers. The court of the mosque, surrounded by a heavy 13th-century masonry arcade, contains pavilions and a fountain and is paved in contrasting marbles. The prayer hall is of relatively modest construction. Its three transverse aisles are roofed with regular masonry cross vaults.

ALEPPO, Citadel
Ayyūbid and Mamlūk periods, 13th–16th centuries

The prehistoric tell at Aleppo was fortified throughout the Muslim period. The great barbican, consisting of a series of gates, provides a winding vaulted approach embodying the full panoply of Islamic defensive systems. Established in its present form in 1209, it changed little in the restorations of 1292, though the intricate stone inlay decoration is of this later date. The barbican

is preceded by a bridge across the moat, its outer end guarded by a gate and outwork erected in 1211 (repaired in 1507). These robust structures, replete with machicolations, panels of decoration and inscriptions, are perhaps the most impressive of all Arab military works in Syria. On the citadel itself are the remains of the palace of the Muslim provincial governors, dating from the 11th century to the 16th. A multi-chambered marble-lined bath (1367), an elaborate throne room of nine domes and an entrance portal (15th century) are the principal indications of the status of the internal structures. All these are now in ruins, though the great square minaret of the mosque still stands like a watch-tower over the city.

ALEPPO, Al-Firdawsī Madrasa
Ayyūbid period, 1234–47

Built by Dayfa Khātūn, regent of the ruler of Aleppo, this madrasa and its auxiliary buildings, including a small mosque and tombs, stand a little outside the ancient walls. The workmanship of the complex is impeccable; ashlar masonry throughout is cut with incised, calligraphic, string-courses and worked into elegant muqarnas forms at the entrance. A bent entrance leads into the courtyard. The original central fountain still survives in the middle of marble paving and the north side of the court is dominated by a single large īwān. The complementary triple-domed prayer chamber focuses upon a mihrāb set in a wall of complex marble inlay in contrasting colours. The lower register of alternating upright panels is surmounted by a complex interlacement of chased strapwork, closely comparable with that of the Zāhiriyya Madrasa.

ALEPPO, Khān al-Wazīr
Ottoman period, mid-17th century

Aleppo was a mercantile city and much of its life focused upon the khāns, of which this example is typical. It is of the open courtyard type with a small, domed, central mosque. Its pride is the great entrance gate with offices, lodges and tally chambers set into the mass of the portal. The gateway is faced in black and white marble and is carefully and chastely worked in relief with muqarnas string-courses and mouldings. Increasing finesse and complexity can be traced in the carving of these later buildings in Aleppo, such as the Khān as-Sābūn and the Khān al-Gumruk, but the discipline and control over the placing of their decoration remains masterly. Despite Mamlūk and Ottoman overlordship there survives in these buildings a quality that relates more to Armenian and Anatolian Seljuq work than to those more distant influences.

BUSRA, Mosque of 'Umar
Umayyad period, 720–1

Probably begun as a new foundation by the caliph, 'Umar II, this mosque was a simplified version of the Great Mosque at Damascus. It was restored at the beginning of the 12th century. It is a courtyard structure with aisles on four sides. The prayer hall consists of two transverse arcades of single range; similar arcades enclose the flanks of the court although, structurally, they are independent of the prayer hall arcades. On the *qibla* axis the transverse arcades are broken by pointed arches, in faint echo of the great central naves at Damascus. The axial emphasis, however, was achieved without adding a longitudinal structure. The mosque is typical of stone building techniques in this region and is roofed with basalt 'planks'. The openings of the minaret are closed with stone shutters, and the external stair is a series of stone cantilevers. The massive tapering square minaret is attached to the north-east corner of the building and has no balcony. It is the earliest-dated tower built for the purpose of the summons to prayer.

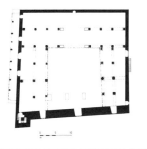

DAMASCUS, Great Mosque
Umayyad period, 709–15

This is the earliest surviving monumental mosque in the Islamic world. The Christian church of St John at Damascus occupied a Roman temple set within a rectangular walled sacred enclosure. At the beginning of the 8th century, Caliph al-Walīd I took over this enclosure, erecting a great triple-arcaded prayer hall on the southern side complemented by double-height arcades of alternating piers and columns around the court. The arcades of the prayer hall run parallel to the *qibla* wall, but, like the Aqsā

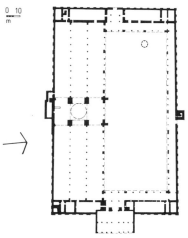

Mosque at Jerusalem, a tall central aisle cuts through them, rising above and terminating in a dome in front of the *mihrāb*. In both mosques the aisles are doubled – arcade rising above arcade. In neither building does the original roof survive; the evidence at Damascus suggests a massively trussed, timber, pitched original roof of a type familiar to Hellenistic Syria. The slightly pointed arch occurs persistently in both mosques; it is found also in the Dome of the Rock at Jerusalem and thenceforth occurs regularly in Islamic buildings. Like these Jerusalem monuments, the Great Mosque at Damascus was heavily embellished with mosaics. The entire courtyard face, and the arcade surrounding it, was mosaic-sheathed above marble-faced lower registers. It was, in fact, the most extensive area of wall mosaic ever laid and, like the Dome of the Rock, was based on landscape motifs. Trees, gardens, rivers and cities are the principal motifs. The square squat corner towers of the Classical enclosure survived to serve as minarets – the first in Islamic architecture. One further

minaret was added in the 12th century. As in other Umayyad mosques, an isolated domed treasury stood in the court; this, the Bayt al-Māl, is supported on six Antique columns and was accessible only by ladder. Externally it was coated in mosaic. The mosaic facings are now being renewed.

DAMASCUS, Citadel
Ayyūbid period, early 13th century

Like many other Muslim fortresses, the form of this citadel was determined well before the Islamic period. Its only natural defence is the bank of the Barada River and it otherwise relies on a heavy enceinte of limestone masonry. Rebuilt by the Umayyads and the Ayyūbids, and also slightly by the Ottomans, it is architecturally remarkable for the massive barbican entered through a portal embellished with *muqarnas*-work. Though the north flank is irregular, owing to the alignment of the river, the east, west and south sides are square. The extensive re-buildings by the Ayyūbid ruler, al-Malik al-'Ādil, gave the citadel its present form. They were probably begun in 1208; an inscription of 1209 fixes the date for one of the machicolated outer towers.

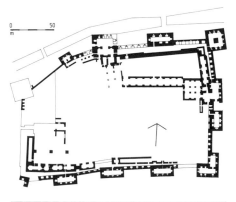

DAMASCUS, Zāhiriyya Madrasa
Mamlūk period, 1279

Completed by the conversion of the courtyard house of the family of Salāh ad-Dīn, this *madrasa* was built as a tomb and a college. Architecturally, it is important for having one of the finest Mamluk portals in the city, with a recessed entrance under a tall and finely worked *muqarnas*-decorated porch, the maturity of which strongly suggests Cairene involvement. The high-domed tomb of the slave-boy who rose to become Sultan Baybars stands in a chamber in the south-east corner of the courtyard. The gold mosaic frieze, which surrounds the chamber at a low level, has designs of trees, wreaths and building motifs, obviously in the tradition of the Great Mosque in the same city, though bolder and coarser in detail: surviving proof of the continuation of the mosaic tradition into the 13th century.

DAMASCUS, Tekke of Süleyman II
Ottoman period, 1560

West of Damascus, in a meadow on the banks of the Barada river, Süleyman's great architect, Sinān, constructed a mosque and dependencies for the sultan, to be used by pilgrims on the route to Mecca. The Tekkiye is a purely Ottoman concept and is the finest example in Syria. It was completed early in the second half of the 16th century, a further *madrasa* being added immediately to the east shortly afterwards in the reign of Selīm II. Both buildings are courtyard complexes with a single-domed chamber on the *qibla* axis and a large open rectangular central tank in the courtyard. This feature is unusual in Ottoman architecture where usually a raised, multifaced, dome-covered fountain holds pride of place in the court. The *tekke* has the single-domed square chamber typical of Ottoman provincial mosques, fronted by the two minarets that indicate royal patronage. The building is remarkable for the bold and powerful but carefully modulated use of contrasting stripes and chequerings of marble in pavements and wall facings. The court is surrounded by a multicelled college and, at

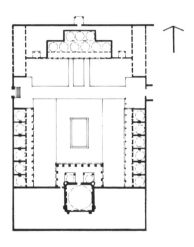

its north, riverside end, boasts the large vaulted halls of the soup kitchens provided for the pilgrims. Joinery, carved marble and locally made faience are of the high craftsmanship typical of the period.

DAMASCUS, Mosque of Dervīsh Paşa
Ottoman period, 1574

Originally standing outside the western city wall, this mosque is named after its founder, governor of the city from 1571 to 1574. Dated by an inscription to his short rule, the mosque has a single-domed prayer chamber preceded by a narrow high-walled ablution courtyard. A porch of five bays fronts the prayer hall, and the regular Turkish construction of the building suggests that an architect trained in the corps of engineers in Istanbul was employed. The cramped forecourt indicates that the building is a replacement of an earlier structure. There is the traditional single minaret attached, and the octagonal tomb of the founder is adjacent. Like the nearby mosque of Sinān Paşa (1585–90), the decoration features panels of local faience influenced by Iznik workshops. The street façade is entirely faced in contrasting courses of marble.

DAMASCUS, 'Azam Palace
Ottoman period, 1749

This building was the home of Āzād Paşa, one of the most distinguished Ottoman governors of Damascus. It is an important, remarkably complete example of a later Ottoman palace in Syria, despite damage in the 20th century. Typically, it is a complex of colonnaded courtyards; in the most important one, a marble pavement surrounds pools and gardens. Paving and walls are striated in contrasting marbles, and stilted arches rise from elaborate *muqarnas* capitals surmounted by multifaceted impost blocks. While there are obvious stylistic allusions to the domestic architecture of both Cairo and Istanbul, this palace shows that Syria had developed its own individual style. The complex intricate and rich joinery of doors, windows, shutters, panelling and ceilings are witness to the high quality of both life and craftsmanship in the city. The palace avoids external display; true to its genre, it presents a reticent face to the city. A comparable palace is that erected in Hama, in 1742, by the same governor. High in the Lebanon mountains at Beit ed-Dīn there is the more eclectic early-19th-century palace of Amir Bashīr.

DAMASCUS, Khān of Āzād Paşa
Ottoman period, *c.* 1750

This, the mightiest of the *khāns* in this great trading city, was originally roofed with nine high domes, covering the courtyard around which were ranged the usual two levels of accommodation: store rooms below, with living quarters above. The columnar structure supporting the domes rose clearly through both levels and, on it, marble-faced pendentives supported the domes carried on high clerestories. Black and white marble banding provided a vigorous system of decoration throughout. Beneath the now-destroyed central dome was set an octagonal marble tank. The entrance from the adjacent *sūq* is through a handsome *muqarnas*-headed multicoloured stone portal.

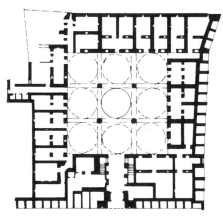

HAMA, Great Mosque
Umayyad and Mamlūk periods, 8th and 13th–14th centuries

The successive creeds and beliefs in Syria are well illustrated in this mosque, which incorporates part of a Roman temple and an Early Christian church. Little remains of the Umayyad alterations, which turned the

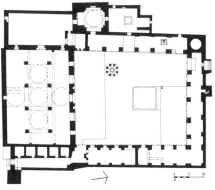

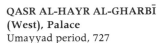

orientation of the prayer chamber from east to south and which added arcades with alternating piers and columns after the model of the Great Mosque at Damascus. The arcades of the rectangular courtyard are probably later replacements. A domed treasury, however, raised on Antique columns, is evidently Umayyad, as may be the base of the square east minaret. The boldly decorated upper sections of the north minaret and the upper structure of the prayer chambers are Mamlūk additions.

QASR AL-HAYR AL-GHARBĪ (West), Palace
Umayyad period, 727

Dated by inscription to the reign of Caliph Hishām, this major Umayyad palace on the road from Damascus to Palmyra was built with the typical central court and outer wall buttressed by half-round towers. It was attached to a pre-Muslim, square, monastic tower and there was also an adjacent caravanserai or barracks. This palace affords the first example in Islamic architecture of extensive façade decoration in carved stucco, an ancient Sasanian technique. The Hellenistic quality of this decoration, however, indicates Syrian workmanship. The outer face of the main entrance was heavily encrusted with finely worked carved stucco, and the court was similarly faced. Carved figurines (some, perhaps, depicting the caliph) and figurative painting were found in the palace. Little now remains *in situ*, as the principal façade and salvaged decoration has been transferred to the National Museum in Damascus.

QASR AL-HAYR ASH-SHARQĪ (East), Palace
Umayyad period, 727–9

The two adjacent buildings that form this palace in the Palmyrene steppes represent Umayyad architecture in a state of evolution. They stand at the head of a valley, which was walled off to form a large game park. The two buildings are both square enclosures, the larger having a central open court faced by internal compartments; there are four axial entrances. One such entrance faces the single entrance of the smaller but taller enclosure, a coherently built structure interpreted by the archaeologists as a caravanserai. It is likely that this smaller enclosure was a caliphal residence, fronted by a military camp formalized into a fort complete with a mosque. Because this latter enclosure can be dated to 729 (and there is even a record of the names of its builders and their place of origin,

Homs in Syria), it is known to have been erected for the caliph, Hishām. Hellenistic details abound in the buildings – in the early machicolations, pointed arches, joggled voussoirs and Byzantine capitals. The 'residence, however, contains clear evidence of Iraqi workmanship in the vaulting, stuccowork and external blind arcading, which decorated the towers flanking the entrance. The artistic resources of the eastern and western domains of the caliph are here juxtaposed.

RAQQA, Walls and Gate
'Abbāsid period, 8th–10th centuries

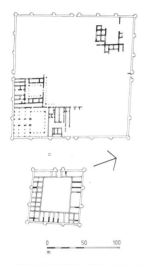

Raqqa was walled by Caliph al-Mansūr in about 772, and is today the only 'Abbāsid urban fortification to have been preserved outside Iraq. A straight section along the presumed north bank of the Euphrates (now running a considerable distance to the south) is completed by a great arc of wall and ditch curving half a mile northwards. The southeast (and probably also the south-west) salient was strengthened with a bastion 18m in diameter faced with baked brick. There were more than one hundred towers in burnt brick on the inner wall. An outer wall, unsupported by towers, was carried round all but the south side. About two thirds of the enceinte survives. A great rectangular cross-vaulted gatehouse stood at the south-east corner of the city on the road to Baghdad,

serving to control the oblique approach to the city. Only the south end of the entrance façade on the east now remains, but this is sufficient to establish its quality and importance. Though often attributed to the 8th century, the gate is unlikely to be earlier than the beginning of the 10th century. The principal evidence for this dating is its four-centred arch, post dating the development of such arches apparent at Samarra. Built in burnt brick throughout, the gate boasts an upper frieze of patterned, cusped, blind arches and areas of brick patterning.

Jordan
MSHATTĀ, Palace
Umayyad period, 744

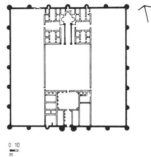

This incomplete rectangular palace in the grassy steppe south-east of Amman is identified as the probable work of Caliph al-Walīd II. The palace had an elaborately decorated rectangular buttressed enceinte wall (now partly removed to the State Museum in Berlin), with an axial approach through a series of courts to a tripartite throne room screened by a triple-arched triumphal arcade. Flanking the throne chambers are completed barrel-vaulted rooms of uncertain, though apparently domestic, purpose. The trilobe forming the throne rooms was completed only up to the springing of the apsidal vaults. The remaining quarters were barely begun though their plans are distinct. The palace mosque was sited in the traditional position, inside and to the right of the main entrance. Throughout, there is a powerful symmetry and axiality in the planning with a tendency for compart-

mentation, often into three sections. The vaulting systems are essentially Iraqi but the stone masonry and carved decoration is Hellenistic; both influences are modified by their interaction, however, and this palace presents the most complete fusion of the two traditions in Umayyad architecture. The outer façade is boldly punctuated by a rhythmic triangular interlace totally covered in vegetal motifs with large projecting rosettes and confronted animals.

QUSAYR 'AMRA, Palace and Bath
Umayyad period, c. 712–15

Among the bath buildings of Umayyad Greater Syria, this example stands out as being of signal importance for its completeness and unique state of preservation. Like the nearby pre-Islamic castle of Kharāna, its wholeness is almost miraculous. It stands in a shallow wadi in curious isolation and probably served as a nomadic caliphal camp in the spring pasturage; equally, it may have been the first of an intended complex, the succeeding palace never having been built. (The baths of the palace at Khirbat al-Mafjar preceded such a palace.) Three parallel vaults roofing the main chamber are carried on broad pointed arches in an essentially Syrian manner. Hellenistic type mosaics survive on the floors, but it is the figurative frescoes in the vaults, depicting animals of the chase, dancing girls and zodiacal arrangements, which make this building so remarkable. Hellenistic in inspiration, these frescoes are indicative of the range of styles and motifs embraced by Umayyad art. A representation of the caliph with other rulers has led to the attribution of this building to al-Walīd I.

JERUSALEM, Dome of the Rock
Umayyad period, 690–2

The Dome holds a unique position in Islamic architectural history as the first Muslim monument of structural, decorative and volumetric maturity. It derives its perfection from the skills of generations of builders in the Near East. Built as a sanctuary, the third

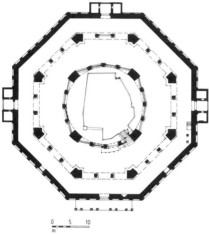

shrine of Islam (after the Kaʿba at Mecca and the Prophet's Mosque at Medina), it was commissioned by the caliph, ʿAbd al-Malik. The building covers a naked rock representing the summit of Mount Moriah, from which the Prophet ascended to heaven, enclosing it with a double octagonal ambulatory. A circular arcade, in which four piers are each separated by three columns, carries the circular masonry drum bearing the wooden double-domed structure. The height to the springing of the dome approximately equals the diameter of this central space. Reaching only half the height are outer octagonal aisles, separated by arcades of eight piers alternating with two columns. The setting-out and interarrangement of these spaces derives from an intricate geometry. Both inside and out, the main body of the masonry was sheathed in bold mosaics with vegetal designs, predominantly gold and green. The dome itself was gilded without and painted within. With the addition of marble casings to the arcades, the interior decoration survives complete (including the remarkable repoussé encasements to the tie-beams), but the present external skin of ceramic tiles and gold-anodised aluminium sheathing is a renewal of the finishes applied by the Ottomans in the 16th century, for by then the original external mosaic had deteriorated.

JERUSALEM, Aqsā Mosque
Umayyad period, 715

In its present form, this mosque is capable of holding about three thousand people and stands on the southernmost ramparts of the Temple Mount. An original but crude building was swept away in 709 to make room for a more substantial structure, completed by al-Walīd. Of this mosque there remain only fragmentary arcades at the south end, the remainder having been lost in the various enlargements and alterations that make up this mosque's chequered history. Altogether, the mosque has been substantially reconstructed six times and has been subject to major repairs on three further occasions. The mosque is similar in many respects to its contemporary, the Great Mosque at Damascus; slender columnar arcades formed a central aisle on the *qibla* axis, terminating in a dome in front of the *mihrāb*. This concept has survived into the present mosque though the length of the building was increased and its width reduced in the ʿAbbāsid period, when the columnar arcades were replaced by piers and cross vaults. Its use as a mosque ceased under the Crusader occupation of Jerusalem, when barrel-vaulted chambers and a Gothic porch were added. The Mamlūk builder, Aybak al-Mushrif, finally gave the building its present form in 1345–50, extending and completing the east side. In 1940 and 1945 further rebuilding took place. There is no integral minaret.

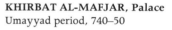

JERUSALEM, Walls, Citadel and Gates
Mamlūk and Ottoman periods, 14th–16th centuries

The defences of the fortress citadel of Jerusalem follow the alignment of walls and scarps in use long before Islam. They form an approximate rectangle enclosing two walled precincts – the citadel and the Temple Mount (Haram ash-Sharīf). The walls were rebuilt in Umayyad times on Byzantine foundations and repaired after the Sāsānids sacked the city in 614. Subsequent conflicts – Crusader, Fātimid, Mamlūk and Ottoman – have left

marks of Christian and Muslim building activity, making the walls, the citadel and the Temple Mount something of an archaeological palimpset. Even so, their present appearance is due, with minor exceptions, to the Ottoman rebuildings of 1537–41. At this time, Süleyman II Qānūnī was at the peak of his imperial power and it was natural that he should refortify Jerusalem, a city enclosing the third shrine of the Faith. The citadel on the east side of the city is a complex of towers of 14th- and 16th-century construction, with massive rusticated masonry, elaborate machicolations and a round minaret. Of the six principal entrances to the city, the Damascus Gate (or Bāb al-ʿAmūd, Gate of the Pillar) is the most formally designed: its vaults incorporate a bent entrance, and the external face is recessed within deep winged returns. It is the only gate in the walls designed fully in accordance with defensive principles.

KHIRBAT AL-MAFJAR, Palace
Umayyad period, 740–50

This unfinished palace, with its elaborate baths, was built under the rule of Caliphs Hishām and al-Walīd II. Representing the height of sophistication reached in late Umayyad architecture, this palace is more purely Syrian and Hellenistic in construction and decoration than almost all contemporary princely works. The complex also includes a mosque and reception courts. The baths were large and magnificent: sixteen piers carried a roof of barrel vaults and domes over a great *frigidarium* enriched with apses, niches, colonnettes and a full range of elaborate entablatures, moulds and decorative string-courses. A rich and vigorous Corinthian order was the stylistic key to the stone masonry. The vaults were of brick, and the floor was formed entirely of the richest geometric mosaic. Highly finished marble and carved stucco were used extensively, particularly in the lavishly ornamented reception room in the north-west corner. Geometric window grilles were used, and medallions containing freely modelled sculptural figures were positioned in niches and supporting pendentives. A central ceiling rosette of great delicacy and complexity was recovered complete from the debris. A remarkable domed octagonal aedicule functioned as a fountain pavilion in the forecourt. The two-storey palace of conventional courtyard form was graced with equally opulent detail – rosettes, rinceaux, acanthus friezes and statuary, including a possible representation of the caliph. Vaulting and domes were in brick with pitched roofs, and floors were in mosaic, marble and other stones. In addition to local craftsmen, Egyptian and Iraqi workmen were used.

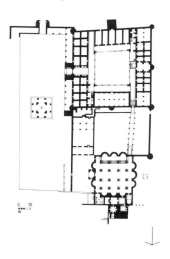

RAMLA, Cistern
'Abbāsid period, 789

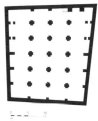

In Ramla, a city of Arab foundation in Israel, there survives a large vaulted cistern, 9m deep. Fifteen cruciform piers carry a double arcade which supports six parallel pointed vaults. The structure is dated by a *kūfī* inscription at the entrance, but is otherwise lacking in decoration. The stone masonry is simple and robust but is accurately dressed. Two-centred pointed arches and vaults were used throughout.

Lebanon
TRIPOLI, Borj as-Spa
Mamlūk period, late 15th century

With the expulsion of the Crusaders, the Mamlūks built a final series of fortifications to secure their coasts against any possible attempts by the Knights, still on Cyprus and Rhodes, to re-establish their foothold. This bastion has a single entrance, well above ground level, a glacis at the foot of the tower, and a prominent series of machicolations. The great chamber is spanned by six groined cross vaults. The massive rectangular keep measures 32m by 22m. In comparison with medieval military architecture of Europe it illustrates parallel developments in the work of Muslim and Christian architects.

Turkey

GODFREY GOODWIN

THE TURKS, a non-Arab people converted to Islam, first entered Anatolia in the 11th century, when the Seljuqs established a powerful state by occupying land originally held by the Byzantine Empire. They remained dominant in Anatolia until the beginning of the 14th century, although another group of Turks, the Dānishmendids, held sway for part of that time in the east and centre. After the Mongol invasions, new Turkish tribes entered Anatolia, notably the Qaramānids and the Ottomans. The latter soon achieved supremacy over their rivals, finally defeated the Byzantines (1453), entered Europe and extended their rule to the Danube. The Ottoman Empire lasted until 1922.

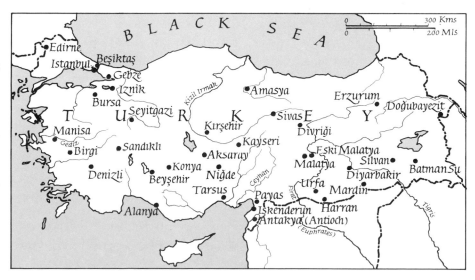

The patronage of independent chieftains and eventually Mongol overlords resulted in different styles of Seljuq architecture in Anatolia. The details of Dānishmendid monuments in Kayseri differ from those of the Artuqid rulers in the south, yet the requirements of religion and war, including the building of bridges and staging-posts across the hinterland, unified them into one distinct group.

In Turkey, the Iranian Seljuq influence from the north encountered that of the Syrian south – as shown in the Great Mosque at Damascus. The cold winter climate of the Anatolian plateau led to enclosed courtyards, which increased the aspect of a pillared hall, as in the early mosques at Konya or Sivas, and also led to a domed fountain area with a wide oculus, persisting well into the Beylik period.

Seljuq minarets were of brick, and therefore thick, but buildings were mainly of stone, following the Anatolian tradition. At Divriği, Iranian motifs were magnified, and translated from plaster into limestone. Part of the decoration there is in a style also found at Sivas, being the work of bands of itinerant masons.

Tombs were connected with major foundations and flourished independently, often in beautiful settings, but they were more modest in height than the tomb towers of Iran. Outwardly, the royal caravanserais had the aspect of fortresses but beyond their ornate portals were private apartments, workshops and halls as vast as cathedrals.

The use of materials from demolished Byzantine buildings made possible the erection of a remarkable number of monuments in a relatively short period; building continued during the Beylik period, when Anatolia was divided against itself under the leadership of rival *beys*, or lords. It was a time of experiment and cross-fertilization, synthesis and refinement. This culminated in the early Ottoman period with the Bursa type of mosque and dervish retreat, which was also associated with government buildings, and colleges and baths of increasing size and significance.

From these beginnings developed the centralized mosque, which rejected the older principle of the pillared hall and the lateral naves. Domes sought to rival in size that of the great church of Hagia Sophia, especially after the conquest of Constantinople in 1453. The concept of the hemispherical vault built upon a cube resulted in the characteristic Ottoman mosque with its portico, and was paralleled by the evolution of the slender stone minaret. The domed unit served the fluidity of form arriving with European Baroque influences in the 18th century. These were best expressed in decorative fountains and waterworks of the period.

The Seljuqs had used tiles as decoration in the Iranian tradition and these were followed by the more varied colours and grander designs of Iznik tiles in Ottoman times. Wood was an important material particularly for secular buildings, where the upper floors of houses were projected outwards to create the characteristic Ottoman street of the 19th century.

The final eclectic period was followed by an attempt at revivalism, but ferroconcrete now dominates the outworn traditions in Turkey, as elsewhere.

CHRONOLOGY

Seljuq period *c.* 1070–1308

Dānishmendid period *c.* 1071–1177

Saltukid period *c.* 1092–1202

Artuqid period 1102–1408

Mengüjükid period 1118–1252

Mongol period *c.* 1243–1335

Qaramāndid period *c.* 1256–1483

Beylik period 14th–late 16th centuries

Ottoman period 1281–1924

AKSARAY, Caravanserai
Seljuq period, 1229

Although heavily restored, this is the grandest caravanserai in Anatolia. It covers an area of 4,500 square metres and was built by Kayqubād I. The great hall of fine ashlar with a rubble core has five aisles and a rebuilt dome; in the forecourt is a richly carved prayer room raised on four arches. On each side are porticos, a *hammām*, workshops and private chambers. The fifteen external buttresses give the appearance of a fortress but, as the 13m-high portal proclaims, this building was a palace that anyone could use as a luxurious staging post when the sultan was absent. Its decoration may be due to Muhammad bin Havlan of Damascus, and certainly it presents a Syrian appearance.

AMASYA, Mosque of Beyazit Paşa
Early Ottoman period, 1414–19

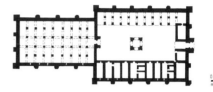

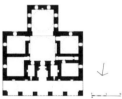

Beyazit Paşa was the vizier of Mehmet I after the Tīmūrid invasion. An inscription names the architect, Yakup bin Aptullah, a slave of the paşa, and probably a Christian. The portico of this mosque is particularly large, and two fountains flank the central entry, which is deeply recessed under a secondary dome and overlooked by two small cells with hearths at second-floor level. Inside, there is an unusual number of *zaviye* rooms. The river served as the ablution fountain.

BATMAN SU, Bridge over the Silvan and Bitlis Rivers
Artuqid period, *c.* 1147

This is the most notable bridge in Seljuq Anatolia, with a central arch that spans 30 m, rising 20 m above river level. The bridge is 150m long and is 7 m wide. There are six subsidiary arches on the Silvan side and one on the Bitlis side, both painted and circular. The caravanserais below the bridge have disappeared but the two guardhouses, or

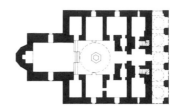

custom-houses, remain. The bridge has been heavily restored and the appearance of the fine ashlar limestone has altered, but part of an inscription in honour of Temür Tash remains. The approaches are bent in the Seljuq manner because the piers are placed in relation to the rock formation, which determined the central span.

BEYŞEHIR, Eşrefoğlu Mosque
Beylik period, c. 1297

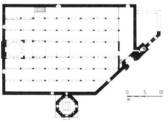

The foremost wooden mosque within ashlar walls in Anatolia, this building has its roof supported on forty-eight wooden columns, giving the impression of a forest. The central court has been reopened during restoration. As the site is irregular, the mosque is entered obliquely through a portal (related to that of the Gök Madrasa at Sivas) beside the minaret. The interior is rich in tiles and glazed brick, as is the *mihrāb*. The walnut *minbar* is signed by the craftsman, Isa. Other Anatolian wooden mosques, as at Bayburt and Kasabaköy, for example, differ considerably from this plan. The adjacent tomb has an interior stone dome with a dazzling display of Seljuq faience mosaic.

BIRGI, House of Çakır Agha
Ottoman period, late 18th century

This mansion (*konak*) is built of wood on a stone and brick foundation. Kitchens, stables and stores opened onto the court below the harem floor, above which is the *piano nobile*. It is built round a projecting seigneurial bower, which is the hub of the house, following a long tradition, expressed in the Chīnili kiosk in the Topkapi palace at Istanbul. Across the broad gallery are the salons, their service vestibules decorated with paintings of idealized cityscapes. The sealed upper windows are for light, the unglazed lower casements with shutters are for air.

BURSA, Hüdavandigār Mosque
Early Ottoman period, 2nd half 14th century

The domed centre court of the mosque is 23m high, with an oculus over the pool and rooms for dervishes on each side. The prayer hall is the climax of the central axis. The unique feature of this foundation of Murād I is the sixteen-cell *madrasa* on the upper floor where the gallery looks down into the court below. Twin passages lead to a domed room above the *mihrāb*. There is a fine loggia above the portico, which is related to those of the Karaman Madrasa at Niğde, to earlier Dalmatian palaces and to the church of Hagia Sophia at Ohrid.

BURSA, Green Tomb
Early Ottoman period, c. 1421

The vizier Haci Ivaz bin Ahi Beyazit built this tomb and the Green Mosque below, both for Mehmet I. The octagonal tomb is clad in green glazed bricks, restored after the 1855 earthquake had split the 15 m-high dome. The tiles of the sarcophagus on its podium constitute the masterpiece of the potters from Tabriz, led by Muhamad 'the Mad', who then went to Edirne to work for Murād II. The *cuerda seca* work of the lofty *mihrāb* matches those of the mosque, as do the wall tile revetments. The whole was designed by Nakkaş Ali. Both the woodwork and the bronze door-furniture are of superb quality.

BURSA, Great Mosque
Early Ottoman period, end 14th century

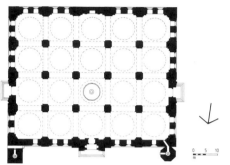

Though built by Beyazit I, the great door of this mosque was probably completed by his conqueror, Tīmūr, and has been recently restored, together with the marble footings of the north wall and the minarets, one of which is an independent addition. Once there was also a grand staircase rising up from the bazaar. The mosque has twenty domes supported by twelve piers in ranks of four and is the final resolution of the pillared hall plan. The interior court, under an oculus, has a large fountain and there is a splendid *minbar*. The giant calligraphy may have been based on original designs but the other decoration is feeble (the Eski Mosque at Edirne is the last important descendant of this style). The mosque was damaged in the 1855 earthquake when all Bursa's minarets had to be rebuilt.

DIVRIĞI, Mosque and Hospital
Mengüjükid period, 1229

This building is remarkable for the originality of its plan, the organization of the hypostyle mosque hall with four rows of four

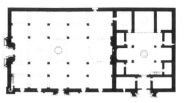

piers (mutilated by restoration), the variety of the vaulting systems, and the carefully balanced proportions of the mosque and hospital areas. The main axis of the mosque leads towards a strongly expressed stone *mihrāb* flanked by a fine *minbar*, signed by Ahmet of Tiflis. The two-storey hospital has four massive central piers supporting a dome, with an oculus over the central pool; the rooms include a tomb chamber. The three external portals and east window are remarkable for the variety and boldness of their carved decoration; no doubt the architect, who may have been Khurshah of Ahlat, employed various groups of itinerant craftsmen.

EDIRNE, Üç Şerefeli Mosque
Ottoman period, 1438–47

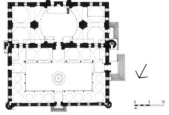

Built for Murād II, this mosque is the first major work in the Ottoman style. Its dome, more than 24 m in diameter, was not to be equalled until the mosque of Mehmet II at Istanbul. The Edirne example rises from a belt of triangular pendentives in the Bursa manner and the pairs of domes on each side represent the old *zaviye* areas. The broad asymmetrical courtyard has a low ablution fountain and its colonnades represent a truly Ottoman approach. There are four minarets built in different styles; one is over 67m high and has three balconies, which give their name to the mosque, another has a spiral design. The tiles in the tympana of the windows may be the last ones executed by the refugee potters from Tabriz.

EDIRNE, Medical Complex of Beyazit II
Ottoman period, begun 1484

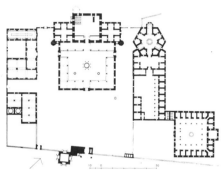

This complex was probably built by the architect Hayrettin Ağa. The square mosque has a lofty dome 20 m in diameter and is flanked by guest rooms reached from inside or out. This design recurs in Beyazit's mosque at Istanbul and that of Selīm I at Edirne. Beyond the mosque court is a large precinct: on its east side is the public kitchen and refectory, facing a spacious store room and a bakehouse, on the west is the hospital. Its outer court has a line of cells for the insane behind a colonnade and service rooms; the inner court leads between the cells to the hall, which has a fountain, four *iwāns* and a long apse. Attached to the hospital is the medical college with eighteen cells. Unlike the Beyazit complex at Amasya, the complex here turns its back on the river.

EDIRNE, Complex of Selīmiye
Ottoman period, 1569–75

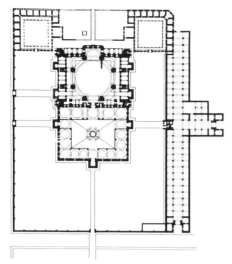

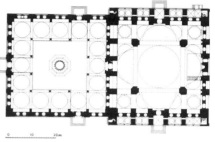

This college is the largest in Anatolia and although built in two periods and never completed, including the carving of columns and capitals, it is a unified conception. The two red-brick fluted minarets on each side of the portico may also be unfinished. There is a fine *muqarnas* vault over the door and a monumental façade with deeply carved trees and birds; these help incorporate the two buttresses that are the minaret bases, but the buttresses of the flanking walls sit less satisfactorily. The court rises through two storeys and there is a large mausoleum faced with marble at the external south end.

Here is the ultimate expression of the domed square, despite the *mihrāb* apse and the strong circular movement of the internal piers, which is accentuated by the centralized singing gallery and recessed arcades. Unsurpassed Iznik tiles are concentrated in the apse and the imperial box, but the workmanship throughout is exceptional, not least the *minbar*. The dome is 42 m high and 31 m in diameter; externally, it dwarfs the complex, except for the marble courtyard, and is contained by the four loftiest minarets in Turkey, each over 70 m high, with three balconies reached by independent stairways. From the 6th-century church of Saints Sergius and Bacchus through the Şehzade Mosque, it was to this climax that the Ottoman imagination had been striving.

ERZURUM, Çifte Minare Madrasa
Seljuq period, begun 1253

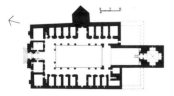

ISTANBUL, Rumeli Hisar
Ottoman period, 1451–2

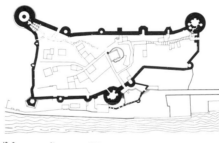

This castle, which commands the Bosphorus, was built by Mehmet II with stone taken from churches and from Anatolian quarries. Reused Byzantine columns act as bonding agents in the masonry. Two towers command the ridge and a third the barbican and gun ports of the shore; originally they had conical caps. The ruined mosque is now a theatre. The walls reach 7 m in thickness in places and one tower is 28 m high. The castle was heavily restored for the capture of Constantinople in 1453. Architecturally, it is cousin to the military traditions of the eastern Mediterranean and to the companion fortress of Beyazit I, opposite across the straits.

ISTANBUL, Complex of Şehzade Mehmet
Ottoman period, mid-16th century

Süleyman I built this complex in memory of his favourite son, and all the inscriptions refer in some way to death. It was Sinān's first major work and the final expression of

the central domed mosque supported by four half-domes. The courtyard is the same area as the mosque but cramped by Murād IV's addition of a canopy to the ablution fountain. The mosque plan derives from the Fātih Paşa Mosque at Diyarbakir, among others, in contrast to the neighbouring Beyazit Mosque, which retains the axial influence of Hagia Sophia. The ashlar masonry is highly decorated and the lateral arcades that mask the buttressing are an innovation. The tomb, with its fluted dome, contains early Iznik *cuerda seca* tiles in which blue, meadow-green and yellow glazes predominate. The complex includes a kitchen-refectory, a hospice for travellers and a *madrasa* in a large precinct shaded by trees.

ISTANBUL, Complex of Süleymaniye
Ottoman period, 1550–7

The complex of Mehmet II at Fātih rivals, but cannot equal, this foundation. Sinān built the complex on land taken from the old palace. It covers 60,000 square metres and includes

241

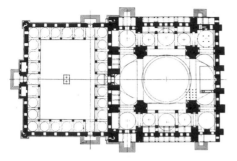

seven colleges, a hospital and asylum, a *hammām*, two residences, hostel, kitchen, tombs, school, fountains, wrestling grounds, shops, piazza and the mosque within its courtyard. The workmanship is exceptional throughout. The whole is raised on great vaults except where the colleges would mask the view. The arcades from the Şehzade Mehmet complex develop here into lateral façades but the courtyard is grandly conceived. The *mihrāb* wall contains stained glass by Ibrāhīm 'the Drunkard' and the earliest tiles from the Iznik workshops. The dome is 53 m high and is the largest of more than five hundred subsidiary domes in this complex.

ISTANBUL, Haseki Hürrem Hammām
Ottoman period, 1556

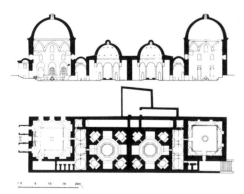

The baths for men and for women are set on a continual axis divided by a wall, which makes a visual link between the Ahmediye complex and that of Hagia Sophia. These are the largest baths built by Sinān and the quality of the details, including the *opus*

sectile paving, is equal to that of the Süleymaniye Mosque. The women's entrance is modestly masked but that for the men has a triple-domed portico leading to the square hall. This is girdled by a sofa under a lofty dome and has a fountain, also a hearth for brewing coffee. The cool room where clothes are washed leads to the ornate room, which is a domed octagon with a marble massage platform. In the angles are domed cells for privacy.

ISTANBUL, Complex of Sokollu Mehmet Paşa
Ottoman period, 1572

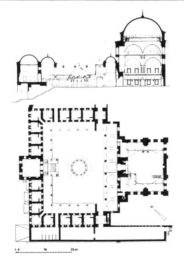

This represents Sinān's perfection of the vizier's mosque. The courtyard is approached up the hillside by a stair, which passes under the lecture hall of the *madrasa* to confront the domed fountain. This enables the hall to achieve its true central position without diminishing the effect of the mosque's portico and entrance. The dome of the mosque is 24.5m high and there are multiple galleries on three sides. Some original paintwork survives and there is a splendid array of tiles from floor to dome with flowers, and bands and wheels of inscriptions. The *minbar* is also hooded in tiles and represents the peak of the Iznik achievement. The 19th-century coloured glass windows also deserve inspection.

ISTANBUL, Complex of Sultan Ahmet
Ottoman period, early 17th century

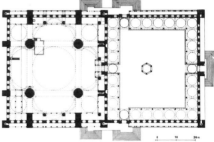

The complex includes the tomb of Ahmet I, a *madrasa*, *imaret* and demolished asylum. It was built on the site of vizerial palaces over the vaults of the Byzantine great palace. A rebuilt pavilion gives access to the royal box. The architect, Sedefkar Mehmet Agha, turned to the Şehzade Mehmet complex for his plan but with a dome too modest for the scale of its supports and the use of triple exedrae. The mosque contains over 20,000 tiles of mixed quality; those in the gallery are the finest. The coloured glass and the flaking blue stencilling are recent but the profusion of plaster *muqarnas* is original. The court is large but its details monotonous and the fountain small. The build-up of the dome and the six minarets is a genuine *tour-de-force*.

ISTANBUL, Topkapi Palace
Ottoman period, various periods

The palace of the 'Gun Gate' was originally double and consisted of summer pavilions at the water's edge – now mainly destroyed by the railway – and the winter palace on the ridge overlooking the city. The courts were arranged in a series: the first contained the armoury in the church of Hagia Irene, and various hospitals and barracks; the second was bounded by the reception hall and inner treasury on one side, and the kitchen on the other; the third was used by the palace school; and the fourth consisted of gardens and various pavilions. On the city side, beyond the barracks of the Halberdiers, was the harem. It was divided into distinct sectors: those for eunuchs, laundry and other services, the queen mother's suite, the sultan's rooms and those of his ladies, and the sacred chamber of the Robe of the Prophet and its pavilion.

ISTANBUL, Revan Kiosk, Topkapi Palace
Ottoman period, 1635

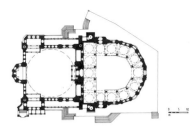

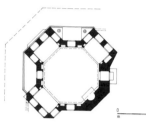

This typical pavilion was built by Murad IV to celebrate the capture of Erivan and projects before the colonnade of the pavilion of the Robe of the Prophet. Designed as a room for contemplative penance its view was later blocked by the grander Baghdad kiosk. It forms a domed octagon with three projecting bays, and a 15m-high hearth is set in the fourth wall. The three sofa ceilings are fine but the dome has been repainted. It is pierced by four windows set in tunnel vaults and spreads externally into broad eaves. The walls are clad in late tiles and marble revetments, haphazardly arranged.

ISTANBUL, Nurosmaniye Complex
Ottoman period, mid-18th century

This is the first major work in the Baroque style imported from France. Formerly recti-linear elements, such as dome buttresses, became curved and *muqarnas* vaults were planned. Yet the mosque remains a domed square, which neither apse nor galleries modify. The horseshoe shape of the court and its arches, however, is unique. The stone minaret caps are not as elaborate as are later examples. A fine stairway and gallery lead to the royal box; the library, *madrasa* and tomb are irregularly grouped within the precinct, which has grandiose portals and a fountain opposite the bazaar. Simeon Kalfa probably was responsible for this mosque while no-minally working under Mustafā Agha. The dome, more than 25m in diameter, was an achievement at a time of a decline in building techniques.

ISTANBUL, Fountain of Ahmet III
Ottoman period, 1728

The fountains built between 1728 and 1732 are the climax of the so-called Tulip phase. This fountain is as large as a house, with a tank (*sabīl*) at each corner where water and sherbet were offered in bronze mugs, and with taps in the middle of each side. The tanks, with their multifoliate arches, carried on slender columns, and the triple curves of their extensive eaves, are Baroque elements but the symmetrical floral decoration in low-relief lacks the essential three-dimensional force. The tiles belong to the short-lived revival at Tekfursaray but are not its finest examples.

ISTANBUL, Büyük Yeni Khān
Ottoman period, 1764

This large commercial *khan* is typical of many built in the capital and elsewhere and was endowed by Mustafā III. At a later date a block of ugly rooms divided the court, which once offered a vista 85 m long. Two tiers of arched galleries are carried above the arcades behind which are ground floor store rooms. The street façade has rooms projecting outwards on corbels above the shops to make use of the irregular site by creating more

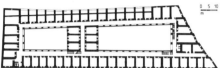

amenable rectangular rooms in the upper storeys. The corbels, the alternating layers of bricks and ashlar, and the dog-tooth mould-ing at roof level go back to Byzantine techniques.

IZNIK, Zaviye of Nilüfer Sultan
Early Ottoman period, 1388

Constructed by Murād I for his mother, who was a Christian by birth, this *zaviye* was an assembly place for the Ahis, or guildsmen. Typical of the period, it is built of one course of ashlar to three of brick in thick mortar, a technique deriving from Byzantine economy methods. The five-arch portico is carried on piers divided by reused Byzantine columns with acanthus capitals half changed into *muqarnas*. Because of their depth the bays are cross-vaulted, except in the centre where a small dome rises from triangular penden-tives. The square hall opens on each side into rooms with fireplaces; the main *īwān* has a lateral *mihrāb* niche and two domes in cradle vaults on each side of a dividing arch.

KAYSERI, Döner Kümbet
Seljuq period, c. 1276

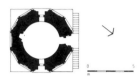

Typical of the Seljuq tombs (*kümbet*) in Anatolia, this building is raised over a burial vault within the stone base and not in the ground. The relationship of this tomb architecture to tents and to the domes and drums of Armenian and Georgian churches is disputed. The trunk of the Döner tomb is divided into panels defined by ribs and arches, which recur on the conical roof. Fanatics defaced the fine decoration, especially the human heads and those of the lions and eagles. At the top, geometric designs lead into the shallow *muqarnas* cornice under the roof. The door into the chamber is out of alignment with the *miḥrāb* within. A marble inscription refers to an unknown lady, Shah Cihan Hatun.

KONYA, Mosque of ʿAlāʾ ad-Dīn
Seljuq period, c. 1156–1220

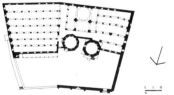

Because of numerous additions and repairs this is a complicated building. The fan-shaped pillared hall with a flat, mud roof supported on six rows of disparate Classical columns may have been the original structure related to the primitive Great

Mosque at Sivas. The western section has a dome before the *miḥrāb* in the Damascus manner and may have been the kernel of the mosque, although distorted by the insertion of two tomb chambers on the courtyard side, and the flanking asymmetrical aisles. The decagonal sepulchre built by Kılıç Aslan II contains fine blue and white inscriptive tiles. The court belonged to the palace rather than to the mosque, and its splendid wall of contrasting coloured stones in the Syrian manner was built by Muhammad bin Havlan of Damascus. The tiled *miḥrāb* is half destroyed but not the ebony *minbar*, built by Menguberti of Ahlat in 1155.

KONYA, Ince Minare Madrasa
Seljuq period, c. 1260–5

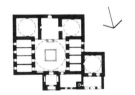

The minaret of this *madrasa* originally had two balconies and was built for the adjoining mosque, which preceded the college, now ruined. The minaret was truncated by lightning in 1901. The minaret of the Taş Madrasa at Aksehir (1250), built by Sahib Ata, was its prototype, but that of the Ince Minare Madrasa was ribbed, and had glazed brick and tile decoration. The name of the architect, Keluk bin Abd Allah, suggests that he was a slave. The T-plan of the *madrasa* had been foreshadowed by the Karatay college and by that of Cacabey in Kirşehir with its large dome over a central court. The dome of the Ince Minare Madrasa is supported on sets of four triangular fan pendentives, but without tiles. The portal is framed with broad bands of concentrated calligraphy, which interlace to form significant structural accents contrasting with the three-dimensional sculptural effect.

MANISA, Muradiye Complex
Ottoman period, 1586

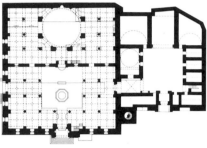

The mosque is remarkable for its unique, inwardly sloping windows at the upper level. It is unlikely that Sinān ever saw his mosque or the minaret in the foreground, while the finely proportioned *madrasa* is not attributed to him. The decorative work in the mosque is very fine, including a beautiful ceiling under the royal loge. Work on the site was delegated to an architect named Mahmud and on his death he was replaced by Mehmet Agha, who may tentatively be identified with the architect of the Ahmediye complex in Istanbul. The Muradiye is the highly sophisticated product of Sinān's old age: in the distance can be seen the Valide Mosque of 1522, with its austere rectilinear forms, combining the breadth that derived from the Damascus school with the domed cube of the Ottomans. Internally, the aggressive central cube supporting the dome is muted by pendentives.

NIĞDE, Ak Madrasa
Beylik period, 1409

The princes of Karamania were the foremost rivals of the Ottomans and this college was founded by ʿAlāʾ ad-Dīn ʿAlī Bey, brother of the amir. It is a two-storey building in fine ashlar and encloses the traditional court. Its arches are defined by corded ribbing. The portal is framed in marble and covered in arabesque decoration and inscriptions. The *muqarnas* vault over the door recedes under an ogee arch, which achieves the appearance of curtains looped open. The portal divides the first-floor loggia in two (unlike that of the Hüdavandigār Mosque at Bursa) and the pairs of pointed arches are divided by ogee arches that spring from reused Byzantine columns. A circular element gives the façade a distinctly Italianate appearance, save for the portal.

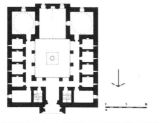

SIVAS, Hospital of Kay Kā'ūs I
Seljuq period, 1218

The first Seljuq hospital in Anatolia had been built at Kayseri in 1205 but the Sivas foundation followed soon after and is the largest of the series. Built of brick and stone, it includes the mausoleum of the prince. The glazed bricks, with the usual Seljuq cobalt predominating, are the work of Ahmad of Marand, north of Tabriz. Over the tomb is a decagonal tower facing the east *iwān* which may once have led to a medical school. The plain external ashlar walls are dominated by

the portal which is highly decorated with interlacing patterns and solar symbols. It admits to a double-vaulted hall forming the third *iwān*. At the opposite end of the court is the main *iwān* with a *mihrāb* niche and flanking chambers. It is likely that there were once ten cells on each side of the court.

SIVAS, Gök Madrasa
Seljuq period, 1271

This college was built facing a rival foundation of the Mongols by Kay-Khusraw III; Kaluyan of Konya, whose name is inscribed twice on the gateway, may also have built the monument. The two-storey college follows the four-*iwān* plan. It has excellent ceramic

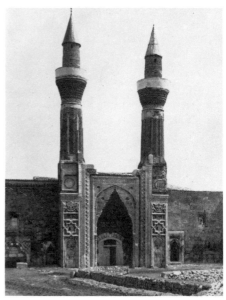

decoration in the mosque. The façade is lavishly carved in marble and possesses the earliest Anatolian example of a fountain incorporated into the wall. The buttresses are integrated into the façade, where foliate motifs dominate over geometric interlacing as in the case of the Çifte Minare Madrasa in Erzurum. Both buildings have several depths of carving, which indicates various groups of workers using different techniques, as at Divriği.

Iraq

HELEN PHILON

In considering the Islamic architecture of Iraq we view, by necessity, the dynasties that sponsored these monuments, covering a period from the 7th to the 15th centuries, ending at a time when, finally, Iranian influences became overwhelming. This architecture falls into fairly distinctive geographic groups: in the north, an essentially stone architecture prevails, while brick is the main building material in central and southern Iraq.

The architecture of the early 'Abbāsids was coloured by pre-Islamic Iranian influences; the adoption of the Iranian concept

of kingship, coupled with the concern for political security, contributed to the creation of the three royal cities at Baghdad, Samarra and Raqqa, as well as to the building of the fortified palace at Ukhaydir. Architectural themes new to the Islamic world appeared at this time. 'Abbāsid architecture is essentially brick built and is characterized by varied vaulting techniques, domes on squinches, lobed arches and the pointed arch, the last originating in eastern Early Christian architecture. In addition, architectural elements were employed for purely decorative purposes and geometric ornamental brickwork (*hazarbāf*) was introduced – destined for great elaboration in Iran. Wood and stucco were used extensively for ornamental panels. Vegetal and geometric motifs became, in time, so abstract that their designs consisted

only of negative and positive visual effects axially organized. The decorative principles here established were to leave an indelible mark on all Islamic art leading to the development of the characteristic arabesque ornamentation.

With the crumbling of the 'Abbāsid dynasty, smaller dynasties mushroomed in Iraq. However, the 'Abbāsids retained titular authority until the Mongol invasion, which destroyed Baghdad in 1258. Under the smaller dynasties, such as the 'Uqaylids, the restrained decorative vocabulary of the early 'Abbāsids was transformed into exuberant stucco decoration. In the Imām Dūr at Samarra, this style reached its apogee in the decoration of the *muqarnas* dome, the first of its type in Iraq.

Historically and geographically, northern

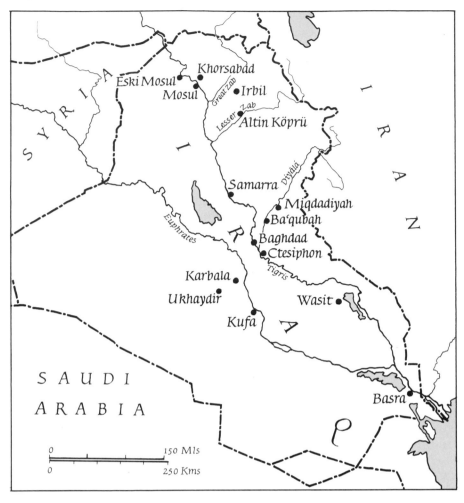

AL KIFL, Minaret and Tomb
Il-Khanid period, 1316

The importance of this complex lies in the unique decoration of the minaret, the vaulting systems of the prayer hall and the pilgrims' hostel and in the double *muqarnas* dome over the tomb, whose exterior does not reflect the inner scheme of the *muqarnas*. The brick minaret (24m high) is set within a projecting semicircular bay, suggesting that the compound was once surrounded by an enclosure wall. Rising from a square base, the cylindrical shaft of the minaret has rows of *muqarnas* decoration carrying a gallery and a narrower shaft covered by a ribbed dome. A staircase built over an arch was once attached to the base of the minaret. The decoration covers only half of the shaft and is divided into horizontal sections decorated with geometric brickwork. The large angular *kūfī* inscription made of small pieces of terracotta is its most impressive feature, the words being formed within alternating upright and inverted triangles. The tomb is covered by a double *muqarnas* dome, the exterior of which does not reflect the inner scheme.

Iraq, with its capital at Mosul, was affiliated to Syria. There, an essentially stone architecture developed, although brick was also used. Distinguished for its pointed pyramidal roofs with interior *muqarnas* domes, and for the extensive use of grey-blue marble, this architecture featured terracotta brick decoration and also glazed tiles, especially on minarets. Marble mosaic-work, later fully exploited in Syria and Egypt, and the inlaying of marble with paste, especially for inscriptions, originated in Mosul in the 12th century. Reserved for *mihrābs*, doorways and wall facings, marble was deeply carved with arabesque designs. During the reign of Badr ad-Dīn Lu'lu', animal and human representations became important elements of the decorative vocabulary.

The later 'Abbāsids produced an eclectic form of architecture by knitting together the *madrasa*, the monumental arched entrances of the Seljuqs and the internal portal scheme (*pīshtāq*), as at Ukhaydir. Pointed and segmented arches and vaults, cross vaults, domical vaults, *muqarnas* vaults and domes were all employed.

Surface decoration was notable for the combination of brick or stucco strapwork set with intricately carved terracotta in bold patterns against a spiralling ground, usually on a single plane. The combination of lines and terracotta inserts creates geometric patterns with three-dimensional effects. The architectural and decorative techniques of the late 'Abbāsids was further refined in subsequent dynasties. By the 14th century, larger surfaces were covered in finely carved terracotta, forming geometric designs in different layers of relief.

Chronology

Umayyad period 661–750

'Abbāsid period 749–1258

Būyid period 945–1048/55

'Uqaylid period 990–1096

Seljuq period 1038–1194

Zangid period 1127–1222

Atabegid period 1222–59

Il-Khanid period 1256–1353

Jalāyirid period 1336–1432

BAGHDAD, Circular City
'Abbāsid period, 762

Founded by al-Mansūr on a site already known as Baghdad, this royal city was called the City of Peace, or Madīnat as-Salām. Imitating Parthian and Sasanian models, Baghdad symbolized the heavenly city, at the centre of which stood the palace of the ruler. Nothing of al-Mansūr's city now remains and knowledge about it is entirely based on literary evidence. At the time of its foundation, and even before the city was completed, the suburb of al Harbiyya, in the north, became a military settlement, while in the south, at Karkh, lived thousands of labourers brought from all the 'Abbāsid lands. Three years after the caliph took up residence within the circular city, the fortified palace complex at Rusafa was built as a second city for al-Mansūr's son and heir. Ten years later, the caliph moved his private quarters outside, to Khuld. These acts define the real function of Baghdad as the ideal vision of a caliphal citadel, the royal and administrative centre of the empire, while military, commercial and residential quarters were segregated from each other and situated outside its circular enclosure. The round city consisted of a double fortified enclosure surrounded by a ditch; between the two circular walls was an intervallum. Within the walls were two circles of habitation followed by the inner royal enclosure. The caliph's palace and mosque were located within a large garden, as were the house of the chief of the guard and the apartments of the chief of police. Four axial arcaded streets with elaborate gateways ran from the royal enclosure to the outer perimeter of the wall.

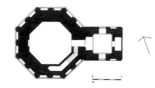

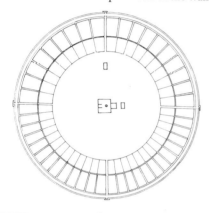

BAGHDAD, Tomb of Sitta Zubayda
Late ʿAbbāsid period, 1179–1225

Built by an-Nāsir for his mother, this octagonal brick tomb is celebrated for its conical *muqarnas* dome, the second of its type in Iraq, after the Imām Dūr at Samarra. The inner space reflects the outer scheme. The important feature of this building is a dome, transforming itself from an octagon into a sixteen-sided figure and back again

through the multiplication and division of the *muqarnas* areas. The dome culminates in a ribbed cupola. *Muqarnas*, pierced to allow light to enter, create a starlit effect inside. Each outside wall of the octagon is divided into four recessed panels and decorated in the *hazarbāf* technique. The deeply carved terracotta with arabesque patterns is set on the same plane as the undecorated brick. The tomb is preceded by a modern square domed building replacing an older one.

BAGHDAD, Minaret of the Jāmiʿ al-Qumriyya
Late ʿAbbāsid period, 1228

According to literary evidence, the mosque that once adjoined this minaret was built by an-Nāsir; therefore, the minaret has been assumed to date from the same period. Built of bricks set in mortar, its base consists of a square polyhedron of projecting triangles transforming a square into a thirty-two-sided figure on which rests the cylindrical shaft. This shaft terminates in a single row of pointed-arched *muqarnas* areas supporting a circular gallery. Above, the minaret was topped by a dome decorated with bricks in the *hazarbāf* technique, replaced recently with glazed tiles. The shaft is decorated with an overall lozenge pattern formed by intersecting recessed lines. The polyhedral base of the minaret is unique in Iraq but is found in tombs at Sivas and Lake Van in Turkey, from the late 13th and early 14th centuries.

BAGHDAD, ʿAbbāsid 'Palace'
Late ʿAbbāsid period, 1230

Thought to have been built by an-Nāsir, this 'palace' is now believed to have been a *madrasa* founded during the reign of al-Mustansir. Its most important features are

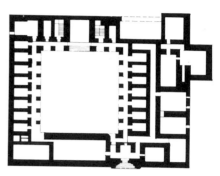

the entrance arrangement, the use of cross vaults, the air-shafts in the inner corridors, the *muqarnas* vaults in the arcades and the unique and finely executed decoration of the *īwān*. The river gates of this two-storeyed brick building flank a blind *īwān*. One gate leads to the courtyard and the other to a passageway known as the *mābayn*, present in large Baghdad houses. The courtyard is surrounded by an arcade covered by a *muqarnas* vault, off which open the student cells. The same scheme was probably repeated on the first floor. The *muqarnas* areas were decorated with terracotta panels carved with arabesques. The decoration of the *īwān*, however, is unsurpassed, the entire surface being covered with brick ornament of various geometric designs.

BAGHDAD, Al-Mustansir Madrasa (Mustansiriyya)
Late ʿAbbāsid period, 1233

The caliph, al-Mustansir, built this *madrasa* for the teaching of the four orthodox Sunnī rites. It is a four-*īwān* courtyard building with a prayer hall, kitchen, student accommodation and baths. The decorated *īwān* on the north-west external wall of the building probably belonged to the Dār al-Qurʾān. The river façade, decorated with a meander pattern, outlined in raised brick plugs adorned with rosettes, has an inscription replacing the original one. This two-storeyed rectangular brick building is composed of eight groups of cells (in two floors) symmetrically arranged around the courtyard. The ground floor contains pointed-arched doorways to the cells while the upper floor

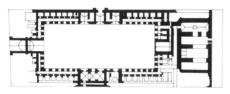

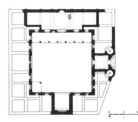

consists of a twelve-sided base with four layers of *muqarnas* decoration carrying a dodecagonal gallery. From this rises the cylindrical shaft with two entrances leading to two staircases spiralling in opposite directions. The shaft is crowned by five rows of *muqarnas* decoration, which carry a second circular gallery and a narrower shaft covered by a pointed dome. The *muqarnas* areas on both the base and shaft were ornamented with terracotta panels with a pattern of split-leaf palmette forms against a finely carved arabesque background. The shaft is decorated with a meander pattern outlined with brick plugs carved with stylized leaf motifs. Below the upper *muqarnas* is a *kūfī* inscription in relief against a fine rosette pattern. Although polyhedral minaret bases are known in Iraq (Sinjar, Irbil and Ana), this is the only one with twelve sides.

opens onto a similarly arched corridor. The arches are set within recessed panels outlined by undecorated horizontal and vertical bands. The *īwāns* are similarly decorated. On the two shorter sides, in between the cells, are single *īwāns*. Their pointed arches on engaged columns are set within undecorated frames rising above the level of the cells. On each of the longer sides is an arrangement of triple doorways, one leading to the *musallā* and the others forming the entrance complex. The arch spandrels and the areas above the doorways are decorated with fine geometric brickwork with carved terracotta arabesque inserts.

BAGHDAD, Sūq al-Ghazl Minaret
Il-Khanid period, late 13th century

This minaret was originally thought to date from 1235, but recent investigation has shown that it belongs to the Il-Khanid period. Built of bricks set in mortar, it

BAGHDAD, Al-Mirjān Madrasa
Jalāyirid period, 1357

This two-storeyed complex contains a school, a mosque and a mausoleum and is built of bricks set in mortar. The combination of these three elements under one roof is unusual in Iraq, but is found extensively in Egypt. Although the building was partly destroyed in 1948, it is notable for its monumental Seljuq type entrance lavishly decorated with terracotta inserts with deep arabesque designs. The entrance is flanked by two semicircular decorated buttresses, one of which forms a minaret. Opposite the entrance was the tomb, now destroyed. The undecorated square chamber was covered by a fluted dome, rare in Iraq, supported on

three rows of *muqarnas* decoration. The slightly pointed dome on the exterior caps a tall drum with engaged columns decorated with bricks of two colours in the *hazarbāf* technique. The prayer hall, situated opposite the *īwān*, was entered through three doors and divided into three areas by pointed transverse arches and covered by domes on pendentives. The pendentives of the dome in front of the *mihrāb* and the areas on either side were decorated with terracotta geometric patterns, set in different planes.

BAGHDAD, Khān al-Mirjān
Jalāyirid period, 1359

Al-Mirjān built this *khān* as a *waqf* for his *madrasa*. Built in brick, this rectangular building has a long vaulted hall (14m high) with a fountain in the middle, onto which the surrounding two-storeyed structure opens. The entrance is similar to that of the *madrasa* of al-Mirjān, and had shops on both sides of it. The first-floor gallery, supported by corbelled *muqarnas* areas, runs round the hall giving access to the rooms. The vaulted hall has eight transverse arches placed at equal intervals, except for the middle bay, which is wider. The vaults rise in stepped stages along the profile of the arch and are topped by domes on squinches. Each stage is pierced with windows opening onto the roof. The plan, vaulting and lighting systems of this *khān* are unique in Islamic architecture.

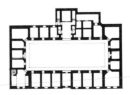

IRBIL, Minaret of the Ulu Jāmiʿ
Zangid or Atabegid periods, early 13th century

The base of this minaret is divided into two parts with two doorways leading to separate spiralling staircases. Built in brick (except for the lower part of the base, which is of limestone and brick), the base, which is in two parts, forms a seven-sided figure with the two longer undecorated sides attached to the mosque (the upper part of the base is octagonal). Each side is decorated with recessed rectangular frames containing pointed-arched niches with geometric brickwork. Above, is a brick band of *kūfī* inscription set against a stucco background. The transition from the octagon (of the base) to the circular shaft is achieved by four rows of *muqarnas* cells, which probably held a gallery with a door opening onto it. The upper part of the shaft is missing. Above the doorway are four wide zones alternating with narrower ones, decorated with variations of the meander pattern containing turquoise-blue glazed tiles. The minaret possibly dates from the rule of Muzaffar ad-Dīn Kūkburī (1190–1232).

KUFA, Mosque and Dār al-Imāra Palace
Umayyad, ʿAbbāsid and Il-Khanid periods, 7th century and 14th–15th centuries

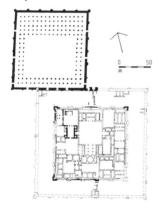

Kufa's first mosque was marked out by Saʿd ibn Abī Waqqās in 638, and was surrounded by a ditch with a covered colonnade on the *qibla* wall. Ziyād ibn Abih, the Umayyad governor of Basra, rebuilt the mosque in 670 and added the palace. The present mosque occupies the ancient site. The Dār al-Imāra is the earliest urban palace preserved in Islam and seems to have been used both as a residence and as an administrative centre. Recently excavated, it is situated on the outside of the *qibla* wall of the mosque and was used and added to by the ʿAbbāsids, remaining in use until the Il-Khanids. So far, it is the only known Umayyad building in Iraq and in its plan and layout is reminiscent of other Umayyad castles and early ʿAbbāsid

palace architecture. It was built of brick decorated with stucco, and surrounded by a double enclosure wall with round corner and intermediary towers. The palace enclosure itself contained a square courtyard into which three *īwāns* opened with porches on two columns. On the south side were the official rooms of the amir, similar to those in the palace at Mshattā. A large hall divided into three aisles by two rows of columns allowed access to a square room with four recesses containing doors.

MOSUL, Mosque of Nūr ad-Dīn
Zangid period, 1170–2

This mosque was recently destroyed; only the minaret, two *mihrābs*, an inscribed marble slab and some stucco decoration survive. It would appear that Nūr ad-Dīn, to whom the mosque is attributed, carried out major alterations on an earlier mosque built by Sayf ad-Dīn Ghāzī I in 1148. From this earlier mosque only an inscribed marble *mihrāb* survives, its deeply carved arabesque decoration set within a geometric pattern. The lyre capitals of the engaged columns of Nūr ad-Dīn's mosque find their parallel in the palace at Raqqa. The complex system of vaults and domes is unique. The marble *mihrāb*, found in the court, and the stucco arcades over the *mihrāb* in the prayer hall probably belong to the restorations of Badr ad-Dīn Luʾluʾ. The brick-built minaret lies in the north-west corner of the mosque courtyard. From a cubical base rises a cylindrical shaft surrounded at the top by a gallery supported on brackets. The base is decorated with geometric brick panels set within decorated rectangular frames, while the shaft is divided into seven wide decorative zones alternating with seven narrow ones all of different geometric brick patterns.

MOSUL, Qara Sarai Palace
Atabegid period, 1233

Built by Badr ad-Dīn Luʾluʾ of stones steeped in mortar, only two out of three *īwāns* opening onto a courtyard survive from this two-storeyed building. The remains of the

stucco decoration on the back wall of the smaller *īwān* consist of a band of intersecting arches containing *kūfī* and *naskhī* inscriptions against intricate leaf arabesque patterns with birds. Above, is a band decorated with broken arches containing human figures. These figural and animal representations seem to be favoured during this period. This is followed by a *naskhī* inscription set against a spiralling leaf and stem arabesque background, the stems of which end in animal heads. Above it, a narrower band contains pairs of facing birds; finally, the whole decorative scheme is capped by a band of *naskhī*.

MOSUL, Tomb of Imām Yahyā
Atabegid period, 1229

Badr ad-Dīn Luʾluʾ held Shīʿī beliefs, which caused the conversion of many *madrasas* and also the erection of new tombs to the Shīʿī *imāms*. This square brick mausoleum is covered by a polyhedral pointed roof with an interior *muqarnas* dome. The façade is symmetrical and decorated with pointed-arched niches with geometric patterns outlined in turquoise-blue bricks, with terracotta inserts carved with arabesques and containing a knotted *kūfī* inscription in cut bricks. The walls of the square tomb chamber have pointed-arched niches set with geometric and arabesque designs. One of the niches contains the doorway. The building is not orientated towards Mecca, the *mihrāb* being placed in a corner. The *naskhī* inscriptions inside are carved in blue-grey marble, the letters being filled with white marble. The marble dado running along the lower part of the wall, with rosettes and a leaf design in high relief, contrasts with the geometric terracotta decoration of the walls. The *muqarnas* dome is a combination of honeycombed niches arranged on a cruciform plan. In order to cover the tall corner areas of *muqarnas* on the outside, four pyramid sections were added.

SAMARRA, Palace of al-Muʿtasim (Jawsaq al-Khāqānī)
ʿAbbāsid period, 836

Overlooking the Tigris, the monumental triple-arched façade of the gateway complex still stands, the only remains of this vast palace, which once contained a throne room, the private quarters of the caliph, a harem, a polo ground, two *sirdābs*, the treasury and a game preserve. This gateway, known as the Bāb al-ʿĀmma, consists of three barrel-vaulted *īwāns*. The two lateral *īwāns* are in two parts – that under the frontal arch was covered by a semi-dome on squinches with a door leading to the rear barrel-vaulted chamber. These did not communicate with the central *īwān*, which was the largest, its pointed frontal arch resting on pilasters, giving access through a rear door to six transverse halls. The square courtyard adjacent to these halls led to the private chambers of the caliph and to the harem, provided with an elaborate sanitary system. To the east, a rectangular court gave access to the throne complex, east of which was the 'Great Esplanade'. The domed throne room was at the centre of four triple-aisled, basilica-like halls admitting light through a clerestory. The palace was decorated with stucco and marble panels, woodcarvings and frescoes; the last depict mainly the activities of the court, the iconography being borrowed from Classical, pre-Islamic Iranian and Central Asian prototypes.

SAMARRA, Great Mosque
ʿAbbāsid period, 847

Built by al-Mutawakkil after his accession to the throne, this is one of the biggest mosques in the Islamic world; however, only its brick enclosure wall now survives, together with the spiral minaret. The building forms an immense rectangle with bastioned walls decorated at the top with a frieze of recessed squares containing concave saucers, the semicircular bastions standing on rectangular bases. The doorways have a shallow relieving arch strengthening the beams. On three sides the mosque was surrounded by an enclosed space (*ziyāda*). The prayer hall had twenty-five aisles formed by rows of piers on square bases, plastered and painted in imitation of marble; each pier employed engaged columns of coloured marble culminating in bell-shaped capitals. The mosque was covered by a flat wooden roof. The windows at the end of the aisles take the form of a five-lobed arch on engaged colonnettes within a recessed rectangle on the interior, and narrow rectangles below the frieze on the exterior, fitted with moulded glass. The *mihrāb* is rectangular and was probably decorated with gold mosaic. The minaret rests on a square base with shallow panels containing niches. On the south side, the spiralling ramp begins, making five complete turns in an anti-clockwise direction before terminating in a cylindrical shaft decorated with pointed-arched recesses. The top platform (50m above the base) was once covered by a small pavilion. Some years later, in 859–61, al-Mutawakkil erected another mosque, that of Abū Dulaf, at Samarra, modelled on this mosque, but with variations in the arrangement of piers and aisles.

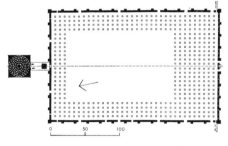

SAMARRA, Qubbat as-Sulaybiyya
ʿAbbāsid period, 892

This is possibly the earliest surviving tomb in the Islamic world. It is situated on the west bank of the Tigris and is built of an artificial composite stone. The building consists of two concentric octagons; the outer has pointed-arched entrances in the middle of each side allowing access to an octagonal barrel-vaulted ambulatory, the vaults resting on sixteen arches springing from the corners of the inner octagon. The square tomb chamber, entered through four doorways, was covered with a dome resting on a drum formed by eight arches, four of which rose above corner squinches. Though the three

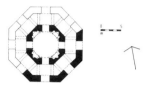

burials discovered here may have been those of three ʿAbbāsid caliphs (and therefore might date the building between 862 and 869), the similarity of the building material to that of the Qasr al-ʿĀshiq palace of al-Muʿtamid (dated 878–82) suggests that this edifice was also built by this ruler as his final resting place.

SAMARRA, Qasr al-Jass
ʿAbbāsid period, 870–92

Caliph al-Muʿtamid built two palaces on the west bank of the Tigris: Qasr al-ʿĀshiq and Qasr al-Jass. The latter is a square brick edifice, with the square throne room located in the centre of a cross, probably covered by a dome. Between the four arms of the cross were arrangements of halls opening into courtyards leading to rectangular chambers and thence to a portico approached by a terrace and stairs. These areas were organized diagonally into identical pairs. The south-west side displays an interesting scheme of units consisting of a courtyard opening into rooms and bathrooms forming self-contained living quarters connected by corridors. The south-east side is more haphazardly arranged, consisting mainly of bath compartments. The palace enclosure has four circular towers at the corners and free-standing rectangular piers, probably connected to the walls by vaults.

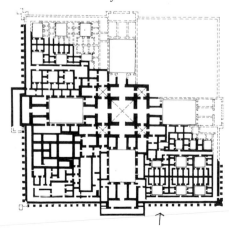

SAMARRA, Imām Dūr
'Uqaylid period, 1085

This is the tomb of Sharaf ad-Dawla Muslim, the 'Uqaylid amir. The square brick mausoleum has four bastioned corners and is topped by a *muqarnas* dome, the earliest of its type in Iraq. The bastions are divided into three zones by narrow bands; above an undecorated zone are two wider ones containing geometric brickwork, the lower is an intaglio of the one above. The plain curtain walls are bordered at the top with three rows of rhomboids outlined in raised brick. The name of the architect, Abū Shākir ibn Abi' l-Faraj, is set in one of them. The tomb chamber is a square domed room. Four corner niches create the transitional octagon on which the *muqarnas* dome rises in five corbelled zones culminating in a fluted cupola. Each zone consists of eight *muqarnas* cells decreasing in height towards the top. The interior stucco decoration is traced to 'Abbāsid prototypes – conches, broken arches on brackets and lobed arches are surrounded by wavy multiple

frames creating an exuberant illogical effect of dizzying forms. This decoration is the most elaborate and accomplished example of what may be termed the Samarran 'Roccoco' style, which appears to predominate in central Iraq under the 'Uqaylids. It is seen in the so-called palace at Raqqa, in two tombs at Haditha, in the minaret at Ana, and in the al-Arba'īn at Takrit.

SAMARRA, Bridge over the Harba River
Late 'Abbāsid period, 13th century

Situated close to Samarra, this bridge was probably built by al-Mustansir in 1228 and is the only known brick bridge in Iraq, most of the others being built in stone or in a combination of stone and brick. The roadway is carried on four wide pointed arches of equal span and height, alternating with narrower arches set within recessed panels. Above the arches and just below the roadway is a brick *naskhī* inscription in relief against a floral background.

UKHAYDIR, Palace
'Abbāsid period, 8th century

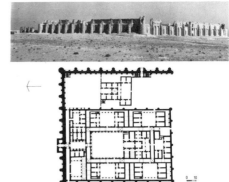

Probably founded by al-Mansūr's nephew, 'Īsā ibn Mūsā, this palace consists of two fortified enclosures built of thin slabs of stone set in mortar. The outer rectangular enclosure has corner and intermediary towers alternating with pairs of blind arches on pilasters. Each gateway is set between half-towers and is provided with a portcullis; that to the south is set between rectangular towers, probably an afterthought of the architect. The palace contains a mosque, a court of honour, audience halls and four *bayts* (self-contained units consisting of a courtyard off which open *īwāns* and flanking rooms on two sides). The entrance hall leads into a square room with a fluted dome, the first of its type in Iraq, followed by a vaulted hall with arched recesses. South of this room is the court of honour, decorated with blind apses, patterned in geometric brick designs. On the south side is the earliest appearance of the arched portal, set within a rectangular frame, rising above the walls of the courtyard (*pīshtāq*). This leads into the official reception rooms of the palace, which are vaulted. The prayer hall of the mosque and two courtyard arcades were covered by a tunnel vault decorated with recessed brickwork, fluted squinches and recessed triangles.

Iran

ANTONY HUTT

Despite an essential feeling of cultural unity, which pervades the entire Islamic world, any discussion of Islamic architecture must inevitably distinguish between western and eastern lands. The eastern part of the Islamic world looks to the Persian language and culture for its inspiration – modern Iran is the heartland of a larger Iranian world, which included Soviet Central Asia and Afghanistan and which spread into the Indian subcontinent. An examination of

architectural developments in Iran must, therefore, be seen in relation to this wider world, where both peoples and artistic ideas easily moved across modern boundaries.

Initially, Iran appears to have accepted western Islamic architectural forms, although a diversity of building materials, coupled with a consummate skill in their use, stemming from earlier traditions, created an Iranian feeling in an essentially Arab style, at an early stage – as in the Tārik Khāna Mosque at Damghan. With the emergence of a local dynasty, the Būyids, in the 10th century, a national awareness began to appear, which was also manifested by the use of Persian as a literary language, culminating in the com-

position of the great national epic, the *Shāhnāmah*, by Firdawsī at the beginning of the 11th century.

This upsurge of national feeling, combined with new ideas and artistic forms that appeared with the invasions of the Central Asian Turks, was responsible for the creation of the great monuments of the 11th and 12th centuries. These peoples, principally the Seljuqs, brought with them a number of creative ideas, including a more solid three-dimensional approach, which were to alter the course of architectural development in Iran. During the Seljuq period appeared the new cylindrical minaret form; the four-*īwān* plan for both mosque and *madrasa* schemes;

tombs were attached to this in a somewhat haphazard manner, but eventually they all were transformed into a more regular complex by the addition of a prayer hall and a new façade for the mosque, which aligned it with the other buildings. The whole of this was clothed with a rich, late 16th-century tile-mosaic, which gave the group further cohesion and a degree of formality.

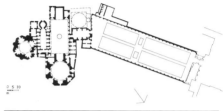

ARDESTAN, Friday Mosque
Seljuq period, 11th and 12th centuries

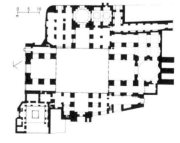

the exteriorization of the structural components of building; an emphasis on large, domed spaces dominating outer façades; and complex brick patterning in a variety of geometric designs. These new ideas, in their realization by local architects and craftsmen, became essentially Iranian creations, an integral part of a national awareness.

Architectural development was hardly interrupted by the destructive Mongol invasions in the 13th century; and, soon after, when the Mongols had simply become another Iranian dynasty, architecture once again resumed its evolution. Considerable refinement in architectural decoration occurred under the Mongols, including a greater use of colour, which had first appeared in a restrained usage on the exteriors of Seljuq buildings. This development continued under the Tīmūrids, who were at first equally as destructive as the Mongols, but who settled down to build some of the finest Iranian monuments, ornamented with superb glazed tile-mosaics. The increased use of colour was associated with a return to the Iranian emphasis on surface rather than structure, in contrast to the Seljuq period, when structural forms were more emphasized.

Under the Safavids, a series of splendid monuments was achieved, particularly at Isfahan, the new capital, where colour was all-pervading, covering almost all the visible surfaces of the buildings. Here, decorated turquoise-blue domes float above many-

tiered façades of equally strong colours. This brilliant façade architecture continued during the 18th and 19th centuries under the Zand and Qājār dynasties.

Chronology

'Abbāsid period 749–932

Būyid period 932–1062

Ghaznavid period 977–1186

Seljuq period 1038–1194

Khwārazm Shāh period c. 1077–1231

Mongol (Il-Khanid) period 1256–1353

Muzaffarid period 1314–93

Tīmūrid period 1370–1506

Turkmen period 1380–1468

Safavid period 1501–1732

Zand period 1750–94

Qājār period 1779–1924

ARDABIL, Shrine of Shaykh Safī
Tīmūrid and Safavid periods, 15th–17th centuries

The tomb of the founder of the Safavid dynasty was held in great veneration by his descendants. The nucleus of the complex is a slender cylindrical tomb tower with a fine tile-mosaic inscription; the walls are covered with glazed brick, forming the name of Allah in square kūfī script. A number of other

Although generally assigned to the Seljuqs, this mosque has had a number of constructional phases, possibly even going back to a Sasanian fire-temple below the chamber in front of the mihrāb. The dome-chamber and the principal īwān, however, date from the Seljuq period, the prayer hall itself from the late 11th century, while the mihrāb is dated 1158 and the principal īwān 1160. The vault of the īwān is overlaid with a fine stucco mesh of half-palmettes, a unique feature, while the delicately carved stucco *mihrāb* is equal to the finest 12th-century *mihrābs* in other Seljuq mosques, although it may have been restored by the Mongols. The decoration of the dome-chamber is very fine with particularly well balanced trilobe squinches dating from exactly the same period as those in the Friday Mosque at Isfahan.

DAMGHAN, Tārik Khāna Mosque
'Abbāsid period, 8th century

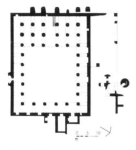

This majestic building, the oldest mosque in Iran, relies on total simplicity for its effect. The almost square courtyard is surrounded by arcades, which deepen to three bays on the *qibla* side; the central aisle is broader and higher than the others. The massive cylindrical brick piers support rows of slightly ovoid arches, which in some cases are slightly pointed, reminiscent of the parabolic curves of Sasanian arches. This powerfully simple mosque, therefore, seems to represent a synthesis of original Iranian techniques with an Arab-inspired plan. Alongside the present circular minaret, which was built in the 11th century, are remains of a square minaret, probably dating from the original construction.

GUNBAD-I QĀBŪS, Tomb Tower
Ghaznavid period, 1007

This is one of the first buildings in Iran that can be associated with the advent of the Central Asian Turks; vibrantly monumental, it presages the great Seljuq buildings of the late 11th century. The tomb was built by order of Qābūs ibn Vashmgīr, a local Caspian ruler, and is a cylindrical tower with a perfect conical roof. Over 51m high, the tower stands on an artificial mound 11m high. The exterior is ornamented with ten

angled buttresses, which merge with the angled base course and the corbelled rim supporting the roof. The only ornamentation on the plain brick surface is two bands of inscription in simple *kūfī*, and the two small *muqarnas* pendentives supporting the half-dome above the entrance. There is no trace of any tomb, which lends credence to the legend that the body of Qābūs was suspended from the roof in a glass coffin.

ISFAHAN, Friday Mosque (Great Mosque)
'Abbāsid to Safavid periods, 8th–17th centuries

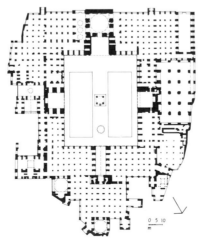

Recent excavations have uncovered vestiges of the earliest mosque on this site, dating back to the 8th century, and there are also considerable remains of the 10th-century Būyid mosque. Most of these were enclosed by the later Seljuq rebuilding, but enough has been revealed to provide plans and details of the original mosque, which was rectangular with colonnades on four sides. The Seljuq mosque of the 11th and 12th centuries consisted of a courtyard surrounded by arcades with a covered santuary. There was one domed chamber in front of the *mihrāb* and another set into the arcades facing it across the courtyard. Both were fronted by deep *īwāns*, and two additional *īwāns* were also set into the side arcades. At this stage, the mosque still retained a compact form which slowly became increasingly complicated as succeeding rulers added to it. One of the side arcades was converted into a prayer hall with a superb *mihrāb* during the Mongol period; a fine *madrasa* was added by the Muzaffarids; and the Tīmūrids incorporated a great winter prayer hall and a fine portal. During the Safavid period the *īwāns* were covered with complicated *muqarnas* vaulting and faced with glazed tilework, and crowning minarets were added to the principal *īwān*. The mosque is thus almost a textbook of Iranian architectural styles. But it is for the fine examples of Seljuq brick patterns, especially in the vaulting systems, and the two great domed chambers, that the mosque is renowned.

ISFAHAN, Royal Mosque (Masjid-i Shāh)
Safavid period, 1612–37

Built by Shāh 'Abbās as the climax of his reconstruction of Isfahan, this mosque has a number of important architectural innovations. The entrance portal to the mosque is at the centre of the south side of the great square (*maydān*), but the mosque itself is turned at an angle, to face Mecca. So successfully did the architects design this change of axis, which occurs within the entrance complex, that it is almost imperceptible; nor is the general aspect from the square unbalanced. The entrance portal is largely covered with tile-mosaic, following the earlier tradition, while the interior is covered with glazed tiles on which the often complicated patterns have been painted with

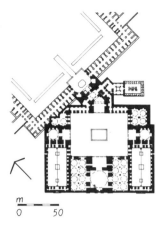

```
m
0      50
```

different coloured glazes. This technique, which is much swifter to apply than tile-mosaic, was much favoured at the time by Shāh 'Abbās. The four-*iwān* mosque form is here brought to a peak of perfection with the *iwāns* and the great dome being reflected in the central pool. The dome-chamber is flanked by two courtyards containing a *madrasa*.

ISFAHAN, Mosque of Shaykh Lutfallāh
Safavid period, 1617

```
0      5 10
m
```

This was the earliest construction to be built around the square, which formed the nucleus of the new urban complex of Shāh 'Abbās. An ingenious corridor entrance enabled the mosque to be oriented so that it would conform to the correct direction of prayer while allowing the outer façade to align itself with the square. The tile-mosaic of the façade

is largely restored but the interior of this single-chambered mosque is entirely covered with its original mosaic. The sunlight filters through a series of double grilles in the drum of the dome, resting on squinches rising directly from the floor. Each of the eight-pointed arches supporting the dome is outlined by a turquoise twisted moulding framing a number of inlays, either inscriptions or flower patterns, enlivened with dark- and light-blue, wine colour and clear lemon-yellow. The interior of the shallow dome is patterned with lozenges which decrease in size as they ascend to the centre.

ISFAHAN, 'Alī Qapu Palace
Safavid period, early 17th century

```
0 5 10
```

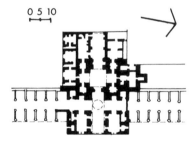

The Iranian concept of a palace had little to do with its European equivalent, where all the various functions were gathered together under one roof. The Safavid concept was modelled on the Classical idea of a park or garden within which a number of different pavilions fulfilled different purposes, sometimes regulated by the seasons rather than by occasions. The 'Alī Qapu was built by Shāh 'Abbās onto an earlier Tīmūrid building and is the entrance to the palace area of Isfahan, overlooking the central square. As the palace gate, it also functions as the major reception area, for the internal privacy of the actual palace buildings would have always been preserved. The high loggia balcony provided a place from which the court would watch proceedings in the square below, while the public rooms and upper music rooms were used for the reception of ambassadors. The symbolic entrance to the royal quarters, the palace had a sacrosanct character; even the shāh dismounted to cross the threshold.

ISFAHAN, Chihil Sutūn
Safavid period, mid-17th century

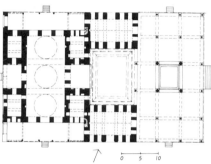

```
0    5   10
```

This is one of the garden pavilions that formed the palace complex. Recent research on the wall-paintings would suggest that the palace was built by Shāh 'Abbās II (1642–66) towards the end of his reign. Like the 'Alī Qapu palace, the Chihil Sutūn has a great portico, the roof of which is supported on twenty high wooden columns. These are doubled by their reflection in the great pool opposite, hence the name Chihil Sutūn, 'forty columns'. The four columns in the centre, surrounding a small basin, rest on carved bases depicting lions, while the alcove at the rear of the portico is decorated with the remains of the mirror-mosaics that, originally, entirely covered the walls. Within the main reception rooms are a series of large historical wall-paintings.

ISFAHAN, Khwajū Bridge
Safavid period, mid-17th century

A number of Iranian bridges have interesting histories, many of them dating back to Sasanian times with subsequent restoration under the Seljuqs or Tīmūrids. The Khwajū bridge, built by Shāh 'Abbās II, is a culmination of this tradition. Not only is this bridge a means of crossing the Zayandeh River, it is also a place to tarry and enjoy the site. Since the river is not navigable, the bridge acts as a weir, the downstream level being much lower, with the water pouring over a series of steps. On the lower level of the bridge the view may be enjoyed in deep shade; above is a roadway lined with arcaded niches that have pavilion rooms looking outwards.

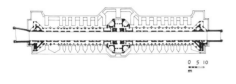

KERMAN, Friday Mosque
Muzaffarid period, 1349 and later additions

This mosque is the oldest surviving building of the Muzaffarids. The plan is of the simple four-*iwān* type with side arcades. There is no chamber in front of the *mihrāb*, but the principal *iwān* is emphasized by being raised above the arcades. There are two important new developments: the high, raised portal and the superb tile-mosaic, which covers the exterior of the portal and the inner courtyard. This mosaic appears astonishingly accomplished, both in technique and in design. The *mihrāb* dates from a 16th-century rebuilding, but the remainder of the *qibla* wall panels are from the original foundation.

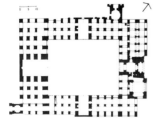

KHARGIRD, Madrasa
Tīmūrid period, 1445

This *madrasa* belongs to the high point of Tīmūrid architecture, and even in its ruined condition compares with the finest contemporary structures. The *madrasa* is of the basic four-*iwān* type, but has a domed chamber at each corner, and is preceded by three domed chambers forming an entrance complex. The vaulting in this entrance area is particularly interesting and shows a considerable development from the previous century. Most of the tile-mosaic has been destroyed, but enough remains to show its excellence. The façade is ornamented with glazed brick panels as well as areas of tile-mosaic, and is flanked with round bastions on polygonal bases, similar to those on the façade of the Gāzur Gāh shrine at Herat. Two other features resemble work in Herat: the vaulting of one of the entrance complex domes, and the five-sided bays that project from the back wall.

KIRAT, Minaret
Seljuq period, 11th century

This isolated minaret is a fine example of the Khurasanian architectural tradition. It has a high octagonal base, which originally supported a balcony entered from the cylindrical shaft. The shaft, which now has a distinct lean towards the north, is unornamented, but the octagonal base has a number of pattern bands that link it to earlier minarets in the area. The balcony was supported on corbelled brick columns with *muqarnas* vaulting, strengthened by wooden beams. A number of the patterns made use of a stucco infill, a technique common during the Seljuq period, but of which only a few traces remain. Despite its present isolation, the existence of a balcony indicates that the call to prayer was given from the minaret; its situation on the crest of a hill, however, indicates that it was also used as a lighthouse

and signal-tower, both to guide caravans travelling at night and to warn of coming dangers.

MASHHAD, Mosque of Gawhar Shād
Tīmūrid period, 1419

During the Tīmūrid period the art of tile-mosaic reached its apogee, and the decoration of this mosque represents the finest remaining example of this technique in Iran. Built on the four-*iwān* plan, the inner walls of the courtyard glow with panels of the richest colours, the whole linked to form a unity of composition by two inscription bands in white on deep-blue, one of which encircles the courtyard, while the other frames the *iwān*. This latter inscription is itself framed by the two minarets that flank the *iwān* and stretch down to the ground. This is the first example of this form in Iran – minarets formerly rose from above the parapets. The idea appears to have originated in India

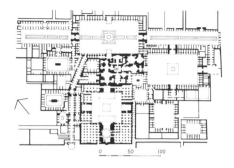

whence it was taken by Tīmūr himself and incorporated in the unfinished mosque of Bībī Khānum at Samarqand (completed 1406).

NAYIN, Friday Mosque
Būyid period, 10th century

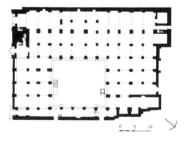

This mosque is still in use and contains the oldest extant minaret in Iran. Its plan, which is that of the simple courtyard hypostyle mosque, has been added to and has undergone considerable alteration. Originally, the minaret on its solid square base abutted the façade, but it was subsequently enclosed by an addition. The almost totally unorna-

mented octagonal shaft represents a transition stage from the square minarets of the western Islamic world to the later 11th- and 12th-century minarets of Iran, creating a new concept in minaret construction. The chief glory of this Friday Mosque, however, is the richness of the carved stucco decoration which adorns the *mihrāb* and surrounding bays. The variety of stucco patterns links earlier Sasanian and 'Abbāsid stucco decoration to that of the Seljuqs, although the use of stucco to conceal rather than to reveal architectural structure relates more to the earlier periods.

RIBĀT-I SHARAF, Caravanserai
Seljuq period, 1114, restored 1154

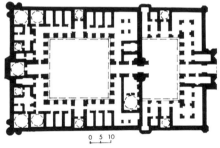

This palatial monument lies in north-eastern Iran on the road to Bukhara and Samarqand, where it constitutes a royal caravanserai. Restored after being sacked by the Oghuz Turks, it is one of the few royal secular constructions remaining from the 12th century. Set in a desolate landscape, it is a rectangular fortress, the interior being divided into two unequal four-*īwān* courtyards. The decoration is opulent, using brick, stucco and terracotta in an imaginative series of combinations. In addition to the usual expected accommodation, the caravanserai has two palatial suites separated by a domed chamber, recalling the throne rooms of earlier palaces, and also two mosques. A huge cistern set below ground in front of the main entrance guaranteed a supply of water throughout the year. The portal, with its external *mihrāb*, enabled travellers arriving after the gates were closed to know the direction for prayer.

SAVEH, Minaret of the Friday Mosque
Seljuq period, 1110

For elegance of composition and quality of decoration this is the finest remaining Seljuq minaret in Iran. It bears a number of pattern bands as well as inscriptions in *kūfī* and *naskhī* script, one of which gives the date. The lower section of the minaret has been restored, the upper section, including the balcony supports, has now disappeared. The decoration of the remaining shaft is organized into three main zones, divided by inscriptions that are separated by a series of delicate guard bands in carved and moulded terracotta. The elements of the inscription bands are interspersed with a number of stucco plugs, many of which are carved with the name of Allah.

SHIRAZ, Vakīl Mosque
Zand period, mid-18th century

This mosque was built during the reign of Karīm Khān Zand (1750–79). Situated alongside the bazaar of the same period, the two-*īwān* mosque has a number of tile-mosaic panels, which still retain many of the designs and colour schemes of the previous Safavid period, but with the introduction of colours (pink especially) that were to become paramount in the succeeding Qājār period. The prayer room rests on five rows of twisted stone columns with acanthus capitals – an unusual feature, which distinguishes this mosque.

SOLTANIYEH, Tomb of Öljeytu
Mongol period, early 14th century

All that is left of the remarkable city founded by Öljeytu (1294–1307) is his mausoleum, its egg-shaped dome still dominating the village that squats uneasily amid its ruins. After founding his new city, Öljeytu wished to have a worthwhile purpose for its existence and decided to remove the body of 'Alī, the Prophet's son-in-law, from its tomb in Iraq and install it as a centre of pilgrimage in Soltaniyeh. The mausoleum was, therefore, originally designed as a great shrine and decorated accordingly; but Öljeytu was induced to reconsider his decision and eventually it became his own tomb, whereupon the interior was less richly endowed. Encircled by eight minarets, the dome of this tomb was once covered with turquoise-blue tile-mosaic and must have proclaimed the power of the Mongol Empire far across the flat landscape. It stands over 50m high and is built of light, pinkish-coloured brick ornamented with panels of turquoise- and lapis-blue. An arcaded gallery beneath the dome has a ceiling richly decorated with coloured stucco and carved terracotta, while the interior is painted white with blue designs.

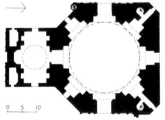

TABRIZ, Blue Mosque
Turkmen period, 1465

Unfortunately, this superb mosque is now in a very ruined state, though indications of its original rich decoration remain. Built as an entirely roofed structure, the central court is domed instead of open. The interior and exterior façades were decorated with some of the finest tile mosaic in Iran, the various panels harmoniously combining the most subtle colours with vivid cobalt-blue, often

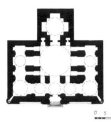

overlaid with gold. Inscriptions border the panels, each letter being raised against the blue background on which a raised flowering arabesque uncurls. The chamber in front of the *mihrāb* had a dado of dark alabaster panels, while its dome was of a rich dark-blue, stencilled with gold patterns. The main doorway with side alcoves retains much of its decoration, giving an idea of the original sumptuous ornamentation.

VARAMIN, Tomb Tower of 'Alā' ad-Dīn
Mongol period, 1289

This tomb tower displays perhaps the finest combination of glazed tilework and massive brickwork prior to the introduction of all-over mosaic tiles. The tomb is a high cylindrical tower with a conical roof; the exterior is created by thirty-two right-angled flanges, while the interior is circular. The flanges rise to the rim of the roof where they meet a band of triangles – similar to those that replaced squinches in Anatolia. The inscription is set in bands on both faces of the flanges. As in all conical roofed towers, there

is an interior dome. Unusually, the tower has two entrances, one cut directly into the south face, the other leading through an extension from the north-west corner.

VARAMIN, Friday Mosque
Mongol period, 1332–6

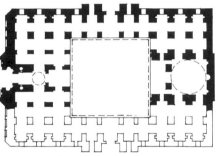

Like the Friday Mosque at Zavareh, this beautifully proportioned mosque was built as a balanced four-*īwān* composition during a single building construction. Unlike any other Iranian mosques, both the portal and entrance are comparatively low so that the whole of the building becomes dominated by the great dome over the chamber before the *mihrāb*. The interior of this chamber shows a development from earlier centuries in that there is a distinct feeling of verticality. The main thrusts of the dome are concentrated at particular points so that the side walls may be pierced with openings giving an increased sense of lightness, anticipating developments in the 15th and 16th centuries. The decoration of the *mihrāb* includes large overblown flowers, typical of the last phases of stucco decoration. Both the entrance portal and *qibla īwān* have semi-domes which were built of *muqarnas* vaulting ornamented with a restrained use of blue glazed bricks highlighting the elements of decoration.

YAZD, Friday Mosque
Muzaffarid period, 1375 and later

The history of this building is complicated because of considerable rebuilding and reconstruction. The *mihrāb* itself is the earliest-dated part of the building and is from the original foundation, as is the dome-chamber. The plan of the mosque is that of a

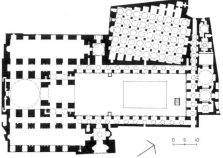

single *īwān* fronting a dome-chamber flanked by oratories thereby creating a triple-*īwān* formula as in Sasanian palaces. The arcaded courtyard has three portals, one of which was rebuilt in the 15th century, when it was

covered with fine tile-mosaic and crowned with a pair of high minarets. Unlike earlier mosques, which tend to be dimly lit and solemn, this mosque has an unexpected lightness and openness owing to the treatment of the side oratories – these are brilliantly white, and are lit by high windows, contrasting dramatically with the rich polychrome decoration of the dome-chamber.

ZAVAREH, Friday Mosque
Seljuq period, 1135–6

This is the earliest preserved Iranian example of a mosque originally built according to the four-*īwān* plan. A simple *kūfī* inscription in brick and stucco in the courtyard gives the date. The minaret is now reduced to a stump but has brick patterns and the remains of bands incorporating ceramic tiles in both dark- and light-blue, the earliest-dated instance of this combination in exterior decoration. The *mihrāb* chamber has considerable elegance with a fine stucco *mihrāb*, but it is the exterior of the dome which perhaps epitomizes the majestic simplicity of the great Seljuq domes. Situated in a small

oasis on the western edge of the central desert, the town is dominated by the silhouette of the dome, which exudes strength and unclouded serenity, resting squarely on its base supported by the firm line of the exteriorized squinches.

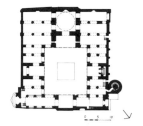

Central Asia and Afghanistan

YOLANDE CROWE

IF AFGHANISTAN AND SOVIET CENTRAL ASIA are grouped together, a geographical and artistic unit emerges alongside the political entity which makes up the early Muslim east, the Mashriq – including Khurasan, Sistan and Transoxiana. As in Syria and India, indigenous building traditions of earlier pre-Islamic principalities continued to evolve within the context of the new religion, which replaced Buddhism and Zoarastrianism; Christian communities survived longer, Jewish ones still exist in this region. To this day mud-brick buildings, wood columns and cross beams, and plaster-decorated walls can still be seen in the making, especially in Afghanistan. Already in the 7th century, at Penjikent, south of Samarqand, squinch arches supporting small domes were skilfully constructed from unbaked bricks. Wall-paintings and stucco carvings in official buildings at this site indicate a vigorous if syncretic tradition readily available for further transformations under Islamic patronage.

In the early centuries of Islam the use of baked brick, a possible Mesopotamian echo,

was limited in official buildings – mosques and fortresses – to a structural function. Soon, however, the brick walls of tombs, mosques and caravanserais were provided with baked-brick patterns, either flush or more often in staggered layers of patterning. By the 12th century, intricate carved terracotta with added turquoise (copper oxide) glazing was used for epigraphy and expand-

ing geometric grids, which completely covered exterior walls. Together with round minarets, domed religious monuments quickly developed, becoming larger and higher as technical advances were made in the handling of baked brick in regular sizes – from the tomb of the Sāmānids at Bukhara to the mausolea of Sanjar at Merv and Ishrat Khane at Samarquand. As soon as glazed tiles were produced on an industrial scale, walls acquired an elaborate revetment of intricate tile-mosaics, with the use of moulded and painted tiles, seen at their best and most varied in the Shāh-i Zinda at Samarqand. If the Kashan potters of Iran originated refined lustre-painted tiles and ceramic *mihrābs* in the 13th and 14th centuries, it is in Central Asia and Afghanistan that the most complete and original repertory of glazed material was created in the 14th and 15th centuries. Later creativity in glazed tilework was taken over by Safavid and Ottoman production.

Among the various types of plans developed for Islamic buildings, it has long been recognized that the four-*iwān madrasa* originated in local 'mansion' houses and Buddhist monasteries of the pre-Islamic era; as can be seen in the excavations of Adzhina Tepe in Tajikistan. As an institution separate from the mosque, the *madrasa* was an innovation of Central Asia, as was the concept of the soaring portal, the *pishtaq*. Placed in front of an *iwān* entrance to a mausoleum, mosque or *madrasa*, the *pishtaq* emphatically stressed the importance of the building and its benefactor.

As in more western parts of the Islamic world, impressive caravanserais as well as public baths and bazaar complexes still bear witness to the way in which local rulers and merchants also sponsored and endowed secular buildings. The main towns of Transoxiana and Afghanistan were the sorting houses of Central and Western Asia as well as of India. To this day, the best example of an Islamic city set within its walls can be seen in Khiva. Although few traces of Tīmūrid gardens survive except in Kabul, it is to them that the Mughal gardens owe their later existence.

As soon as the centralized power of the 'Abbāsids began to wane in the 10th century, the local Sāmānids took over part of Afghanistan and Central Asia. The following Turkic dynasties – Ghaznavids, Ghūrids, Tīmūrids and, for a short time, Mughals – re-established political control over the area, which had once been united under the Graeco-Bactrian, Kushan and Hephtalite rulers. Although the dominions of the Qarakhanids and the Shaybānids remained north and west of the Oxus river, their buildings, as did those of other dynasties, related closely together and formed a distinct architectural unity.

Chronology

'Abbāsid period before 819

Sāmānid period 819–1005

Ghaznavid period 977–1186

Ghūrid period 1000–1215

Tīmūrid period 1370–1506

Mughal period 1526–1666

Khwārazm-Shāh period 915–1231

Seljuq period 1038–1194

Qarakhanid period 992–1211

Shaybānid period 1500–98

Soviet Central Asia
ANAU, Complex of Jamāl-ad-Dīn
Tīmūrid period, 1452–6

This unique religious complex consists of a commemorative mosque, a *madrasa*, a *khānaqāh* and lodgings for pilgrims; it stands inside the walls of the fortress, and was sponsored by the dissolute Tīmūrid ruler Abu'l-Qasīm Bābur for the holy man Jamāl-ad-Dīn. A high *pishtaq*, about 19m, at one time with two decorative minarets above, hides the double dome of the mosque. The striking spandrels above the entrance arch are filled with the animated arabesque of two huge white dragons on a dark-blue ground. The gradual introduction of deep niches, here in two tiers on either side of the *pishtaq*, to act as a transition towards the wings, forecasts more elaborate examples in the Mughal architecture of India. The two, ruined double-storeyed wings lie on either side of the mosque at right angles. It has recently been almost totally destroyed by an earthquake.

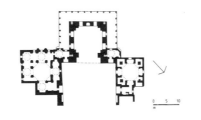

BAKU Complex of Shīrvān-Shāhs
Shīrvān-Shāh period, 15th century

The importance of Baku, on the western shores of the Caspian, grew throughout the Middle Ages until the Shīrvan-Shāhs (Khalīl Allāh and Farrukh Yasār) established their residence on a rocky outcrop overlooking the lower part of the town. The main buildings consist of a reception hall of unusual shape, a mosque with a dated minaret (1441–2) and the mausoleum of the Shīrvan-Shāh rulers

(1425–6), all in fine ashlar with intricate carvings; by contrast, the tomb of Sa'īd Yahyā Bakuvi is faced in plain stone. In spirit, the architecture remains closer to that of eastern Anatolia than to that of the main Iranian plateau, in the same way as the 12th–13th-century tomb towers of Azerbaydzhan.

BUKHARA, Tomb of the Sāmānids
Sāmānid period, 10th century

Orthodox Islamic burial usually follows a very simple ritual from which practices in Central Asia deviated soon after the coming of Islam, when earlier traditions reasserted themselves. The monumental tomb of the first local Muslim dynasty is one of the

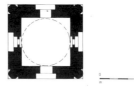

earliest in Islamic architecture (one tombstone belongs to as-Saʿīd Nasr II, 914–43). Besides its structural function for walls and a spacious dome, the use of standardized baked brick for overall decoration instead of stucco is a significant innovation. Corner columns buttress the slightly tapering cube. Inside, the transition from the square to the dome, more than 7m in diameter, is achieved by a corner arch – a new solution. The presence of an internal gallery running around the drum of the dome, is expressed on the outer elevation by a series of arcades that finalizes the 'basket weave' brick patterning of the walls, and conceals the lower part of the dome. Brick beading frames the entrances on four sides, the spandrels being filled with a dog-tooth pattern of diagonally set end bricks.

BUKHARA, Kalyān Mosque
Shaybānid period, completed 1514

After defeating the last of the Tīmūrids, the Uzbek Shaybānids, in turn, indulged in self-glorification and sponsored a number of good if not unduly remarkable religious constructions and public markets. Under ʿAbdallāh I (1512–39), the congregational mosque of Kalyān was given its final outline. Its splendid brick minaret, 46m high and dated 1127, survives an earlier 12th-century mosque. The plan follows the traditional layout of a four-īwān mosque with a raised pishtaq to emphasize the qibla and a high dome over the mihrāb hall. Another lesser pishtaq indicates the entrance. A system of stone pillars and some 288 small domes makes up the rest of the monument with arcades surrounding the courtyard. The building is said to be large enough to hold 120,000 worshippers. The glazed tile decoration is in no way spectacular. A planned grouping of public buildings in association with the mosque was consciously implemented and the Mir Arab Madrasa was built opposite in the 1530s, also according to a four-īwān plan with one hundred cells.

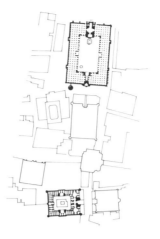

BUKHARA, Madrasa of ʿAbdal-Azīz Khan
Uzbek, 1645–80

This is one of the later madrasas at Bukhara, when it again became a capital. Built opposite to the madrasa of Ulugh Beg, it is remarkable for its large size, elongated pishtaq and refined decoration. On either side of the entrance, two halls, the summer mosque and an assembly room, recall the Ulugh Beg madrasa layout, as does the double gallery of rooms around the courtyard. The four-īwān plan and diagonal bridging of the courtyard corners improve the balance of the large open space. Various techniques make up a freer attitude to decorative treatment: tile-mosaics, with the use of more yellow, cover the pishtaq and gallery façade. In the summer mosque and assembly hall, walls and elaborate vaultings evolved from the 15th-century faceted grid are covered with blue, white and russet wall-paintings, emphasizing fan and star shapes, as well as muqarnas decoration with touches of gold. Garden pavilions and kiosks sparsely decorate some panels. The relief plasterwork inside the entrance pishtaq also shows a very high standard of craftsmanship.

BUKHARA, The Namāzgāh
Various periods, 12th–17th centuries

Not unlike the musallā of the Arab world and usually sited outside town, a namāzgāh, or open-air place of prayer, can accommodate large crowds of worshippers on important feast days. A simple border indicates the limits of the dedicated area. The surviving namāzgāh of Bukhara consisted at first of a baked brick qibla wall, over 38m long and divided into three by the central mihrāb and two side blind arches. The space just in front of it could have been roofed, as suggested by similar buildings in Nissa and Merv. The fine geometric brick and terracotta patterns are 13th century. Glazed tiles were inserted in the 15th century and finally, in the 17th century, a new façade with a cental pishtaq (15.3 m high in front of a dome) was added as well as a brick minbar with canopy, placed in the open on the south side. The whole monument stands on a stone plinth south of the old town walls.

DAYAKHATYN, Caravanserai
Seljuq Period, 11th century

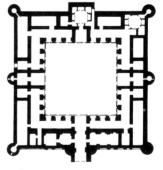

During the increasing prosperity under Ghaznavid and Seljuq rule, an important network of caravanserais was built across Afghanistan and Central Asia to link the area with India, Kiev and the Mediterranean. This square caravanserai is one of a series, including the Ribāt-i Sharaf and Rībāt-i Malik in Khurasan, and stands halfway between Bukhara and Khiva on the Amu

Darya (Oxus) River. The fortified walls of baked brick enclose a single square court-yard with four *iwāns* linked by arcades; behind are large rooms and storage areas, including two domed halls with central skylights. Brick pendentives appear beneath the decaying plaster decoration and both domes are set within the thickness of the roof. Brick decoration emphasizes both the entrance portal and the walls on either side; blind arches alternate with panels filled with angular *kūfī* composed of diagonally set bricks. All other outer walls are finished in plain brick coursings with an upper band of terracotta motifs and single brick design in relief.

MERV, Tomb of Mu'izz-ad-Dīn Sanjar
Seljuq period, early 12th century

Once second only to Baghdad, Merv flourished under the Seljuqs and in particular under Sanjar (1118–57), who sponsored a number of projects including a huge irrigation dam on the Murghab River. He was buried in this tomb, which is 36m high and was built by Muhammad ibn Aziz from Sarakhs. Unlike other massive-looking tombs in that town, which stood on their own, with its prominent entrance *iwān*, Sanjar's mausoleum (very much revered and often redecorated) was linked by a grille window to a mosque on its west side, now vanished. The large, square, brick mass is lightened by the high, arched gallery above it (a variation of the one in the tomb of the Sāmānids at Bukhara) and the drum rises behind it, emphasized by two rows of blind arcades. Its original turquoise outer dome could be seen a day's journey away but has now disappeared. Surprisingly, the terracotta patterns in the intrados of the gallery, and the brick decoration of the panels, have lost much of the vigour of earlier similar work, although inside the dome the central eight-pointed star strikes a bolder note.

SAMARQAND, Bībī Kānum Mosque
Tīmūrid period, begun 1399

'If it were not for the sky and the Milky Way, its dome and entrance arch would be unique,' wrote al-Yazdi, in the 15th century, about this mosque. With an inner court measuring 87m × 63m, the Bībī Khānum

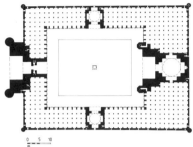

Mosque was even greater in its time than the Quwwat al-Islām Mosque, *c.* 1191, at Delhi, which had just been conquered by Tīmūr. This grandiose construction in Samarqand remained unfinished after Tīmūr's death. The hastily built fabric with brick decoration, *banā'ī*, and tile-mosaic decoration, shaken by earthquakes, soon began to deteriorate and it was no longer in use by the 17th century. The four L-shaped halls are now being restored, including 480 stone columns and domes. The *pishtaq* of the mosque, on the opposite side to the entrance portal, soars to the height of 41m, completely hiding the great dome. When seen on their own, the two domed lateral chambers appear huge, but they do not dwarf the mosque because of the subtle modular proportioning used throughout the building.

SAMARQAND, Madrasa of Ulugh Beg, Market-Place
Tīmūrid period, 1417–20

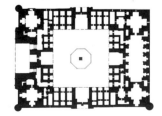

According to the Spanish Ambassador, Clavijo, Tīmūr ordered the cutting of a new bazaar street from the 'Iron' Gate (north), passing the Bībī Khānum Mosque and caravanserai, leading to the registan, the sandy market-place. From an earlier group of mosques, *khānaqāhs*, and caravanserais conceived by Ulugh Beg, only his *madrasa* survives. Across the registan (70 m × 60 m) now stands its 17th-century counterpart, the Shīr Dār (Lion Bearer) Madrasa, and between them, the Tīlā Kārī (Gold Decorated) Madrasa, in part the congregational mosque. Ulugh Beg's earlier *madrasa* at Bukhara (1417) is smaller and lacks the four-*iwān* plan, the four, corner, domed halls and the impressive *pishtaq*, as in the Samarqand *madrasa* planned by an architect from Shiraz. With room for over one hundred students and a learned body of teachers lodged in cells on two levels round the courtyard, the *madrasa* became the centre for theology and science for a time. Some of the best *banā'ī* technique has been applied to the monument, and in particular to the side panels of the entrance *iwān*. Large hexagonal-shaped inlays of carved marble are added to the tile-mosaics of the expanding star grid in the spandrels of the *pishtaq*. The corner minarets are now purely ornamental.

SAMARQAND, Shāh-i Zinda Complex
Tīmūrid period, 14th–15th centuries

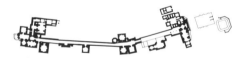

Kusan ibn 'Abbās, cousin of the Prophet, brought Islam to Smarqand in 676 and is said to have been buried at the top of the Shāh-i Zinda (Living King) complex. Opposite it, recent archaeological work has brought to light a possibly 11th-century *madrasa*, one of the earliest buildings at this site. Only the shrine itself must have escaped Chingiz Khan's destruction of the city in 1220, and it was handsomely restored between 1334 and 1360. A narrow alley, some 70m long, leads up to it across what used to be the pre-Mongol city walls at the level of the 'new' southern gate. On both sides, funeral buildings were erected between 1360 and 1434, after which Ulugh Beg added a monumental entrance to the whole complex. Varied domes, some still shining with turquoise tiles, crown surprisingly small constructions. The decoration in the whole complex is the most elaborate for the period, not withstanding Tīmūr's palace at Shahr-i Sabz built by an architect from Khwarazm. Tile-mosaic with added gold leaf, glazed, carved terracotta, *cuerda seca*, painted tiles, woodcarvings, wall-paintings, coloured glass and stucco decoration exemplify the best production of the time.

SAMARQAND, 'Ishrat Khāne
Tīmūrid period, 1464

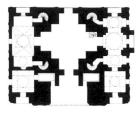

The wife of the Tīmūrid ruler Abū Sa'īd endowed the 'Ishrat Khāne by *waqf* to ensure maintenance of the building as a burial place for the women of the family. The ruined tripartite mausoleum, behind its high *pishtaq*, exemplifies the original evolution of Tīmūrid architecture: massive foundations against earthquakes, a marble paved central hall and a crowning dome on a system of transverse arches. The area between two perpendicular arches and their pillars was filled with a network of elongated and broadened lozenges, similar to the fractured plane of inner facets of a polyhedron contained within the hall. Such a vaulting system was also used on both sides of the hall, in the mosque and in the *miankhane*. The general effect is that of greater space without undue soaring heights. Coloured glass filled the windows, and painted stucco in subtle relief, *kundal*, permitted precise vegetal and epigraphic compositions in frames, cartouches and medallions.

SAMARQAND, Gūr Emīr Complex, Tomb of Tīmūr
Tīmūrid period, 15th century

This complex originally consisted of a *madrasa*, a *khānaqāh* and further halls on three sides of a square court marked by four

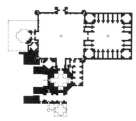

corner minarets. When Muhammad Sultan, the grandson and heir of Tīmūr, died of wounds after the battle of Ankara in 1402, Tīmūr ordered the building of an octagonal mausoleum on the site of the halls, and its further alteration in 1404 in the spirit of the Bībī Kānum Mosque at Samarqand. A gigantic *kūfī* inscription runs around the drum of the double dome, melon-shaped and brilliantly tiled, some 34 m high. The monumental portal at the entrance of the courtyard was commissioned by Ulugh Beg and was signed by Muhammad ibn Mahūd al-Isfahānī in 1434. The square cenotaph room, with its soaring cupola, painted pendentives, gold leaf decoration, and onyx dado, befits, by contrast, Tīmūr's dark-green nephrite cenotaph and the surrounding seven marble ones, all of which are inside a delicately carved marble railing. In the crypt below, plain marble inscribed slabs cover the real tombs.

SAMARQAND, Observatory of Ulugh Beg
Tīmūrid period, 15th century

After Tīmūr's death in 1405, the centre of culture and politics moved to Herat. By the middle of the 15th century, however, Ulugh Beg had made Samarqand the meeting place of learned men, and men of science. This ruler is best remembered for his work in astronomy. In order to carry out his research,

Ulugh Beg built an observatory on a rocky hill – for solid foundations – north of the Tīmūrid town. The observatory was circular, enclosing a hexagonal construction; at the centre, a deep trench, with steps marked in degrees, contained the gigantic curve of a sextant by which the movements of the sun, the moon, planets and stars could be studied and recorded. Around the sextant, large halls, corridors and special rooms were arranged on three floors to keep instruments and lodge the staff. Paintings representing spheres, optical instruments, the known world and celestial bodies covered the walls. Like the tiled garden pavilions and palaces of the Tīmūrid period, only the writings of historians now recall these splendours.

URGENCH, Tughtabeg Khatun Tomb
Sufi period, *c.* 1370

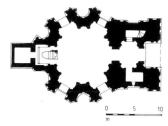

The memory of the short-lived dynasty of Sufi still survives in the most original family shrine. Built less than fifty years after the nearby tomb of Najm-ad-Dīn Kubra, this unique tomb has an ambitious plan which transforms the traditional massive shape into an elegant ensemble with lighter buttressing. Although a high *pishtaq* was already a common feature in Khurasan, here the added vestibule opens the way to the main part of the shrine. Seen from outside, the overall width of the vestibule is the same as one of the eight facets of the shrine itself. Because of this extra space, the main dome stands independently, with its high drum framed by terracotta panels. Most of the turquoise dome has gone. The triumphant tile-mosaic inside the dome (about 9 m in diameter) surpasses any geometric expanding decoration previously created in that medium, including work in Yazd. Moulded terracotta patterns, glazed in shades of turquoise, fill the arched panels inside the drum.

Afghanistan
BALKH, No Gunbad (Nine Dome) Mosque
'Abbāsid period, late 9th century.

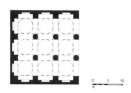

The square is related to local architecture such as the Chahār Sutūn at Termez with its pairs of axial pillars. A system of pointed arches connects these pillars to double columns engaged on three sides; the fourth side, opposite the *qibla* wall, is open. The structural elements are of baked brick, loosely bonded, entirely covered in carved stucco in bold decorative compositions. This technique derives from the Buddhist tradition of Central Asia and, in the new Islamic style, coincides with a more geometric vocabulary emanating from Iraq, the centre of power. Expanding leaf scrolls, with roundels in high relief, fill the spandrels of the arches; intrados decoration is based on circular, quatrefoil, square or star grid systems with enclosed palmettes, leaves, cones and buds in spacious compositions, more pleasing than those in the mosque at Nayin.

BALKH, Mosque of Abū Nasr Parsā
Tīmūrid period, after 1460

The funerary mosque in front of the tomb of the Sūfī saint Abū Nasr Parsā belongs to a series starting in the 12th century; 15th-century examples exist in Khurasan, such as at Tayabad (1444), but differ slightly following local traditions. In this mosque at Balkh, there are three entrances into the square chamber within the octagonal exterior. Were it intact, the *pishtaq* and its minarets would completely hide the ribbed and tiled double dome. The height of the inner dome is almost half of the total height (about 29 m) and it is supported by a system

of arches and interval pendentives. The light colour scheme of the decoration, rusty-red motifs and emphatic blue curves, and the added light through the windows, increase the feeling of space. Deep arched niches, no longer blind ones, on two levels, animate every second facet of the outer octagonal wall. The tile-mosaics of their spandrels, as well as the twisted torus of the *pishtaq*, combine with great felicity arabesques and Chinese-looking blossoms.

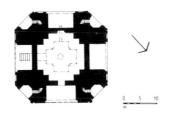

GHAZNI, Minaret of Bahrām Shāh
Ghaznavid period, early 12th century

Although at an altitude of over 2000 m, Ghazni was at the crossroads on the way to India and was the capital of the Ghaznavids; for a time it was the centre of Islamic art and culture in the East. Bahrām Shāh (1118–52) sponsored the building of the second of two noble minarets, as the monumental inscription at the top of the shaft indicates, as well as the mosque that went with it, now vanished. Terracotta ornaments in panels of expanding grids and eight-pointed stars make up most of the dignified decoration; the obtuse angle enclosed between two consecutive points of the star-shaped shaft gives each panel the aspect of a wide-open book. Earlier minarets of the same type have been found in the Iranian province of Kerman; this type of shaft would

have been the first stage for a further cylindrical shaft comparable to that of the Jar Kurgan minaret near Termez dated 1108.

HERAT, Gāzur Gāh
Tīmūrid period, 1425

The Sūfī saint 'Abdallāh Ansārī died in 1089, and his memory was perpetuated in this shrine outside Herat. Redesigned by the master builder Qivām ad-Dīn of Shiraz for Gawar Shād, during the building of her *madrasa* in Herat, it was subsequently added to and restored at least three times. Its plan is unique: it combines a meeting place for learned theologians with a special burial place. The 30m-high *pishtaq*, with its two lanterns facing west, towers over the tomb, in front of it and the many handsome tombstones of the 15th century in the courtyard. Although the layout appears to be that of a four-*īwān madrasa*, the cells are located only in the western half on opposite sides. There are two areas with transverse ribs and vaulting on each side of the entrance hall: a mosque and an assembly hall. Great

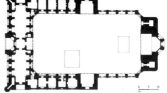

schemes of tile-mosaic, *banā'ī*, wall-paintings and stucco-work combine to create a sense of pleasing harmony, not unduly flamboyant. Gāzur Gāh has sometimes been called a *hazīra*, an enclosed burial ground uncovered by a domed structure. Later outbuildings are scattered in the walled garden.

HERAT, Madrasa of Gawad Shād
Tīmūrid period, completed 1437

This four-*īwān madrasa* was built by the same architect as Gāzur Gāh. Only one of the entrance minarets, covered in tile decoration, and the three-shell domed mausoleum, over 20m high in the western corner, still stand. The mausoleum was completed by 1432. Baysonqur, the gifted son of Gawad Shād, was the first of a group of male members of the Shāh Rukh family to be buried there. Such a burial place in a *madrasa* for important tombs had become the rule by this time, replacing the usual corner teaching hall. The dome with its sixteen-sided drum rises 9.5m above the cenotaphs and illustrates the early handling of transverse arches, spreading the load and leading it down to the four corner pillars. More or less expanding fan-shaped pendentives, and fillings with occasional groups of *muqarnas* vaults, are all painted blue and rusty-red on a white ground, creating an impression of a light textile canopy.

JAM, Minaret
Ghūrid period, 12th century

Completely preserved to its full height, about 65m, this minaret stands on its own by the Hari Rud River on the central Afghan east-west road. It was probably associated with the Great Mosque at Firuz Koh, the new capital of the Ghūrids. The octagonal base, with splendid calligraphy, is buried to a depth of about 4 m in rubble and earth. A double spiral staircase built around a brick and mortar core leads to the first balcony. The circular shallow shaft above is reinforced inside by four separate vertical brick ribs that act as anchors for the square brick platforms and steep steps between them. A lantern crowns the summit, above two further balconies with ruined wooden corbels. The remarkable proportions and decoration of the minaret make it an outstanding example of 12th-century brick architecture. Unfolding bands of calligraphy up and down the circular shaft (Sūra xix of the Qur'ān) enclose geometric patterns in eight successive areas. An impressive glazed inscription gives the name of the founder, Ghiyāth ad-Dīn Muhammad (1163–1203).

LASHKARI BĀZĀR, Southern Castle
Ghaznavid and Ghūrid periods, 12th and 13th centuries

The huge ruined settlement spreads for 7 km along the Helmand River north of Bust and includes the southern castle, or winter palace of the sultan, a warmer residence than his fine palace at Ghazni. Rectangular in shape, with outer walls buttressed by massive towers, it was built round a central courtyard with two levels of blind arcading and four *īwāns*. The north *īwān* is higher than the others and leads into the audience hall. After a fire at the time of the Ghūrid take-over in 1150, the west side of the palace was enlarged and rooms were added to the northeast side, though the audience hall was made smaller. Painted fragments from the dado in the audience hall were recovered – as many as forty-four figures, now headless, stand as a symbolic bodyguard in a frontal position, wearing caftans in shades of red and blue. The walls above retain traces of a geometric brick grid filled with stucco motifs. Splendid mud-brick elliptical vaultings still bridge lofty passages, and keyhole-shaped windows open up tall thick walls.

Indian subcontinent

GARRY MARTIN

Islam, born in the deserts of Arabia in the 7th century, spread through Iran, Central Asia and Afghanistan to the subcontinent, arriving in northern India in the 12th century. The architecture that had evolved in those countries was based on brickwork (both mud and fired) with glazed tile decoration; these Islamic building-types had already been well established in their countries of origin when invading Muslim armies entered India. A mature theory of structural mechanics was introduced, utilizing the pointed arch, the vault, the squinch and the true dome together with decorative themes based on calligraphy, the arabesque and geometric patterns.

India at the end of the 12th century was a wealthy civilization with a complex structured society determined by the religions of Hinduism and Jainism. Structurally, Hindu architecture was based on the post-and-beam system, mainly in stone, the manipulation and plastic treatment of which had been mastered by Indian craftsmen for over a thousand years. Monumental temples were covered in a sculptured array of gods and goddesses and were constructed in conformity with sacred texts, which laid down the essential components of buildings and their geometric and symbolic relationships. It was from the interaction of these two building traditions, the Hindu and Islamic, and their expressions in building, that the genius of Indo-Islamic architecture emerged.

The stylistic development of Islamic architecture in India is traditionally divided into that of the Delhi sultanates, the independent regional developments, and the great achievements of the Mughals. From 1206, northern India was dominated by a series of independent sultanates centred on Delhi, comprising a number of successive dynasties ('Slave', Khaljī, Tughluq, Sayyid and Lōdī), whose consolidation of power was expressed through large-scale building projects ranging from mosques and tombs to palaces and forts. Building styles evolved through many experimental stages blending Islamic architectural forms and building-types with indigenous Hindu architectural and craft traditions.

At the same time, significant regional developments occurred in architecture as outlying provinces seceded from the central authority at Delhi. Projects were conceived that relied heavily on indigenous traditions, such as the architecture of Gujarat, Bengal and Kashmir; on the influence of Delhi sultanate styles, as evidenced by the mosques of Jaunpur; or on influences derived directly from Iran and Central Asia, such as the buildings in the Punjab and the Deccan (Bijapur).

In 1526, Bābur, a descendant of both Chingiz Khan and Tīmūr, defeated the last Lōdī emperor at the battle of Panipat and ushered in the Mughal (Persian for 'Mongol') domination of northern India for the next 250 years. Mughal architecture begins with Humāyūn's tomb, in Delhi, which is essentially an Indian stone version of an Iranian tiled mausoleum, and the first major example in India of an ornamental tomb garden. The great mosques and tombs that followed experimented with the formal relationships of building elements – particularly the *īwān*, courtyard, domes and minarets. Fortresses and palaces were also built, echoing the caravanserais and tent cities of the Mughals' nomadic ancestors.

At the end of the 16th century, Akbar conceived the new royal city of Fatehpur Sikri, outside Agra, where free reign was given to the skills of Hindu craftsmen. The red sandstone architecture of this period gave way in the early 17th century, during the reign of Jihāngīr, to the white marble architecture of Shāh Jihān, whose master-piece, the Tāj Mahal, is the ultimate expression of Mughal architecture.

The brilliance of Indo-Islamic architecture lies in the successful blending of Iranian and Hindu building traditions. The dispersal of indigenous craft guilds by Aurangzēb in the early 18th century and the subsequent disintegration of the Mughal Empire, separated architecture from its traditional sources of inspiration and patronage. Later buildings, such as the 18th- and 19th-century Oudh architecture of Lucknow, were hybrid creations parallel in period and consequence to the revival styles that dominated European architecture at this time.

Chronology

DELHI SULTANATES

'Slave' period 1206–90

Khaljī period 1290–1320

Tughluq period 1320–98

Sayyid period 1414–51

Lōdī period 1451–1526

REGIONAL SULTANATES

Bengal 1336–1576

Kashmir 1346–1589

Deccan 1347–1527

Gujarat 1391–1583

Jaunpur 1394–1479

Malwar 1401–1531

Bijapur 1490–1686

Sūrī period 1540–55

Mughal period 1526–1858

India
AGRA, Jihāngīrī Mahal
Mughal period, c. 1570

Akbar built a series of red sandstone palaces within the walls of the Red Fort at Agra of which the Jihāngīrī Mahal is the only surviving example. The building is a curious fusion of Hindu and Islamic design and detailing. An enclosed central courtyard is surrounded by symmetrically arranged

265

rooms, similar to such Hindu palaces as the Man Mandir at Gwalior, built in the 15th century. This symmetry is interrupted on the east side by another courtyard arranged in the Iranian manner of three inward-facing *īwāns*. The front elevation and the three-*īwān* courtyard are Islamic in feeling with arches, arcades and niches of red sandstone with white marble inlay. On the other hand, the enclosed central courtyard is entirely Hindu in treatment with heavily carved brackets in the form of serpentine volutes and steps, eaves and massive rectangular piers overlaid with a lace-like veil of carved geometric and floriated designs.

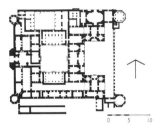

AGRA, Tomb of I'timād ad-Dawla
Mughal period, 1628

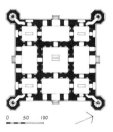

Jihāngīr's queen, Nūr Mahal Begum, erected this tomb for her father, a high court official, on the banks of the Jumna River. The design, modelled on that of a dwelling house, denotes the transition from the red sandstone architecture of Akbar to the white marble constructions of Shāh Jihān. A square chamber with attached octagonal towers is surmounted by a pavilion with finely carved lattice-work screens surrounding it. The whole marble surface of the building is covered with an elaborate inlay (*pietra dura*) of semiprecious stones – geometric designs alternate with floral traceries in lapis, onyx, jasper, topaz and cornelian. This technique, used earlier in the temples of Rajasthan, was evolved to a state of perfection in this Indian interpretation of an Iranian tiled tomb. Four red sandstone gateways enclosing a square garden provide a splendid foil for the white marble tomb at its centre.

AGRA, Tāj Mahal
Mughal period, 1632–54

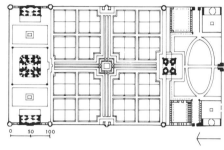

When Shāh Jihān's favourite wife, Mumtāz Mahal, died, the bereaved emperor assembled designers and craftsmen from all over India, Iran and Central Asia to construct a tomb that was to prove the ultimate achievement of Mughal architecture. The Tāj Mahal harmoniously combines the great building traditions of Central Asia, Iran and India, all of which placed great emphasis on the geometrical relationships contained within a building. The plan further develops the theme of Humāyūn's tomb by an arrangement of a central chamber with four corner chambers and corridors concentrating their axes on the single central focal point: the cenotaph. This focus is given vertical expression by an inner dome and an outer dome set on a high drum behind the raised central *īwāns*. The tomb is raised on a podium and framed and balanced by four detached minarets. Arch spandrals, inscriptions and cenotaphs are all inlaid with semiprecious stones in decorative themes superbly executed and integrated with the overall design. A 'tomb mosque' and identical reception hall, gateways and pavilions and walkways are all constructed in red sandstone to provide a monumental setting of contrasting themes for the white marble tomb. A long garden leading up to the tomb platform is subdivided by canals, reflecting pools, paths and *parterres*, originally full of flowers and once lined with cyprus trees and flowering fruit-trees. Here, immortality and regeneration are alternately emphasized.

AHMADABAD, Friday Mosque
Gujarat sultanate, 1423

Gujarat had a rich heritage of Hindu and Jain architecture, which is clearly illustrated in the Islamic buildings of Ahmadabad where many traditional Hindu features were incorporated directly into the design of mosques and tombs. The sanctuary of this mosque, erected by Ahmad I, combines a screen of arches linked by a pillared portico of post-and-beam construction. Exquisitely carved minarets (the tops now missing) flank a large central arch, which frames two tall columns joined by a cusped arch – a feature taken directly from the entrance gateways of temple complexes. Behind the arched façade, closely set columns support mezzanine galleries, whose changes of level are emphasized internally by a diffused light admitted by carved stone screens of the clerestory, and articulated outside by alternating large domes with clusters of smaller ones. The plain masonry of the external walls is beautifully integrated with the profusely carved features of the minarets, columns and string-courses.

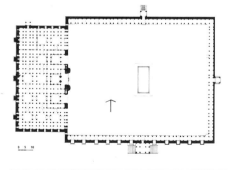

BIJAPUR, Ibrāhīm Rauza
Bijapur sultanate, 1615

The 'Ādil Shāhī rulers of Turkish and Iranian origin, evolved a separate and distinctive style of architecture centred around their capital at Bijapur. The tomb and mosque complex of Ibrāhīm II is set within an enclosed garden and employs many features distinctive of this style. Arches springing from low imposts are articulated by domed finials, which rise above a heavily decorated parapet. A wide eave encompasses each building, supported on closely set ornate

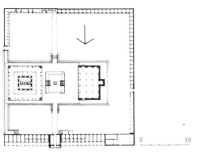

brackets. The central domes are three-quarter spheres set within the folds of large lotus-petal mouldings, as are the smaller domes which cap the slender minarets rising from the corners of the building. Extensive use is made of carved plasterwork in the execution of calligraphic inscriptions, geometric designs and medallions of local innovation.

BIJAPUR, Tomb of Muhammad ʿĀdil Shāh
Bijapur sultanate, 1626–56

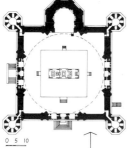

Popularly known as the Gul Gunbad (Round Dome) this tomb has a single dome, which spans the largest floor area of any building in the world. The tomb is a gigantic cube with octagonal turrets attached to the corners and surmounted by a huge hemispherical dome. This is supported by an ingenious system of intersecting arches, transferring the shape of the square chamber to the circular drum from which the dome springs. These arches also support a circular platform slightly projecting over the chamber, masking the springing of the dome, which gives the impression of the dome hovering high above the observer. The decoration was never finished, owing to the death of the builder, but the elevations display in moulded plaster two characteristic decorative features of Bijapur architecture: a foliated apex to the arch and a circular medallion supported by a voluted bracket.

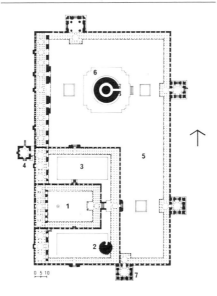

Qutb Minar Enclosure: (1) Original mosque 1197, (2) Qutb Minar 1199, (3) Extension to mosque 1229, (4) Tomb of Iltumish 1235, (5) Later extension 1296, (6) Unfinished minār 1316, (7) ʿAlāʾī Darwāza 1305.

DELHI, Quwwat al-Islām (Might of Islam) Mosque
'Slave' period, c. 1197

Built by Qutb ad-Dīn Aybak, this first great mosque in India was constructed inside a captured Hindu citadel on the platform of a demolished temple site. A central courtyard was surrounded by arcades of reused columns and slabs salvaged from the destruction of twenty-seven Hindu and Jain temples. In 1199, a tall free-standing arched screen was constructed across the face of the west arcade to lend emphasis to the *qibla* direction. Although structurally unrelated to the earlier arcades, its arches and decoration expressed building forms familiar to the Muslims. Hindu masons, however, unfamiliar with these new Islamic architectural forms constructed them in their own tradi-

tional techniques by corbelling the arches, providing them with an ogee profile, and constructing the arcade domes as shallow corbelled vaults. The entire screen façade was superbly carved by Hindu craftsmen in low-relief bands of *naskhī* inscriptions, spiral floral designs and lotus patterns.

DELHI, Qutb Minār
'Slave' period, 1199

This enormous minaret, 72.5m high, was erected by Qutb ad-Dīn Aybak as a tower of victory, a symbol of the supremacy of the new religion of Islam, which was eventually to conquer almost the whole of Hindu India. The minaret adjacent to the Quwwat al-Islām Mosque originally had four storeys, tapering from 15m diameter at the base to 3m at the top, crowned by a pillared kiosk. The two upper rounded storeys were erected by Fīrūz Shāh Tughluq, in 1368, after lightning had struck the minaret. The three lower fluted storeys were constructed of red sandstone, each level exhibiting different combinations of circular and stellar shapes in plan. Each storey is separated by a balcony on corbelled bracketing carved in intricate patterns of recessed arches. The shafts of the minaret exhibit alternating bands of Arabic inscriptions and stylized geometric and floral patterns.

DELHI, Tomb of Iltutmish
'Slave' period, c. 1235

In 1229, Shams ad-Dīn Iltutmish doubled the size of the Quwwat al-Islām Mosque by

adding new arched screens and arcades arranged co-axially with the original mosque. His own tomb, a square, domed chamber with a subterranean crypt, was added adjacent to the north-west corner of the mosque. Traditional Hindu methods of construction are demonstrated by the corbelled form of the squinch vaulting and arch profiles. The roof, now fallen, was a shallow dome formed by concentric rings of corbelled masonry. The inside walls covered in carved low-relief patterns are reminiscent of Persian rugs and hangings – intricate patterns in two dimensions. Bands of inscriptions in *kūfī* and *naskhī* scripts are interwoven with stylized lotus and vine patterns and bands of geometric ornament. All are carved in red sandstone relieved by white marble inserts in the *qibla* wall.

DELHI, ʿAlāʾī Darwāza (Gateway)
Khaljī period, 1305

ʿAlāʾ ad-Dīn Khaljī planned further to enlarge the Quwwat al-Islām Mosque in 1296. His death in 1316 terminated the project and only foundation courses and the unfinished

rubble core of the first storey of a gigantic minaret remain. The south gateway of the complex was completed, however, and indicates how the whole scheme was to be executed. The use here of the true arch and dome with voussoirs and squinches demonstrates a familiarity with building techniques not previously seen in India. The façades of the gateway are divided into rectangular panels within which are set horseshoe-shaped arches and carved screens framed by alternating bands of inscriptions and floral and geometric designs, executed in red sandstone and white marble. The richness, colour and texture of the elevations again exhibit the two-dimensional qualities of Persian carpets. The methods of walling and the horseshoe-shaped arches with spearhead fringes are features that were to determine the stylistic development of Delhi sultanate architecture.

DELHI, Tomb of Ghiyāth ad-Dīn Tughluq
Tughluq period, 1325

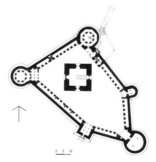

Ghiyāth ad-Dīn Tughluq constructed the massive fortifications of the fourth city of Delhi, Tughluqabad. His own tomb was set in an artificial lake as a fortified outwork of the main city, connected to it by an arched bridge. The tomb enclosure is an irregular pentagon with projecting bastions. The battering of these bastions is reflected in the sloping walls (75°) of the square red sandstone tomb. The central bays of the elevations are raised on three sides, and a four-centred arch with spearhead fringe frames an entrance doorway. Each doorway displays a curious combination of arcuate and trabeate traditions, an arch reinforced at its springing by a bracketed lintel. A single dome of white

marble is crowned by a ribbed finial comprised of a fruit and water pot motif, traditional Hindu elements associated with fertility and good fortune. The sloping walls, arch and lintel doorways, and finials were to become typical stylistic features of later Indo-Islamic architecture.

DELHI, Tomb of Khān-i Jihān Tilangānī
Tughluq period, 1368–9

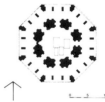

This small tomb, built for the prime minister of Firuz, Shāh Tughluq, within its own fortified enclosure, is the first example of an octagonal mausoleum in India. The octagonal central chamber is surrounded by an arcaded verandah, each façade of which has three four-centred arches shaded by a wide eaves-stone (*chajja*). The central arch in each face is articulated by a small cupola set above and behind the running merlon on the parapet. A single dome rises over the central chamber surmounted by a ribbed fruit and water pot finial. Unlike the stone architecture of earlier tombs, the main construction has a rubble core with plaster covering and bands of inscriptions and medallions worked in stucco. This combination of octagonal plan, arcaded verandahs, eave-stones and cupolas was used as a model for future tomb designs.

DELHI, Begampūr Mosque
Tughluq period, c. 1370

Built during the reign of Fīrūz Shāh Tughluq this mosque is raised on a high plinth with three entrance gateways approached by flights of steps. The plan illustrates a version of the Iranian four-*īwān* mosque; a large rectangular courtyard is surrounded by arcades, at the centre of each side is a projecting raised *iwān* framing the gateways and entrance to the prayer hall. The arched arcades are reflected in the arched openings of the external walls and the pointed domes, which rise in serried ranks above the arcades. A notable feature, repeated in future mosque architecture, is the tall arched pylon framing the triple entrance to the prayer hall with two attached octagonal tapering turrets. The raised pylon completely masks the raised pointed dome over the main chamber introducing a problem of the co-ordination of arched *iwān* and dome that was to be approached in many ingenious ways by Indian builders.

DELHI, Khirkī Mosque
Tughluq period, *c.* 1375

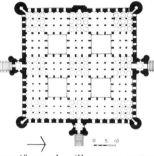

This cruciform plan illustrates an inventive synthesis of the open, courtyard style and the totally covered mosque. The mosque is raised on a substructure of arches with three projecting entrances, each of which displays and arch-and-beam combination first seen at Ghiyāth ad-Dīn Tughluq's tomb. Tapering turrets frame the entrances, which echo the circular, sloping bastions set at each corner of the mosque giving the whole structure a fortress-like appearance. Inside, the surrounding arcades are joined by two arcaded aisles intersecting to form four open light-wells. Each corner and intersection is marked by clusters of nine small domes whose stuccoed surfaces were once brilliantly coloured. The construction is of coarse rubble masonry covered by layers of stucco, the standard method of building in this period.

DELHI, Chotte Khān Kā Gunbad Tomb
Sayyid and Lōdī periods, 15th century

During the Sayyid and Lōdī periods many tombs were built to a standard pattern, of

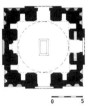

which this unascribed but locally named tomb is an example. The building is square in plan with three entrances constructed in the arch-and-beam manner emphasized by being framed by raised rectangular panels. The side bays are divided into two storeys with arched recesses and are surmounted by pillared domed kiosks (*chatrīs*) set alongside the drum of the main dome. The exterior is executed in coarse masonry and was originally covered in stucco. Inside the tomb, squinch arches and recessed wall arches support a sixteen-sided triforium drum and domed ceiling. The extrados of the arches, framing panels, borders and drum have bands of inscriptions carved in stucco while the dome has a carved and painted design representing an eight-pointed star with circular medallions.

DELHI, Moth-ki Masjid
Lōdī period, 1505

This beautifully proportioned and modelled prayer hall displays cantilevered balconies and open-arched two-storeyed towers at its corners, tending away from the fortress-like quality of earlier mosques. Five diminishing

recessed arches open into the main prayer hall; the central arch is framed by a projecting pylon, here contained within the line of the parapet. This enables the three raised domes to dominate the composition and to articulate the three projecting *mihrāb* bays in the west wall. Tapering turrets are here used to frame the central *mihrāb* bay in the west wall instead of the central entrance arch to the prayer hall, as at the Begampūr Mosque. *Muqarnas* pendentives support the side domes while squinch arches are used in the central domed chamber. Red sandstone, white marble, glazed tiles and finely cut plaster medallions provide the decorative scheme.

DELHI, Humāyūn's Tomb
Mughal period, 1565

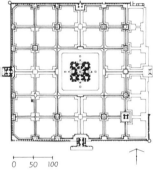

After Humāyūn's death in 1556, his wife, Hājjī Begum, assembled designers and craftsmen, both Iranian and Indian, who created a tomb that was to prove a turning point in the construction of mausolea in India, and was a clear synthesis of Iranian and Indian building traditions. Four, cubic, outer chambers are linked geometrically to a central chamber but are independent – visually and spatially – a fusion of the Hindu idea of an enclosed sanctuary and an Iranian sequence of rooms. An inner dome covers the central chamber placed midway between the floor and the top of the marble cased outer dome – the first major use of this Central Asian type of construction in India. The elevations are well balanced compositions of arcades, *iwāns*, arches, pinnacles and kiosks, all visually integrated by the large white marble dome. The masterly construction in red and yellow sandstone with white marble inlay is an Indian version in stone of an Iranian tomb with decorated glazed tiles. An important innovation is the setting of the tomb in an ornamental square garden based on the Persian *chār bāgh* principle.

DELHI, Red Fort
Mughal period, 1638

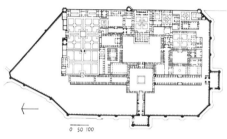

Shāh Jihān transferred his capital from Agra to Delhi in 1638 and constructed the new fortress-capital of Shāhjahānābād. The Red Fort to the east of the city, was laid out in a series of squares surrounded by massive, red sandstone, fortified walls and gateways. Progression into the centre of the fort was through bazaars, a music pavilion gatehouse and a large garden, at the back of which was set the Public Audience Hall (Dīwān-i-'Amm), a single-storey pavilion of red sandstone with cusped arches. On either side were gardens flanked by white marble constructions overlooking the Jumna River. These open single-storey ̦pavilions were built as inter-connecting courts linked and cooled by channels of water flowing through them under delicately carved dividing screens into shallow marble basins such as the lotus-shaped pool of the Rang Mahal. Cusped arches, curved cornices, bulbous domes and highly decorated flat ceilings, in gilt overlaid with sinuous serpentine patterns and naturalistic flower designs, were features of this architecture.

DELHI, Friday Mosque (Jāmi' Masjid)
Mughal period, 1644–58

This was the royal mosque for the new Shahjahanabad and is one of the largest

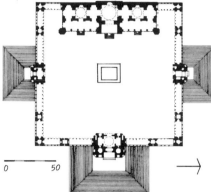

courtyard style mosques in India. It is raised on a high plinth with its surrounding arcades open at the sides linked by gateways and kiosks. The prayer hall advances into the main courtyard and is independent from the surrounding arcades. Its front elevation is framed between two four-stage minarets. Three bulbous white marble domes with red sandstone stripes are raised on their drums and set well back from the raised central *īwān* to avoid any imbalance caused by the close proximity of *īwān* and dome, as seen in Iranian and earlier mosques in India. The decoration is simple with alternating areas of red sandstone and white marble used to emphasize the domes and minarets. Inside, simple niche and arabesque patterns in white marble are set in the red sandstone walls.

DELHI, Pearl Mosque
Mughal period, 1662

This small mosque of polished white marble was built as a chapel for the private worship of the emperor, Aurangzēb. Constructed

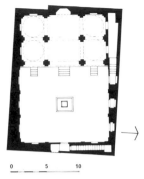

within the Red Fort, whose axes faced the cardinal points, the outer walls of the mosque were aligned to these axes while the inner walls skewed to face Mecca. In contrast to the serenity of the Pearl Mosque at Agra, this mosque is characterized by the predominance of a sinuous contour illustrated by the curved Bengali cornice and the bulbous domes crowned by exaggerated lotus mouldings and finials. All surfaces are decorated with sinuous lines whose decorative themes tend to blur the distinctions between the separate building forms and elements. This tendency was to characterize later Mughal architecture and was also a feature of contemporary Rococo architecture in Europe.

DELHI, Tomb of Safdār Jang
Mughal period, 1753

This last great Mughal tomb was erected in Delhi for the second nawāb of Oudh. A long avenue, and two centuries, separate it from Humāyūn's tomb, the first Mughal building in India. The tomb is raised on a platform and set in an ornamental garden, but its proportions and the arrangement of its formal elements highlight the disintegration that was occurring in Mughal architecture as well as in the whole empire. The monumental character of Mughal tombs depended on a subtle balance of forms. Here, the vertical proportions are emphasized; the form of the elevation is derived from the entrance gateway to the Tāj Mahal while the details are an eclectic amalgamation. It was a last attempt at a building in the traditional grand manner before the complete degeneration of architectural traditions, which took place in the 18th and 19th centuries.

FATEHPUR SIKRI, Palace
Mughal period, 1569–74

One of the most remarkable monuments in India is this great ceremonial capital built by Akbar at Sikri, the hermitage retreat of his spiritual guide, Shaykh Salīm Chishtī. The Town of Victory (Fatehpur) has no streets as such, the palace consisting of a series of interlocking courtyards set to the cardinal points. No symmetrical axes or monumental approaches are used; instead, asymmetry seems to have been deliberately incorporated into the setting-out and design of colonnades, pavilions and other buildings scattered around the complex. All the buildings – the palaces, the treasuries, the harem, the guest houses, the bath houses, the guards' quarters – are in characteristic rich red sandstone, using traditional Hindu trabeate construction and detailing but with a lightness and simplicity that suggests Islamic pavilions or tents rather than the traditional massiveness of Hindu architecture. Hanging awnings and rugs added shade and colour and, too, warmth to the otherwise open buildings. A unique structure is the so-called Dīwān-i Khāss, where Akbar is said to have assembled exponents of all religions for the eventual formulation of his own eclectic beliefs. A single square high chamber contains a central monolithic column, thickly clustered with ornate projecting brackets supporting a circular platform approached by four narrow bridges.

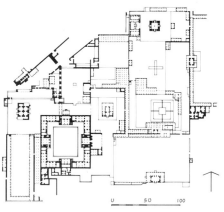

FATEHPUR SIKRI, Friday Mosque
Mughal period, 1571

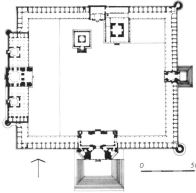

In contrast to the Hindu construction of the rest of Fatehpur Sikri, this royal mosque uses the traditional Islamic forms of central courtyard, arched arcades and domes. The prayer hall has three separate enclosed sanctuaries, each surmounted by a dome and linked by arcades; a tall central īwān masks the raised dome behind. The surrounding arcades are lightened by rows of pillared kiosks set against the skyline on top of the parapets. In 1596, one of the entrance gateways was replaced by Akbar with a victory gate, the Bulāwand Darwāza. This superb composition of a large īwān, chamfered sides, arched recesses, pinnacles and kiosks is constructed in red and yellow sandstone with white marble inlay outlining the span of the arches. Such monumental architecture clearly demonstrates the assured control and skill of the designers. In the courtyard of the mosque stands the tomb of Shaykh Salīm Chishtī, reconstructed in white marble some years later by Shāh Jihān, exhibiting superbly carved, pierced marble screens and serpentine brackets.

GAUR, Tantipara (Weavers') Mosque
Bengal sultanate, 1480

The influence of the humid, monsoon climate of Bengal is reflected in the later types of brick mosques, designed as covered rectangular halls with octagonal turrets at the corners – without an arcaded courtyard. Built by Mirsād Khān, this mosque is divided into two aisles by squat piers, looted from a demolished Hindu temple, with corbelled brick pendentives which originally supported ten domes. The five lancet arches of the front elevation are crowned by a heavy moulded cornice, the curved origin of which lies in the traditional Bengali bamboo-framed thatched roofs whose exaggerated downwards curve quickly shed the monsoon rains. Curved string-courses divide the elevation into rectangular panels housing niches of cusped arches surrounded by flowing floral patterns of vine tendrils, lotuses and hanging pendant designs, all executed in terracotta. The mihrābs in the qibla wall echo the carvings of the external niches.

GULBARGA, Friday Mosque
Deccan sultanate, 1367

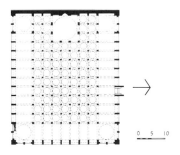

In the Deccan, independent sultantates evolved an architecture which sprang directly from Iran and the influences of Delhi sultanate architecture, wholly independent of local Hindu building traditions. The Iranian architect of this mosque evolved a scheme composed entirely of domes and arches, almost devoid of ornament, which is unique in all of India. The conventional design of the open courtyard is here abandoned in favour of an entirely covered area – a forest of columns supporting small domes. The surrounding cloisters are spanned by a

271

single wide arch springing from a very low impost (contrasting with the more slender span of the courtyard arches), and are roofed by barrel vaults similar to the form of the arches. Lighting and ventilation were achieved by opening the sides of the cloisters and raising the main dome over a square clerestory section.

HYDERABAD, Chār Minār (Four Minarets) Gateway
Deccan sultanate, 1591

One of the finest examples of a style of architecture that developed under the Qutb Shāhī dynasty, this triumphal archway was built by Muhammad Qulī at the junction of four roads leading to the four quarters of the old city. Four, tall, well proportioned minarets are engaged at the corners of the archway, hence the name. As is typical of this style, the lower elevations containing the archways and shafts of the minarets are relatively simple and unadorned. Above the cornice run heavily ornamented arched trioforiums and bracketed eaves in successive layers. The minarets are clustered with arcaded balconies and capped by small domes rising out of foliated petal mouldings – a feature, also, of the buildings of Bijapur.

JAUNPUR, Atala Mosque
Jaunpur sultanate, 1408

Constructed by Shams ad-Dīn Ibrāhīm on the site of the Hindu temple, Atala Devi, and on foundations prepared by Fīrūz Shāh Tughluq, this mosque demonstrates a unique architectural development that evolved during the Sharqī period. The west sanctuary is preceded by a massive arched pylon 23m high, whose sloping sides recall an Egyptian propylon. This pylon is repeated in smaller form on either side and again echoed in the three entrance gateways to the courtyard. Arched openings, which pierce the central screen, both allow light into the domed hall at the level of the supporting squinches and link the screen visually to the dome, otherwise hidden behind the massive pylon.

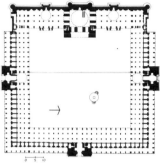

The shape of the central arch, with its spearhead fringe, the sloping sides of the pylon and the rear *mihrāb* projections, with their sloping buttresses and turrets, demonstrate the influence of Tughluq architecture from Delhi.

MANDU, Jahāz Mahal
Malwar sultanate, c. 1460

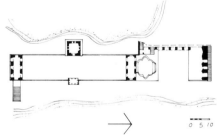

During the 15th century, the capital of Malwar was transferred from Dhar to Mandu, built on a vast plateau surrounded by massive fortifications. Mosques, tombs and palaces, constructed largely of stone, were erected by workmen imported from Delhi, trained in the traditions of building current during the Tughluq period. Typical of the many pleasure palaces erected at Mandu is the Jahāz Mahal (Ship Palace), so called because it is long and narrow and set between two beautiful lakes. It is assigned to the reign of Muhammad Khaljī. Pillared

kiosks on the roof take advantage of the views and cooling breezes. The great variety in roof shapes, the brightly painted plaster, and brilliantly glazed tiles of yellow and blue around the bases of the domes enhance this picturesque palace, set in a landscape of great beauty.

SASARAM, Tomb of Shīr Shāh Sūr
Sūrī period, c. 1540

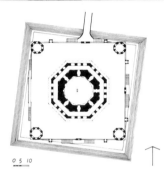

The octagonal tomb, which began with that of Khān-i-Jihān Tilangānī at Delhi and underwent development during the Lōdī period, achieved its most perfect expression during the brief reign of the Afghan, Shīr Shāh Sūr, who constructed his own tomb in the middle of an enormous artificial lake. A square platform rises from, and is set at an angle to, a stepped platform that leads to the lake. The octagonal tomb is surrounded by an arcaded verandah above which rise two levels of hexagonal pillared kiosks opening onto a central dome surmounted by an enormous lotus and water pot finial. The superb blending of dome, kiosks and arcades demonstrates the complete assurance the designers had achieved with the octagonal form. Grey chunar sandstone, painted merlons, glazed tiles on the cupolas and in the arch spandrels, a white main dome and gold-painted finial combined to create a magnificent spectacle rising out of the waters of the lake.

SIKANDRA, Akbar's Tomb
Mughal period, 1604–13

This tomb takes the form of a tiered pyramid, perhaps inspired by earlier Buddhist monasteries. The grave is placed in a crypt directly above which are three ornamental sarcophagi, the uppermost being a marble cenotaph set on a platform open to the sky,

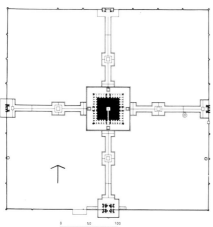

surrounded by perforated marble screens. The upper storeys are built of pillared kiosks, linked by eaves in the Hindu manner. They seem to indicate a change of conception after the construction of the ground storey, which has arched arcades and prominent central *iwāns*. There is speculation as to whether the open tomb platform was intended to be surmounted by a dome or pavilion. The tomb is set in a *chār bāgh* garden whose south entrance gateway exhibits superbly executed inlaid decoration with both floral and geometric patterns in coloured marbles and stones. Rising above the parapet of the gateway are four beautifully proportioned minarets, making their first appearance in Indian architecture in a fully developed form.

SRINAGAR, Friday Mosque
Kashmir sultanate, 1398

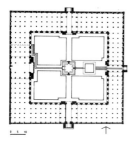

The mountains of Kashmir, with their abundant forests, led to the evolution of a distinctive wooden architecture, which was continued by the first Muslims who settled there in the 14th century. This mosque, erected by Sikandar But-Shikan, was originally constructed of horizontal courses of timber, dovetailed at the ends, but was three times destroyed by fire; its present construction dates only from 1674, but its timber and brickwork faithfully follow the original form. The interior cloisters are crowded with tall columns of deodar pine, supporting timber ceilings. The square plan of the cloisters is interrupted by four cubic halls surmounted by pyramidal roofs from which rise steeples and finials in carved timberwork, reminiscent of the pagoda and *stūpa* forms of Buddhist architecture that once flourished in these regions but are now only found in neighbouring Nepal.

Pakistan
LAHORE, Jihāngīr's Tomb
Mughal period, 1627

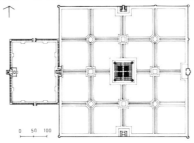

Located just outside Lahore, at Shadera, this tomb is set in an ornamental garden; there are paved causeways, canals and reflecting pools, with four entrance gateways of red sandstone. The long, low, arcaded structure has four octagonal minarets engaged at the corners, their shafts patterned with chevrons and crowned by domed kiosks. The central octagonal chamber is separated from the outer surrounding arcades by walls 19m thick. Over this central chamber, on the roof, is a square platform that once supported a marble pavilion, now destroyed. Decorative themes are worked in fresco, marble inlay and mosaic tiles, forming geometric patterns and panel designs of flower vases, whose origins are distinctly Iranian. The marble cenotaph is one of the finest in India with inlaid semiprecious stones set in naturalistic floral designs and calligraphy inscribing the Ninety-Nine Names of God.

LAHORE, Wazīr Khān Mosque
Mughal period, 1634

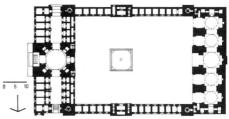

A separate and distinct style of Mughal architecture evolved in the Punjab, influenced by Safavid Iran. Buildings were constructed in baked brickwork and used glazed tiles for decoration. Unlike Safavid buildings, which were totally covered in glazed tiles, the decoration of this mosque is subordinated to the architectural elements. Octagonal minarets, walls, kiosks and gateways are divided into rectangular panels framed by bands of plain brickwork. These panels are filled with mosaic tilework forming floral and geometric patterns in vivid greens, oranges, blues and browns. Inside, the walls and ceilings are entirely covered in sinuous patterns and floral designs, painted in tempera in rich shades of magenta, dark-green and ochre.

LAHORE, Shalimar Gardens
Mughal period, 1633–42

The idea of the formal enclosed garden was brought from the lands of Tīmūr, the favourite form being the *chār bāgh*, a garden divided into four by axial canals or walkways. This concept was adopted and developed for formal tomb gardens during the Mughal period and was also used as a basis for the planning of pleasure gardens, of which a great many were laid out at Lahore, Delhi, Agra and Kashmir. The Shalimar

Gardens were designed as three separate terraces arranged in descending levels, making the maximum use of waterfalls and cascades. Two terraces are set in the form of *chār bāghs* and the central rectangular terrace is a large reservoir, in and around which were positioned marble pavilions and kiosks. Water directed by axial canals swirled down honeycombed chutes and cascaded over small walls lined with niches.

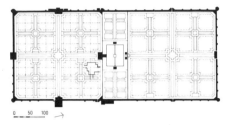

LAHORE, Bādshāhī Mosque
Mughal period, 1673–4

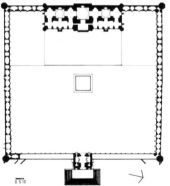

This great royal mosque attached to Lahore fort is the largest in area in the subcontinent. The elevation of the prayer hall was modelled on that of the Friday Mosque at Delhi with a few significant changes: the tall framing minarets at the corners have been replaced here by octagonal turrets crowned by kiosks and set at each of the four corners of the prayer hall, rendering it a free-standing structure separate from the arcades enclosing the courtyard. Tall minarets are placed at each corner of the courtyard, visually framing and articulating the whole complex. The red sandstone of the prayer hall and minarets is offset by the white marble of the bulbous domes, cupolas and the delicate inlay decoration. The gateway to the mosque has a chamber containing relics of the Prophet and his family.

MULTAN, Tomb of Shāh Rukn-i ʿĀlam
Punjab style, 1320–4

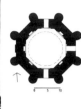

The architecture of Multan blossomed from a blending of indigenous Indian building traditions and cultural links with southern Iran maintained by the ruling dynasties. This building was originally erected by Ghiyāth ad-Dīn Tughluq as his own tomb. On ascending the throne he constructed another tomb for himself at Delhi and made over this tomb to his spiritual guide. The octagonal shape, the sloping walls for better stability, the sloping tapering buttresses, which rise to become domed turrets above the parapets, and the ornamental finials were all features that were to influence the development of Islamic architecture at Delhi. The tomb is constructed of sand-coloured fired bricks bonded at intervals with courses of carved shisham wood following an indigenous form of construction dating back to the prehistoric Indus Valley civilization. The elevations are ornamented with panels and string-courses of carved brickwork, glazed tiles and raised patterns in glazed brickwork of white, dark-blue, turquoise-blue and sky-blue, adding both shadow and colour to the sumptuous composition.

TATTA, Friday Mosque
Mughal period, 1644

Built by Shāh Jihān as a memorial to his stay in Tatta, this courtyard mosque with its four inward-facing *īwāns*, brick construction and glazed tile decoration reflects the strong cultural ties that Sind shared with Iran. The great east gateway and twin courtyards were added in 1658. The main chamber has three features unusual in Indian Islamic buildings: a domed *īwān*; light admitted into the central chamber through screened openings at floor level in the *qibla* wall; and a dome supported on a series of intersecting arches forming squinch nets. The walls, arches and dome of the central chamber are totally covered in glazed tilework. Square painted tiles and mosaic tiles are combined, forming a sumptuous array of geometric patterns in white, cobalt-blue, turquoise-blue and red. The dome exhibits a central medallion around which revolve concentric rings of stellar patterns, each with its own constellation of stars.

West Africa

ALLAN LEARY

The history of Islam in Africa south of the Sahara is one of interaction between two cultures – Islamic and African. In conditions of considerable ethnic and geographical diversity, distinctive West African mosque-types evolved – a synthesis of Muslim and African architectural concepts.

Islam came into West Africa by the Saharan caravan routes in about the 9th century. Two main directions of influence can be identified: western routes, linking the Maghrib with Berber-African gold-trading centres in the western Sudan, where close relations were established with the black pagan Soninke state of Ghana; and eastern routes, bringing the kingdoms of the central Sudan – Kanem, Bornu and the Hausa states – into contact with Tripoli, Tunis and Egypt.

The earliest known West African mosques were those at Koumbi Saleh and Tegdaoust, Arabized Berber settlements occupied between the 9th and 13th centuries and tentatively associated with ancient Ghana and Awdaghost. Recent excavations confirm their resemblance to existing stone and mud mosques in the Adrar and Hawd regions – simple combinations of courtyard, sanctuary and square minaret (*sawmaʿa*).

Ancient Ghana fell to the Almoravids in the 11th century and it was not until the rise of the black Muslim kingdom of Mali and its successor state, Songhai, in the 13th and 14th centuries, that Islam spread effectively into the savanna region and the Djenne-Timbuktu area became the centre of Islamic diffusion. Here developed a type of clay mosque often referred to as 'sudanic'. The introduction of Muslim architectural forms and techniques was a many-stranded phenomenon – some, the square minaret, for example, were adapted to local technologies, while others, such as fired brick construction or arch forms in dressed stone, were never widely used. The diffusion of these techniques and forms depended as much on non-Arab Muslims as on direct Arab influences.

The diffusion of the building of clay mosques to the south and east of the Niger bend occurred through the trading and missionary activities of black Mande groups – the Dyula, who, from the 14th century, established Muslim settlements along their trade routes from Djenne to the Akan goldfields; and the Wangarawa, who first introduced Islam to the Hausa states in the 14th and 15th centuries. The form of the Dyula mosques, especially their pinnacled, buttressed and trabeated construction, reveals their Djenne origin. The Hausa-Fulani mosques, however, with multidomed roof systems, suggest a local technology influenced not only by Mali and Songhai but more directly – through the central Saharan caravan routes – by North African forms. The role of the 19th-century Fulani reformers was also significant, not only in Hausaland but throughout Muslim West Africa.

The 'sudanic' mosque was the dominant Islamic structure in West Africa. Islamic sources for secular architecture are less readily identified but it is probable that the elaborate palace complexes of the Hausa, and flat-roofed mud construction in general, owed something to Muslim influences.

Chronology

WESTERN SUDAN

Ghana empire *c.* 8th–11th centuries

Mali period 13th–14th centuries

Songhai period mid-15th–late-16th centuries

Dyula influence *c.* 14th–19th centuries

Masina-Fulani influence 19th century

CENTRAL SUDAN

Kanem-Bornu period *c.* 11th–19th centuries

Hausa period *c.* 11th–18th centuries

Hausa-Fulani period 19th century

Niger
AGADEZ, Great Mosque
Songhai-Hausa influence, 16th–19th centuries

Founded by the Tuareg in the early 15th century, in an area then occupied by Hausa groups, Agadez came under Songhai influence with its conquest in 1501–16 by Askiā al-Hājj Muhammad. The first mosque is thought to date from then. It was rebuilt in 1844–9, by which time the main economic and political links were with the Hausa states

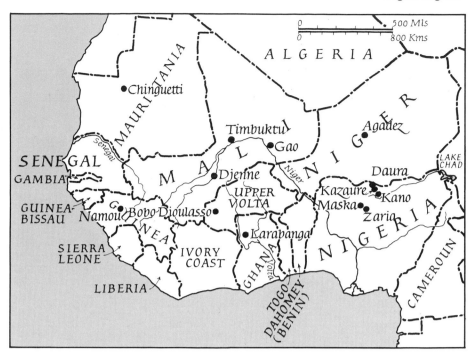

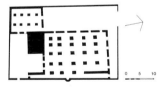

further south. Projecting 'dum'-palm beams on the minaret recall the Mande-Songhai mosques, while the single apsidal *mihrāb* and the absence of a tower above the *mihrāb* point to an element of Hausa influence.

Nigeria
DAURA, Palace
Hausa period, ?18th century

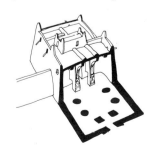

According to tradition, Daura was the capital of one of the earliest Hausa states. The entrance hall (*zaure*) of this ruler's palace is of considerable age. The roof was rebuilt in 1959, but most of the structure is regarded as pre-Fulani, dating possibly from the 18th century. Formal entrance buildings, which, with domed audience chambers, were a feature of Hausa-Fulani palaces, probably developed at the same time as rectangular mud mosques during the 15th and 16th centuries. Although living in 'decorated palaces' was condemned by the Fulani at the beginning of the 19th century, these buildings were retained and occupied after the Fulani conquest of the Hausa states.

KANO, Friday Mosque
Hausa-Fulani influences, 15th–19th centuries

Many Hausa clay mosques were characterized by heavy tower-minarets derived from the square North African form. Anathema to the Fulani reformers, they were mostly replaced by mosques with stair-minarets during the 19th century. The Kano minaret, demolished in 1937–8, and the Friday Mosque of Katsina, which survived until the early 20th century, are evident exceptions. The age of this mosque and its minaret is uncertain, though its foundation is ascribed to Muhammad Rumfa, the Hausa ruler of Kano (1463–99). The mosque seems to have fallen into disrepair and to have been rebuilt by a Fulani ruler between 1855 and 1883. The height of the minaret was about 20m; the adjoining sanctuary was a low flat-roofed structure within a walled enclosure.

MASKA, Friday Mosque
Hausa-Fulani period, late 19th century

On the southern fringes of the Katsina emirate, Maska was an important weaving and dyeing centre. This mud-brick mosque, which replaced an early pre-19th-century structure with a tower-minaret, was built for the Fulani ruler between 1890 and 1897. Oral tradition suggests that it was erected by Dahiru, a son of the builder of the Friday Mosque at Zaria. Although it is smaller than the Zaria building and undecorated, its formal and structural qualities tend to confirm this attribution.

ZARIA, Friday Mosque
Hausa-Fulani period, early 19th century

Built during the reign of the Fulani emir ‘Abd al-Karīm (1834–46), this mosque is attributed to a famous Hausa builder, Mallam Mika’ilu Babban Gwani. Before its reconstruction, in 1975, it consisted of a multi-domed sanctuary with an adjoining court, surrounded by a walled enclosure and built like all Hausa-Fulani buildings of oval mud-

bricks. The spaces within the sanctuary are spanned by complexes of mud arches, reinforced with corbels of palm beams. Supporting piers and part of the qibla wall are decorated in relief. Apart from the sanctuary, preserved within a new concrete mosque, most of the old building has been demolished. Four modern minarets stand at the corners.

Mauritania
CHINGUETTI, Great Mosque
Berber-Arab, ?13th–15th centuries

On the western Saharan caravan route, this town was an important Muslim centre from the 13th century onwards. This mosque is of split stone and clay with a roof of palm beams on stone piers. Twin mihrāb and minbar niches, characteristic of other Saharan mosques – Walata, Tichitt, Nema – and found also in many of the Mali-Songhai clay mosques, are built into the qibla wall. A square minaret of the sawma‘a type rises from the south-west corner of the courtyard. Recent excavations verifying the existence of previous mosque structures on the site suggest an early foundation date. The remains of similar mosques, in use between the 9th and 12th centuries, have been uncovered at Koumbi Saleh and Tegdaoust.

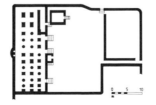

Mali
GAO, Mosque-Tomb of Askiā al-Hājj Muhammad
Songhai period, early to mid-16th century

Askiā al-Hājj Muhammad ruled over the Songhai empire from 1493 until 1528. The date of the building of his tomb is not recorded but was probably soon after his death in 1538. The present mud-brick structure, evidently dating from the 19th century, consists of a massive stepped tower-minaret with projecting poles, standing in a walled courtyard with a narrow-aisled sanctuary to the east. It differs markedly from that described by Barth in 1854. The central seven-stepped tower that he saw was 18m to 20m high; the present three-storeyed structure is about 11m high. The mihrāb tower has now disappeared. Within the qibla wall are twin mihrāb and minbar niches; this form does not occur further to the east.

DJENNE, Great Mosque
Mali-Songhai-Fulani influences, ?14th–15th and 20th centuries

The present mosque was built in 1909 under French supervision. Together with the Great Mosque at Mopti, built in 1935, it represents a new architectural syncretism – the beginnings of an ‘official’ ethnic style – widely accepted throughout this part of Africa for secular buildings. The previous structure was described briefly by Caillié, who saw it in 1827. It was largely demolished about 1830 by the Masina-Fulani leader, Sheku Ahmadu, who built a simpler Friday mosque near by. A conjectural reconstruction of the earlier building, based on a survey of the ruins and on oral accounts, was published by Dubois, in 1896, and shows a mosque rather different from the present version. No certain date can be given for its foundation, although the 14th century seems likely.

Djenne builders used both oval and rectangular bricks. The arch form seems not to have been adopted here prior to the colonial period.

TIMBUKTU, Great Mosque
Mali–Songhai periods, 14th century

The mosque is constructed of round dried mud-bricks and stone rubble with clay rendering, with a flat sanctuary roof supported on arcades of mud piers. Three of the arcades incorporate quasi-horseshoe arches constructed from stone voussoirs. The minaret is about 16m high with an internal stair, accessible from a smaller courtyard by external steps to the roof terrace. A conical tower with projecting poles rises above the *mihrāb* and *minbar* niches. Adjoining it over the *mihrāb* is a rudimentary clerestory structure. The foundation of the mosque, in 1325, is attributed to Mansa Musa, king of Mali, and major reconstruction was undertaken in 1569–71 for the Timbuktu *qādī*, al-'Aqīb. Further modifications are recorded over the next two hundred years but substantial alterations seem to have occurred between 1828 and 1853, during a period of Masina-Fulani dominance.

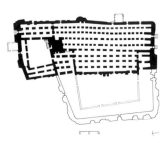

TIMBUKTU, Sankore Mosque
Mali–Songhai periods, 14th–15th centuries

Similar in construction to the Great Mosque at Timbuktu, this mosque has a number of distinctive features. The courtyard is surrounded on three sides by enclosed arcaded galleries, there is a single *mihrāb* niche and the minaret is heavily buttressed. Stone-voussoired arches occur in the sanctuary. No foundation date is recorded in the local histories but the mosque was known as a centre of learning from the early 15th century. Various reconstructions are recorded, notably that by al-'Aqīb in 1578. The original form of the mosque, as described in 1828 by Caillié, seems to have resembled that at Chinguetti. The galleries were probably added, and also the buttressing of the minaret, when the building was repaired by a Kunta Arab leader, Shaykh Ahmad al-Bakkā'i, in the late 1840s.

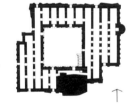

Upper Volta
BOBO-DIOULASSO, Friday Mosque
Dyula influence, 19th century

This town was an early Mande-Dyula settlement about two hundred miles south of Djenne on the route to Kong and to the Akan goldfields. The inhabitants were Muslims at an early period, but later apostatized and were reconverted in the 19th century. The

present Friday Mosque dates from between 1850 and 1885 and consists of a heavily buttressed sanctuary about 11m long, constructed of rectangular mud-bricks, the flat roof supported by clay piers; there is a single *mihrāb*. Courtyard enclosures are often lacking in the Dyula mosques, which, throughout Upper Volta, the Ivory Coast and northern Ghana, can be seen as variations on the Djenne form.

Ghana
LARABANGA, Friday Mosque
Dyula influence, 17th–19th centuries

This ancient Mande-Dyula trading settlement, important as a centre of Islamic diffusion, is located about 350 miles southeast of Djenne. Local traditions associate the foundation of the Friday Mosque with a Dyula cleric during the reign of one of the Gonja kings, Jakpa (1622/3–1666/7). The rectangular building, with heavily pinnacled buttresses and square pyramidal towers with projecting beams, is constructed from rectangular sun-dried bricks. It is thought to have been reconstructed in the 19th century.

Guinea
NAMOU, Friday Mosque
Masina-Fulani influence, 18th–19th centuries

The mosques of the Futa Jalon, a highland region of Guinea where Muslim Fulani from Masina became politically dominant in the 18th century, serve to illustrate the modifications to mosque design that occurred in association with vernacular traditions in areas of higher rainfall. The plan of the sanctuary remained square under a dome-like thatch. A similar solution to the problem, in an area conquered by the Fulani in the 19th century, was recorded by Frobenius in 1907 at Mokwa, in Nigeria.

East Africa

RONALD LEWCOCK

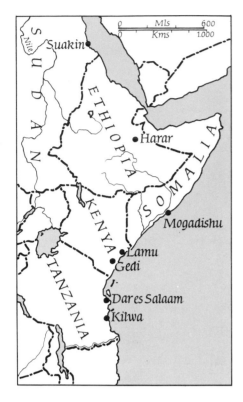

East African mosques exhibit close parallels with early mosques in southern Arabia. Both have the same longitudinal prayer halls with small courtyards used mainly for open-air ablution, narrow spans and flat roofs; in particular, a characteristic feature of many of them is the presence of a central row of piers in line with the *mihrab*. In view of the close relationship between Aden and the East African ports in the 12th and 13th centuries, it is hardly surprising that the South Arabian mosque-type was adopted, nor that it resisted change during subsequent periods when external influences (Indian and Portuguese, in particular) were altering other characteristics of the architectural styles along the coast.

The style, typified by the alterations to the Great Mosque at Kilwa in the 13th and 15th centuries, is markedly Indian. This style was ultimately derived from earlier styles in Iran and Iraq, but the immediate and near-contemporary parallels to the developments on the East African coast in dome and vaulting design and architectural decoration may be seen in the Indian mosques of the 14th century, notably those built during the Tughluq period, such as Nizam ad-Din's *khan* and the tomb of Ghiyath ad-Din Tughluq, both at Delhi. The Shish Gunbad, also at Delhi, and the 15th-century mosques at Jaunpur have rows of square panels as crowning friezes, like those that are characteristic of the East African architectural styles.

East African arches are not true arches with radiating voussoirs, but are Indian corbelled arches, meeting at the top without a central voussoir.

Although little remains of the external façades of mosques, palaces and houses, it is possible to reconstruct what they were like by referring to the miniature façades of the pillar tombs, which reproduced the current vocabulary of the larger buildings. In the case of the great pillar tomb at Malindi near Gedi, and in the tombs at Gedi, dressed stone mouldings outline the rectangular frames of doors and windows and culminate in horizontal friezes of square coffers, with precious porcelain bowls often set in their centres.

The splendid wooden doors have elaborately carved frames and central cover strips, and are decorated with rows of projecting iron or brass bosses. Rosettes play a prominent part in the designs.

Chronology

Muslim in 'Zanj' 9th–mid-12th centuries

Dynasties at Mogadishu and Kilwa mid-12th century

Minor local dynasties late 13th–14th centuries

Rise of Malindi, Paté and Mombasa early 15th century

Portuguese seizure of principal towns early 16th century

Somalia
MOGADISHU, Mosque of Fakhr ad-Din
13th century

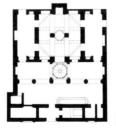

This mosque is said to have been founded by the first sultan of Mogadishu and almost the whole of the present building is likely to date back to the 13th century. Clearly the work of an architect, the mosque is sophisticated both in form and decoration. A façade with three doorways and panelled marble decoration leads through an ablution lobby to a transverse courtyard, beyond which an arcaded portico fronts the square prayer hall and large flanking rooms on both sides. In the prayer hall a high dome rises in the central bay of the nine, square, ceiling bays; two polygonal columns carry the longitudinal beams that support the ceiling and the dome. A second dome, of the Anatolian conical type, rises out of the centre of the arcaded portico. The *mihrab* is of north Indian manufacture and carved in marble; it contains the ancient motif of a lamp hanging on a chain surrounded by an inscription giving the date (1269) and a name, which may be that of the artist.

Kenya
GEDI, Walls, Houses and Palace
15th century (mainly)

This deserted Arab-Bantu town lies about five miles from the coast. The site was occupied from the 13th century, but the surviving ruins are principally of the 15th century. The town covered an area of about eighteen hectares and the town wall, the palace, the Great Mosque, seven smaller mosques, three fine pillar tombs and a number of private houses substantially survive, although without their roofs, and in some cases without their upper walls. The walls are of coral rag and mortar, with door openings framed in fine cut coral and roofs of coral tiles covered in lime and carried on squared timbers. Three gates penetrated the town walls – that to the north leading to an open square in front of the palace. The streets in this area seem to have been laid out originally on a grid orientated roughly north-south and east-west. The plan of a typical house shows a spatial progression from the narrow street through a large doorway into a private courtyard and thence into a series of transverse rooms, which become increasingly private and smaller. The palace was an ordered cluster of such units, one of which served as the reception hall; an imposing portico flanked by seats led into the palace.

LAMU, Houses, Pillar Tomb and Fort
?15th century

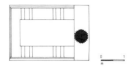

One of the best preserved Islamic towns on the East African coast, Lamu was reputedly founded in the time of 'Abd al-Malik, the Umayyad caliph (699). Europeans seldom reached there, and the coastal Arabs achieved a wealth and luxury that is witnessed by the fine deserted mansions surviving around the harbour, containing walls of tiered decorated niches lining the reception rooms. There is a fluted pillar tomb, perhaps of the 15th century, and more than twenty whitewashed mosques cluster along the narrow streets. The towering fort alongside the central square was begun by the last great sultan of neighbouring Paté, in 1809, and completed by governors sent by the Omani sultan of Zanzibar, in 1820.

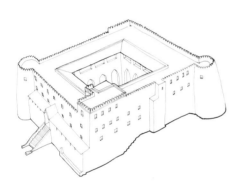

Tanzania
KILWA, Great Mosque
Late 12th century, 13th century

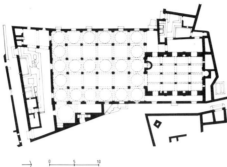

Kilwa was founded in the 9th century. The Great Mosque, which survives in a ruined state, was built in two main stages – the smaller north prayer hall first, and the greater south enlargement later. The north prayer hall had originally a coral and plaster roof on wooden rafters supported on polygonal wooden pillars. The arched south hall was reroofed with barrel vaults and domes over alternate bays in the period 1420–40. A good deal of the south hall and the surrounding walls remains intact. Ibn Battūta, who visited Kilwa in 1331, described it as 'one of the most beautiful and well constructed towns in the world. The whole of it is elegantly built.'

KILWA, Palace of Husuni Kubwa
1245

This palace is attributed to al-Malik al-Mansūr ibn Sulaymān, one of whose inscriptions has been found there. With well over one hundred rooms, courtyards, terraces, ornamental swimming pool, vaults and domes of various shapes, and carved decoration, this was the most magnificent Islamic architectural complex in Africa south of the Sahara. Situated on a high sandstone headland, with views over the entrance to the harbour of Kilwa to the north and the town to the west, the layout of the palace follows closely the shape of the headland; the vaulted private quarters of the sultan at the tip, the public reception rooms and *dīwān* in the centre, and a great forecourt on the inland side. The latter resembled an Iranian caravanserai with *īwāns* in the centre of its four sides; on the upper level on the north and west sides there was a suite of richly decorated reception rooms with a variety of stucco vaults and domes. A great fortress-like enclosure on the neighbouring headland may have been the barracks for the royal troops, and seems to have contained a mosque. Kilwa was abandoned after the last sultan was deported to Muscat in 1843; by then the palace had been unused for many centuries.

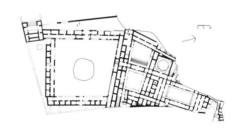

The Far East

GEORGE MICHELL

More than one third of all Muslims live east of India, but the Islamic architecture of China and South-East Asia still remains little known and poorly documented, probably because Islamic architecture in these areas did not adopt distinctive forms, techniques or decoration. Certain modifications were, of course, incorporated into Far Eastern buildings in order to adapt them to the requirements of a mosque, but these modifications did not substantially alter the indigenous character of the architecture. Even so, these buildings are part of the architecture of the Islamic world and deserve, therefore, to be included here.

It was probably not until the influxes of the 8th and 9th centuries that Muslims arrived in China (by both land and sea) in any numbers. Though the foundation of several mosques (such as Canton) may go back to this early period, most Islamic architecture in China is more recent. It is also typically Chinese – solid timber columns, with elaborate systems of projecting corbels, support gabled tiled roofs that have the characteristic upward sloping corners; walls and gateways are of masonry. Mosques are enclosed by walls with imposing portals that sometimes function as minarets (Hang-Chou and Peking). The interior is conceived in the traditional Chinese manner as a sequence of colonnaded halls opening onto courtyards; there may also be an ablution fountain or open pavilion for seating. The prayer hall is indicated by a simple *mihrāb* in the rear wall,

mostly a semicircular-headed niche, beside which there is often a timber *minbar*. Arabic and Chinese inscriptions, carved in relief and/or painted, are the only adornment. There is generally no minaret; the mosque at Canton, with its plain tapering cylindrical tower, perhaps dating from the beginning of the 10th century, is exceptional.

Islam only spread to the Indonesian archipelago during the 15th and 16th centuries but few mosques belong to this period. Like Chinese mosques, those of Java are surrounded by enclosure walls broken by gateways occasionally developed into high porches. The prayer hall, an open square gallery, is characterized by its massive pyramidal roof rising to a point, usually in three or five storeys, to create a pagoda-like effect (Jogjakarta). The structure is traditional – horizontal and vertical timbers support the sloping roof, there being no inclined beams. The verandahs in front of many mosques are later additions, sheltering accessory activities. Mosques are frequently combined with cemeteries and tombs in a complex of interconnecting walled courts (Sendangduwur). The minaret is mostly a simple wood and bamboo construction, the brick example at Kudus being unique. Related to this architecture of pyramidal tiered roofs are the mosques of other regions, which reflect similar indigenous forms and techniques. At Acheh in northern Sumatra, Kuching in Sarawak, and in the southern islands of the Philippines, the monumental thatched mosques are almost identical to secular buildings, especially village meeting halls.

An important phase of Far Eastern Islamic architecture is that belonging to the Colonial period and many of the mosques in Malaysia, Indonesia and the Philippines are built in an eclectic European style. The open tiered roof construction is frequently replaced by neo-Classical façades (Johore, Malaysia) and by Indian, Mughal-influenced domes (Singapore and Kuala Lumpur); minarets are even modelled on Dutch lighthouses (Bantam, Java). It is noteworthy that Middle Eastern and Indian influences in the mosque architecture of South-East Asia only appear in recent times.

China
CH'ÜAN-CHOU, Mosque
1310

Possibly the oldest extant mosque in China, many of its features are atypical. A series of arched portals and vestibules lead to a staircase from which the prayer hall is entered. The walls are of masonry, un-adorned except for ogee-headed niches, one of which functions as a *mihrāb* in a rect-angular bay. Similarly shaped arches also appear above the portals, their corbelled construction recalling Indian Islamic archi-tecture. The doors have stone lintels sup-ported by corbels carved with Chinese designs. A timber roof was once supported on stone columns but has now disappeared. Openings in the prayer hall walls provide access to the cemetery, in which a typically Chinese pavilion shelters several tombs.

HANG-CHOU, Great Mosque
?15th century

This mosque is described in an official 15th-century report but has probably been renovated many times since. The entrance has an unusual imposing high portal with a slightly pointed opening and an Arabic inscription above. A frieze of *muqarnas*-like mouldings and merlons surmount the portal, which is raised up in front of a pagoda structure like an *īwān*. Two staircases ascend to the upper pavilion, which functions as a minaret. A covered way leads to the col-umned hall with two diminutive courts. The prayer hall is divided into three bays with a *mihrāb* and a *minbar*. A lacquered table at the centre of the mosque supports an inscribed tablet wishing the emperor long life, even eternity.

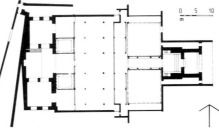

Indonesia
SENDANGDUWUR (East Java), Mosque
?16th century

This complex, possibly built on the site of a Hindu temple, consists of a square mosque with a triple-tiered roof (modern replace-ment), several adjacent tomb structures, a walled cemetery and a number of elaborately decorated stone gateways. Located on a terraced hill, the complex doubtless in-corporates old Javanese connections be-tween spirits of ancestors and mountains. Steps and gateways to the north of the mosque lead down to a Hindu-styled water-tank. The gateways are provided with bird-like 'wings', unique in Indonesian archi-tecture, incorporating various Hindu motifs such as ferocious masks, wish-fulfilling trees, peacocks and eagles.

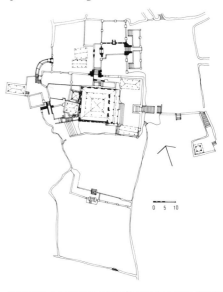

KUDUS (Central Java), Minaret
Early 16th century

Built of red brick with inserted ceramic dishes, the ornamentation of this square tower (about 15m high) is restricted to stepped mouldings and framed niches imitat-ing the form of a traditional Javanese Hindu temple. This minaret also appears to be related to Balinese towers where signal drums are sounded – drums are beaten to announce prayers. The pavilion above is a modern addition.

Glossary

JAMES DICKIE (Yaqub Zaki)

adhān: summons to prayer
'ain (ayin in Turkish*)*: dervish ceremony
'āmma: uneducated, working class
arasta: row of shops attached to a religious structure
bādgīr: wind-tower
bāgh: garden or pleasure pavilion
baraka: spiritual power which surrounds a holy man or object, blessing
barīd: postal service
bedesten: central and most secure part of a market area
birka: ablution tank
buq'a: monastic retreat
çardak: summer reception room
çesme (Turkish): drinking fountain
chahār bāgh: four-fold plot
chahār-sūq: place of intersection of two *sūqs*
dār al-Islām: 'Abode of Islam', totality of Islamic believers
dargāh: portal
darīh: tomb
dergāh (Persian and Turkish): dervish lodge. (Persian for 'a royal court')
dhikr: dervish ceremony (literally 'remembrance of [God]')
dikka: respondents' platform
dīwān: government department or royal reception chamber
fawāra: fountain with jet
fisqīya: ablution tank
fundūq: warehouse or inn
ghatā: coping stone running longitudinally along the top of a recumbent gravestone
ghusl: total ablution
hadīth: prophetical tradition
hadra: dervish ceremony
hajj: pilgrimage
hammām: bath
han (Turkish): caravanserai
hanafiyya: ablution fountain
haram (English, harem): private quarters of a house or sanctuary of a mosque
haud: ablution tank in centre of *sahn* (q.v.)
hisba: craft or market law
hujra: chamber, cell
hunkar mahfil: imperial loge in an Ottoman mosque
'Īd: festival
'īdgāh: place of community prayer
ijmā': the principle of communal consensus
imām: leader, especially prayer leader
imām khatīb: preacher cum prayer-leader
imām rātib: prayer-leader
īwān: roofed or vaulted hall open at one end
jabāna: cemetery
jāinamāz (Persian): prayer-rug
jali: perforated stone screen
jamā'a: congregation, assembly
jāmi' masjid: congregational mosque
kalima: 'words' of the *Shahāda* (q.v.)
khān: caravanserai
khānaqāh: monastery
khāssa: educated, wealthy class

khatīb: a prayer-leader qualified to preach
khutba: sermon, homily, address
ksar: fortified hamlet
kūfī: a rectangular script used for monumental purposes
kula: defensive town house
külliye (Turkish): complex centred on a mosque but embodying medical, charitable and educational facilities
kursī: chair or lectern (any kind of support, from a plinth in architecture to the folding legs of a tray)
kursī's-Sūra: Qur'ān lectern
lahd: burial vault or niche
ma'adhdhana: minaret (from *adhdhana*, 'to call to prayer')
mabkhāra: thurible, censer. (Both kinds, swinging and stationary, are used in Islam. The stationary kind can take an architectural form.) Also: minaret top or corner turret in the shape of a censer
madfan: mausoleum ('place of burial')
madhhab: legal school (literally, 'way')
madrasa: collegiate mosque (literally, 'place of study')
mafraj: reception room
mahfil: congregation, assembly
maida (coll): ablution zone or fountain
majli: reception hall
malqaf: wind-catcher
manāra: minaret (from *nāra*, 'to shine forth, to glow')
maqabriyya: recumbent gravestone, usually of the prismatic variety
maq'ad: loggia
maqbara: cemetery
maqsūra: enclosure near the *mihrāb* in early mosques. Intended to protect the ruler against assassination, its visible legacy is the *hunkar mahfil* (q.v.). Also the screen enclosing the grave in an important mausoleum
māristān: infirmary (*bīmaristān*: 'place of *bimar*', Persian for 'a sick person')
marqad: grave (literally 'resting place')
mashhad: shrine or shrine mosque (literally, 'place of witness', i.e. *martyrium*)
masharabiyya: screen or grille of turned wood
masjid: district mosque
masjid-i Jum'a: congregational mosque (literally 'Friday mosque')
mastaba: stone bench
maydān: ceremonial open space
mazār: mausoleum ('place of visitation')
medina: 'city'
menzel: courtyard house
mihrāb: niche whether concave or flat indicating the *qibla*
mijmar: thurible, censer
minbar: pulpit (pronounced *mimbar*)
mu'adhdhin: summoner to prayer (Eng. muezzin)
mu'allaq: literally 'a hanging mosque', i.e. one suspended

over shops on the ground floor
muballigh: respondent (literally, 'informant') in a mosque
mulhaq: appenage
muqarnas: 'stalactite' or 'honeycomb' ornament or vaulting made up of small concave segments
muqrī: Qur'ānic cantor
musallā: place of community prayer. Also 'prayer-rug' and 'oratory'
mutribkhāna (Turkish *mutribhane*): tribune reserved for orchestra in a *samā'khāna* (q.v.)
namāzlik (Turkish): prayer-rug
namāzgāh: oratory
naskhī: a cursive script
nasta'līq: a cursive script
pendentive: curved or faceted inverted triangle of masonry supporting a dome
pīshtāq: monumental portal
qabr: grave
qabrstān (Persian): cemetery
qalamdān: coping stone in shape of pen-box (*qalamdān*), usually found in India and denoting the tomb of a male
qārī: Qur'ānic cantor
qasaba: citadel, capital, metropolis
qasr: castle
qaysāriyya: central and most secure part of a market area
qibla: direction of prayer. Also synonymous in some contexts with *mihrāb*
qiblīyya: *iwān* serving as oratory in a *madrasa*
qubba: dome. Also, by substitution of the part for the whole, signifies mausoleum
rābita: hermitage
rauda: mausoleum (literally, garden: hence, 'funerary garden')
ribāt: fortified monastery
riwāq: portico, usually one side of a *sahn* (q.v.)
sabīl: drinking fountain
saff: serial prayer-rug (literally, 'row'), row of worshippers
sahn: courtyard (of a mosque)
sahrījī: grille
sajāda: prayer-rug
samā'khāna (Turkish *semahane*): ceremonial hall in a *khānaqāh*
saqāya: ablution tank
sawmā'a: minaret (from *sama'a*, 'to climb')
shadūf: device for lifting water
shāhid, shāhida: vertical stone (literally 'witness'). *Ash-shāhid al-awwal*: headstone; *ash-shāhid ath-thānī*: footstone
Shahāda: 'Attestation of Faith'
sharī'a: place of community prayer
shubāk: window or grille
sihrij: ablution tank
sirdāb: basement
squinch: an arch-shaped element spanning a corner, forming the octagonal base of a circular dome
suffa: stone platform, usually to support tombs (English 'sofa')
sūq: street of a market
tābūt: wooden catafalque usually marking the grave of a saint
tajwīd: cantillation of the Qur'ān
takkiyya (Turkish *'tekke'*): monastery (also hospice)

tarkība: recumbent gravestone ('construction')
tā'wīdh: headstone (anything on which a religious formula is inscribed)
thuluth: a cursive script
turba: mausoleum ('dust') (Turkish *türbe*)
ulu cami (Turkish): great mosque
waqf: charitable endowment
wudū': partial ablution
zāhir: recumbent stone ('the apparent')
zakāt: poor-tax
zāwiya (Turkish *zaviye*): small monastery
ziyāda: extension to a mosque
ziyāra: mausoleum ('visitation')

CHAPTER 3

Supplementary notes to the text

p. 97, column 1, para 2. Qur'ān verses are quoted from N. J. Dawood's translation, Penguin Classics, 1974
p. 98, column 2, para 3. The quotation from Herodotus is from A. de Sélincourt's translation, Penguin Classics, 1972
p. 100, column 2, para 1 . . . 'a much paraphrased passage'. See *The Travels of Ibn Battuta*, translated and edited by Sir H. A. R. Gibb, Vol II, 1962, p. 508. The hierarchy of the Islamic marketplace and location of wares was first stated by G. Marçais in 'L'Urbanisme Musulman', *Mélanges d'histoire et d'archéologie de l'occident Musulman*, Algiers, 1957, pp. 230–1
p. 101, column 1, para 3. For Ibn Battūta, see Gibb, *op. cit.* Vol I, 1958, pp. 71–2
p. 102, column 1. The study on which all further work on Anatolian caravanserais must rest is that made by the Erdmanns, *Das anatolische Karavansaray des 13 Jahrhunderts*, Istanbul, 1976
p. 107. For a recent study of the Ottoman *bedesten* see G. Goodwin, *A History of Ottoman Architecture*, London, 1971, pp. 86–7

CHAPTER 5

Supplementary notes to the text

p. 162, column 1, para 3 . . . 'questions and answers are finely balanced'. Dr Dickie, in an important lecture at the Commonwealth Institute, London, on 'Islamic Architecture: motion and equilibrium', 1976, has pointed out the rightness of E. M. Forster's definition of Islamic architecture in his *A Passage to India*: 'It is an architecture of questions and answers.'
p. 164, column 2, para 4 . . . 'based on another mathematical progression'. See G. Marçais: 'Remarques' and 'Nouvelles remarques sur l'esthetique musulmane' in *Annales de l'Institut d'Etudes orientales*, VI, 1947, pp. 31–52 and IV, 1938, pp. 56–71
p. 169, column 1, para 2 . . . 'the figural decoration in Christian buildings'. See O. Grabar: *The*

281

Formation of Islamic Art, London, 1973, and E. Dodd: 'The Image of the Word', *Berytus*, VIII, 1969
p. 170, column 1, para 1 . . . 'square, triangle or polyon.' See I. El-Said, *Geometric Concepts in Islamic Art*, London, 1976
p. 170, column 1, para 2 . . . 'multiplicity in unity'. See Y. Massignon, *Les méthods de réalisation artistiques des peuples de l'Islam*, 1928, and T. Burckhardt, *Art of Islam*, London 1976
p. 171, column 1, para 2 . . . 'geometric arabesque'. For example, E. H. Hankin, *The Drawing of Geometric Patterns in Saracenic Art*, Calcutta, 1925, p. 3
p. 173, column 1, para 3 . . . 'a vibration of light'. T. Burckhardt, *op. cit.*
p. 175, column 2, para 4 . . . 'The Grammar of Ornament', London 1856, p. 67

KEY MONUMENTS
Arabia section text © 1978 Geoffrey King and Ronald Lewcock
Spain section text © 1978 Geoffrey King
Iraq section text © 1978 Helen Philon

Supplementary notes on Iraq
Kufa, Zāwiya (*see p.* 249)
Under the mosque courtyard, an underground *zāwiya* (14th–15th C.), built of brick and mortar, opens onto an octagonal well through eight barrel-vaulted *īwāns*. At the intersection of the four southern *īwāns*, a polygonal dome is preserved, together with some of its decoration. The dome is built of horizontal brick courses with brick plugs carved with rosettes. The *miḥrāb* on the southernmost *īwān* is set within a rectangular frame and is composed of two-pointed arched recesses; the spandrels being decorated with arabesque motifs in low relief.

Select Bibliography

GENERAL WORKS

BOSWORTH, C. E. *The Islamic Dynasties* (Edinburgh, 1967)
BURCKHARDT, T. *Art of Islam: Language and Meaning* (London, 1976)
CRESWELL, K. A. C. *Early Muslim Architecture*, 2 vols. (Oxford, 1932, revised 1969; 1942)
Early Muslim Architecture (London, 1958)
A Bibliography of the Architecture, Arts and Crafts of Islam (Cairo, 1961, supplement 1973)
The Encyclopaedia of Islam (1st edn, Leiden, 1913–42; 2nd edn, Leiden and London, 1960–)
GRABAR, O. *The Formation of Islamic Art* (New Haven and London, 1973)
GRUBE, E. J. *The World of Islam* (New York and Toronto, 1966)
HOAG, J. *Islamic Architecture* (New York, 1977)

LEWIS, B., ed. *The Cambridge History of Islam*, 2 vols. (Cambridge, 1970)
The World of Islam (London, 1976)
MONNERET DE VILLARD, U. *Introduzione allo studio dell'archeologia islamica* (Rome, 1966)
PAPADOPOULO, A. *L'Islam et l'art musulman* (Paris, 1976)
PEARSON, J. D., ed. *Index Islamicus* (Cambridge, 1958–)
ROGERS, M. *The Spread of Islam* (London, 1976)
SOURDEL-THOMINE, J. and SPULER, B., eds. *Propyläen Kunstgeschichte: Die Kunst des Islam* (Berlin, 1973)

CHAPTER ONE

THE QURʾĀN

ARDALAN, N. and BAKHTIAR, L. *The Sense of Unity* (Chicago and London, 1973)
ANDRAE, T. *Muhammad, the Man and his Faith* (London, 1936)
GIBB, H. A. R. *Muhammadanism* (New York, 1962)
GOLVIN, L. *La Mosquée* (Algiers, 1960)
GOTTHEIL, R. J. H. 'The Origin and History of the Minaret' in *Journal of the American Society*, 30 (1909–10)
GRABAR, O. 'The Islamic Dome' in *Journal of the Society for Architectural Historians*, 22 (1963)
'The Case of the Mosque' in *Middle Eastern Cities* (Berkeley, 1969)
GRUNEBAUM, G. E. VON *Classical Islam* (Chicago, 1970)
MACDONALD, D. B. *Development of Muslim Theology, Jurisprudence and Constitutional Theory* (New York, 1903; reprinted Lahore, 1960; Beirut, 1964)
MACDOUGALL, E. B. and ETTINGHAUSEN, R. eds. *The Islamic Garden* (Dumbarton Oaks, 1976)
SCHACHT, J. 'An unknown type of minbar' in *Ars Orientalis*, II (1957)
SCHACHT, J. and BOSWORTH, C. E., eds. *The Legacy of Islam* (Oxford, 1974)
SERJEANT, R. B. 'Mihrāb' in *Bulletin of the School of Oriental and African Studies*, XIII (1960)
SOURDEL, J. 'Mosquée et madrasa' in *Cahiers de civilisation médiévale*, 13 (1970)
WATT, W. M. *Muhammad, Prophet and Statesmen* (London, 1961)

CHAPTER TWO

DADASHEV, S. A. and USEINOV, -. M. A. *Ansambl Dvortza Shirvanshahov v Baku* (Moscow, 1956)
DAVIS, E. F. *The Palace of Topkapi* (New York, 1970)
DUDA, D. *Innenarchitektur Syrischer Stadthäuser* (Beirut, 1971)
GABRIEL, A. *Châteaux turcs du Bosphore* (Paris, 1943)
GABRIELI, F. 'Il palazzo hammadita' in *Festschrift für Ernst Kühnel* (Berlin, 1959)
GRABAR, O. 'Mshattā, Wasit,

Baghdad' in *Studies in honour of P. K. Hitti* (London, 1959)
KHADR, M. 'Deux actes de waqf' in *Journal Asiatique*, 255 (1967)
LEZINE, A. *Le Ribat de Sousse* (Tunis, 1956)
LLOYD, S. and RICE, D. S. *Amasya* (London, 1958)
MINASIAN, C. O. *Shah Diz* (London, 1912)
REMPEL, L. I. and AHRAROV, I. *Reznoi Shtuk Afrasiyaba* (Tashkent, 1971)
SOURDEL, D. 'Questions de cérémonial 'abbaside' in *Revue des Études islamiques*, XXVIII/1 (1960)
STARK, F. *The Valleys of the Assassins* (London, 1934)

CHAPTER THREE

BASTANI-PARIZI, M. 'L'ensemble de Ganj Ali Xan à Kerman' in *Memorial Volume of Congress VI of Iranian Art and Archaeology* (Tehran, 1976)
ÇULPAN, C. *Türk Taş Köprüleri* (Ankara, 1975)
ÉCOCHARD, M. and LE COEUR, C. *Les Bains de Damas*, 2 vols. (Beirut, 1942–3)
ERDMANN, K. *Das anatolische Karavansaray*, 3 vols. (Berlin, 1961, Istanbul, 1976)
GRUNEBAUM, G. E. VON 'The Structure of the Muslim Town' in *Islam, Essays in the Nature and Growth of a Cultural Tradition* (London, 1955)
KIEL, M. 'The Ottoman Hammām and the Balkans' in *Art and Archaeology Research Papers*, 9 (1976)
MARÇAIS, G. 'L'urbanisme musulman' in *Mélanges d'histoire et d'archéologie de l'Occident musulman* (Algiers, 1957)
ÖZDEŞ, G. *Türk Çarşıları* (Istanbul, 1953)
SAUVAGET, J. 'Les caravansérails syriens du hadjdj de Constantinople' in *Ars Islamica*, IV (1937)
'Caravansérails syriens du moyen age' in *Ars Islamica*, VII (1940)
La poste au chevaux dans l'empire des Mamelouks (Paris, 1941)
SIROUX, M. *Caravansérails d'Iran et petites constructions routières* (Cairo, 1949)
Anciennes voies et monuments routiers de la region d'Ispahan, suivie de plusieurs autres édifices de cette province (Cairo, 1971)
'Caravansérails seldjoucides iraniens' in *The Art of Iran and Anatolia from the 11th to the 13th century AD* (London, 1974)
TERRASSE, H. 'Trois bains Mérinides du Maroc' in *Mélanges William Marçais* (Paris, 1950)
WIRTH, E. 'Zum Problem des Basars (*sūq, çarşı*)' in *Der Islam*, 51–2 (1974–5)

CHAPTER FOUR

BULATOV, M. S. 'The Tomb of Sultan Sanjar' in *Architectural Heritage*, XVII (in Russian, Moscow, 1964)

CRESWELL, K. A. C. 'The Origin of the Persian Double Dome' in *The Burlington Magazine*, XXIV (1913–14)
FISCHER, K. *Dächer, Decken und Gewölbe indischer Kulstätten und Nutzbauten* (Wiesbaden, 1974)
GOITEIN, S. D. *Studies in Islamic History and Institutions* (Leiden, 1966)
JONES, D. and MICHELL, G. 'Squinches and Pendentives: Problems and Definitions' in *Art and Archaeology Research Papers*, 1 (1972)
KPYUKOV, K. S. 'The Module in Monuments of Central Asian Architecture' in *Architectural Heritage*, XVII (in Russian, Moscow, 1964)
LÉVI-PROVENÇAL, E. *Séville musulmane au début du XIIè siècle* (Paris, 1947)
LEVY, R. *The Maʿālim al-Qurba of Ibn al-Ukhuwwa* (London, 1938)
MAINSTONE, R. J. *Developments in Structural Form* (London, 1975)
MAYER, L. A. *Islamic Architects and their Works* (Geneva, 1956)
Islamic Woodcarvers and their Works (Geneva, 1958)
Islamic Metalworkers and their Works (Geneva, 1959)
ROSENTHAL, F. *The Muquddimah of Ibn Khaldūn* (London, 1958)
SERJEANT, R. B. 'Building and Builders in Hadramawt' in *Le Muséon*, LXII (1949)
'A Judeo-Arab House-Deed from Habbān' in *Journal of the Royal Asiatic Society*, 3–4 (1953)
WILBER, D. N. 'Builders and Craftsmen of Islamic Iran: the Early Period' in *Art and Archaeology Research Papers*, 10 (1976)
WULFF, H. *The Traditional Crafts of Persia* (Cambridge, Mass., 1966)

CHAPTER FIVE

BOURGOIN, J. *Precis de l'art arabe et materiaux pour servir à la théorie et à la technique des arts de l'Orient musulman* (Paris, 1892)
Les élements de l'art arabe: Le trait des entrelacs (Paris, 1897)
CABANELAS, D. 'La antigua policromia del techo de Comares en la Alhambra' in *Al Andalus*, XXXV (1970)
CHRISTIE, A. H. *Traditional Methods of Pattern Designing* (Oxford, 1910)
DODD, E. 'The Image of the Word' in *Berytus*, XVIII (1969)
EL-SAID, I and PARMAN, A. *Geometric Concepts in Islamic Art* (London, 1976)
GOLDIN, A. 'Islamic Art: the Met's generous embrace' in *Art Forum* (March 1976)
GRABAR, O. 'An art of the object' in *Art Forum* (March 1976)
HANKIN, E. H. 'On some discoveries of the methods of design employed in Mohammedan Art' in *Journal of the Society of Arts*, LIII (1905)
The Drawing of Geometric Patterns in Saracenic Art (Calcutta, 1925)
HILL, D. and GRABAR, O. *Islamic Architecture and its Decoration*

A.D. 800–1500 (London and Chicago, 1941)

JONES, O. *The Grammar of Ornament* (London, 1856)

KÜHNEL, E. *Die Arabeske: Sinn und Wandlung eines Ornaments* (Wiesbaden, 1949)

MARÇAIS, G. 'Nouvelles remarques sur l'esthétique musulmane' in *Annales de l'Institut d'Études orientales*, VI (1947)

MASSIGNON, Y. *Les methodes de réalisation artistiques des peuples de l'Islam* (Paris, 1928)

REMPEL, L. I. *Arkitekturnyi Ornament Uzbekistana* (Tashkent, 1961)

ROGERS, M. 'The eleventh century: a turning point in the architecture of the Mashriq?' in *Islamic Civilization 950–1150* (Oxford, 1973)

SCHERR-MOSS, S. P. and H. C. *Design and Colour in Islamic Architecture* (Washington, 1968)

SHAFI'I, F. *Simple Calyx Ornament in Islamic Art* (Cairo, 1956)

CHAPTER SIX

ABDULAK, S. and PINON, P. 'Maisons en pays islamiques: modèles d'architecture climatique' in *L'Architecture d'Aujourdhui*, May/June (1973)

BEAZLEY, E. 'Some Vernacular Buildings of the Iranian Plateau' in *Iran*, XV (1977)

COLES, A. and JACKSON, P. *A Windtower House in Dubai* (London, 1975)

COSTA, P. and VICARIO, E. *Yemen: Paese di Construttori* (Milan, 1977)

GREENLAW, J. P. *The Coral Buildings of Suakin* (Stocksfield, 1976)

HOURANI, A. H. and STERN, S. M., eds. *The Islamic City* (Oxford, 1970)

JACQUES-MEUNIÉ, D. *Greniers-Citadelles au Maroc*, 2 vols. (Paris, 1951)

Architecture et habitats du Dades (Paris, 1962)

KING, G. 'Architecture of south-west Arabia' in *Architectural Association Quarterly*, 8/1 (1976)

KÖMÜRCÜDĞLU, E. A. *Das Alttürkische Wohnhaus* (Wiesbaden, 1966)

PAUTY, E. *Palais et maisons de l'epoque musulmane au Caire* (Cairo, 1932)

PETHERBRIDGE, G. 'Vernacular Architecture in the Maghreb' in *Maghreb Review* 3 (1976)

PRUSSIN, L. 'The Architecture of Islam in West Africa' in *African Arts/Arts d'Afrique*, 1/2 (1968)

RAGETTE, F. *Architecture in Lebanon: The Lebanese House during the 18th and 19th Centuries* (Beirut, 1974)

RAINER, R. *Traditional Building in Iran* (Graz, 1977)

REVAULT, J. *Palais et demeures de Tunis (XVIe et XVIIIe siècles)* (Paris, 1967)

ROCHE, M. *Le Mzab: Architecture ibadite en Algérie* (Paris, 1970)

WENZEL, M. *House Decoration in Nubia* (London, 1972)

Key Monuments of Islamic Architecture

ARABIA

ESIN, E. *Mecca the blessed, Madinah the radiant* (London, 1963)

GALDIERI, E. 'A Masterpiece of Omani 17th century Architecture' in *The Journal of Oman Studies*, 1 (1975)

LEWCOCK, R and SMITH, G. R. 'Two Early Mosques in the Yemen' in *Art and Archaeology Research Papers*, 4 (London, 1973)

'Three Medieval Mosques in the Yemen' in *Oriental Art* (1974)

MOUSALLI, M. S.; SHAKER, F. A.; MANDILY, O. A. *An Introduction to Urban Patterns in Saudi Arabia* (London, 1977)

SAUVAGET, J. *La Mosquée omeyyade de Médine* (Paris, 1947)

SERJEANT, R. B. and LEWCOCK, R. *San'a', an Arabian Islamic City* (London, 1978)

SPAIN

BURCKHARDT, T. *Moorish Culture in Spain* (London, 1972)

CALVERT, A. *Moorish Remains in Spain* (London, 1906)

GOMEZ-MORENO, O. 'Arte Arabe Español Hasta los Almohades' in *Ars Hispaniae*, III (Madrid, 1951)

JONES, O. and GOURY, J. *Plans, elevations, sections and details of the Alhambra* (London, 1842)

MALDONADO, B. P. *Arte Toledano, Islámico y Mudéjar* (Madrid, 1973)

El Arte Hispano-Musulman en su Decoración Geometrica (Madrid, 1975)

STERN, H. *Les mosaiques de la Grande Mosquée de Cordoue* (Berlin, 1976)

TERRASSE, H. *L'art hispano-mauresque* (Paris, 1932)

Islam d'Espagne (Paris, 1958)

TORES BALBAS, L. 'Arte Almohade, Nazari, Mudéjar' in *Ars Hispaniae*, IV (Madrid, 1949)

NORTH AFRICA

BASSET, H. and TERRASSE, H. *Sanctuaires et forteresses almohades* (Paris, 1932)

DOKALI, R. *Les Mosquées de la période turque à Alger* (Algiers, 1974)

HILL, D.; GOLVIN, L; HILLENBRAND, R. *Islamic Architecture in North Africa* (London, 1976)

HUTT, A. *Islamic Architecture: North Africa* (London, 1977)

Islamic Art and Architecture in Libya (Catalogue of an exhibition held at the Architectural Association, London, 1976)

LEZINE, A. *Architecture de l'Ifriqiya: recherches sur les monuments aghlabides* (Paris, 1966)

MARÇAIS, W. and MARÇAIS, G. *Les Monuments arabes de Tlemcen* (Paris, 1903)

MARÇAIS, G. *L'Architecture musulmane d'Occident: Tunisie, Algérie, Maroc, Espagne et Sicile* (Paris, 1954)

MEUNIÉ, J.; TERRASSE, H.;

DEVERDUN, G. *Nouvelles Recherches archéologiques à Marrakech* (Paris, 1957)

TERRASSE, C. *Medersas du Maroc* (Paris, 1927)

EGYPT

ABU-LUGHOD, J. *Cairo* (Princeton, 1971)

BRANDENBURG, D. *Islamische Baukunst in Ägypten* (Berlin, 1966)

BRIGGS, M. S. *Muhammadan Architecture in Egypt and Palestine* (Oxford, 1924)

CRESWELL, K. A. C. *The Muslim Architecture of Egypt*, 2 vols. (Oxford 1952, 1959)

HAUTECOUR, L. and WIET, G. *Les Mosquées du Cairo*, 2 vols. (Paris, 1932)

KESSLER, C. 'Funerary Architecture within the City' in *Colloque international sur l'histoire du Caire* (Cairo, 1974)

The carved masonry domes of mediaeval Cairo (London, 1976)

MINISTRY OF WAQFS *The Mosques of Egypt*, 2 vols. (Cairo, 1949)

MOSTAFA, S. L. *Kloster und mausoleum des Farağ ibn Barqūq in Kairo* (Glückstadt, 1968)

PARKER, R. S. and SABIN, R. *A Practical Guide to the Islamic Monuments in Cairo* (Cairo, 1974)

RUSSELL, D. *Medieval Cairo and the Monasteries of the Wadi Natrun* (London, 1962)

SYRIA, JORDAN, ISRAEL, LEBANON

ALMAGRO, M.; CABALLERO, L.; ZOZAYA, J.; ALMAGRO, A. *Qusayr 'Amra* (Madrid, 1975)

BERCHEM, M. VAN 'Notes archéologiques sur la mosquée des Omeyyades' in *Bulletin d'Etudes orientales*, VII–VIII (1937–8)

GRABAR, O. 'The Umayyad Dome of the Rock' in *Ars Orientalis*, III (1959)

HAMILTON, R. W. *The Structural History of the Aqsa Mosque* (Jerusalem, 1947)

HAMILTON, R. W. and GRABAR, O. *Khirbat al-Mafjar* (Oxford, 1959)

HERZFELD, E. 'Damascus: Studies in Architecture' in *Ars Islamica*, IX–XIII (1942–3, 1946, 1948)

RICHMOND, E. T. *The Dome of the Rock in Jerusalem* (Oxford, 1924)

SAUVAGET, J. *Les Monuments historiques de Damas* (Beirut, 1932)

Alep (Paris, 1941)

'Châteaux omeyyades de Syrie' in *Revue des Etudes islamiques*, XXXV (1967)

SCHLUMBERGER, D. *Les Fouilles de Qasr el-Heir el-Gharbi* (Damascus, 1939)

WULZINGER, K. and WATZINGER, C. *Damaskus II: die islamische stadt* (Berlin and Leipzig, 1924)

TURKEY

ASLANAPA, O. *Turkish Art and Architecture* (London, 1971)

GABRIEL, A. *Les monuments turcs d'Anatolie*, 2 vols. (Paris, 1931, 1934)

Une capitale turque, Brousse (Bursa) (Paris, 1958)

GABRIEL, A. and SAUVAGET, J. *Voyages archéologiques dans la Turquie orientale* (Paris, 1940)

GOODWIN, G. *A history of Ottoman architecture* (London, 1971)

KURAN, A. *The mosque in early Ottoman architecture* (Chicago, 1968)

LEVEY, M. *The World of Ottoman Art* (London, 1975)

STRATTON, A. *Sinan* (London, 1972)

ÜNSAL, B. *Turkish Islamic Architecture in Seljuk and Ottoman times* (London and New York, 1973)

VOGT-GÖKNIL, U. *Living Architecture: Ottoman Architecture* (London, 1966)

YETKIN, S. K. *L'architecture turque en Turquie* (Paris, 1965)

IRAQ

AL-HADITH, A. 'Kifil Minaret' in *Sumer*, XXVIII (1972)

'Khan Mirjan and its restoration' in *Sumer*, XXX 1/2 (1974)

BELL, G. L. *Amurath to Amurath* (London, 1911)

Palace and Mosque at Ukheidir (Oxford, 1914)

HERZFELD, E. and SARRE, F. *Archäologische Reise im Euphrat und Tigris Gebiet*, 4 vols. (Berlin, 1911–20)

HERZFELD, E. *Geschichte der Stadt Samarra* (Hamburg, 1943)

LASSNER, J. *The Topography of Baghdad in the Early Middle Ages* (Detroit, 1970)

LE STRANGE, G. *Baghdad during the 'Abbāsid Caliphate* (London, 1900)

MACADAMS, R. *Land Behind Baghdad* (Chicago and London, 1965)

MASSIGNON, M. L. *Mission en Mésopotamie: 1907–1908*, 2 vols. (Cairo, 1912)

PREUSSER, C. *Nordmesopotamische Baudenkmäler altchristliche und Islamische Zeit* (Leipzig, 1911)

REITLINGER, G. 'The Medieval Antiquities West of Mosul' in *Iraq*, V (1938)

IRAN

DIEZ, E. *Persien, Islamische Baukunst in Churasan* (Darmstadt, 1923)

GALDIERI, E. *Isfahan: Masğid-i Ğum'a*, 2 vols. (Rome, 1972)

GODARD, A. 'Les anciennes mosquées de l'Iran' in *Arthar-e Iran*, 1, 2 (1936)

The Art of Iran (London, 1965)

ISFAHAN COLLOQUIUM, proceedings of the *Studies on Isfahan* (Harvard University, Cambridge, Mass., 1974)

MATHESON, S. A. *Persia: An Archaeological Guide* (London, 1972)

POPE, A. U. and ACKERMAN, P., eds. *A Survey of Persian Art*, 6 vols. (London and New York, 1938–9)

POPE, A. U. *Persian Architecture* (London, 1965)
WILBER, D. *The Architecture of Islamic Iran: The Il-Khanid Period* (Princeton, 1955) *Persian Gardens and Garden Pavilions* (Rutland, 1962)

CENTRAL ASIA AND AFGHANISTAN

BRANDENBURG, D. *Samarkand* (Berlin, 1972)
COHN-WIENER, E. *Turan – Islamische Baukunst in Mittelasien* (Berlin, 1930)
GOLOMBEK, L. ''Abbāsid Mosque at Balkh' in *Oriental Art*, 15 (1969) *The Tīmūrid Shrine at Gazur Gah* (Toronto, 1969)
GOMBOS, K. *The Pearls of Uzbekistan* (Budapest, 1976)
KNOBLOCH, E. *Beyond the Oxus* (London, 1972)
MOSLEM RELIGIOUS BOARD OF CENTRAL ASIA AND KAZAKHSTAN, TASHKENT *Historical Monuments of Islam in the USSR* (Tashkent, 1962)
PUGACHENKOVA, G. A. and REMPEL, L. I. *Istoriia Iskussto Uzbekistana* (Moscow, 1965)

INDIA

BROWN, P. *Indian Architecture (Islamic Period)* (Bombay, 1968)
BURGESS, J. *The Muhammadan Architecture of Ahmedabad*, 2 vols. (London, 1900–5)
CARR, S. *The Archaeology and Monumental Remains of Delhi* (Calcutta, 1876)
COUSENS, H. *Bijapur and its Architectural Remains* (Bombay, 1916)
CROWE, S. and others *The Gardens of Mughal India* (London, 1972)
DANI, A. S. *Muslim Architecture in Bengal* (Dacca, 1961)
FUHRER, A. *Sharqi Architecture of Jaunpur* (London, 1909)
PAGE, J. A. *A Historical Memoir on the Qutb, Delhi* (Calcutta, 1926)
SMITH, E. W. *Mughal Architecture of Fathpur Sikri*, 4 vols. (Allahabad, 1894)
TOY, S. *The strongholds of India* (London, 1957)
VOLWAHSEN, A. *Living Architecture: Islamic Indian* (London, 1970)
WETZEL, F. *Islamische Grabbauten in Indien aus der zeit der soldatenkaiser 1320–1540* (Leipzig, 1918)
YAMAMOTO, T. *Delhi: Architectural Remains of the Delhi Sultanate Period*, 3 vols. (Tokyo, 1968)
YAZDANI, G. *Mandu: The City of Joy* (Oxford, 1929)

WEST AFRICA

AJAYI, J. F. A. and CROWDER, M. *History of West Africa* (London, 1971)
BARTH, H. *Travels and Discoveries in North and Central Africa in the years 1849–1855* (London, 1857)
CAILLIÉ, R. *Journal d'un voyage à Temboctou et à Jenné dans l'Afrique centrale pendant les années 1824–1828* (Paris, 1830)

MARLES, E. F. *Mosque research project: report no. 1* (Legon, 1967)
MAUNY, R. *Tableau Géographique de l'Ouest Africain au moyen age* (Dakar, 1961)
MEUNIÉ, D. J. *Cités anciennes de Mauretanie* (Paris, 1954)
MOUGHTIN, J. C. 'The Friday mosque, Zaria City' in *Savanna*, I 2 (1972)
SCHACHT, J. 'Sur la diffusion des formes d'architecture religieuse musulmane à travers le Sahara' in *Travaux de l'Institut de Recherches sahariennes*, XI and XVII (Algiers, 1954, 1958) 'Islam in Northern Nigeria' in *Studia Islamica*, VIII (1957)
STEVENS, P. F. *Aspects of Muslim Architecture in the Dyula region of the Western Sudan* (Legon, 1968)

EAST AFRICA

ALLEN, J. DE V. 'Swahili Ornament: A study of the decoration of the 18th century plasterwork and carved doors in the Lamu region' in *Art and Archaeology Research Papers*, 3 and 4 (1973)
CHITTICK, N. *Kilwa* (Nairobi, 1974)
GARLAKE, P. S. *The Early Islamic Architecture of the East African Coast* (Nairobi and London, 1966)
KIRKMAN, J. *The Arab City of Gedi – Excavations at the Great Mosque* (Oxford, 1954) *Gedi – the Palace* (The Hague, 1963)
LEWCOCK, R. 'Zanj – the East African Coast' in *Shelter in Africa* (London, 1971) 'The Indian Ocean' and 'Architectural Connections between Africa and parts of the Indian Ocean' in *Art and Archaeology Research Papers*, 9 (1976)

THE FAR EAST

ARNAIZ, G and BERCHEM, M. VAN 'Les Inscriptions arabes de Ts'iuan-tcheou' in *T'oung Pao*, XII (1911)
BERNET KEMPERS, A. J. *Ancient Indonesian Art* (Amsterdam, 1959)
BROOMHALL, M. *Islam in China* (London, 1910)
CAMIWADA, H. 'L'Architecture religieuse de l'Islam à Java' in *En Terre d'Islam*, VII (1935)
LEGEZA, L. 'Chinese and Islamic Influences in the Philippines' in *Arts of Asia*, VII 5 (1977)
PIJPER, G. F. 'The Minaret in Java' in *India Antiqua: A Volume of Oriental Studies presented to Jean Philippe Vogel* (Leiden, 1947)
VISSIÈRE, A. 'L'Islam à Hang-Tcheou' in *Revue du Monde musulman*, XXII (1913)

Index

Page numbers in *italic* refer to illustrations and their captions. Page numbers in **bold** refer to countries and monuments in the 'Key Monuments' section. Abbreviations: a. architect/artist; h. historian; p. period; r. ruler; w. writer.

'ABBĀSID (p.), 36, 38, *58*, 66–7, 106, 135–7, 139, *154*, 165, 170, 209–11, 215, 222–3, 230, 235–7, 245–7, 249–53, 256, 259
al 'Abbāsiya, palace, 216
'Abd al-Malik (r.), *15*, 16, 33, 236
'Abd ar-Rahmān I (r.), 212
'Abd ar-Rahmān II (r.), 214
'Abd ar-Rahmān III (r.), 213
ablution fountain, 20–2, 27, 35, 102, 104, 109, 167, 173, 216, 221–2, 228, 233, 240–1, 279
Abū Bakr (r.), 36, 208
al-'Adil Kitbughā (r.), 225
'Adil Shāhī (p.), 266
aesthetics, 13–4, 161–4, 174
Afghanistan, 69, 75, *84*, *88*, 98, 105, 130, 132, 165–7, *180*, *192*, 193, 204, 207, 251, **258–9**, 264
Afrasiab, 72, 78
Agadez, Great Mosque, **275**
Aghlabid (p.), 216, 220–1
Agra, 95, 133, 270, 273
  Pearl Mosque, 270
  Red Fort, 63, **265–6**
  Tāj Mahal, 46–7, *56*, 76, 132–3, *146–7*, *154*, 163, 167, 174, **266**, 270
  Tomb of I'timād ad-Dawla, *148*, 161, **266**
Ahmad ibn Tūlūn (r.), 71, 222–3
Ahmadabad, Friday Mosque, **266**
  Tomb of Sīdī Sa'īd, *155*
Ajdabiya, palace, **221**
Akbar, *29*, *31*, 46–8, *63*, 72, 265–6, 271
Aksaray, 80
  caravanserai, **238**
Aksehir, Taş Madrasa, 244
'Alā' ad-Dīn Kayqubād (r.), 80, *88*, 103
Alanya, 70, *84*, 103
'Alawid (p.), 216–9
Aleppo, 71, 100–1, 106–7, 111, 134, 225
  citadel, *51*, *54*, 68, *69*, 78, 100, **231**
  al-Firdawsī Madrasa, **231**
  Great Mosque, *108*, **231**
  Khān al-Gumruk, 111, 231
  Khān Ozdemur, *90*
  Khān al-Sābūn, 231
  Khān al-Wazīr, **231**
  Madrasa Shād-Bakht, 142
  sūq, *93*, *108*, 111
  al-Zāhiriyya Madrasa, 231
Alexander the Great, 69
Alexandria, 99, 106
  Basīlī Mosque, *22*
  Ramla Station Mosque, 40
Algeria, 167, *181*, *190*, 193, *200*, 206, 208, 215–16, **218–19**
Algiers, Great Mosque, 219
  Mosque of the Fishery, **218–19**
'Alī (r.), 97, 257
Aliabad, caravanserai, 98–9, *105*
Almohad (p.), 212–9
Almoravid (p.), 212, 215–17, 219

Amasya, Mosque of Beyazit Paşa, **238**, 240
'Amr (r.), 222
Ana, minaret, 248, 251
Anatolia, 39, *58*, 65, 77, *84*, *88–9*, 98, 102–3, 106–7, 111, 131, 135, 143, 168, *183*, 199, 206, 231, 237–9, 241, 244, 257, 259
Anau, Complex of Jamāl ad-Dīn, **259**
animals (in art), 50, 68–9, 77, 103, *120*, *158*, 165, 171–2
Antioch, 100, 103, 136
Arab conquest, 33, 80, 168, 193–5, 212, 220, 222
arabesque, *154–5*, 162, 170–2, *171*
Arabian Peninsula, 97–8, 103–4, *118*, 135–6, *180–2*, 194, 197, 199, *200*, 201, 204–6, 208, **209–11**, 278
arch, 67, *87*, 106, *118*, *124*, *126–7*, 133, *136*, 141–2, *142*, *146–7*, 162–4, 166, 174, 212, 215–6, 218–20, 223–4, 230, 232, 234–7, 253, 266–71, 273, 276–8
architects, *114*, 129–3, 224, 238, 240, 242, 244, 251–2, 261–3, 276
architectural drawing, *114*, 129, 132, 174
architectural treatise, 133, 174
Ardabil, Shrine of Shaykh Safī, **252**
Ardestan, 161
  Friday Mosque, **252–3**
Armenia, 66, 107, 231, 244
Artuqid (p.), 102, 130, 238
Ashir, fortress, 77
al-Ashraf I and II (r.), 211
astronomy, 130, 165, 235, 264
Atabegid (p.), 246, 249
Atlas Mountains, 69, *82*, 205–6
audience hall, *54*, *60*, *62–3*, 68–9, 72–3, 76, 262, 270–1, 275
Aurangabad, Tomb of Rabī'a ad-Dawrānī, 46
Aurangzēb (r.), 265, 270
Ayyūbid (p.), 40, *71*, 102, 133, 138, 166–7, 222–5, 230–2
Āzād Paşa (r.), 233–4
Azerbaydzhan, 206, 259
BĀBUR (r.), *114*, 132, 259, 265
Badr ad-Dīn Lu'lu' (r.), 246, 249
Baghdad, *29*, 38–9, *57*, 67, 70–2, 78–9, 99, 106, 132, 137, 195, 202–3, 212, 235, 245–8
  'Abbāsid 'Palace', *116*, **247**
  Khān al-Mirjān, **248**
  al-Mirjān Madrasa, **248**
  Mosque of al-Qumriyya, **247**
  Mustansiriyya Madrasa, *24*, 39, *148*, **247–8**
  Nizamiyya Madrasa, 38–40
  Sūq al-Ghazl minaret, **248**
  Talisman Gate, 50, 79
  Tomb of Sitta Zubayda, **246**
Baku, *53*
  Complex of Shīrvān Shāhs, 68, **259**
Balkans, 107, *187*, 199–201, 204–6
Balkh, 165
  Mosque of Abū Nasr Parsā, **263**
  No Gunbad Mosque, **263**
Bam, citadel, *54*, 67, *178*, 194–5
baraka, 16, *31*, 37, 42–4, 97, 207
Barqūq (r.), 130, 227
Basra, 70, 249
bath (*hammām*), 12, *54*, 68–9, 72, 76, *93*, *95*, 97, 101, 104–6, 109–12, 165, 213–14, 218–19, 228, 231, 235–6, 238, 242, 259, 271
Batman Su, bridge, **238–9**
Battle of the Ditch, *28*, 44
Baybars (r.), 40, 103, 105, 129, 233
Baysonqur (r.), 262

bazaar, 10, *86*, *92–4*, *96*, 99–100, 104, 107, *108–9*, 195, 259, 270
bedesten, *94*, 100, 106–7, *108–9*, 111
Beit ad-Din, palace, 233
Bektashī, *26–7*, 41
Bengal, 265, 270–1
Berbers, 66, 205, 216, 274
Beşiktaş, Tomb of Barbarossa, 47
Beyazit I (r.), 239, 241
Beyazit II (r.), 110–11, 138
Beylik (p.), 238–9
Beysehir, 103
  Eşrefoğlu Mosque, **239**
Bihzad (a.), *30*, 45, 175
Bijapur, 265, 272
  Ibrāhīm Rauza, **266–7**
  Tomb of Muhammad 'Ādil Shāh (Gul Gunbad), 46, **267**
Birgi, house, **239**
Bistam, 42, 130
Bobo-Dioulasso, Friday Mosque, **277**
Bosphorus, *53*, 69, 73, 78, *179*
brickwork, *53*, 67, 78, 100, 102, 104–5, 107, 109, *113–6*, *122*, *126*, 132, 134–7, 141, 143, *148*, 161, 163, 165–7, 173, 175, 195, 212, 235, 245, 253, 260–3, 271, 273–4, 277
bridge, 11–12, *51*, 68, *69*, 73, 77, *84–5*, 97–9, 105–6, 231, 238–9, 251, 254–5
Buddhism, *26*, 36, 41, 172
Buddhist architecture, 99, 258–60, 272–3
building construction, 65, 76, 78, *113–16*, *122*, *126*, 129, 131, 133–43, *136*, *139*, 141–2, 174
Bukhara, 68–9, *92–3*, 102, 106, *137*, 166–7, 256, 258, **259–60**, 262
  Kalyān Mosque, **260**
  Madrasa of 'Abdal-Azīz khan, **260**
  Mir Arab Madrasa, 260
  Namāzgāh, **260**
  Tomb of the Sāmānids, 76, *116*, *132*, 137, 166–7, 258, **260**, 262
burial, *29–30*, 44–6
Bursa, 39, 101, 106–7, 238
  Birinc Han, 110
  Gcyvc Han, 110
  Great Mosque (Ulu Cami), **240**
  Green Mosque (Yeşil Cami), 110, 130, *239*
  Green Tomb (Yeşil Türbe), *117*, **239**
  Hüdavandigār Mosque, **239**, 244
  Koza Han, 110–1
  Mosque of Murād I, 135
  Mosque of Murād Paşa, 135
  Mosquc of Orkhān, 111
  Tomb of Osman, 47
Būyid (p.), 38, 77, 105, 230, 246, 251–3
Busra, 39
  Mosque of 'Umar, **232**
Büyükçekmece, bridge, 106
Byzantine (p.), 66–7, 70, 72, 100, 102, 134–6, 140–3, 165, 172, 212–3, 230, 236–7, 242–3
CAIRO, 38, 44, 66, 70–2, *71*, 75, 77–9, 88, 100–1, 103, 106–7, *121*, *127*, 130, 133–4, *158*, 167, 171, *179*, *185*, 198, 200–1, 203, 211–2, 221, 233
  al-Aqmar Mosque, 12, *71*, *150*, 169, **224–5**
  al-Azhar Mosque, 38, *71*, *127* **233–4**
  Bektashī foundation, 26
  Caravanserai of Qānsūh al-Ghūrī, *90–1*, **229**
  citadel, 55, 68, 224, 226, 229

Fountain and School of 'Abd ar-Rahmān Katkhudā, **229**
Funerary Complex of Sultan Ināl, **228**
Funerary Complex of Sultan Qāyitbāy, **228**
Hospital, Mausoleum and Madrasa of Qalā'ūn, *71*, **225**, 227
Kāmiliyya Madrasa, 40, *71*
Khān al-Khalīlī, 107
Khānaqāh of Baybars, 41
Khānaqāh and Mausoleum of Sultan an-Nāsir Fāraj (Barqūqiyya), *26*, *31*, 41, *124*, **227–8**
Madrasa of Amir Mithqāl, *71*, **227**
Madrasa of Baybars (Zāhiriyya), 40, *71*
Madrasa of Barqūq, **227**
Madrasa of al-Malik as-Salih Najm ad-Dīn Ayyūb, **225**
Madrasa and Mausoleum of an-Nāsir Muhammad, *71*, **225–6**
Mausoleum of Abū Mansūr Ismā'il, 40
Mausoleums of Amirs Salār and Sanjar al-Jāwlī, **226**
Mausoleum of Imām ash-Shāfi'ī, 225
Mausoleum of Umm Qulthūm, *142*
Mosque of Ahmad ibn Tūlūn, 132, 166, **233**, 234
Mosque of Amir Altunbugha, **226–7**
Mosque of 'Amr ibn al-Ās, 107, *127*, 136, *171*, **223**, 225
Mosque of al-Hākim, *71*, *143*, 171, 223, **224**, 225
Mosque of al-Mu'ayyad Shaykh, *23*, 138, **228**
Mosque of Muhammad 'Alī, 55, 226, **229**
Mosque of an-Nāsir Muhammad, 226, 227
Mosque of as-Sālih Talā'i', *154*, 166
Mosque of Sayyida 'Ātiqa, 142
Mosque of az-Zāhir Baybars, *118*, **225**, 226
Mosque-Madrasa and Mausoleum of Qānsūh al-Ghūrī (Ghūriyya), 40, *71*, *96*, 97, **228–9**
Mosque-Madrasa of Sultan Hasan, 12–13, 40, 100, 138, *149*, 169, **227**, 228
Nilometer of Roda, 130, **223**
Qarāfa cemetery, *56*, 76
Qusūn Mosque, *71*, 131
Rifā'ī Mosque, *22*, 43
Tomb of Aqsunqur, *155*
Tomb of Barsbay, 41
walls and gates, *51*, *71*, 78–9, 131, **224**
Calligraphy, 14, *50*, *116*, *123*, 137, 144, *146–7*, *150–1*, 161–4, 167–9, 172–4, 240, 244, 262
Canton, 279
Cappadocia, 42, *183*, 418
caravan, *82*, 97, 100, 103–4, *107*, 111, 274
carpentry, 112, *113*, 133–4, 138
carpets, *20*, 161, 163–4, 167, 208
Caspian Sea, 69–70, 104, 259
Caucasus, 66, 68–9
ceiling, *121*, 138, *149*, *160*, 161–2, 164, 167, 173–4, 210–11, 220, 222, 229
Çekirge, Tomb of Süleyman Çelebi, 47
cemetery, 11, *28–31*, 44–7, 280

Central Asia, 12–13, 66, 69–70, 76, 78, 80, *92*, 97–9, 102, 104, 111, 132, 162, 167, 170–1, 174, 250–1, 253, *258–62*, 265–6, 269
ceramic, 144, *148*, *151–2*, 163, 167, 219
Chah-i Siyah, caravanserai, *86*, 101, 104
chahār bagh (fourfold plot), 47, 270, 273–4
China, 69, 72, 98–9, 106, 132, 161, 170–1, 279, **280**
Chingiz Khan (r.), 263, 265
Chinguetti, Great Mosque, *276*, 277
Christian architecture, 33, 36, 99–100, *124*, 131, 135, 143, 165, 169, 210, 212, 214–15, 230–2, 234, 236, 239, 241–2, 244–5
Christians, 34–6, 40–1, 43, 45, 75, 134, 172, 204, 211, 215, 236, 238, 258
Ch'üan-Chou, mosque, **280**
circumambulation, 16, 42–3, 210
cistern, 68–9, 206–7, 214, 216–17, 219, 237, 256
citadel, *54–5*, 66, 68–70, 78, 205, 213–14, 222, 231–2, 236
city, 10, 66–7, 70–2, 77–8, *82*, 99, 139–40, 195, 199, 202, 208, 217, 246–7, 271
Cizre, bridge, 106
Classical architecture, 12, 66–7, 76, *95*, 99–100, 107, 109–10, 140, 206, 211, 230, 236–7, 254
Classical art, 77, *154*, 165–6, 168, 170–3, 235, 250
clay walling (pisé), 112, *113*, *115*, *122*, *137* 138, 195, 202, 204–6, 274–5
colour, 144, *145*, *148–9*, *157*, 161, 164, 166–7, 170–1, 173, 252, 256
column, 135, 162–4, 211–2, 218, 221, 233, 254, 256, 273, 279
commemoration, 11, 43–4, 99
commercial architecture, 71, *84*, *86–94*, 97–107, *108–9*, 109–11, 194
'concrete', 135, 143, 218
Constantinoplc, 98, 100, 210, 212–13, 230, 238
  Hagia Sophia, 143, 238, 241–2
Coptic (p.), 33, 165, *171*
corbclling, 136–7, 141–2, 267, 2*7*1
Cordoba, 106, 130–1, 216
  Great Mosque, 34, 65, 106, *125*, *127*, 135, 143, *155*, 162, 165–7, 171, 212, 214–5, 219
  Madīnat al-Zahrā' palace, 72, *213*
  Minaret of San Juan, *212–3*
cosmogony, 15, 47
courtly ritual, 72, *158*
courtyard, 10, *18–21*, *24–5*, 35, 38, *60*, *62*, *86*, *88*, *90–1*, 101–2, 104–5, *157*, 164, 169, 173–4, *181*, *184–5*, 197–203, 205, *209–226*, 228–9, 231–4, 236, 240–4, 247, 249–51, 253–4, 256, 258, 260–1, 263–4, 265–8, 270–2, 274, 276–80
courtyard house, 38, 198–201, 209
Creswell, K. A. C., 34, 135
Crusaders, 69, 78, 222–3, 225–6, 230, 236–7
Ctesiphon, 227
DAMASCUS, 34, *58*, 70–2, 101, 103, 106–7, 138, 172, 199, 222, 230
  'Azam palace, 78, **233**
  citadel, 67–8, **232**
  Great Mosque, 11, 40, *124*, 133, 135–6, *154*, 165, 172, 210, 223, 231, **232**, *233–6*, 238, 244
  Hammām al-Bzouria, 101, 109, *110*

Hammām al-Sultan, 110
Khān of Āzād Paşa, **234**
Mosque of Dervīsh Paşa, **233**
Mosque of Sinān Paşa, 233
Nūriyya hospital, 39
al-Qadam Mosque, 44
sūq, 109
Tekkiye of Süleymān II, 104, **233**
Damghan, Tārik Khāna Mosque, *148*, 251, **253**
dancing, 41–2
Dānishmendid (p.), 237–8
dār al-Islām, 65, 97–8, 102
Daura, palace, **275**
Dayakhatyn, caravanserai, **260**
Deccan, 265, 271–2
defensive architecture, *58–9*, 66–70, *86*, *88–9*, *186–7*, 204–5
Delhi, 272–3
  'Alā'ī Darwāza, gateway, *118*, 167, **268**
  Begampūr Mosque, **268–9**
  Chotte Khān Kaň Gunbad tomb, **269**
  Friday Mosque, *21*, 65, **270**, 274
  Khān of Nizām ad-Dīn, 278
  Khirkī Mosque, **269**
  Moth-ki Masjid, **269**
  Pearl Mosque, **270**
  Qutb Minār, 75, *150*, **267**
  Quwwat al-Islām Mosque, 166–7, 171, 263, **267**, 268
  Red Fort, *156*, 174, **270**
  Shīsh Gunbad, 12, 278
  Tomb of Ghiyāth ad-Dīn Tughluq, 47, **268**, 269, 274, 278
  Tomb of Humāyūn, *32*, 47, 167, 265–6, **269–70**
  Tomb of Iltutmish, **267–8**
  Tomb of Jahānārā, *31*
  Tomb of Khān-i Jihān Tilangānī, **268**, 272
  Tomb of Safdar Jang, **270**
Derbend, gates, 68
dervish, *26–7*, 40–3, 45, 239
Dezful, bridge, *85*, 105
Dhur, Māder-i Shāh caravanserai, 104
dikka, *22–3*, 37, 138
Divriği, mosque and hospital, 230, **240**, 245
Diyarbakir, 130
  citadel, *52*, 66–7, 78–9, 224
  Fatih Paşa Mosque, 241
Djerba, *188*, *190*, 198–9, 207
Djenne, 275
  Great Mosque, 275, **276–7**
Doğubayazit, Palace of Işaq Paşa, *58*, 77
dome, 10–4, *18–9*, 34, 38–8, 42, 47, 70, 72, 76–9, *88*, 104, 107, 109–10, *114*, 117, *124–6*, *141*, 141–3, *149–50*, *155*, 162–3, 167, 171, 173, *180–1*, *190*, 208, 210–2, 215–22, 224–30, 234, 236, 238, 240–2, 244, 246–9, 251, 254, 257–8, 260, 262–74, 277–8
domestic architecture, 10, 12, 65, *121–2*, *131*, 133, 138, 140, 173, 176, *177–87*, 193–205, *200–1*, 208, 216, 239, 278
doors, *120*, 138, *149*, 166–7, 197, 202, 209–10, 222, 239, 278
Dubai, 197, 209
Dura Europos, 98
Dyula (p.), 275, 277
EAST AFRICA, 136, 197, 209, **278–9**
Edirne, 98, 239
  cemetery, *28*
  Complex of Beyazit II, *126*, **240**
  Complex of Selīm II, *22*, 39, 111, **240–1**

Kavaflar Arasta, 111
Üç Şerefeli Mosque, 39, **240**
education, 24–5, 37–9
Egypt, 37, 39, 42, 67–8, 98–9, 101, 103, 135–6, 138–9, 162, 164–5, 167–8, 170–2, 174, *190*, 193, 198–9, 201–2, 212, **222–9**, 230, 246, 274
environmental control, *121*, *181–2*, *188–9*, 194, 199–204, 209
Erzurum, *158*
Cifte Minare Madrasa, **241**, 245
Eski Mosul, bridge, 106
Ethiopia, 197, 199, 204
Euphrates, 66–7, 98–9, 102, 166, 198, 201, 235
European architecture, 13, *53*, 69, 73, 76–8, 103, 134, 136, 170–1, 174–5, 207, 216, 221, 223, 225, 229, 237–8, 243, 254, 265, 270, 280
Europeans, *23*, *60*, 98, *178–9*, 193, 196–7, 203, 206, 209, 276–7
Evdır Han, 98
expression of power, 39, 48, *49–64*, 65–79, 111, 172
FAR EAST, 106, 209, **279–80**
Fatehpur Sikri, *49*, 72, 104–5, 265
Friday Mosque, **271**
Palace, 13, **271**
Tomb of Shaykh Salīm Chishtī, *152*, 167, 173, **271**
festivals, *19*, 35, 199, 208
Fez, 20, 98, 106
al-'Attārīn Madrasa, *128*, 129, 164
Bū-'Ināniyya Madrasa, *148*, 151, 166, 174, **216–17**
Qarawiyyin Mosque, **216**
figurative art, 77, *158–9*, 162, 165, 169, 172–3, 234–5, 237, 246, 249, 262
Firdawsī (w.), 251
Firuz Koh, Great Mosque, 262
Fīrūz Shāh Tughluq (r.), 267–8, 272
foliation, 14, *123*, 144, *150*, *154–5*, 162–3, 165–73, 175, 200
fortification, 11, *50–3*, 65–70, 98, 205, 210, 213–14, 218, 222, 224, 235–6, 247, 251, 268, 270
fortress, 48, *58–9*, 69–70, 76–8, 101–2, 111, 133, *180–1*, *186–7*, *192*, 193, 202, 204–5, 207, 210, 219–21, 237–8, 241, 262, 265, 268–70, 279
fountain, *61*, *156*, 172–4, 195, 200, 213–16, 218, 221–2, 229, 231, 233, 238, 240, 242–3, 245
four-*īwān* plan, 12–13, 38–40, 101, 225, 227–8, 240, 245, 251, 253, 255–63, 268, 274
Fulani (p.), 275–7
funerary garden, 33, 43, 46–7, 265–6, 273
furniture, 161, 199
Fustat, 70–1, 106–7, 194, 198–9, 203, 222–4

GARDEN, 72–3, 77–9, *132*, *156*, 163, 173–4, 200, 212–13, 216–17, 232–3, 242, 254, 259, 262, 266, 270, 273–4
gateway, 11, 48, *49–51*, 66–71, 73, 76, 78–9, 100, 163, 172, 197, 216, 218, 224–5, 228–9, 231, 235–6, 250, 254, 266, 268, 270–4, 279–80
Gao, Mosque-Tomb of Askiā al-Hājj, **276**
Gaur, Tantipara Mosque, **271**
Gaz, caravanserai, *89*
Gebze, Complex of Obanmustafa Paşa, 104
Gedi, 278

geometry, 14, 130–2, *132*, 135–7, 144, *148–50*, 162–3, 166, 168–75
Georgia, 134, 244
Ghana, **277**
Ghana (p.), 274–5
Ghaznavid (p.), 252–3, 259, 261–2
Ghazni, 263
Minaret of Bahrām Shāh, 166, **263**
Ghiyāth ad-Dīn Muhammad (r.), 262
Ghūrid (p.), 259, 262
glass, 139, *152*, 170, 173, 242, 264
glazed tile, *61*, *117*, 137, 139, *154*, *159*, 161, 164–70, 172–3, 175, 213, 216–7, 219–20, 222, 226–9, 233, 238–9, 244, 246, 252–3, 255–9, 261, 263–4, 273–4
Granada, 100, 171, 215–6
Alhambra palace, 14, *50*, *54*, *62*, 66–9, 73, 76, 79, *125*, *152–3*, *156*, 164, 166, 169, 172, 174, 212, **213**, 214–5
Generalife Gardens, **213**
granary, 68, *180–1*, *187*, *205*, 206–7
Guinea, **277**
Gujarat, 106, 265–6
Gulbarga, Friday Mosque, **271–2**
Gunbad-i Qābūs, 39, 47, *56*, 134, 208, **253**
Güzel Hisar, caravanserai, *88–9*
HĀFIZ (w.), 47
Hafsid (p.), *90*, 216, 220–1
hajj, 16, 35, 80, *82–3*, 97–8, 103, 105, 110–11, 197, 209
Hājjī Bektash, *khānaqāh*, 27, 41–2
al-Hakam II (r.), 212
Hama, 103, 206
'Azam Palace, *64*, 65, 78, 233
Great Mosque, 135, **234**
Mosque of the Serpent, *22*
Hamadan, gates, 68
Hammādid (p.), 216, 219
han, 80, 102–3, 107, *108–9*, 109, 111
Hang-Chou, mosque, 279, **280**
harem (*haram*), *60*, 104, *179*, *182*, 196, 199, 204, 239, 242, 250, 271
Harīm al-Rashīd (r.), 67, 77
Harran, Great Mosque, 135
Hausa (p.), *182*, *190–1*, 274–6
Herat, 114, 203, 263
citadel, *55*, 67, 69
Friday Mosque, 144, *145*
Gāzur Gāh, 44, 255, **263–4**
Madrasa of Gawad Shād, **264**
Hindu architecture, 171, 264–9, 271, 273, 280
Hishām (r.), 65, 234–6
Hisn Kayfa, bridge, 68, 106
Homs, 68, 103, 235
Great Mosque, *118–9*
hospital, 39, 71, 225, 240, 242, 245
Humāyūn (r.), 47, 269–70
Hyderabad, Chār Minār gateway, **272**
IBN BATTŪTA (w.), 98, 100–1, 194, 279
Ibn Khaldūn (h.), 41, 132, 137, 139–41, 193–4, 201, 208
ice-house, *189*, 206–7
'īdgāh, *18–19*, 33, 35
Idrīsid (p.), 216
Ikshīd (p.), 223
Il-Khanid (p.), 133, 226, 245–6, 248–9, 252
imām, *20*, 22, 33–4, 36–7, 39–40, 47
India, 37, 39, 42, 45, 72, 76, *92*, 97–9, 104, 106, 135–6, 164, 166–71, 173, 175, 200, 208–9, 251, 255, 258–9, 261, **264–73**, 278–80
Indonesia, 161, 279, **280**

industrial architecture, *188–9*, 206–7
inscription, 11, 78–9, 131, *150–1*, 164, 166, 168–9, 197, 212, 214–5, 220, 255–6, 258, 261, 267–9
Iqbal (w.), 29
Iran, 12–13, *19*, 35, 37–9, 45, 65, 67–9, 72, 77, *82–3*, *88–9*, 98–9, 102–7, 111, *117*, 130–1, 133, 138–9, 141, 161–2, 164, 166–8, 170–3, 175, *182*, *188*, 202–4, 206–9, 227, 238, 245, **251–8**, 259, 264–6, 268–9, 271, 273–4, 278
Iraq, 42, 65, 70, 72, 77, 97–9, 102–3, 105, 130, 133–4, 172, 196, 202, 207, 212, 220, 223–4, 234, 236, **245–51**, 257, 260, 278
Irbil, Minaret of the Ulu Jāmi', 248, **249**
Isfahan, 39, 67, 71–3, *73*, 76, 78, 99, 104–5, 111, 142, *184*, *188*, *196*, 207–8, 252
'Alī Qapu palace, 73, *121*, *160*, 161–2, **254**
Allāharandi Khān bridge, 73, 106
Chahār Bāgh, 73
Chihil Sutūn, 73, 174, **254**
Friday Mosque, 13, 65, 142–3, 161–2, 166–7, **253**
Hasht Bihisht, *62*, 73
Khwājū bridge, *85*, **254–5**
Māder-i Shāh caravanserai 100–1, 104–5
Madrasa-i Shāh, 25, *117*, *120*, **253**
Madrasa of the Māder-i Shāh, *86*
Maydan-i Shāh, 73, 100, 104, **253**
Mosque of Shaykh Lutfallāh, 73, *152*, **254**
Royal Mosque, *19*, 73, *126*, 167, **253–4**
Israel, 105, 230, **235–7**
Istanbul, 39, 46, *53*, 67, 100–1, 106, 111, 131, 143, 166, 201, 211, 233
bazaar, *94*, 100, 107, *109*
Büyük Yeni Khan, *90*, **243**
Çağaloğlu Hammām, *95*
cemetery, 46
Complex of Şehzade Mehmet, 229, **241**, 242
Complex of Sokollu Mehmet Paşa, 34, **242**
Complex of Sultan Ahmet, *18*, 130, 229, **242**, 244
Fountain of Ahmet III, **243**
Haseki Hürrem Hammām, **242**
Kapali Çarsı, 109
Khirqa-yi Shērif Mosque, 44
Köprülü Tomb, *31*, 45
Laleli Complex, 111
Mosque of Beyazit, **240–1**
Mosque of Mehmet II, 240
Mosque of Mehmet Fātih, 104, 241
Mosque of Rustem Paşa, 170, 175
Nurosmaniye Complex, **243**
Rumeli Hisar, *53*, 241
Şişli Mosque, 29
Süleymaniye Complex, 110, 132, *152*, **241–2**
Tiryakı Çarşı, 110
Topkapi palace, 13, *60–1*, 73, *74–5*, 78–9, *82*, *154*, 170, 239, **242–3**
Tomb of Abū Ayyūb al-Ansārī, 46
Yeni Cami, 29
Yeni Valide, 110
īwān, 11, *18–19*, 24, 26, 38–41, 46, 72, 103, 109, *126*, *184*, 199, 208, 222, 225, 231, 243, 245, 247–8, 250, 253, 255, 259, 265–6, 269–71, 273

Iznik, *61*, *154*, 229–30, 233, 238, 241–2
Zaviye of Nilüfer Sultan, **243**
JABRIN, Palace of Imām Bal'arab ibn Sultān, **211**
Jalāl ad-Dīn Rūmī (w.), 27, 42
Jalāyrid (p.), 245–6, 248
Jam, minaret, 75, 166, **264**
jāmi', *22*, 35–6, 38–41
Jaunpur, 265, 278
Atala Mosque, **272**
bridge, *84*, 106
Java, 279–80
Jazira, 102, 106
Jerusalem, 33, 71, 230
Aqsa Mosque, 136, 232, **236**
Dome of the Rock, 11–12, 16, 34, 42, 75, *76*, 135–6, 143, 165, 168, 171, 225, 232, **235–6**
walls, citadel and gates, *50*, *55*, 67–8, **236**
Jews, 134, 212, 258
Jidda, 209
Jihāngīr (r.), 47, 265–6
Jones, Owen, 175
Jordan, 76, 165, 230, **235**
Judaism, 75
KA'BA, 16, *17*, 33–4, 42–3, 166, 194, **209–10**, 236
Kabul, 204, 259
kalima, 15–6
Kano, Friday Mosque, *182*, **275–6**
Kashan, *94*, 203, 206, 259
Kashmir, 112, *113*, 265, 273
Kayqubād (r.), 42, 238
Kayseri, *88*, 208, 238, 245
Complex of Khwānd Khatūn, 39, 46
Döner Kümbet, **244**
Kenya, **278–9**
Kerman, 99, *120*, *189*, 261
Friday Mosque, **255**
Ganji 'Alī Khān, *95*
Masjid-i Malik, 99
Khaljī (p.), 265, 268
khān, *82*, *88–91*, *93*, 97–101, 103, 106–7, *107–8*, *109–11*, 230–1, 234, 243, 248
khānaqāh, 26–7, 38–9, 40–3, 71, 97, 101, 111, 226–8, 259, 263–4
Khargird, madrasa, 39, **255**
Khirbat al-Mafjar, palace, 76, *158*, 165, 172–3, **236–7**
Khirbat al-Minya, palace, 76, 235
Khiva, 69, 259, 261
Khurasan, *24*, 38, 66, 99, 104, 165, 206–7, 254, 258, 260–1, 264
Khwarazm, 98, 263
Khwārazm Shāh (p.), 252, 259
Al Kifl, minaret and tomb, **246**
Kilwa, Great Mosque, 278, **279**
Palace of Hunsuni Kubwa, **279**
Kirat, minaret, 99, **255**
kitchen, *61*, 73, 103–4, 233, 239–42, 247
Konya, 80, 134, *159*, 238
Büyük Karatay Mosque, 39, *118*, *124*, 142, 244
Gömech Khātūn Mausoleum, 46
Ince Minare Madrasa, 39, *151*, **244**
Mawlawiyya Khānaqāh, 27, 42
Mosque of 'Alā' ad-Dīn, 12, **244**
Sirçali Madrasa, 39, 139
ksar, *186*, 195, *205*
Kudus, minaret, **280**
Kufa, 70, *185*
Dar al-Imāra, 72, **249**
kūfī, *51*, *61*, *150–1*, 168, 220, 246
kursī, *23*, 37–8, 138
Kuwait, *120*
LAHORE
Bādshāhī Mosque, **274**

fort, *159*
Harīm Minār, *157*
Shalimar gardens, **273–4**
Tomb of Jihāngīr, 47, **273**
Wazīr Khān Mosque, **273**
Lamu, 279
landscape, 47, *156–7*, 163, 167
Larabanga, Friday Mosque, **277**
Lashkari Bāzār, *59*, 73, 176, **264**
law, 16, 133–4, 139–40, 194, 197–8, 202
Lebanon, 134, 138, 200–2, **230**, 233, **237**
Libya, 167, *181*, *186–7*, 202, 205–6, 208, 215–16, **221–2**
light, 129, 144, *148*, *152–3*, 162, 165, 168, 173–4
literary sources, 77, 98, 133, 193–4, 204, 246, 164
liturgical furniture, *22–3*, 34–7, 138
Lōdī (p.), 265, 269, 272
Luleburgaz, Complex of Sokullu Mehmet Paşa, 111
madrasa, 10, *18–19*, *24–6*, 35, 37–41, 43, 46, 71, 77, 97, 101–2, 105, *108*, 111, 173, 211, 216–17, 222–33, 238–9, 241–9, 253, 255, 259–63
Maghrib, 201, 205, 215–16, 218, 274
magical protection, *50*, 67, *158–9*, *182*, 208
Mahan, Khānaqāh of the Niʿmatallāhiyya order, 42
Mahdia, 70
Great Mosque, 216, **219–20**, 224
Mali, **276–7**
Mali (p.), 275–7
Mamlūk (p.), 40, *71*, **90–1**, 100, 103, 109–10, *121*, *123*, 135, 165–8, 170–1, *185*, 209–10, 223–32, 234, 236–7
Mandu, Jahāz Mahal, **272**
Manisa, Muradiye Complex, **244**
al-Mansūr (r.), 195, 246, 251
manuscript illustration, *29–30*, *63*, *82*, *92*, *95*, *113–4*, 132, 144, 164, 167–8, 170, 172–3, 175, *185*
al-Maqrīzī (h.), 41, 129, 194
maqsūra, 46, 65, 138, 220
Marīnid (p.), 101, 216, 218–19
market (*sūq*), *82*, *92–4*, 97–100, 103, 106–7, *108–9*, 109–11, 140, 221–2, 263
Marrakesh, 68, 172, 218
Bādīʿ palace, 217
gateways, 78, 216
Kutubiyya Mosque, 215–6, **217**
Qubba al-Baʿad, **217**
Tomb of the Saʿdīans, **217**
Yūsuf Madrasa, *157*
Marsh Arabs, 198, *201*
martyr, 44, 46–7, 97
masharabiyya, *121*, 173, 196, 201, 227
Mashhad, 105
Mosque of Gawhar Shād, **255–6**
Shrine of Imām Riza, 104
Masina (p.), 277
masjid, *18*, 22, 27, 35–6, 43–4, 102, 109, 208
Maska, Friday Mosque, **276**
mathematics, 130–1, *132*, 133, 168–71, 173, 176
Mauritania, **276**
mausoleum, 13, *29*, 34, 41–2, 46–7, *56–7*, 76, 79, 207, 225–9, 241, 248–9, 257, 259, 262–5, 268–9
maydān, 71–2, *73*, 100, 104, 109, 253
Mecca, 15, *30–1*, 33–5, 40, 42, 45, *58*, 77, *83*, 97, 104, 165, *183*, 194,

201, 204, 233
Mosque of the Haram, *17*, **209–10**
Medina, 33–4, 42, 44, 110, 165, 194, 208–9
Mosque of the Prophet, 33, 36, 135, **210**, 236
Mosque of the Two Qiblas, 33
Mediterranean, 97, 99, 168, 199, 212, 216, 230, 241, 261
Mehmet I (r.), 110, 130, 238–9
Meknès, Palace of Maulāy Ismāʿīl, **217**
memorial mosque, *28*, 35, 43–4
Mengüjükid (p.), 238, 240
Merdivenköy, Bektashī *khānaqāh*, 27, 42
Mérida, Alcazaba citadel, 214
Merv, 66, 72, 261
Tomb of Muʿizz ad-Dīn Sanjar, 258, **261**
Mesopotamia, 38, 79, 99, 105–6, 141, 166, 171, 194, 230
metalwork, *120*, 129, 134, 136, 138, 144, *149*, 197
Meyadin, Tomb of Shaykh Shiblī, 251
mihrāb, 13, 16, *18–19*, 22, *28*, 33–7, 39, 46, 103, *123*, 132, *155*, 162–4, 166, 169, 173, 208, *210–12*, 214–20, 222, 226, 231, 253, 257–9, 261, 275–8
military architecture, *50–3*, 66–70, 97–9, 103, 172, *220–1*, 230–1, 234, 237–8, 241, 246–7
minaret, *18*, *20*, *24*, 34, 38–40, 42, 70–1, 75–6, 79, 99, 111, *117*, *127*, 132, 135, 141, *143*, *148*, *151*, 166, 168, 210–12, 214–26, 231–4, 238, 240–2, 244, 246–51, 253, 255–6, 258, 260–2, 265–7, 272–7, 279–80
minbar, *18*, *22–4*, 36–7, 138, 208, 211, 216, 220, 239–40, 242, 276–7, 279
minor arts, 161–3, 167, 170–2, 174–5
al-Mirjān (r.), 248
Mogadishu, Mosque of Fakhr ad-Dīn, **278**
Monastir, *ribāt*, 216, 220
Mongol (p.), 35, 72, *83*, 103, 134, 170, 206, 223, 231, 237–8, 245, 252–3, 257, 263, 265
Mopti, Great Mosque, **276**
Morocco, *53*, *58*, 66, 69, *92*, *122*, 134, 173, *186*, 195, 199, 201, 204–7, 215–8
mortar, 134–5, *136*, 137, 141, *142*
mosaic, 77, 79, 135, 139, *148*, *155*, 162, 165–8, 171–2, 210, 212, 222, 230–3, 236, 252, 254–60, 262–3, 273
Mosul, 246
Mosque of Nūr ad-Dīn, **249**
Qara Sarai Palace, **249**
Tomb of Imām Yahyā, **249**
Mount Muqattam (Cairo), Bektashī *khānaqāh*, 26, 40–1
Mosque of al-Juyūshī, 43, 47, 75–6
Mshattā, palace, *59*, 76, 136, 165, 171, **235**, 249
mud-brick, 66–7, 98, 100, 105, 137, *176*, *182*, *189*, 195, 207–9, 219, 258, 276–7
muezzin, *20*, 22, 34, 37, 99
Mughal (p.), *21*, *29*, 33, 45, 47, 72, 75, *92*, *95*, 104, 106, *114*, *118*, 135–6, 161, 167–70, 173–5, 259, 265–6, 270–4
Muhammad, the Prophet, 15, *28*, 33–4, 36, 40, 44, 46, 97, 168, 194, 197, 199, 202, 208–10, 236, 274

Multan, Tomb of Shāh Rukn-i ʿĀlam, **274**
Mulūk at-Tawāʾif (p.), 212, 214
muqarnas, 14, 77, 79–80, *93*, 103, *116*, *118*,*125*, *142*, *152–3*, 162–3, 166–7, 173, 211, 216–18, 222, 229, 231–2, 242, 245–8, 251
Murād II (r.), 43, 239–40
musallā, 33, 35, 44, 208, 248
Muslim community, 15–16, 47, 97, 109, 195
Mustafā III (r.), *90*, 111, 243
al-Mustansir (r.), 247, 251
Muzzaffarid (p.), 252–3, 255, 257
NAMĀZGĀH, 44, 260
Namou, Friday Mosque, **227**
Nāsir-i Khusrau (w.), 98, 106–7
naskhī, *150*, 168
Nasrid (p.), 212–13, 215
nastaʿlīq, 169
Natanz, 127
Tomb of Shaykh ʿAbd al-Samad al-Isfahani, 12, 42, *151*
naturalism, *154–5*, 170–1
naval architecture, 70
Nayin, 78, 165
Friday Mosque, **256**, 260
Niğde, Ak Madrasa, **244–5**
Karaman Madrasa, 239
Niger, *182*, **275**
Nigeria, *182*, *191*, 208, 275–6
Nile, 106, *178–9*, *182*, 206–7, 222
nomad, *82*, *182*, *192*, 193–4, 197–8, 201–2, 205
Norman (p.), 212, 216, 222
North Africa, *18*, 66, 77, *90*, *92*, 98–9, 101, 107, 136, 162, 165–8, 172, *187*, 195, 206, 208, 212–13, **215–22**, 275
Nubia, 66, 176, 199
Nūr ad-Dīn (r.), 101, 231, 249
OBSERVATORY, 39, 264
Oman, 197, 203, 208–9, **211**
orientation, 13, 16, *22*, 33–4, 201–2, 253–4, 270
Orkhān (r.), 107, 111
Orontes, 206
Ottoman (p.), *18*, *21*, *28*, 37, 39, 41, 45, 47, *53–4*, *60–1*, 69, 71, 75, 77–9, *82*, *94*, 98, 100, 103–4, 106–7, 109, 111, *118–19*, *124*, 129–32, 135, 143, 166–7, 170, 175, *179*, 199, 202, 204, 209–10, 216, 218–21, 223, 229–34, 236–44, 259
Oxus, 259, 261

PAKISTAN, 204, 208, **264–5**, **273–4**
palace, 10, 13–14, 39, *58–64*, 65–6, 68, 72–3, *74–5*, 76–9, 103, 111–12, 162, 166, 168–9, 173–4, 204, 211–17, 219, 221–2, 230, 233–7, 242–3, 246, 249, 250–1, 254, 265, 270–2, 275, 278–9
Palermo, 212
Ziza palace, 222
Palestine, 67, 76, 101, 103, 134, 165, 167, 230
palm beams, *190–1*, 271
Palmyra, 13, 77, 98, 234
Paradise, 34, 46–7, 169
Payas, 103
caravanserai of Selīm II, 103
Peking, 279
pendentive, 67, 124, 141–3, *142*, *158*, 163, 172, 210, 219, 222, 240, 243–4, 248, 261–2
Petra, 98, 100–1
pietra dura, 135, 266
pigeon-tower, *179*, *188*, 207
pillar tomb, 278–9
Pīr-i Bakrān, *khānaqāh*, 11, 42, 161
pīshtāq, 246, 251, 259–64

polychrome effect, *118–9*, 135–6, *148*, 166–8, 170–1, 212, 222
popular shrine, 44, *190*, 207–8
portal, 10–11, 13, 39, *49*, *81*, *86*, 90, 101–4, *118*, *146–7*, *151*, 162–4, 166–9, 176, *177*, 197, 210–11, 216–17, 224–5, 229, 231–4, 238, 240–1, 243–6, 251, 253, 255–7, 261–9, 272, 279–80
prayer, *28*, 33–7, 43
prayer-rug, *18*, 34, 36
pre-Islamic architecture, 11–13, 33–4, 36, 68, 76, 78, *84*, 90, 98–9, 135–7, 139, *140*, 141–3, 168, 202, 210, 235, 250, 258, 274
privacy, 196–7, 198–9
prostration, *20*
Punjab, 265
QAIROUAN, Great Mosque, *18*, 65, 136, 143, 166, 216, **220**, 221
Mosque of Sīdī ʿUkba, *171*
Mosque of the Three Doors, **220**
waterworks, 216
Qāyitbāy (r.), 37, 110, 224
Qājār (p.), 77, 98, 104–5, 111, 167–8, 173, 252, 256
Qalʿa of the Banī Hammād, 77
palace, 216, **219**
tower, **219**
Qalāʾūn (r.), 110, 225–6
Qarakhanid (p.), 259, 263
Qaramānid (p.), 237, 238
Qaramānlī (p.), 237
qasāriyya, see *bedesten*
Qarraqan, tomb tower, 116, 161
Qasr al-Hayr East, 65, 73, 77, 101, 135–6, **234–5**
Qasr al-Hayr West, 76, 101, 165, 172, **234**
Qazvin, 94
qibla, 13, *18–9*, *22*, *30–1*, 33–9, 42, 44–6, 133, 169, 202, 208, *210–12*, 217–21, 223–4, 226, 261, 267
Qum, 98, 202
Mausoleum of Shāh ʿAbbās II, 46
Qurʾān, 15–6, *22*, 33–4, 37, 43–6, 76, 97, 133, *150*, 168, *171*, 196, 207, 247, 262
Qusayr ʿAmra, 76, 143, *158*, 165, 172, **235**
Qutb Shāhī (p.), 272
RABAT, gateways, *50*, 78, 216, **218**
necropolis at Chella, 101, *218*
Mosque of Hasan, *118*, 215–6, **218**, 219
Rajasthan, *184*, 266
Ramla, cistern, 237
Raqqa, 67, 136–7, 166, **235**, 245, 249
Raqqāda, palace, 216
Rashīdī (p.), 209–10
Rasūlid (p.), 209, 211
Rayy, *madrasa*, 39
reception room, 10, 168–9, *179–82*, 196, 198–9, 203, 205, 213, 215, 221, 242, 250–1, 254, 259, 279
Red Sea, 103, *167*, 194, 197, 209, 223
ribāt, 11, 40, 70, 79, 101–2, 111, 216, 220–1
Ribat-i Malik, 102, 261
Ribāt-i Sharaf, 102, **256**, 261
Riyadh, **210**
Roman architecture, 66, 68, 103, 106, 135–7, 142–3, 214, 232, 234
Rome, 72, 75, 78–9, 98–9, 102, 136, 181, 202, 205, 230
Ronda, bath, 214
royal patronage, 40, 43, 48, *56–7*, 60–3, 65, 69–72, 76–80, 101, 103–4, 106, 109–11, 129, 131, 133, 169, 172–3, 210–29, 231–77, 279

Rustamid (p.), 216
SA'DĪ (p.), 216–17
Safavid (p.), *21*, 39, 65, 73, 75, 79, 104–6, 111, 162, 167, 170, 172, 175, 252–4, 256, 259, 273
Sahara, 195, 206, 274–6, 279
saint, 30, 44–5, 205, 207–8, 260–1
Salāh ad-Dīn ibn Ayyūb (Saladin) (r.), 40, 222, 224, 232
Salalah, 198, 201
Saltukid (p.), 238, 241
Sāmānid (p.), 76, 106, 259, 260
Samarqand, 72, 77, 103, 131–2, 256
    Bibi Khānum Mosque, 256, **261**
    Gūr Emīr Complex (Tomb of Tīmūr), 43, 76, *150*, *155*, **262**
    'Ishrat Khāne, 258, **262**
    Madrasa of Ulugh Beg, 260, **261**
    Observatory of Ulugh Beg, **262**
    Shāh-i Zinda Complex, 76, 259, **261**
    Shir Dor Madrasa, **261**
    Tilla Kari Madrasa, **261**
Samarra, 71–2, 134, 139, 154, 162, 165–6, 202, 223, 235, 245
    bridge, **251**
    Great Mosque, **250**
    Imām Dūr, 245–6, **251**
    Mosque of Abū Dulaf, **250**
    Palace of al-Mu'tasim, **250**
    Qasr al-'Āshiq, **250**
    Qasr al-Jass, **250**
    Qubbat as-Sulaybiyya, **250**
San'a', 101, *122*, *131*, 194, 204, 206
    Great Mosque, 136, **210**
    Mosque of al-Bakīriyya, **210–11**
Sandikh, Ulu Mosque, 130
Saragossa, Aljaferia Palace, 212, **214**
Sarajevo, 107, 199
Sasanian (p.), 66, *85*, 98–9, 105–6, 139, 141, 165, 171–3, 211, 227, 230, 234–6, 246, 252, 255–6, 258
Sasaram, Mausoleum of Shīr Shāh Sūr, 12, *56*, **272**
Sā'ūdi (p.), 209–10
Saveh, Friday Mosque, **256**
Sayyid (p.), 265, 269
sculpture, *50*, 68–9, *158–9*, 165, 170, 172–3
Scutari, Yeni Valide, 45
Selīm I (r.), 223, 230
Selīm II (r.), 103–4, 106, 111, 131, 210, 233
Selīm III (r.), 41, *60*
Seljuq (p.), 35, 38–40, 65, 80, *84*, 98–9, 102–3, 106–7, 111, *116*, *118–19*, 131, 135, 137, 143, 165–6, 172, 222, 225, 230–1, 237–9, 244–6, 248, 251–3, 255–6, 258–9, 261–2
Sendangduwur, mosque, **280**
Seville, Alcázar, **215**
    Giralda, 212, **214–15**
    Great Mosque, **214**
Sfax, 130
    Great Mosque, 216, **220**
Shāh 'Abbās I (r.), 72, 100, 104, 106, 253–4
Shāh 'Abbās II (r.), 254–5
Shāh Jihān (r), 47, *63*, 133, 266, 270–1, 274
Sharqī (p.), 272
Shaybānid (p.), 259–60
Shibam, mosque, 204, **211**
Shī'ism, 38–9, 46, 65, 105, 168, 222–3, 249

Shiraz, 104, 263
    Shāh Hamza 'Alī Mausoleum, *152*
    Tomb of Hāfiz, 47, *149*
    Vakīl Mosque, *126*, **256**
Sicily, 164, 174, 215–6, 222
Sikandra, Akbar's Tomb, *31*, 46–7, *148*, 167, 272–3
Sinān (a.), *28*, 39, 45, 104, 106, 111, 129, 130–1, 175, 229, 233, 241–2, 244
Sind, 203, 274
Sinjar, minaret, 248
Siraf, 101
Sistan, *188*, 194, 207, 258
Sivas, *88*, 103, 106, 238, 247
    Gök Madrasa, 39, 239, **245**
    Great Mosque, 244
    Hospital of Kay Kā'ūs I, **245**
'Slave' (p.), 265, 267
society, 129–31, 133, 139–40, 206–7, 176, *182*, 193–202, 205, 208
Soghdia, 66, 98
Soltaniyeh, Mausoleum of Öljeytu, *57*, 72, 76, 143, **257**
Somalia, 278
Songhai (p.), 275–7
Sousse, Great Mosque, 216, 220
    ribāt, 70, 101, 216, 220–1
South Arabia, 211
South-East Asia, 97, 279–80
space and decoration, 144, *156–7*, 161–4, 177
Spain, *18*, 40, 46, 66–7, 72, 78, 106–7, *125*, 131, 134, 136, 139, 143, 161–2, 165–8, 173–4, **212–15**, 216
Srinagar, Friday Mosque, **273**
squinch, 67, *124*, *141–2*, *141–3*, 163, 220–2, 245, 258, 268
stable, 101–4, 162, 204–5, 217, 239
stonework, *49*, 67, 77–8, 80, 98, 100, 102, *113*, *115*, *118–19*, *122*, 129, 134–7, 141–3, *148*, *151*, 161, 166–8, 171–4, *182–3*, 199, 202, 212, 216, 221–4, 226–7, 229–34, 237, 245–5, 264, 266, 268–71, 278, 280
street, 71, *93*, 99, 107, 109, 195, 197, 199–200, 224
stucco-work, 77, 102, *115*, *123*, *128*, 135, 138–9, *148*, *154*, 161–6, 168, 170–3, 199, 208, 211–13, 216–17, 222, 224, 226–7, 234–5, 237, 251–3, 255–6, 258, 260, 264, 267–9
Suakin, *107*, 197–8, 208
Sudan, *107*, 176, 195, 198, 202, 221, 274
Sūfism, 15, 40–3, 174, 227–8
Süleyman II, 'the Magnificent' (r.), 103–4, 109, 130
Sultan Han, 80, *81*, 102–3
Sumatra, 280
Sunnism, 38, 41, 222, 247
Sūrī (p.), 265, 272
symbolism, 11–2, 33–4, 41–2, 46–7, *50*, 65–9, 70–2, 75–6, 79, 135, 162, 170–3, 176, 197–8, 200–1, 205, 208, 225–6, 246, 254, 267
Syria, 13, 39–40, 67–8, 73, 76–7, 97–9, 101–4, 107, 109, 133–4, 136, 138, 141–2, 165, 167, 171–2, 174, *180–1*, 204, 212–14, 222–5, 227, **230–5**, 236, 238, 246, 258
Syrian Hajj Route, 104, 109

TABRIZ, 72, 131, 239–40
    Blue Mosque, **257**
    Mosque of 'Alī Shāh, 131
Ta'if, 194, 209
Ta'izz, Ashrafiyya Mosque, **211**
ta'līq, 169
Tanzania, 279
Tatta, Friday Mosque, 274
technique of building, *113–6*, *118*, *120–5*, 129, *133–43*, *139*, *141–2*, 176, 194, 195, 201, 203–4, 207, 264, 268
technology, 140–1, *188–9*, 195, 206–7, 223
Tekkiye (*tekke*), 40, 104, 233
tent, 12, 80, *82–3*, 100, 103–4, 161, *180*, *192*, 197, 198, 201, 262, 244
Termez, Chahār Sutūn, 263
textiles, 34, 45, 106–7, 109, 144, 161, 166, 170–1, 174–5, 208, 268, 271
Thousand and One Nights, 72
throne room, *63*, 214, 231, 250, 256
thuluth, *150*, 168
tie-beam, *127*, 135–6, *142*, 143, 220
Tigris, 71, 102, 198, 201, 250
Timbuktu, *178*
    Great Mosque, **277**
    Sankore Mosque, **277**
Tīmūr (Tamerlane) (r.), 43, 72, 76, 131, 240, 256, 263–5, 273
Tīmūrid (p.), 35, *54*, 131, 167, 238, 252–5, 259–64
Tinmal, Friday Mosque, **218**
Tlemcen, Great Mosque, 216, **219**
    Mosque of al-Mansūr, 219
Toledo, 131, 212
    Mosque of Bāb Mardūm, 143, **215**
tomb, 10–13, 16, *27–32*, 33, 41–8, *56–7*, 111, 131, 166, 173, *190*, 202, 207–8, 210–11, 216–18, 221–3, 225–8, 230–3, 238–40, 243–7, 249–53, 257–8, 260–70, 272–4, 276, 278–80
'tomb mosque', 43–4, 46, 266
tomb tower, 11–12, 39, 47, 253, 257
tombstone, *28–31*, 34, 45–6, *154*, 167, 262
Tophane, Tomb of Kiliç Ali Paşa, 47
Transoxiana, 39, 68, 258–9
travel, 80, *81–3*, 97–9, 102–4, 106, 134, 195, 209
treasury, 210, 232, 234, 242, 250, 271
Tripoli (Lebanon), **237**
Tripoli (Libya), *90*, *93*, 220, 274
    Complex of Ahmad Pasha, **222**
Tughluq (p.), 265, 268–9, 272, 278
Tūlūnid (p.), 212, 223, 230
Tunis, 133, 274
    Mosque of Sīdī Mahriz, 219
    Mosque and Tomb of Hamūda Pasha, **221**
    Zaytūna Mosque, 216, 220, **221**
Tunisia, 166, 167, *181*, *183*, 202, 206–7, 215–16, **219–21**
Turkestan, 42, 166, 206
Turkey, 36–7, 42, 45–7, *82*, 100, 102–3, 105–7, *117*, 131, 133, 138–9, 166–7, 170, 172, 174, *179–81*, 199, 201, 204–5, 216, 225, **237–45**, 247, 266
Turkman (p.), 252, 256
UKHAYDIR, *58*, 137, 166, 245–6, 251
'Umar (r.), 36, 210, 232

Umayyad (p.), 12, 33–4, 70, 72, 76–7, 79, 103, 106, 110, 131, 135, 143, 165–6, 170–3, 209, 212–5, 223, 230, 232, 234–6, 246, 248
underground architecture, 202
university, 24, 38, 216
Upper Volta, 276
'Uqaylid (p.), 245–6, 251
urban setting, 10–12, 41, 66–73, 76–8, *90–1*, *93–4*, 97–101, 106–7, *108–9*, 109–11, 139–40, *178–81*, *183*, 194–5, 197, 200–2, 204, 207, 222, 224–5, 228
Urgench, Tughtabeg Tomb, **264**
'Uthman (r.), 66, 194, 210
Uzbeck (p.), 260
VARAMIN, Friday Mosque, **257**
    Tomb Tower of 'Alā ad-Dīn, **257**
Vasari, 172
vaulting, *31*, 67, 78, 80, 107, 109, *115–16*, *124–5*, *140–2*, *141–3*, *181*, *187–8*, 206–8, 214, 216–19, 221, 224, 227, 235, 240, 245–6, 248, 251, 253, 255, 257, 262–4, 271, 278
vernacular architecture, 76, 176, *177–92*, 193–208, 277
Visigoths, 212, 214–15
Vitruvius, 133, 136, 140, 174
voussoir, *118*, 135–6, *136*, 162, 167, 212–13, 268
WADI HALFA, 176, *177*
al-Walīd I (r.), 133, 135–6, 210, 232, 235–6
al-Walīd II (r.), 235–6
wall-painting, *58*, 77, 79, *158*, 165, 168, 172–3, *177*, *182*, 230, 235, 254, 262, 264
waqf, 43, 45, 77, 97, 101, 105–6, 110–11, 229, 247, 269
watch-tower, 11–12, *82–3*, 97, 99, *186–7*, 221, 231, 280
water, 79, 97, 101, 106, *156–7*, 162, 173–4, 213–14, 270, 272, 274
water-mill, *189*, 206
West Africa, *200*, 208, **274–7**
Western interpretation, 175
wind-catcher/tower, *179*, *189*, 202–4, *203*, 206
windmill, *188*, 207
windows, *121*, *123*, 136, 138–9, *146–7*, *152–3*, *155*, 164–6, 168–70, 173, *183*, 197, 211, 214, 216–7, 222, 230, 240
woodwork, 67, *96*, 100 *121*, *128*, 129, 133–4, 138, 143–4, *148–9*, *154*, 163–8, 170, 172–3, *179*, *183*, 211, 216–17, 227, 233, 238–9, 273
YA'QŪB AL-MANSŪR (r.), 217–19
Ya'rubid (p.), 209, 211
Yazd, 77, *189*, 203, 264
    citadel, *53*, 67
    Friday Mosque, **257–8**
Yemen, 42, 97–8, 101, *122*, 139, *180–1*, *187*, 194, 204, 206, **210–11**
Yugoslavia, 106, *182*, *189–90*, 200, 202
Yunesi, caravanserai, *87*
ZAND (p.), 252, 254
Zangid (p.), 40, 101–2, 165, 222, 230, 246, 249
Zanzibar, 209
Zaria, Friday Mosque, *190–1*, **276**
Zavareh, Friday Mosque, 39, 257, 258
zāwiya, 40, 216, 218, 238, 240, 243
Zīrid (p.), 216, 220–1

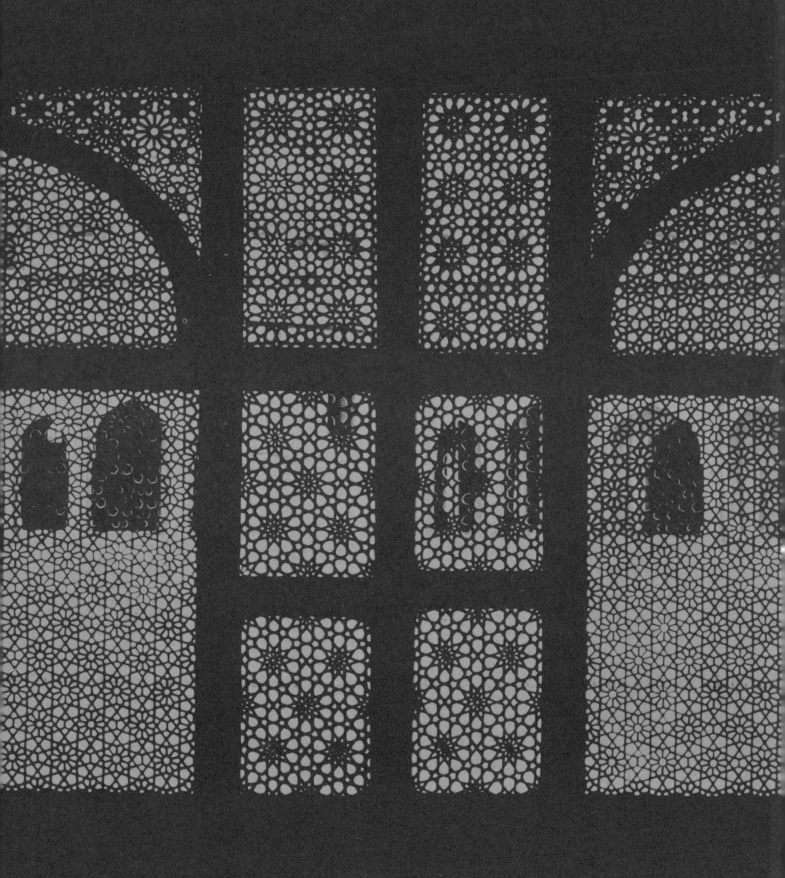